Inference and Consciousness

Inference has long been a central concern in epistemology, as an essential means by which we extend our knowledge and test our beliefs. Inference is also a key notion in influential psychological accounts of mental capacities, ranging from problem-solving to perception. Consciousness, on the other hand, has arguably been the defining interest of philosophy of mind over recent decades. Comparatively little attention, however, has been devoted to the significance of consciousness for the proper understanding of the nature and role of inference. It is commonly suggested that inference may be either conscious or unconscious. Yet how unified are these various supposed instances of inference? Does either enjoy explanatory priority in relation to the other? In what way, or ways, can an inference be conscious, or fail to be conscious, and how does this matter? This book brings together original essays from established scholars and emerging theorists that showcase how several current debates in epistemology, philosophy of psychology, and philosophy of mind can benefit from more reflections on these and related questions about the significance of consciousness for inference.

Anders Nes is Associate Professor of Philosophy at the Norwegian University of Science and Technology. He has written on cognitive phenomenology, inference, and perception in various journals and edited collections. He has previously been a Researcher at the CSMN, University of Oslo, and a Career Development Fellow at Oxford University.

Timothy Chan was Researcher at the CSMN, University of Oslo. He had been a lecturer at the University of East Anglia and taught at several other universities. He edited *The Aim of Belief* (2013) and published research articles in journals including *Canadian Journal of Philosophy*, *Philosophical Studies*, and *Synthese*.

Routledge Studies in Contemporary Philosophy

Moved by Machines
Performance Metaphors and Philosophy of Technology
Mark Coeckelbergh

Responses to Naturalism
Critical Perspectives from Idealism and Pragmatism
Edited by Paul Giladi

Digital Hermeneutics
Philosophical Investigations in New Media and Technologies
Alberto Romele

Naturalism, Human Flourishing, and Asian Philosophy
Owen Flanagan and Beyond
Edited by Bongrae Seok

Philosophy of Logical Systems
Jaroslav Peregrin

Consequences of Reference Failure
Michael McKinsey

How Propaganda Became Public Relations
Foucault and the Corporate Government of the Public
Cory Wimberly

Philosophical Perspectives on Contemporary Ireland
Edited by Clara Fischer and Áine Mahon

Inference and Consciousness
Edited by Anders Nes with Timothy Chan

For more information about this series, please visit: www.routledge.com/
Routledge-Studies-in-Contemporary-Philosophy/book-series/SE0720

Inference and Consciousness

Edited by
Anders Nes with Timothy Chan

NEW YORK AND LONDON

First published 2020
by Routledge
52 Vanderbilt Avenue, New York, NY 10017

and by Routledge
2 Park Square, Milton Park, Abingdon, Oxon OX14 4RN

Routledge is an imprint of the Taylor & Francis Group, an informa business

© 2020 Taylor & Francis

The right of Anders Nes and Timothy Chan to be identified
as the authors of the editorial material, and of the authors for
their individual chapters, has been asserted in accordance with
Sections 77 and 78 of the Copyright, Designs and Patents Act
1988.

All rights reserved. No part of this book may be reprinted
or reproduced or utilised in any form or by any electronic,
mechanical, or other means, now known or hereafter invented,
including photocopying and recording, or in any information
storage or retrieval system, without permission in writing from
the publishers.

Trademark notice: Product or corporate names may be
trademarks or registered trademarks, and are used only for
identification and explanation without intent to infringe.

Library of Congress Cataloging-in-Publication Data
A catalog record for this book has been requested

ISBN: 978-1-138-55717-8 (hbk)
ISBN: 978-1-315-15070-3 (ebk)

Typeset in Sabon
by ApexCovantage, LLC

Contents

Introduction: Inference and Consciousness   1
ANDERS NES

PART I
Unconscious Inference in Cognitive Science and
Psychiatry   13

1   Unconscious Inference Theories of Cognitive
Achievement   15
KIRK LUDWIG AND WADE MUNROE

2   A Realist Perspective on Bayesian Cognitive Science   40
MICHAEL RESCORLA

3   The Role of Unconscious Inference in Models of
Delusion Formation   74
FEDERICO BONGIORNO AND LISA BORTOLOTTI

PART II
Inference in Speech Comprehension   97

4   Seeing and Hearing Meanings: A Non-Inferential
Approach to Speech Comprehension   99
BERIT BROGAARD

5   Metacognition and Inferential Accounts of
Communication   125
NICHOLAS ALLOTT

vi *Contents*

PART III
Inference, Structure, and Generality 149

6 Non-Inferential Transitions: Imagery and Association 151
JAKE QUILTY-DUNN AND ERIC MANDELBAUM

7 Knowledge of Logical Generality and the Possibility
of Deductive Reasoning 172
CORINE BESSON

PART IV
Conscious Non-Demonstrative Inference 197

8 Fore- and Background in Conscious Non-Demonstrative
Inference 199
ANDERS NES

9 Morphological Content and Chromatic Illumination
in Belief Fixation 229
DAVID HENDERSON, TERRY HORGAN, AND MATJAŽ POTRČ

PART V
Inference and Perceptual and Introspective Knowledge 253

10 Experience and Epistemic Structure: Can Cognitive
Penetration Result in Epistemic Downgrade? 255
ELIJAH CHUDNOFF

11 The Transparency of Inference 275
RAM NETA

Contributors 290
Index 291

Introduction
Inference and Consciousness

Anders Nes

Inference seems to be central to the life of thought. It allows old thoughts to give birth to new ones, in a way answering to logical and evidential relations legitimizing the offspring. It extends the scope of knowledge, broadening it beyond what is registered by the senses. It makes our minds non-accidentally sensitive to relations of coherence and consistency. To be sure, thoughts can interact also non-inferentially, for instance by association. Nevertheless, it is tempting to think that inference is of basic importance to how thoughts qua thoughts can matter. At least, this is so in so far as thoughts are more or less fully fledged, having conceptual structure, and bearing a range of logical or evidential relations to each other. One might, indeed, doubt to what extent it would make sense to attribute thought to a creature without assigning it a capacity for inference.

Still, the nature of inference as a mental phenomenon has received comparatively little attention in philosophy.[1] Much industry has of course been devoted to articulating the standards for valid, rational, justified, coherent, or otherwise appropriate inference, of various types. Yet the nature, or natures, of the inferential mental acts, events, structures, or processes to which these standards apply have not been explored in comparable depth and detail. It is interesting to compare, here, with the situation for such notions of truth and justification, on the one hand, versus those of propositions and beliefs, on the other. Philosophical logicians and epistemologists have, respectively, explored truth and justification at length. Yet this has not been to the neglect of inquiries into the nature of the propositions or beliefs that bear these features. Philosophical work on inference seems in comparison more lopsided towards the standards.[2]

The question of the psychological nature of inference is complicated by the varied ways in which inference has been supposed to play out in mind. Many different types of inference have been distinguished: theoretical versus practical, deductive versus non-deductive, and formal versus material, to name but three. In this collection, however, the nature of inference will be approached via another notable distinction among its manifestations, viz. that between conscious and unconscious inference.

2   Anders Nes

The class of conscious inferences seems to have comparatively clear instances. They would presumably include inferences drawn by a person, who is aware of whatever is inferred as something that follows from or is supported by such-and-such considerations, from which it is inferred, and who has a disposition to give voice to the inference, marking its status as such with words such as 'so', 'therefore', or 'then'. In the philosophical tradition, inference has often been understood in broadly this vein. At least, inferences have been viewed as intellectual acts within the power of humans only. They have been taken to be the preserve of distinctively rational, discursive creatures. Thus, Aristotle and, following him, Aquinas viewed inference as one of the characteristics of our rational soul, as opposed to the appetitive and perceiving soul shared with animals.[3] Kant, following a traditional view of early modern logic, identified the 'highest' cognitive or intellectual ability, reason, as the 'faculty of inference'.[4]

The category of unconscious inference may not have equally clear or uncontroversial instances. A historically influential candidate case, however, are inferential processes hypothesized to underlie and explain perceptual states, such as states of seeing the shapes of nearby objects.[5] Such inferences are not, or not clearly, attributable to the subject of consciousness who ends up seeing the shapes in question – they are perhaps more aptly assigned to some subpersonal part of the perceiver. Awareness of the inferences is to be had only via, in effect, reverse engineering the perceptual capacities in question. The perceiver need not have the words or, arguably, concepts to articulate grounds or conclusion in such a way to make it intelligible how the former could be supposed to support the latter.

These respective examples of conscious and unconscious inference seem, then, to differ psychologically in important ways: personal-level status, awareness, conceptual articulation, and possibly in other respects. This encourages the question to what extent is there an interesting category of inference in common between these examples. More generally: to what extent is there such a category in common between supposed cases of inference that differ in ways relevant to their classification as conscious or otherwise? Relatedly, may talk of 'inferences' in accounts of perceptual or other psychological states that seem not to arise from conscious reasoning be understood strictly and literally? To answer these questions is to take a stand, implicitly if not explicitly, on the significance of consciousness for inference.

In approaching the question of the significance of consciousness for inference, it would be useful, if only as a preliminary, to have a nuanced overview of the various ways or senses in which inferences might be supposed to be conscious or unconscious. When the distinction between conscious and unconscious inference is brought up in philosophical contexts, there is a tendency to have in mind extreme representatives of each group: e.g., self-conscious, fully explicit deductions, on the one hand;

Introduction 3

subpersonal processes underlying vision, on the other. Yet there are putative inferences that seem to lie somewhere between these extremes on dimensions relevant to consciousness. They include inferences in fluent speech comprehension – including pragmatic comprehension – as well as abductive inferences, more or less fluently drawn, in other domains of daily life. How does consciousness figure in these 'middling' cases?

The chapters of this collection cast light on inference from diverse angles. They do so, moreover, by variously bearing on the question how consciousness may or may not be of significance to or figure in inference. Some contributors articulate skepticism about the coherence or explanatory value of positing inferences far removed from consciousness. Such doubts are set out by Kirk Ludwig and Wade Munroe in their chapter, and are also voiced by Berit Brogaard in hers. Michael Rescorla meanwhile defends the value of invoking unconscious inference, notably within the context of Bayesian cognitive science, advocating a realistic construal of such accounts. Federico Bongiorno and Lisa Bortolotti, in their contribution, also affirm the value of appeals to unconscious inference, specifically in accounts of delusions. The chapter by Jake Quilty-Dunn and Eric Mandelbaum offers support for unconscious inference from a slightly different angle, in as much as they defend a proposal on the nature of inference on which consciousness plays no essential role.

Other chapters in the collections focus on the contents or structure of consciousness in inferences that are, at least, not entirely unconscious or subpersonal. Corine Besson addresses conscious deductive reasoning, examining what forms of personal-level propositional knowledge of logic that may be implicated in, or required for, such inference. Nicholas Allott considers inferences in pragmatic comprehension of speech. He proposes that such inferences should be seen to have a metacognitive aspect. He argues, however, that this is consistent with their being executed with little awareness. The chapters by Anders Nes and by David Henderson, Terry Horgan, and Matjaž Potrč, like that by Allott, also look at inferences that inhabit roughly the 'middling' territory hinted at earlier. Specifically, these chapters consider abductive or other non-demonstrative inferences at the personal level (of which pragmatic inferences arguably is a special case). In particular, they address how consciousness may extend over the rich stocks of information to which such inferences seem to be sensitive.

The two final chapters of the collection bear on how inference relates to two forms of knowledge with which it often has been contrasted, viz., respectively, perception and our reflective access to our own mind. Elijah Chudnoff defends the claim that perceptual experience, as a source of justification for belief, is epistemically unlike inferentially acquired belief, and that this is so even if experience is subject to cognitive penetration (arguably a form of unconscious inference); at least, this difference holds, he argues, for the basic, 'presentational' aspects of experience. Ram Neta,

4 *Anders Nes*

finally, objects to the conception of self-knowledge as a form of inference that is advanced in Alex Byrne's recent influential work; Neta also seeks to identify and account for an interesting parallel between self-knowledge of belief and of inference.

What follows gives a somewhat fuller presentation of the themes, questions, and arguments pursued in the contributions to the collection.

1. Unconscious Inference in Cognitive Science and Psychiatry

The first part the collection focuses on unconscious inference, as posited to explain facets of normal, or abnormal, psychology.

Kirk Ludwig and Wade Munroe's chapter, 'Unconscious Inference Theories of Cognitive Achievement', critically examines appeals to unconscious inference in cognitive science. Specifically, they take aim at the idea that there are modular, subpersonal systems, underpinning personal-level cognition, that strictly and literally engage in inference. They argue inferences could be ascribed to such systems only if the system harbored a cognitive agent equipped with propositional attitudes. Yet we could attribute such agential powers to the relevant modules only if we could, inter alia, attribute possession of the concepts in terms of which the contents of the inferential transitions are specified; Ludwig and Munroe contend however that we cannot attribute such concepts. In any case, attribution of agential powers to modules is homuncular, raising a worry of vicious regress. Ludwig and Munroe anticipate the response that unconscious inference theories do not, or should not, purport to posit strict and literal inferences. May not these theories be content with hypothesizing processes *akin* to inferences, or what Ludwig and Munroe dub 'inference facsimiles'? The authors ask however what content, and theoretical utility, the appeal to such facsimiles might have, concluding it has, at best, a heuristic role: it offers a sketch of the sort of causal-functional structure we should be looking for when seeking to uncover the mechanism that relate sensory input to personal-level output.

The next chapter, 'A Realist Perspective on Bayesian Cognitive Science' by Michael Rescorla, is more sanguine about the explanatory power of the appeal to unconscious inference – especially unconscious Bayesian inference – in accounts of cognition. Rescorla gives an account of the methodology of Bayesian cognitive science, distinguishing three elements: (i) articulating a normative Bayesian model of the task, (ii) specifying its free parameters, and (iii) checking how the so-specified model fits actual performance. The methodology is committed to some approximate fit between actual performance and Bayesian norms, but not perfect fit. Now, Bayesian inferences are transitions among credal states. As Rescorla observes, little is yet established as to their neural realization (though the matter is subject of ongoing research). A putative worry arises, though, even with regard to the mere possibility of their realization, viz. the intractability of many of the Bayesian computations relevant to explanations in Bayesian cognitive science. In response, Rescorla reviews approximation schemes, arguing that computationally limited systems could approximately implement intractable computations. Rescorla ends with favorably contrasting realist with instrumentalist interpretations of Bayesian cognitive science. Instrumentalists have advertised their view as being (inter alia) more in tune with the merely approximate, idealized character of Bayesian models, and with scientific practice. Rescorla argues however that realism makes better sense of certain possible changes in the Bayesian priors posited by Bayesian models. For example, repeated exposure to fasts-moving stimuli can alter the 'slow motion' prior that is hypothesized to account for various perceptual phenomena. Likewise, realism allows, Rescorla argues, for a principled explanation for the sequence of inference, in Bayesian models with iterated inference.

The final chapter in this part, by Federico Bongiorno and Lisa Bortolotti, entitled 'The Role of Unconscious Inference in Models of Delusion Formation', shifts focus from explanation of normal to accounts of abnormal cognition, specifically to accounts of delusions. Their chapter addresses the roles of conscious and unconscious inference in these psychiatric processes. They compare two rival accounts of delusion formation. According to *explanationism*, delusions are beliefs purporting to explain anomalous experience. According to *endorsement theory*, delusional beliefs manifest the acceptance of certain anomalous experiences as being veridical. On the face of it, the former but not the latter view is committed to an inferential step in the generation of delusions. Bongiorno and Bortolotti question, however, how deep this putative difference runs. They argue both accounts are compatible with Bayesian models that hold delusions to result from a Bayesian inference. Concentrating on Coltheart's influential Bayesian model, they argue it cannot be subsumed neatly under one as opposed to the other of either explanationism or endorsement theory.

2. Inference in Speech Comprehension

The second part of the collection turns to the role of inference in the comprehension of speech. This is an interesting domain to explore, with a view to the various forms of inference, with varying degrees or forms of consciousness, that may or may not be in play. On the one hand, speech comprehension is often enough an achievement that seems to rely on consciously available stocks of knowledge. For example, many who read the sentence, 'When the policeman arrested the robber, he was masked', will interpret the pronoun 'he' as co-referential with 'the robber'. It is plausible to think this interpretation relies on their knowing, or assuming, robbers to be more likely to be masked than police officers.[6] On the other hand, the immediacy that typically characterizes fluent comprehension (even of pragmatic aspects of understanding) may seem to make it more akin to processes of perception than ones of conscious inference.

Berit Brogaard's chapter, 'Seeing and Hearing Meanings: A Non-Inferential Approach to Speech Comprehension', stresses the perception-like character of fluent understanding of speech. She marshals empirical and theoretical considerations in favor of a non-inferential view. Comprehension exhibits, she contends, inter alia such features as the Stroop effect, stimulus satiation, immediacy, automaticity, amodal completion, and evidence insensitivity. These features are arguably characteristic of perceptual processes. Now, it might be objected that, even if comprehension has these marks of perceptual processes, it could still be inferential, since inference, on well-known 'constructivist' views, is operative even in such paradigmatically perceptual (specifically, visual) processes as size and color constancy (cf., e.g., Rock, 1982). Brogaard responds, however, that inference cannot take place at an entirely subpersonal level. Rather, inference subsumes only mental transitions that are accessible to consciousness and that contribute to making behavior intelligible in terms of norms of rationality. Brogaard allows, though, that 'Type 1', or 'System 1', cognitive processes, as posited by dual-process theories of cognition, may contribute to comprehension. Yet she argues that these processes are associative or based on heuristics rather than inferential.

In his chapter, 'Metacognition and Inferential Accounts of Communication', Nicholas Allott concentrates on pragmatic aspects of language comprehension. Several influential accounts of such comprehension agree in viewing it as an inferential achievement: this goes both for Grice's account and that in relevance theory. Indeed, as Allott points out, pragmatic comprehension may seem not only to be inferential but also to manifest features of so-called 'System 2' reasoning, notably in that it seems to be informationally unencapsulated. At the same time, in normal, smooth communication, pragmatic comprehension is, nevertheless, quick and seemingly effortless (a point also stressed by Brogaard in her chapter). In the latter respect, comprehension is more akin to paradigm 'System 1' inferences. These features of pragmatic interpretation, which seemingly pull in opposite directions, can be reconciled, Allott argues, if we take such interpretation to manifest a form of inference that is subject to a certain minimalist kind of metacognition. The metacognitive aspect of these inferences consists in the fact that they are subject to a form of monitoring and control. The metacognition implicated is nevertheless minimalist, in that subjects are not consciously aware of the monitoring or control in question, and in that it does not involve meta-representation of the target inferential process. As Allott notes, such a process would share key features with procedural metacognition, as conceived by Joëlle Proust (2013). Allott argues that cognitively realistic inferential accounts of utterance interpretation require there to be metacognitive

Introduction 7

feedback, even in normal smooth communication. He reviews, moreover, two separate sets of experimental results that show that feedback occurs in comprehension without hearers being aware of this.

3. Inference, Structure, and Generality

The third part of the collection comprises two chapters that address the importance of structure and generality to inference.

Jake Quilty-Dunn and Eric Mandelbaum, in their chapter 'Non-Inferential Transitions: Imagery and Association', address inference by examining mental processes with which it putatively contrasts, such as certain imagistic and associative processes. As Quilty-Dunn and Mandelbaum remind us, imagery and association have historically been given very prominent roles in accounts of mind, e.g., in Humean empiricism and Pavlovian associationism. Although the latter approaches may have gone too far in downplaying inference, they may well have been right to allow that there are these putatively non-inferential mental processes. How, then, do they differ from inference? Quilty-Dunn and Mandelbaum proposes that a certain structural or formal character distinguishes inference. Their proposal here is bound up with a conception of inference as a natural psychological kind of mental transition, the paradigm cases of which include such deductive forms as modus ponens. While they do not claim that inference, so understood, is limited to the personal level, or requires a potential accessibility to consciousness, they do take it to be narrower, at least in intension or conception, than what they describe as a broad Helmholtzian notion of inference, on which low-level computations in vision by definition qualify as inferences. Quilty-Dunn and Mandelbaum allow that such low-level processes could, as an empirical matter, turn out to exemplify the natural psychological kind, inference, that they purport to characterize: the point is that they would not do so just by virtue of being a sort of computational processes. To qualify, the computations would have to be transitions among discursive representations, subject to formal, content-independent rules (as exemplified, say, by the inference rules of first-order logic). It follows, they argue, that transitions among iconic representations are not inferential, since they are not governed by such rules. Association, moreover, is best understood as a bare propensity of coactivation of different mental representations ('bare' in that it has no psychological explanation). It is not governed by structure-sensitive rules, and so not inferential.

Corine Besson's chapter, 'Knowledge of Logical Generality and the Possibility of Deductive Reasoning', also engages with the traditional thought that inference – at least deductive inference – is structural or formal, and that it, as such, abstracts away from or generalizes across content. In particular, Besson considers the ramifications of this traditional thought for the logical competence of reasoners. Now, Besson does

8 *Anders Nes*

not purport to address inference quite generally as much as inference or reasoning as a mental phenomenon at the personal level, asking what sort of logical knowledge such inference requires on the part of the reasoner. On a cognitivist view, deductive reasoning requires propositional logical knowledge. In keeping with the noted traditional thought, that inference is formal and as such abstracts away from or generalizes over contents, cognitivists have often assumed that this logical knowledge would have to take the form of knowledge of general logical principles. For example, it would consist in knowledge of such principles as modus ponens or universal instantiation. This cognitivist view has been held to run into a circularity problem, which Besson dubs the 'general/particular circularity threat'. Roughly, the worry is this. If deductive inference requires knowledge of logical principles, this must be because the latter knowledge needs to be applied in the mental act of inference. Yet applying this general propositional knowledge itself seems to be an inferential step very much like the inferential mental act it was supposed to account for. Besson critically examines two recent versions of the general/particular circularity threat, due respectively to Romina Padro and Paul Boghossian, arguing that they fail to disprove the idea that deductive reasoning requires knowledge of logical principles. However, Besson shares their skepticism that deductive inference manifests application of knowledge of such general principles. She offers, to cognitivists, the proposal that any knowledge of logic applied in inference may be specific to the inference at hand. Knowledge of general principles, in so far as that possession thereof is indeed required, may be explained by, rather than explain, competence in drawing the specific inference at hand.

4. Conscious Non-Demonstrative Inference

When philosophers have inquired into inference, the lion's share of their attention has been devoted to demonstrative inference – especially to such varieties thereof as has been studied in such familiar branches of logic as propositional, first-order, or modal logic. However, non-demonstrative inference, notably including abduction, poses distinctive questions for the understanding of inference. In particular, it poses distinctive questions when it comes to clarifying the various ways or senses in which inference may or may not be conscious. The chapters in this section do not address the possible roles for non-demonstrative inference at entirely unconscious or subpersonal levels. Instead, they explore how consciousness unfolds within personal-level instances of non-demonstrative inference. Such inferences may seem to be sensitive to, or dependent on, rather broad ranges of information possessed by the thinker. Yet it has often been supposed that occurrent consciousness has a narrowly circumscribed scope – that one can consciously entertain only a very limited number of objects or 'chunks' of information at any moment, say about four.[7]

As Anders Nes notes in his contribution, 'Fore- and Background in Conscious Non-Demonstrative Inference', it is a common thought that one can distinguish between certain fore- and background assumptions in inference – that a conclusion may be drawn from some salient grounds, that as it were stand out from a receding terrain of background assumptions also relied upon. Nes distinguishes a 'Boring' and an 'Interesting' view on such fore-v-background structures. On the former, they can be captured by specifying, for the various grounds or assumptions of the inference, whether they are phenomenally conscious, or access conscious, or else how easily available they are to such consciousness; on the latter, there are fore-v-background structures over and above such classifications. Nes points to reasons for thinking that the Interesting View at least merits exploration. He takes stock of recent contributions to such a view from Sebastian Watzl, on which attention makes for a 'centrality structure' in consciousness, and from Terence Horgan, Matjaž Potrč, and co-workers, who suggest information can be backgrounded in consciousness by figuring within certain 'looming potentialities'. Drawing on aspects of this work, as well as some remarks from Husserl, and the role of 'schemas' or 'gists' in memory, Nes proposes that background assumptions can figure in consciousness by being condensed into a consciously, though inattentively, entertained notion of their overall thematic gist. The latter gives, he argues, the drift of an elucidation of how or why such-and-such salient grounds mean, or imply, or support, that so-and-so conclusion holds. Having in mind such a thematic gist explains why, upon offering such an elucidation, one might have a sense of filling out, or making implicit, something already had in mind or assumed in drawing the inference.

In their chapter, 'Morphological Content and Chromatic Illumination in Belief Fixation', David Henderson, Terry Horgan, and Matjaž Potrč emphasize the epistemic role of background information in abductive inference. Taking their cue from Dennett's discussion of the frame problem in artificial intelligence, and from Fodor's remarks on the 'Quineian' and isotropic character of central cognition, they argue the rationality of abductive belief formation require that be sensitive to rich stocks of pertinent evidence possessed by the subject. Much, or even most of this evidence is taken into account in belief-formation, they argue, not by virtue of being explicitly represented but rather by being implicitly accommodated in the guise of what they term 'morphological content'. Is this implicitly accommodated constitutively relevant to consciousness? According to what Henderson, Horgan, and Potrč dub 'The Explicit Occurrent Content (EOC) assumption', it cannot be. The EOC assumption thus implies that the epistemic role of this content must then be either entirely non-experiential, or at best indirect, via feeding into some brute feelings of 'seeming rightness', that are evidentially blind as to any further specifics as to why a given conclusion seems right. Neither view

10　*Anders Nes*

is attractive, they argue. An alternative to the EOC assumption is available, however, if background assumptions can 'chromatically illuminate' conscious belief fixation, being implicitly, yet in some sense nevertheless consciously, appreciated in inference. The metaphor is that of sources of chromatic light, themselves unseen, modulating how objects before one appear. The authors develop here earlier work by Horgan, Potrč, and collaborators, on the idea of chromatic illumination (with which Nes's chapter also engages). They argue this conception makes available a novel, and attractive, version of experiential evidentialism about doxastic justification, dubbed chromatic-experiential evidentialism.

5. Inference and Perceptual and Introspective Knowledge

The final part of the collection continues in an epistemological vein. Epistemologists have generally been interested in inference as a means to knowledge or justified belief. When so looked at, inference has often been contrasted with such means to knowledge or justification as perception and introspection.[8] The two chapters in the final part of the collection cast light on ways in which inference may or may not relate to, or have a role in, the two latter epistemic means.

Elijah Chudnoff's chapter, 'Experience and Epistemic Structure: Can Cognitive Penetration Result in Epistemic Downgrade?', engages with the following question. If you believe someone is angry because you are unjustifiably worried they may well be, your belief would not typically justify further judgements as to their mood. However, if someone looks angry to you because your visual experience is cognitively penetrated by a similarly unjustified worry, would your visual impression still justify judgements as to their mood? Susanna Siegel (2017) has recently answered 'No', arguing the perception and belief are epistemically alike here: the visual state, just like the belief, should be seen as a step in an inferential chain, subject to similar threats of vicious circularity. Chudnoff allows that a negative verdict, like Siegel's, may be appropriate when to *non-presentational* aspects of visual phenomenology are subject to cognitive penetration by unjustified states (examples of non-presentational aspects include those due to amodal completion, i.e. when objects seem to continue in certain ways behind occlusion). He resists this verdict, however, for *presentational* aspects. Chudnoff thus defends the traditional view of perceptual experience as epistemically distinct from inferentially acquired belief, at least as far as the basic, presentational aspects of experience go.

The final chapter, Ram Neta's 'The Transparency of Inference', deals with our reflective access to our own minds. Gareth Evans (1982, p. 225) famously claimed that I can 'get myself in a position to answer the question whether I believe that p by putting into operation whatever procedure I have for answering the question whether p'. Neta agrees this is a rational route to self-attribution of belief (though not necessarily the only such route). How, though, can Evans's route be rational – how can one rationally move from settling a question about the non-psychological world (assuming 'p' is non-psychological) to ascertaining the putatively quite different matter of one's psychology? Alex Byrne (2011) has proposed to solve this puzzle by construing Evans's route as involving a certain inferential step, albeit of a special sort. Neta objects that Byrne's strategy here is not as general as he purports it to be – in particular, it fails to extend to an analogous, Evans-like route to self-attribution of inference – and that Byrne's would-be inferences violates a plausible constraint on inference, viz. that the inferences be such that the thinkers in question could be committed them as good inferences. A better and simpler account of the rationality of Evans's route is available, Neta proposes: we are entitled to assume that what we believe about some issue is determined by the conclusion of our reflection on the evidence concerning the issue, for, quite simply, that assumption is credible on our total (including empirical) evidence.[9]

Notes

1. One telling observation is that there is no general entry on 'inference' at either the Stanford, Routledge, or Internet encyclopedias of philosophy.
2. To make this comparative claim is of course not to deny that there are numerous streams of invaluable work in philosophy, of varying vintages, on the psychological nature of inference. Moreover, there are signs that philosophical interest in the nature of inference is picking up, including the very recent collections by Juhl and Schechter (2018) and Balcerak Jackson and Balcerak Jackson (2019).
3. For Aristotle, see Barnes, 1984, pp. 427b7–427b27. For Aquinas, see Oesterle, 1962, p. 17.
4. See Kant, 1998, pp. A130–1/B169, A299–305/B355–362. See also Longuenesse, 2005, p. 95 and Merritt, 2011, p. 23, nt. 31.
5. Such appeals to unconscious inference are often traced back to Helmholtz, 1867/1924. However, as Hatfield (2002) argues, related ideas go back at least to Alhazen.
6. The example is due to Stanley, 2005, pp. 1–2.
7. For the number four, see Cowan, 2000. Miller, 1956 is an earlier influential paper taken to suggest a figure of seven. These studies are couched in terms of limits on short-term or working memory, not directly in terms of consciousness. Implications for the latter thus depend on whether consciousness is limited by such memory capacities, as argued by Carruthers (2015) among others, or whether at least some forms of consciousness may overflow the latter, as argued by Block (2008).
8. 'Introspection' here adverts merely to the distinctive ways we have of knowing our own minds, by which we cannot in the same way know the minds of others.
9. Acknowledgements: Work on the collection started at CSMN, a research center at the University of Oslo. Support from its various fellows and staff, in particular from CSMN director Olav Gjelsvik, and core group members Jennifer Hornsby and Deidre Wilson, has been invaluable. Special thanks to CSMN colleagues Nicholas Allott and Eline Busck Gundersen who were

12 Anders Nes

essential to nurturing the idea of the collection, and who have offered detailed input at several stages along the way. Support from RCN grants 213068 and 240645 is gratefully acknowledged. Thanks also to Joëlle Proust; to Alexandra Simmons; to all who have taken part at talks or workshops related to the collection; and, not least, to the contributing authors. Thanks, finally, to CSMN colleague Timothy Chan: Timothy was crucial to formulating the original concept and outline of the collection, including getting some of our early contributors on board; much to his regret, he had to withdraw from later work on the collection for reasons of ill health. This book would not have happened without him.

References

Balcerak Jackson, M., & Jackson, B. Balcerak (Eds.) (2019). *Reasoning: New Essays on Theoretical and Practical Thinking*. Oxford: Oxford University Press.

Barnes, J. (Ed.) (1984). *The Complete Works of Aristotle. Vol. I*. Princeton: Princeton University Press.

Block, N. (2008). Consciousness and Cognitive Access. *Proceedings of the Aristotelian Society*, 108, 289–317.

Byrne, A. (2011). Transparency, Belief, Intention. *Aristotelian Society Supplementary Volume*, 85, 201–221.

Carruthers, P. (2015). *The Centered Mind*. Oxford: Oxford University Press.

Cowan, N. (2000). The Magical Number 4 in Short-Term Memory: A Reconsideration of Mental Storage Capacity. *Behavioral and Brain Sciences*, 24, 87–185.

Evans, G. (1982). *Varieties of Reference*. Oxford: Oxford University Press.

Hatfield, G. (2002). Perception as Unconscious Inference. In D. Heyer & R. Mausfeld (Eds.), *Perception and the Physical World*. London: Wiley.

Helmholtz, H. von. (1867/1924) *Treatise on Physiological Optics* (Ed. J. P. C. Southall.) Menasha, WI: Optical Society of America.

Juhl, C., & Schechter, J. (Guest Eds.) (2018). *Philosophical Issues 28: Philosophy of Logic and Inferential Reasoning*. London: Wiley Periodicals.

Kant, I. (1998). *Critique of Pure Reason* (Trans. & ed. by P. Guyer & A. Wood.). Cambridge: Cambridge University Press.

Longuenesse, Béatrice. (2005). *Kant and the human standpoint*. Cambridge: Cambridge University Press.

Merritt, M. McBay (2011). Kant's Argument for the Apperception Principle. *European Journal of Philosophy*, 19(1), 59–84.

Miller, G. A. (1956). The Magical Number Seven, Plus or Minus Two: Some Limits on Our Capacity for Processing Information. *Psychological Review*, 63(2), 81–97.

Oesterle, J. T. (Ed. & trans) (1962). *Aristotle on Interpretation. Commentary by St. Thomas and Cajetan*. Milwaukee: Marquette University Press.

Proust, J. (2013). *The Philosophy of Metacognition*. Oxford: Oxford University Press.

Rock, I. (1982). Inference in Perception. *PSA: Proceedings of the Biennial Meeting of the Philosophy of Science Association*, II, 525–540.

Siegel, S. (2017). *The Rationality of Perception*. Oxford: Oxford University Press.

Stanley, J. (2005). Hornsby on the Phenomenology of Speech. *Aristotelian Society Supplementary Volume*, 79, 131–145.

Part I

Unconscious Inference in Cognitive Science and Psychiatry

1 Unconscious Inference Theories of Cognitive Achievement

Kirk Ludwig and Wade Munroe

The Ethiops say that their gods are flat-nosed and black,
While the Thracians say that theirs have blue eyes and red hair.
Yet if cattle or horses or lions had hands and could draw,
And could sculpt like men, then the horses would draw their gods
Like horses, and cattle like cattle; and each they would shape
Bodies of gods in the likeness, each kind, of their own.

– Xenophanes

1. Introduction

What explains cognition and perception? What explains how the world looks to us, why we are subject to systematic illusions? What explains our capacity to speak and to understand language? The ultimate infrastructure for personal level cognition and perception lies in the physical construction of our bodies. But description at the level of fundamental physics doesn't promise much insight into the mechanisms of cognition and perception. We want rational insight, so to speak, into the infrastructure of cognitive achievement. We are tempted to seek an explanation not in terms of a family of concepts disjoint from those under which we bring the explananda but in terms of the same or allied concepts.

How does a research team solve a problem that none of its members is able to solve alone? It institutes a division of labor, in which different members of the team carry out different portions of the task, drawing on complementary skills and knowledge. When we have a specification of the division of labor, the subtasks and the processes by which they were carried out, and the organization of the team members that explains how their several contributions are combined into a complete solution, we understand the mechanism by which the research team solved the problem. This gives us rational insight into its cognitive achievement. This gives us one model for how to understand personal level cognitive achievement, namely, in terms of a division of labor into subtasks conceived of as problems to be solved at the subpersonal level. It promises rational insight into cognitive achievement, provided that the operation of these subpersonal processes can be characterized in terms of the same concepts as personal level cognitive operations, that is, in terms of rational problem-solving or inferential reasoning, of some form or other. Since these processes are to explain personal level cognitive achievement, they are conceived of as being strictly subpersonal. Insofar, they are unconscious inference theories of personal level cognitive achievement.

This chapter considers the allure and prospects for unconscious inference theories of cognitive achievement (henceforth, 'UIT'). UITs explain various conscious, perceptual, and cognitive phenomena by postulating inference-like processes that operate over unconscious representational states. They subdivide into positions that hold (a) that these unconscious representational states and inference-like processes are in principle accessible to consciousness, and therefore are personal level states and processes, and (b) that they are strictly subpersonal and in principle inaccessible to consciousness (access or phenomenal (Block, 1995, 2002)). Our interest lies in the latter. UITs in category (b) subdivide into those that hold that the inference-like processes are (i) genuine inferences or (ii) not inferences but merely inference-like, inference facsimiles. We subdivide UITs in type (b.ii) into those that hold inference facsimiles are defined over genuine representational states and those that hold they are defined over a theory-internal concept of representation. These divisions are represented in Figure 1.1.

We argue that the only tenable UITs are ones that employ a theory internal technical notion of representation (lower right in Figure 1.1) but that once we give cash-value definitions of the relevant notions of

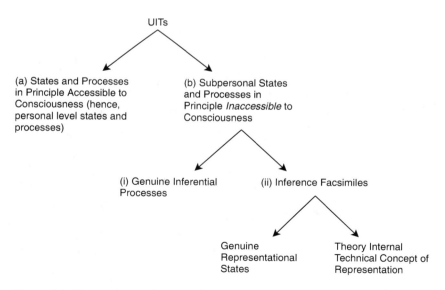

Figure 1.1 Unconscious Inference Theories

representation and inference, it is difficult to see that much is left of the ordinary notion of representation. We suggest that the real value of talk of unconscious inferences lies in (a) their heuristic utility in helping us to make fruitful predictions, such as about illusions, and (b) their providing a high-level description of the functional organization of subpersonal faculties that makes clear how they equip an agent to navigate its environment and pursue its goals.[1]

In Section 2 we characterize the kinds of unconscious inference that we are concerned with. In Section 3 we review desiderata on what kinds of processes can count as inferences. In Section 4 we apply the desiderata to argue that there are no genuine modular subpersonal inferences. First, we argue that if they are inferences, they require a homunculus as their subject (Section 4.1). Next, we argue that the conditions required for this are not met by subpersonal modular capacities (Section 4.2). Finally, we argue that even waiving these points, UITs face a dilemma: they are committed to either an explanatory regress or the explanatory dispensability of unconscious inferences. In Section 5 we consider a retreat that merely requires inference facsimiles at the subpersonal level. We look at input-output representations (Section 5.1) and structural representations (Section 5.2) in Ramsey's sense (2007), and argue neither provide a genuine notion of representation suitable for use in a UIT. We then turn to cash-value definitions that make no pretense to connect with ordinary notions and suggest that they do not add new explanatory power, though talk of representations and inferences can play a useful heuristic role in theorizing about cognition and perception (Section 5.3). Section 6 summarizes.

2. Subpersonal Modular Inferences

Typically unconscious subpersonal inferences are treated as taking place in modular systems that serve narrowly defined functions. UITs of perceptual achievement (veridical representation of the environment) and linguistic understanding are paradigm examples. Although most of our discussion focuses on perception, the points carry over to other theories that treat information processing subsystems as inferential.[2]

While UITs of perceptual achievement have an ancient pedigree (Hatfield, 2002), contemporary theories trace their lineage back to Helmholtz (1867). Classic examples include (Barlow, 1990; Brunswik, 1981; J. A. Fodor, 1983; R. L. Gregory, 1966, 1980, 1997; Irvin Rock, 1983, 1984; Wandell, 1995). As Helmholtz puts it, the inferences that the perceptual system engage in

> are in general not conscious, but rather unconscious. In their outcomes they are like inferences insofar as we from the observed effect

on our senses arrive at an idea of the cause of this effect. This is so even though we always in fact only have direct access to events at the nerves, that is, we sense the effects, never the external objects.

(1867, p. 430)

Similarly, according to Rock:

Although perception is autonomous with respect to such higher mental faculties as are exhibited in conscious thought and in the use of conscious knowledge, I would still argue that it is intelligent. By calling perception 'intelligent', I mean to say that it is based on such thought like mental processes as description, inference, and problem solving, although these processes are rapid-fire, unconscious, and nonverbal. 'Description' implies, for example, that a perceptual property such as shape is the result of an abstract analysis of an object's geometrical configuration, including how it is oriented, in a form like that of a proposition, except that it is not couched in language. Such a description of a square, for example, might be 'a figure with opposite sides equal and parallel and four right angles, the sides being horizontal and vertical in space'. 'Inference' implies that certain perceptual properties are computed from given sensory information using unconsciously known rules. For example, perceived size is inferred from the object's visual angle, its perceived distance, and the law that geometrical optics relating the visual angle to object distance. 'Problem solving' implies a more creative process of arriving at a hypothesis concerning what object or event in the world the stimulus might represent and then determining whether the hypothesis accounts adequately for, and is supported adequately by, the stimulus.

(1984, p. 234)

More recently, UITs have been given new life by the idea that the brain is a predictive engine, and, more specifically, a Bayesian reasoner, which engages in probabilistic inference about the hidden causes of sensory input with the goal of reducing sensory prediction errors (Clark, 2016; Hohwy, 2013).[3] As Hohwy puts it: 'The brain infers the causes of its sensory input using Bayes' rule' (2013, p. 18).[4] According to Clark, 'the predictive processing story, if correct, would rather directly underwrite the claim that the nervous system approximates a genuine version of Bayesian inference' (2016, p. 41). Rescorla notes that the inferences involved are strictly subpersonal:

Perceptual processes are subpersonal and inaccessible to the thinker. There is no good sense in which the thinker herself, as opposed to her perceptual system, executes perceptual inferences. For instance, a normal perceiver simply sees a surface as having a certain colour.

Even if she notices the light spectrum reaching her eye, as a painter might, she cannot access the perceptual system's inference from retinal stimulations to surface colour.

(2015, p. 695)

At the level of our discussion, differences between classical and Bayesian inference theories will not be significant. The problem lies in the transference of concepts (i.e., the concepts of inference and representation) from one domain to another without taking seriously the conditions for their application. Details with respect to the nature and content of the postulated inferences make no difference.

Let's look at how a UIT might explain perceptual constancy. Perceptual constancies are described by a function that yields a constant value (perceptual representation) while its arguments (sensory stimuli) change. When the value is constant while inputs change, we have the representation of sameness of size, shape, color, and so forth through changes of proximal stimulus. The UIT strategy is to explain how the perceptual system achieves constant representation of the relevant property by giving it knowledge of the function and knowledge of the appropriate arguments. For example, Emmert's Law states that the perceived linear size of an object is proportional to the product of its perceived distance and the angle subtended on the retina. There are analogues for constancy of represented shape through rotation relative to the observer, constancy of lightness and color through variations in illumination conditions, constancy of position relative to movement of the perceiver, and so on. The perceptual system gets information about, for instance, perceived distance (inferred from more basic cues) and the angle subtended by an object in the visual field and then infers using Emmert's Law a size that is to be represented in perceptual experience. Inferential mechanisms are also used to explain illusions. For example, in the Ponzo illusion illustrated in Figure 1.2, the black bars are the same length but the depth cues provided by the receding track generate a visual representation of the upper bar as longer than the lower.

For our purposes, the key features of the supposed inferential processes involved in UITs are that:

(1) they operate over representations that bear semantic relations to one another;
(2) they are modular in that they are relatively autonomous from personal level cognition, intention, belief, and reasoning;
(3) they are postulated to explain specific perceptual and cognitive capacities;
(4) their inputs are paradigmatically not personal level cognitive states but subpersonal representations, so that they are not conceived of

Figure 1.2 Ponzo Illusion (background photo from https://pixabay.com/photos/railway-rails-rails-gleise-train-711567/)

simply as mediating personal level cognitive states as input and conscious output; and
(5) they are not in principle accessible to the person whose cognitive and perceptual capacities they subserve because their functional role is to precede and to explain modifications of consciousness.

3. What Are Inferences?

In this section we review the central desiderata on an account of personal level inference (PLI). We identify features generally accepted as necessary for inference. This sets the stage for asking whether subpersonal modular processes subserving personal level cognition are plausibly thought of as inferential.

PLI involves a transition from one set of propositional attitudes (e.g., beliefs, intentions, suppositions) to another. Inferences can terminate in a new attitude – a new intention in practical inference or belief in theoretical inference. Alternatively, they can terminate in an alteration of current attitudes – for example, an inference may result in relinquishing an intention or strengthening a belief. Attitudes whose contents support the attitudinal shift are *premise attitudes*, the new or altered attitudes that result are *conclusion attitudes*.

Practical and theoretical inferences are distinguished by the attitude types of their premise and conclusion states. For theoretical inference, the premise and conclusion attitudes have mind-to-world direction of fit. For practical inference, two kinds of attitudes are required, those with mind-to-world direction of fit (beliefs) and those with world-to-mind direction of fit (preferences). In practical inference, means-end beliefs provide premises, while preferences provide comparative evaluative judgments, such as that vanilla ice cream is better than chocolate.

An inference must involve states that have modes appropriate for its type. For example, a sequence of wishes whose contents are related by a logically valid argument form is not an inference, despite logical relations between their contents. We focus on theoretical rather than practical reasoning, in which transitions occur between states with mind-to-world direction of fit. This excludes treating modeless representations as figuring in inferential processes.

It is widely accepted that a successful account of PLI must satisfy the following three desiderata (Boghossian, 2014; Broome, 2013, 2014):[5]

(1) It must distinguish PLI from other types of transition in thought.

Not just any transition between propositional attitudes (even of the correct types) constitutes an inference. For example, an associative shift between two attitudes is not an inference. A change in attitudes must be caused 'in the right way' to constitute inference. Therefore, the fact that the attitude contents have logical relations between them suitable for epistemic support is not sufficient for a mental transition to constitute an inference. For example, although A follows from A *and* B, one might come to believe A from believing A *and* B by associating A with B rather than inferring it from A *and* B.

(2) It must allow that one can make a mistaken or non-normative inference, that is, one which still counts as an inference despite its not being a good inference.

Roughly, a mistaken inference is one in which the premise attitudes provide little or no support for the conclusion attitudes. People do not always reason correctly. An adequate analysis of PLI must allow that individuals can make inferences even when they commit the base-rate fallacy or affirm the consequent. So the fact that someone's attitude transitions do not conform to Bayesian norms on belief updating (e.g., conditionalization) does not entail that the person has failed to infer. Putting this together with (1), descriptively conforming to, e.g., Bayesian norms in attitude transitions is neither necessary nor sufficient for engaging in inference.

(3) It must explain how PLI is something we do and not merely something that happens to or within us.

22 Kirk Ludwig and Wade Munroe

We make inferences and *we* update our attitudes in doing so. An adequate account of PLI must allow for inference to be a controlled process as opposed to something that merely happens to a person.

Much of the contemporary literature on PLI focuses on what Paul Boghossian (2014) calls the Taking Condition (TC):

[TC] Inferring necessarily involves the thinker taking her premises to support her conclusion and drawing the conclusion because of that fact.[6]

TC is regarded by many as central to satisfying conditions (1)–(3). TC distinguishes inference from other thought transitions by requiring that inference involves the reasoner *taking* her premises to support her conclusion and drawing the conclusion in virtue of this (desideratum 1). An associative transition does not depend on one's taking there to be an epistemic support relation between one's premises and conclusion. Furthermore, TC makes room for incorrectly taking one's premises to support one's conclusion. In consequence, one can count as inferring a conclusion even when it is not supported by one's premises (desideratum 2). Finally, because TC implies that a transition in thought only constitutes an inference when it is responsive to its subject taking the premises to support the conclusion, inference is properly something that can be attributed to the subject, rather than something that merely happens to or within her (desideratum 3).

TC requires clarification. A full account would need to explain:

(1) What *taking* one's premises to support one's conclusion consists in, for instance, whether taking is an intentional state like belief or intuition, or whether it is something like a disposition to judge that one's premises support one's conclusion.[7]
(2) What the content of the taking is.[8]
(3) What it is to *draw* one's conclusion in virtue of taking one's premises to support it, that is, what is required beyond the premise attitudes causing the conclusion attitudes.

Most contemporary work on inference either (i) focuses on answering one (or more) of the these questions or (ii) challenges TC as a necessary condition of inference. However, extant objections to TC assume that taking constitutes an intentional or representational state (McHugh and Way, 2016; Rosa, 2019; Wright, 2014). Thus, these are not objections to TC per se but to a certain way of explaining it.

The dominant account treats inference as a causal process that constitutes rule-following. For example, Boghossian (2014) adopts a rule-following account in which inferring just is following a rule of inference in moving from a set of premise attitudes to a conclusion

Theories of Cognitive Achievement 23

attitude. Roughly, we can think of a rule as an instance of the following schema:

> If antecedent conditions, C, hold, then it is permitted/required to do/accept/believe A.[9]

In a rule-governed theoretical inference the antecedent conditions will be the possession of certain premise attitudes, and the rule will indicate which attitude(s) one is then permitted/required to adopt. Boghossian argues that in following a rule (rather than merely conforming to it) one takes the antecedent conditions as reason to perform the permitted/required action. So, if a person follows a rule of inference, nothing additional is needed for her to take her premises to support her conclusion. The taking falls out from the rule-following; no additional occurrent, intentional state constitutes the taking.

We treat TC as a fourth requirement on an adequate account of PLI, aimed in part at satisfying requirements (1)–(3). It expresses a relation of the reasoner to a process involving intentional states that makes sense of its being normatively appropriate from the point of view of the reasoner. We formulate this as follows:

TC*: For a transition between premise states to conclusion states to count as an inference, their subject must take the premises to support the conclusion, whether this is a matter of an explicit intentional attitude with that content, the process being explained by the subject following a rule appropriate for the type of inference, or the subject being disposed to regard or act as if the inference is correct or justified.

We are deliberately non-specific to allow for various ways theorists have tried to make TC more precise. Notice that even if inference is construed as a matter of following a rule, when that is not understood in terms of a propositional attitude about the transition, since the rule is defined over the states involved in the transition, it requires the agent to be sensitive in its cognitive operations to the contents of those states.

4. Are There Modular Subpersonal Inferential Processes?

By subpersonal modular inferential processes (SMI) we mean processes which are genuinely inferential and not merely treated *as if* they were, or *modeled* by inferences (we return to 'as-if' talk in Section 5). We focus on the claim that there are modular processes involved in vision, language understanding, and other cognitive processes that (i) operate over states with intentional content and subserve personal level cognitive and perceptual processes by delivering appropriate personal level intentional

24   Kirk Ludwig and Wade Munroe

states and (ii) constitute inferences on the part of the modular system itself as opposed to the personal level subject (PLS).[10]

In this section, we develop an argument against the plausibility and theoretical utility of SMI processes, construed as outlined in the previous paragraph.

(1) First, we argue that if inferential, SMI must be treated as inferences of a cognitive agent with propositional attitudes.

(2) Second, we argue that the conditions required to attribute SMI to subpersonal units conceived of as cognitive agents are not met.

(3) Third, we argue that even if conditions required to attribute SMI to subpersonal units were met, this would amount to a homuncular explanation of personal level cognitive achievement, and that, to avoid a regress, the explanation of the cognitive capacities of the homunculi would have to be given in different terms. Then the same style of explanation could be applied for personal level cognitive achievement, showing the homuncular explanation to be gratuitous. The explanation offered is therefore defective because it is in principle replaceable and there is no non-question-begging reason not to replace it at the first stage of explanation.

4.1. Modular Inferences Require Homunculi

If SMI are genuine inferences but not by the PLS, they must be inferences of a subpersonal level agent. We will say a *homunculus* is a subpersonal agent whose cognitive work subserves personal-level cognitive achievements. Thus, if SMI are genuine inferences, they require homunculi.

First, for SMI to be genuine inferences, we must be able to make sense of their being taken to be correct by their subject. This requires us to conceive of their subject as taking intentional attitudes toward the inferences or at least to be disposed to take such attitudes toward them, or to be involved in rule-following of the sort that would support the idea that the subject takes a normative stance toward the relevant transitions. This is what it is for a cognitive agent to be making inferences. If the subject of SMI is not the PLS, it must be a homunculus.

Second, inferences involve transitions among propositional attitudes. Propositional attitudes have agents as their subjects. Moreover, SMI are theoretical inferences. Therefore, they require attitudes with mind-to-world direction of fit, that is, belief-like states.[11] The functional role of belief is to guide behavior, broadly construed, in the light of system goals. We can get a grip on states having mind-to-world direction of fit only if we are prepared to attribute to the system goals as well, and at least some form of rudimentary agency, in which its activities are directed in accordance with its beliefs and preferences. These are not personal level psychological states. They are not part of the psychological economy of the PLS. They therefore require a subpersonal agent.[12]

Third, the attribution of attitudes with contents presupposes that the concepts involved in the attitudes are possessed by their subject. Concept possession requires having the capacity to deploy concepts appropriately in relation to evidence and to reason in accordance with the requirements of their application conditions. Since these concepts are not and need not be possessed by the PLS in virtue of having the relevant modular capacity, as the case of children and non-human animals show, they are not concepts of the PLS – even if the PLS has the concepts independently. There must therefore be a distinct cognitive agent who possesses them.[13]

4.2. SMI Are not Homuncular Inferences

The main argument against homuncular SMI is that attributions of inferential capacities require commitments that are not met by subpersonal processes subserving personal level cognition and perception.[14] We raise two problems, the holism of attitude attribution, and the holism of concept attribution.

First, inferences are not defined over representations but over attitudes with psychological modes appropriate for the forms of inference. In the case of theoretical inferences (about how things are) this requires a mode with mind-to-world direction of fit. But attitudes with mind-to-world direction of fit are part of a pattern that includes attitudes with world-to-mind direction of fit.

The reason that attribution of belief takes place in the context of attribution of desire and intention is that the canonical role of belief is to guide action in the light of preference. This is what gives us the idea that a state is a state *whose job it is* to represent something in the world as opposed to one that is merely lawfully correlated, like tree rings, with changes in the world. The difficulty with homunculi engaging in SMI is that there is no point in attributing to them any preferences or intentions, any more than there is to attributing preferences and intentions to trees. Trees do not engage in flexible goal directed behavior guided by representations of their environment. Neither do subpersonal cognitive faculties. We might attribute to a subpersonal module a *function*, relative to its contribution to cognition, but this is not to attribute a goal to the module itself. There is *no more* point to attributing goals to subpersonal modules that have functions subserving cognition and perception than to the heart or lungs or small intestines, all of which have biological functions as well.[15]

The second problem is connected. There are holistic constraints also on the attribution of concepts. The inferences typically attributed to modular faculties require sophisticated conceptual resources and reasoning capacities that there is no evidence that subpersonal modules possess, as opposed to those theorizing about them. This is one reason we do not want to attribute these inferences to PLS. The operations of subpersonal mechanisms subserving cognition are insensitive to whether the PLS possesses the competencies required by the concepts deployed in SMI. But then it is *even less plausible* to attribute these competencies to subpersonal agents that do not have the capacity to deploy these or even simpler concepts. Even as simple an inference as that involved in deploying Emmert's Law for linear size constancy requires geometrical concepts of angle, distance, size, and space, as well as the concept of equivalence and mathematical product – and this is just a beginning.[16]

Concept possession is constituted by competence in correct application. Vision theorists and linguists have these concepts because they can deploy them across different domains. Their attribution to theorists is supported by attribution of a range of supporting concepts, for vision theorists, of number, sum, cardinality, color, light, and so forth and for linguists, of language, meaning, compositionality, rule, scope, domain, binding, and so forth. *None* of these *general* capacities can be attributed to subpersonal modules. The concepts attributed are only postulated to be deployed in a limited domain. No one thinks that the competencies required for possession of these concepts by the theorists who deploy them in describing SMI are possessed by subpersonal modules. But since the competencies are required to possess the concepts, the modules themselves do not possess the concepts. Therefore, they are not capable of performing inferences over contents involving them, since having the attitudes involved in the inference requires having the concepts they involve.

The attribution of SMI to subpersonal modules is a form of theoretical projection. If a vision scientist were to explain to someone how one might extract the relevant information present in, e.g., visual representation of the environment, from physical stimuli, given background knowledge of how the world works, she might use the sort of inferential account attributed to the visual system itself. Seeing the visual system as doing what the vision scientist is doing is supposed to make intelligible how the visual system does it: it does it just like that, like a vision scientist with tunnel vision, who cannot make any other inferences, who cannot think about anything in general, who cannot deploy the relevant concepts in any other domain. But the light at the end of the tunnel goes out when we see that having the concepts cannot be divorced from the general capacities that constitute competence in their deployment.

4.3. *Explanatory Regress or Explanatory Dispensability*

If we could find a subject for SMI, would we have an explanation of our cognitive achievements? The short answer is: Yes. But if we explain how cognition is possible in one agent by appeal to others engaging in cognition on its behalf, we have not explained how cognition as such is possible. It might be said that we can do better than this because we can explain the cognitive achievements of the subpersonal modules as well. But how? One might reapply the strategy of breaking the task down into subtasks performed by a second, deeper level of cognitive agents. Would this explain adequately the cognitive achievements of the first level of subpersonal cognitive agents? Yes . . . but only by postponing again the question of how cognition as such is possible.

One reply is homuncular functionalism (Dennett, 1978, p. 80): as we go down levels, we make an explanatory advance because the homunculi get successively dumber as they are given successively simpler inferences to make.[17] Yet even agents who are not very clever, if they are making even simple inferences, have to meet the holistic constraints on attitude and concept possession. Moreover, one needs to specify, at each level, exactly what the inferences are. It is unlikely that their content becomes less sophisticated as we go down the hierarchy, as they involve the concepts that theorists use to describe input and output. Consequently, simple inferences or not, we are postulating sophisticated cognitive agents.

One might reply that SMI were never intended to explain cognition as such. One could accept the force of the regress argument but still maintain that some explanatory progress has been made. This comes with a commitment to explain the subpersonal level cognition without adverting to further levels of subpersonal inferential processing. But now there is a dilemma. Suppose that putative SMI can be explained without appeal to further underlying subsubpersonal level inferences. We would then have an explanation of how cognition works which does not ultimately require appeal to cognitive operations. Why can't we apply this strategy at the first sublevel of processing? If we can, then the postulation of SMI is gratuitous because it is explanatorily dispensable. The only support that can be provided for it, since it is by hypothesis inaccessible to the PLS, is that if it were true, it would partially explain personal level cognition. Thus, if SMI are not explanatorily dispensable, they set us off on an explanatory regress. If they set us off on an explanatory regress, then they cannot provide an explanation of cognition as such. If the regress can be stopped, then SMI are explanatorily dispensable. Thus, SMI are either explanatorily dispensable or we cannot provide an explanation for cognition as such.

5. Inference Facsimiles

Surely it is a mistake to suppose the sorts of inferences appealed to in UITs are intended to be inferences in the ordinary sense! Similarly, surely the representations over which unconscious inferences are defined were never intended to be ordinary representations. Thus, we do not need a subject of the inference who takes their premises to be support for their

28   Kirk Ludwig and Wade Munroe

conclusions, and we do not need to worry about holistic constraints on attitude attribution or concept possession. From the standpoint of the working scientist, these criticisms are an example *par excellence* of the attempt to constrain the development of concepts appropriate for theoretical explanation to those developed in the domain of commonsense, which would frustrate the search for theoretical explanations across *every* domain in which science operates.

It is doubtful that all theorists who invoke unconscious inferences to explain cognitive achievements think of them as different from ordinary inferences in any respect other than being in principle unconscious and subserving personal level cognition and perception.[18] But a natural fallback is to suggest that the notions of inference and representation deployed in UITs should be understood in a different sense than the vernacular. On this view, to talk of 'unconscious inferences' in the context of a UIT is not to talk about unconscious *inferences*, but about, as we will put it, unconscious inference facsimiles, like, in some respects, but not the same as, inferences. This leaves us with two questions. First, what is the content of such UITs, given their reliance on unconscious inference facsimiles, since we cannot rely on our antecedent understanding of 'inference' and 'content'? Second, in what does their theoretical utility lie: how are they to help us understand cognition and perception?

There is a hard and a soft line on the first question. The hard line maintains that while not subject to the usual holistic constraints, the states over which SMI are defined are genuine representations. The processes defined over them that subserve personal level cognition and perception are inferential insofar as the states in the processes bear semantic relations to one another that mimic inferential processes. Thus, the status of the processes as substantively inference-like depends on the states involved being genuine representations. The soft line relinquishes the idea that there need be anything of our antecedent notion of representation left and treats talk of representations as a proxy for something that could be explained without appeal to intentionality. We address the hard line first, then the soft line, which leads to the second question.

5.1. The Hard Line: IO-Representations

What constraints are there on genuine representation? Ramsey (2007) notes that it is not enough for the *theorist* to assign representational content to states, as when we treat voltage levels in transistors as representing 1 or 0. These make sense relative to tasks we design a machine to implement. It doesn't give the machine the task or intrinsic intentionality. The notions we appeal to, as Ramsey says, 'must in *some* way be rooted in our ordinary conception of representation; otherwise, there would be little point in calling a neural or computational state a representation' (p. 25). But they can't be observer relative. We must make sense of the states

Theories of Cognitive Achievement 29

having content *and* of their functioning as representations *for the system* containing them. Ramsey distinguishes two notions of representation for subpersonal cognitive processing that can be detached from propositional attitude psychology, input-output representation, or IO-representation (2007, sec. 3.2), and structural representation, or S-representation (2007, sec. 3.3). We deal with IO-representations in this section and S-representations in the next.

IO-representation applies to a system that already has representations as inputs and as outputs. If intervening processing can be explained by state transitions that, by an assignment of content to them, represent the process as involving semantically sanctioned transitions from input to output, then those internal states have IO-representations. Ramsey claims that IO-representations are genuine representations *for* the system, and so not merely observer relative. But there are two problems with this. First, there is no evident inconsistency in *denying* that the assignment of representations to internal states characterized neutrally captures something intrinsic to the system. For it is not inconsistent to claim that what mediates input and output is *simply causal-functional organization*. One might *stipulate* that *if* there is a semantic mapping, *then* mediating states are IO-representations. But this is a merely verbal maneuver and so not ampliative. Second, even if Ramsey were correct, IO-representation can't be applied to perceptual processing since it presupposes that both input and output independently have representational content – and although the output of perceptual systems is independently representational, the input is not (or not solely). Thus, this notion of representation for the perceptual system would rely on an observer relative assignment of representation to inputs to the perceptual system. This would give the intervening states IO-representational content, but they would be observer relative as well, and not representations *for* the system.

5.2. *The Hard Line: S-Representations*

S-representations are structural representations. The idea is illustrated by a map. Points on the map correspond to areas on the terrain (within a margin of error). The distance between points corresponds to the distance between the areas on the terrain. When we use a map, we exploit what we know about its structure and the mapping function to learn about the terrain. Put most generally, it is the idea of a modeling system consisting of elements (m-elements) and relations between them which are isomorphic to a target system with its elements (t-elements) and its relations in the sense that there is a mapping from m-elements to t-elements, and a mapping of m-relations to t-relations, such that for any m-relation, r, relating a sequence, s, of m-elements, the image of r in the target system relates the image of the sequence of m-elements in the target system. The image of a relation or element of the modeling system in the target system is what it is mapped onto. The idea is that subpersonal processes may extract information from models in this sense to guide what representations are produced at the personal level.[19]

The difficulty lies in the idea that a subpersonal process *extracts* information to *guide* a process. What gives substance to this idea? It is not that there is an isomorphism between elements of the system and something outside it. Isomorphism is not representation. The cars in one row in a parking lot may be isomorphic with those in the next. But neither row represents the other. Isomorphism is symmetric, representation is not. When we use a map to locate a restaurant, we are the ones who, by exploiting what we know of its structure and relation to a city, use it as a representation. This presupposes an agent who uses it as a representation for a purpose. For subpersonal processes hypothesized to exploit S-representations, however, there is no one who uses them. By hypothesis the PLS does not use them. And having set aside the appeal to subpersonal agents as implausible, unsupported, and pointless, there is no one else to use them either. We are left with a structure isomorphic with some bit of reality that plays a causal role in the production of appropriate personal level representations. We could define this as an S-representation! But, again, this is not ampliative. The adoption of the language of representation may give the impression of depth of explanation. But the definition accomplishes only an abbreviation.[20]

5.3. *The Soft Line*

This leads us from the hard line to the soft line. The hard line maintained that the states over which SMI are defined are genuine representations. The soft line treats talk of representations as a proxy for something that entails no commitment to genuine intentionality. But then why bother? The answer is that even if talk of representations and unconscious inferences plays no fundamental explanatory role, it can play a useful heuristic role. But what does it come to and how could it play a heuristic role?

The answer is that, to borrow an apt expression from Brunswik (1956, p. 141), even if to different purpose,

> if we can see processes subserving perception and cognition as ratiomorphic, we gain insight into *how* they perform a function serving personal level perception and cognition.

Processes subserving perception are ratiomorphic if (i) they have the formal or functional features of a bit of reasoning, under an appropriate mapping, but not the semantic content, and (ii) the processes having that structure, in the organism's environment, yield a largely effective updating of perceptual representations of its environment. This removes

Theories of Cognitive Achievement 31

commitment to the processes involving genuine representations. But it keeps everything that is important for understanding. More precisely:

> A process is (thinly) *ratiomorphic* if there is an isomorphism from its causal-functional structure to a system of rules and representations which shows how, from input described in a certain way, the system generates appropriate personal level representational output, where appropriateness is judged in terms of its general usefulness in guiding the consuming system's cognition and action, given its goals and purposes.

Why is it useful to think of subpersonal processes as ratiomorphic? There are at least four connected reasons.[21] (i) First, it gives us a way of thinking about the causal-functional structure of a process in terms of a familiar conceptual scheme with which we have great facility. It provides, in Egan's terms, a 'function-theoretic' characterization of a mechanism subserving perceptual and cognitive capacities.[22] (ii) Second, it is an aid to discovery because it aids in thinking about the perceptual system from the design perspective. Thinking of processes as ratiomorphic helps us to see how the system could be structured to produce appropriately and dynamically changing output in response to stimuli given the environment and history of the organism's interaction with it. (iii) Third, it is an aid in making predictions because it involves adopting the intentional stance toward a subsystem, conceived as an oddly limited reasoner.[23] (iv) Finally, as Egan notes, it can 'serve as a temporary placeholder for an incompletely developed computational theory of a cognitive capacity and so guide the discovery of mechanisms underlying the capacity' (forthcoming, p. 13). This shows in what sense the function-theoretic structure identified is explanatory: it quantifies over realizations that implement it, providing insight into what the actual realizers contribute to the functioning of the system of which they are a part.

Cognition and perception are subserved by subpersonal processes. There are constraints on those processes given that they are supposed to deliver to the PLS, for the most part, accurate representations of the immediate environment. In the case of perception, this requires a causal-functional organization of the system that generates at the output a perceptual representation whose intrinsic nature reflects in its structure (even if structure alone is not sufficient for representation) a structure of similar complexity in the world (like a map and what it maps). The question that needs an answer is how the structure of the one is transmitted to the other.

When it is a design problem, we know what the target is, we know the nature of the environment, and we know what the input is. We can then seek to construct a mechanism that exploits structure in the input to transform it into the output we want, given the environment and a

32 Kirk Ludwig and Wade Munroe

history of interaction with it. We understand how the system goes from physical input to a representation of the environment when we have an account of a mechanism that generates it from structure in the input. Since the input inevitably underdetermines the appropriate output, part of what we want insight into is how the system is structured to yield from input appropriate output. This requires something to be supplied by the mechanism that constrains the relation of input to output in a way that is sensitive to what is likely to be producing the input given the environment. This is what makes it apt for description as ratiomorphic.

If we think of the task as assigned to a person who has knowledge of general features of the environment and how the system is situated in it, and then is given knowledge of the input, we can think of an inferential process that would generate an appropriate output representation. This gives us a description of a functional-causal organization that will do the job. And if we implement the design in a physical system, then we will have an explanation of how that system does the job (assuming we have representations as output). What is crucial for understanding how the job is accomplished is not that there be representations and rules of inference in the system itself but only that its structure be isomorphic to a system of representations and rules of inference. Thus, thinking of the process as ratiomorphic (seeking to see it under a mapping) helps both (i) to formulate hypotheses about the functional-causal organization of a subsystem and (ii) to grasp it.

Once we have a hypothesis about a ratiomorphic structure, (iii) it can help us to make predictions. For example, from Emmert's Law we can predict that manipulating depth information will yield incorrect representations of object size, as is born out, for example, in the Ames Room Illusion. Thinking of the process as ratiomorphic makes the prediction particularly vivid because we think of someone deducing from incorrect premises a conclusion that follows from it. Conversely, thinking of illusions as generated by ratiomorphic processes provides additional clues to the structure of those processes. For example, the Muller-Lyer illusion, the Ponzo illusion (Figure 1.2), and the moon illusion provide clues to the functional-causal structure of the visual system, which we can seek to make intelligible from the design perspective, which encourages looking for ratiomorphic processes in the system.

Finally, what a hypothesis about ratiomorphic structure gives us is an account of the causal-functional structure of a mechanism relating input to the perceptual system (or its subsystems) and output, which explains, given ceteris paribus laws connecting features of the environment with input, why for the most part the output is appropriate for the organism. The causal-functional structure is a kind of mechanism sketch. The sketch is filled in by finding a realization of it in a lower level description of the system, and ultimately a description in terms of the neurophysiology of the brain. Thus, (iv) the hypothesis guides investigations into more detailed mechanisms underlying the functional relationship between environment, input, brain mechanism, and perceptual representation.

When the ratiomorphic approach is appropriate, representational talk doesn't add anything to our understanding of the nature of the process as such. Yet it does give us insight. It provides insight both into the causal-functional organization of the system that does the causal-structural translation job and into how it is fitted for the job that it does. The assignments make *perspicuous* to us how the system preserves or generates or selects *relevant* causal-structural information. It makes clear to us how it subserves a function for the system we explain in terms of goals or representations – but crucially it does so without our having to take seriously the idea that the mechanisms themselves have representational content.[24] In this sense the role is heuristic.

6. Conclusion

Serious use of the terms 'inference', 'content', 'representation', and 'concept' must pay attention to their application conditions or supply operational definitions. Attention to their application conditions makes clear that modular systems subserving personal level cognition do not engage in inferences, they do not involve, except in their output, representations, and they, as opposed to the system which they subserve, do not possess concepts. It is natural to respond by declaring that philosophy should not attempt to put a priori constraints on the development of theoretical concepts in the pursuit of scientific understanding. But that's not the point. If words are being used in their usual sense, we must respect their application conditions. If new theoretical concepts are being deployed, we must make clear what their nature is. When we provide operationalized definitions, it becomes clear that talk of inference and so on, is basically unrelated to the ordinary personal level notions, and supplies no explanatory power over what can be said without appeal to them, though the vocabulary retains a heuristic function.

Notes

1. Nico Orlandi has developed a critique of inferentialist or constructivist accounts of perceptual accomplishment in a series of papers and a recent book (2011a, 2011b, 2012, 2013, 2014, 2016). Orlandi argues that inferentialism is not *the best explanation* of the success of the visual system. Orlandi advocates an embedded view (EV) of perception. 'According to EV, the visual system has physical features that make it act in a lawful manner. We should refrain from thinking of such features as representing anything. The features are biases shaped by environmental contingencies in the evolutionary past *and in the present*, and we can appeal to such contingencies to explain what we see' (2014, p. 57). We focus on whether the conditions for attributing inferences to subpersonal systems can be met in the first place, but we argue that there is heuristic value in inferential talk because identifies

causal-functional structure that helps explain successful representation. We suggest that this construal of inference talk converges with the approach that Orlandi recommends on empirical grounds.

2. For example, unconscious inference theories of linguistic cognition look back to Chomsky's work (1965, 1988) on the structure of the language faculty. Though Chomsky has claimed that it is a misreading to attribute to him a UIT, his followers have embraced it:

> the unconsciousness of mental grammar is still more radical than Freud's notion of the unconscious: mental grammar isn't available to consciousness under any conditions, therapeutic or otherwise.
>
> (Jackendoff, 1994, p. 9)

> The cognitive unconscious is the massive portion of the iceberg that lies below the surface, below the visible tip that is consciousness. It consists of all those mental operations that structure and make possible all conscious experience, including the understanding and use of language . . . it is completely and irrevocably inaccessible to direct conscious introspection.
>
> (Lakoff and Mark, 1999, p. 103)

UITs have been extended to unconscious processing of semantic rules for interpretation as well at the level of LF (see also (Larson and Segal, 1995)). On this view, language processing involves a faculty that possesses innate knowledge of grammatical principles and principles of interpretation that are applied both to input when a child is learning a first language and in language processing subsequently.

3. Orlandi (2014, 2016) argues that the Bayesian approach is better characterized as an ecological approach than as an inferential theory.

4. Hohwy represents the error minimization theory being a successor of inference theories that stretch back to Helmholtz that differs in its account of the inferences involved. Hohwy thinks it obvious that there is unconscious inferential processing: 'We can in fact engage in such inference, since we can perceive' (2013, p. 14), as if perception could not occur when proximal stimuli underdetermine distal causes without *inferential* processes being involved. The interesting question, on his view, is the kind of inference.

5. We don't claim these desiderata are exhaustive, only that they are of central importance. See Hlobil (2014, 2016) for discussion.

6. Boghossian notes a historical precedent for the Taking Condition in Frege, who claims, '[t]o make a judgment because we are cognizant of other truths as providing a justification for it is known as inferring'. (1979, p. 3). See Hlobil (2016) for more on historical antecedents.

7. Neta (2013) argues that taking is a judgement, Valaris (2014, 2017) that it is a belief, and Chudnoff (2014) and Dogramaci (2013) that it is an intuition or intellectual seeming. In contrast, Hlobil (2016) and Boghossian (2014) (and arguably Broome, 2013) deny that it is an intentional state.

8. Nes (2016) claims that in inferring some proposition, p, from some set of propositions, Q, one has 'the sense' that Q *means that* p where 'means' is taken to be natural meaning in Grice's sense of the term. Broome (2013) claims that the content of taking is that *the contents of one's premise attitudes imply the contents of one's conclusion attitude*. Valaris (2017) argues that the content of taking is that *the contents of one's conclusion attitude follows from the content of one's premise attitudes*, where taking consists in *realizing* that all (relevant) possibilities that make one's premise attitudes true, make one's conclusion attitude true. Finally, Neta (2013) claims that the content of a taking state is that *one's premise attitudes propositionally justify one's conclusion attitude*.

Theories of Cognitive Achievement   35

9. See Boghossian (2008) on epistemic rules.

10. Modular inferences are subpersonal. It is prima facie consistent with their being unconscious and modular that they are inferences made *by* the person in whom they take place. We do not address this view here because (i) it is implausible and (ii) it is unlikely that those advocating for an unconscious inference theory of perceptual achievement attribute, e.g., the inferences supposedly being drawn by the visual system to the agent herself as subject. For example, many of the inferences would involve concepts that the PLS (which may be a child or non-linguistic animal) clearly does not possess.

11. Many theorists attribute genuine beliefs to subsystems in the brain. For example, 'It asserts that at some level of description all creatures of the same phenotype share the same prior beliefs about what their sensory input should be' (Hohwy, 2013, p. 86). Here the sensory inputs are not conscious level but stimulus at the sensory surfaces, of which the PLS is ignorant.

12. Could one argue that the goals are not goals of the module but of the system that contains it? (Thanks to Anders Nes for this question.) First, since the behavior being guided is that of the subsystem, the goals are directed at what the subsystem does rather than the containing system, and so are at the wrong level to be personal level goals. Second, as we note next, the concepts deployed in the subsystem representations cannot be generally assumed to be available to the containing system. These concepts will be involved in goal specification for the subsystem as well.

13. Are we overlooking the possibility of non-conceptual content? Non-conceptual content has been claimed for perceptual experiences, but we are not here entertaining views that attribute perceptual experiences to subpersonal modules. However, subpersonal computations have also been said to have non-conceptual content because they traffic in representations whose correctness conditions would be specified using concepts the PLS does not possess (Evans, 1982, p. 104, n 122). However, we are here concerned with the view that SMI involve genuine inferences of just the sort that occur in the PLS except for being subpersonal. (See the quotations in Section 2 and notes 11 and 18 in this connection.) We will consider fallback positions in Section 5, where we conclude that there is no case for a subsystem having states that are representations *for* the subsystem itself rather than a grid projected onto it by the theorist.

14. We pass over some problems related to conclusions and premises of SMI. The conclusion is in a different subject than the premises, is an experience rather than belief, and contains more information than the premises. The first is the most serious problem because there is no one subject to take the premises to support the conclusion. For the premises, how are the general principles, some of which are not innate, learned by subsystems, if they do not have access to information possessed by the PLS, and how do subsystems learn of what is going on at the sensory surfaces? Magic?

15. On this topic, it is useful to note a feature of Bayesian models of perception. The Bayesian inference from perceptual input to, e.g., shape, yields a probability distribution, but perception is determinate. This is usually handled by invoking a utility function, which may be task dependent, that reflects the penalty for making a mistake (rather than just choosing the hypothesis with the highest posterior probability). The determinate output is the one that maximizes expected utility. However, first, this undercuts the idea that an *inference* is being made to what the environment is like. If you accept Pascal's Wager, you are not inferring that God exists, but reaching the practical judgment that belief in God maximizes expected utility. Second, whose utility? Not the perceptual system, but the PLS, since it is potential harm or benefit

36 *Kirk Ludwig and Wade Munroe*

to the whole system that is taken into account. But then we have an action with no proper agent.

16. The prediction error minimization project treats the perceptual system as a hierarchy of levels at each of which inferences are performed. At the lowest level it treats inputs to the inferences as involving information about physical stimulation of the sensory surfaces. 'The brain does have access to the sensory data that impinges on it' (Hohwy, 2013, p. 50). The brain is also said to engage not just in first-order Bayesian reasoning but also in 'second order statistics that optimizes its precision expectations', which is a matter of 'perceptual inference about perceptual inference' (p. 66). This involves more conceptual sophistication than most people possess. It is a good thing the brain is smarter than the person it serves. Notably, the more sophisticated the theorist becomes, the more sophisticated the brain is said to be. The history of inferential accounts, which have become more and more sophisticated over time, suggests that the inferences lie in the eye of the beholder.

17. Dennett's proposal was bound up with his advocacy of the Intentional Stance as foundational in understanding propositional attitude attributions. See note 23 in this connection. See also Hornsby (2000, p. sec. 4) for how Dennett's development of intentional systems theory led him away from an early strict division between personal level attributions of psychological states and subpersonal mechanisms.

18. See the quotation from Rock in Section 2, and Fodor (1984): 'what mediates perception is an inference from effect to causes. The sort of mentation required for perception is thus not different in *kind* – though no doubt it differs a lot in conscious accessibility – from what goes on in Sherlock Holmes's head when he infers the identity of the criminal from a stray cigar band and a hair or two' (p. 31). In this connection see also the discussion in (Bennett and Hacker, 2003, pp. 23–33).

19. This is very much the idea in the prediction error minimization account that attributes Bayesian reasoning to the perceptual system. The brain has a model of the environment which is used to make a prediction and revised to minimize error between the prediction and environment (Hohwy, 2013, ch. 2).

20. Ramsey defends S-representations against the related charge that isomorphism is promiscuous by arguing that 'components of the model become representations when the isomorphism is exploited in the execution of surrogative problem-solving' (2007, p. 96). One might think this solves the problem just outlined. But the question is still how to make sense of its being *exploited* in any sense other than playing a causal role in producing appropriate personal level representations, or of *problem solving* going on in any sense other than that an appropriate personal level representation results. Repeating a question begging description is not an argument.

21. See Ludwig (1996, p. sec. 7). Frances Egan's (2010, 2012, 2013, 2017) two-part pragmatic deflationary account of representations in cognitive neuroscience separates mathematical from cognitive content in computational accounts of cognitive function. Our discussion focuses on what Egan calls the intentional gloss. The mathematical function gets into the picture only as more detailed mechanisms for realization of the 'inferential processes' are proposed.

22. Egan introduces this term (2013, 2017) to characterize a neural mechanism as computing a mathematical function, but it applies equally well to inferential theories at a higher level of functional organization.

23. We treat the intentional stance as a matter of treating a system as-if it had intentional states. Dennett's intentional systems theory holds that the distinction between as-if intentionality and original intentionality is ill-motivated (2009). We reject this. The concept of the intentional stance presupposes intentionality

since it presupposes an intentional agent who takes it up. If intentional systems theory maintains that a system has genuine intentional states if someone can usefully take the intentional stance toward it, it makes the explanans presupposes an understanding of the explanandum. Thus, the truth of the biconditional itself has to be settled on the basis of an independent analysis of intentionality. For further critical discussion, see (Bennett and Hacker, 2003, appendix 1).

24. Assigning representational contents to states is analogous to assigning numbers to physical magnitudes like mass, energy, and momentum. We use the numbers and their structure to keep track of relations among the states that we assign them to. Similarly, to treat a state, say, as representing 1, or an edge, is to keep track of its role in the system, relative to a systematic assignment of contents to states and semantic relations to transitions.

References

Barlow, H. B. (1990). Conditions for Versatile Learning, Helmholtz's Unconscious Inference, and the Task of Perception. *Vision Research*, 30, 1561–1571.

Bennett, M. R., & Hacker, P. M. S. (2003). *Philosophical Foundations of Neuroscience*. Malden, MA: Blackwell Pub.

Block, N. (1995). On a Confusion About a Function of Consciousness. *Brain and Behavioral Sciences*, 18(2), 227– 247.

Block, N. (2002). Some Concepts of Consciousness. In D. Chalmers (Ed.), *Philosophy of Mind: Classical and Contemporary Readings* (pp. 206–219). Oxford: Oxford University Press.

Boghossian, P. A. (2008). Epistemic Rules. *Journal of Philosophy*, 105(9), 472–500.

Boghossian, P. A. (2014). What Is Inference? *Philosophical Studies*, 169(1), 1–18.

Broome, J. (2013). *Rationality Through Reasoning*. Wiley-Blackwell.

Broome, J. (2014). Comments on Boghossian. *Philosophical Studies*, 169(1), 19–25.

Brunswik, E. (1956). *Perception and the Representative Design of Psychological Experiments*. Berkeley, CA: University of California Press.

Brunswik, E. (1981). Levels of Perceptual Organization. In M. Kubovy & J. R. Pomerantz (Eds.), *Perceptual Organization* (pp. 255–278). Hillsdale, NJ: Lawrence Erlbaum Associates.

Chomsky, N. (1965). *Aspects of the Theory of Syntax*. Cambridge, MA: MIT Press.

Chomsky, N. (1988). *Language and Problems of Knowledge: The Managua Lectures*. Cambridge, MA: MIT Press.

Chudnoff, E. (2014). The Rational Roles of Intuition. In A. Booth & D. Rowbottom (Eds.), *Intuitions*. Oxford: Oxford University Press.

Clark, A. (2016). *Surfing Uncertainty: Prediction, Action, and the Embodied Mind*. Oxford: Oxford University Press.

Dennett, D. C. (1978). *Brainstorms: Philosophical Essays on Mind and Psychology* (1st ed.). Montgomery, VT: Bradford Books.

Dennett, D. C. (2009). Intentional Systems Theory. In A. Beckermann, B. P. McLaughlin, & S. Walter (Eds.), *The Oxford Handbook of Philosophy of Mind* (pp. 339–350). Oxford: Oxford University Press.

Dogramaci, S. (2013). Intuitions for Inferences. *Philosophical Studies*, 165(2), 371–399.

38 Kirk Ludwig and Wade Munroe

Egan, F. (2010). Computational Models: A Modest Role for Content. *Studies in History and Philosophy of Science Part A*, 41(3), 253–259.

Egan, F. (2012). Representationalism. In E. Margolis, R. Samuels, & S. Stich (Eds.), *The Oxford Handbook of Philosophy and Cognitive Science*. Oxford: Oxford University Press.

Egan, F. (2013). How to Think About Mental Content. *Philosophical Studies*, (1), 1–21.

Egan, F. (2017). Function-Theoretic Explanation and the Search for Neural Mechanisms. In D. M. Kaplan (Ed.), *Explanation and Integration in Mind and Brain Science* (pp. 145–163). Oxford: Oxford University Press.

Egan, F. (Forthcoming). *A Deflationary Account of Mental Representation*. In Joulia Smortchkova, Krzysztof Dolega,Tobias Schlicht (Eds.), *What are Mental Representations?* New York: Oxford University Press.

Evans, G. (1982). *The Varieties of Reference*. Oxford: Clarendon Press.

Fodor, J. A. (1983). *Modularity of Mind: An Essay on Faculty Psychology*. Cambridge, MA: MIT Press.

Fodor, J. A. (1984). Observation Reconsidered. *Philosophy of Science*, 51(1), 23–43.

Frege, G. (1979). *Logic. Posthumous Writings*. Oxford: Blackwell.

Gregory, R. L. (1966). *Eye and Brain: The Psychology of Seeing*. New York: McGraw-Hill.

Gregory, R. L. (1980). Perceptions as Hypotheses. *Philosophical Transactions of the Royal Society B: Biological Sciences*, 290(1038), 181–197.

Gregory, R. L. (1997). Knowledge in Perception and Illusion. *Philosophical Transactions of the Royal Society B: Biological Sciences*, 352, 1121–1128.

Hatfield, G. (2002). Perception as Unconscious Inference. In D. Heyer & R. Mausfeld (Eds.), *Perception and the Physical World: Psychological and Philosophical Issues in Perception* (pp. 113–143). Hoboken, NJ: John Wiley and Sons.

Helmholtz, H. v. (1867). *Handbuch der physiologischen Optik*. Leipzig: Voss.

Hlobil, U. (2014). Against Boghossian, Wright and Broome on inference. *Philosophical Studies*, 167(2), 419–429.

Hlobil, U. (2016). *What Is Inference? Or the Force of Reasoning* (PhD - Doctor of Philosophy Unpublished Doctoral dissertation). University of Pittsburgh Retrieved from http://d-scholarship.pitt.edu/28130/

Hohwy, J. (2013). *The Predictive Mind*. Oxford: Oxford University Press.

Hornsby, J. (2000). Personal and Sub-Personal; A Defence of Dennett's Early Distinction. *Philosophical Explorations*, 3(1), 6–24. doi: 10.1080/13869790008520978

Jackendoff, R. (1994). *Patterns in the Mind: Language and Human Nature*. New York: Basic Books.

Lakoff, G., & Mark, J. (1999). *Philosophy in the Flesh: The Embodied Mind and Its Challenge to Western Thought*. New York: Basic Books.

Larson, R. K., & Segal, G. (1995). *Knowledge of Meaning: An Introduction to Semantic Theory*. Cambridge, MA: MIT Press.

Ludwig, K. (1996). Explaining Why Things Look the Way They Do. In K. Akins (Ed.), *Perception*. Oxford: Oxford University Press.

McHugh, C., & Way, J. (2016). Against the Taking Condition. *Philosophical Issues*, 26(1), 314–331.

Nes, A. (2016). The Sense of Natural Meaning in Conscious Inference. In T. Breyer & C. Gutland (Eds.), *Phenomenology of Thinking* (pp. 97–115). London: Routledge.

Neta, R. (2013). What Is an Inference? *Philosophical Issues*, 23(1), 388–407.

Orlandi, N. (2011a). Ambiguous Figures and Representationalism. *Phenomenology and the Cognitive Sciences*, 10(3), 307–323.

Orlandi, N. (2011b). The Innocent Eye: Seeing-as without Concepts. *American Philosophical Quarterly*, 48(1), 17.

Orlandi, N. (2012). Embedded Seeing-as: Multi-Stable Visual Perception without Interpretation. *Philosophical Psychology*, 25(4), 1–19.

Orlandi, N. (2013). Embedded Seeing: Vision in the Natural World. *Noûs*, 47(4), 727–747.

Orlandi, N. (2014). *The Innocent Eye: Why Vision Is Not a Cognitive Process.* Oxford: Oxford University Press.

Orlandi, N. (2016). Bayesian Perception Is Ecological Perception. *Philosophical Topics*, 44(2), 327–351.

Ramsey, W. M. (2007). *Representation Reconsidered.* New York: Cambridge University Press.

Rescorla, M. (2015). Bayesian Perceptual Psychology. In M. Matthen (Ed.), *The Oxford Handbook of Philosophy of Perception* (pp. 694–716). Oxford: Oxford University Press.

Rock, I. (1983). *The Logic of Perception.* Cambridge, MA: MIT Press.

Rock, I. (1984). *Perception.* New York: Scientific American Books, Inc.

Rosa, L. (2019). Reasoning without Regress. *Synthese*, 196(6), 2263–2278.

Valaris, M. (2014). Reasoning and Regress. *Mind*, 123(489), 101–127.

Valaris, M. (2017). What Reasoning Might Be. *Synthese*, 194(6).

Wandell, B. A. (1995). *Foundations of Vision.* Sunderland, MA: Sinauer Associates.

Wright, C. (2014). Comment on Paul Boghossian, 'What is inference'. *Philosophical Studies*, 1(1), 1–11.

2 A Realist Perspective on Bayesian Cognitive Science

Michael Rescorla

1. Bayesian Modeling of the Mind

Bayesian decision theory is a mathematical framework for modeling inference and decision-making under uncertain conditions. It has two central notions: *subjective probability* (or *credence*), which reflects the degree to which an agent believes that a state of affairs obtains; and *utility*, which reflects the degree to which an agent desires an outcome. At the heart of the framework lie norms governing credence and utility:

- The *probability calculus axioms* constrain how to allocate credence at any moment.
- *Conditionalization* dictates how to reallocate credence in light of new evidence.
- *Expected utility maximization* dictates what the agent should do in light of her current credences and utilities: namely, choose the action that maximizes expected utility.

The Bayesian framework has proved remarkably fruitful within a wide range of disciplines, including statistics (Berger, 1985), philosophy (Earman, 1992), physics (Trotta, 2008), artificial intelligence (Thrun, Burgard, and Fox, 2006), and medical science (Ashby, 2006).

The Bayesian framework attained its modern form in the work of Ramsey (1931) and de Finetti (1937/1980), who conceived of it in normative terms. The goal was to capture how agents *should* proceed. Subsequent researchers have often deployed the Bayesian framework for descriptive ends (e.g., Arrow, 1971; Luce and Suppes, 1965), maintaining that it helps us describe actual humans in an idealized way. There are long-standing debates about how well it serves this purpose (Kahneman and Tversky, 1979).

The debate has recently been transformed by the advent of *Bayesian cognitive science*, which constructs detailed Bayesian models of *perception* (Knill and Richards, 1996), *motor control* (Wolpert, 2007), *causal reasoning* (Gopnik et al., 2004), *social cognition* (Baker and Tenenbaum, 2014), *intuitive physics* (Battaglia, Hamrock and Tenenbaum, 2013; Sanborn, Masinghka, and Griffiths, 2013), *human and nonhuman navigation* (Madl et al., 2014; Petzschner and Glasauer, 2011), *natural language parsing* (Levy, Reali, and Griffiths, 2009), and many other psychological domains. Bayesian modeling postulates mental activity that approximately conforms to Bayesian norms. Often, the postulated activity is *subpersonal*: executed by a mental subsystem rather than the individual herself. For example, Bayesian perceptual psychology treats the perceptual system as executing a Bayesian inference from proximal sensory stimulations (such as retinal stimulations) to perceptual estimates of shape, size, color, and other distal conditions. The inferences are not consciously accessible. No amount of introspection or soul-searching will reveal the credences or credal transitions instantiated by one's perceptual system. The emerging picture is that unconscious Bayesian inference underlies many core mental phenomena, including perception.

Bayesian cognitive science elicits diverse critical reactions. Critics charge that it gives no insight into neural implementation mechanisms and so is unexplanatory (Jones and Love, 2011; Herschbach and Bechtel, 2011), or that it is vacuous because it can fit any dataset through artful setting of parameters (Bowers and Davis, 2012; Glymour, 2011), or that its putative explanations are flawed because they do not specify how initial credences arise (Orlandi, 2014), or that it does not accurately describe how the mind works even though it fits some experimental results (Block, 2018; Colombo and Seriès, 2012; Glymour, 2011), or that many mental phenomena violate Bayesian norms (Colombo, Elkin, and Hartmann, forthcoming). All these critics deny that we have good reason to postulate unconscious Bayesian inferences.

I favor a different line. Bayesian models vary widely in their scientific merit, but many strike me as non-vacuous, well-confirmed, and explanatorily superior to non-Bayesian alternatives. We have good reason to believe that these models are approximately true. As you can see, I advocate a *realist* viewpoint towards Bayesian modeling of the mind. I have defended my realist viewpoint in previous writings (Rescorla, 2015a, 2016). Here I will clarify what the realist viewpoint involves, and I will bolster my earlier defenses of it. Section 2 reviews basic aspects of Bayesian perceptual psychology. Section 3 broadens attention to Bayesian modeling beyond perception. Sections 4–5 clarifies the goals and methods of Bayesian cognitive science. Section 6 rebuts some widely discussed objections to Bayesian modeling. Sections 7–9 favorably compare my realist perspective with an *instrumentalist* view on which Bayesian models are predictive tools that we should not construe even semi-literally.

2. Perception as Unconscious Bayesian Inference

The phrase 'unconscious inference' traces back to Helmholtz (1867), who highlighted an *underdetermination problem* endemic to perception. The perceptual system cannot directly access conditions in the distal environment. It has direct access only to proximal sensory stimulations, which underdetermine their distal causes. How does perception solve this underdetermination problem? How does it estimate distal conditions based upon proximal sensory input? Helmholtz hypothesized that proximal stimulations trigger an unconscious inference regarding the most likely distal cause of the stimulations. Bayesian perceptual psychology builds upon Helmholtz's approach, postulating an unconscious Bayesian inference from proximal stimulations to perceptual estimates (Knill and Richards, 1996; Rescorla, 2015a).

A Bayesian perceptual model features a *hypothesis space*, where each hypothesis h concerns some aspect of the distal environment. h might concern shape, size, color, etc. The *prior probability* $p(h)$ is the initial credence assigned to h. The *prior likelihood* $p(e \mid h)$ is the conditional credence in proximal sensory input e given h. Upon receiving input e, the perceptual system reallocates credence over the hypothesis space in accord with Conditionalization, computing the *posterior probability* $p(h \mid e)$: the conditional credence in h given e. Bayes's Theorem states that

$$p(h \mid e) = \eta p(h) p(e \mid h),$$

where η is a normalizing constant to ensure that probabilities sum to 1. Based upon the posterior, the perceptual system selects a privileged estimate $\hat{h}$ of distal conditions. Usually, although not always, $\hat{h}$ is selected through expected utility maximization, where the utility function reflects the cost of an incorrect perceptual estimate. The selected estimate $\hat{h}$ informs the final percept.

Bayesian perceptual psychology has produced numerous well-confirmed models of perceptual processing. An acclaimed example is the motion perception model offered by Weiss, Simoncelli, and Adelson (2002). The model assumes a 'slow motion' prior, that is, a prior probability that favors slow distal speeds. One notable feature of the model is that, when stimulus contrast is low, computation of the posterior assigns higher weight to the slow motion prior, resulting in a slower speed estimate. This explains the well-known *Thompson effect*: perceived speed is slower when stimulus contrast is low (Thompson, 1982). The model explains a range of additional motion illusions that had previously resisted explanation within a single unified framework.

Another good example is the object-tracking model offered by Kwon, Tadin, and Knill (2015). The model applies when a perceiver visually tracks an object covered with a textured pattern (e.g., a soccer ball) that rotates as it moves through space. The model divides time into discrete stages separated by interval Δt. At time t, the perceptual system receives retinal input e_t and on that basis estimates three distal variables: x_t, the object's position at time t; v_t^{obj}, the object's translational velocity at time t; and $v_t^{pattern}$, pattern motion within the object. To form these estimates, the perceptual system employs priors that treat objects as likely to decelerate over time. This generalizes the slow motion prior from (Weiss, Simoncelli, and Adelson, 2002). The priors also treat object motion as more likely than pattern motion. Finally, the priors enshrine reasonable assumptions about environmental dynamics, such as that

$$(*) \quad x_t = x_{t-1} + \Delta t \times v_{t-1}^{obj}$$

and about the interface between perceiver and environment. At time t, the perceptual system computes the posterior

$$p(x_t, v_t^{obj}, v_t^{pattern} \mid e_1, e_2, \ldots, e_t)$$

and selects privileged estimates $\hat{x}_t$, $\hat{v}_t^{obj}$, and $\hat{v}_t^{pattern}$. The posterior at t and retinal input e_{t+1} jointly determine the posterior at $t+1$:

$$p(x_{t+1}, v_{t+1}^{obj}, v_{t+1}^{pattern} \mid e_1, e_2, \ldots, e_{t+1}).$$

The result is a sequence of posteriors, each based on its predecessor and on current retinal input.

The object-tracking model explains an impressive range of phenomena. Consider *motion-induced position shift* (MIPS): a stimulus with a moving pattern appears shifted in the direction of pattern motion. A video of a typical MIPS stimulus is available online.[1] According to the Bayesian model, MIPS reflects the perceptual system's attempt at disambiguating inherently ambiguous retinal input. Retinal texture motion is jointly caused by translational velocity v_t^{obj} and pattern motion $v_t^{pattern}$. The perceptual system must disentangle how much retinal texture motion is due to v_t^{obj} and how much to $v_t^{pattern}$. When stimuli appear in the center of the visual field, position estimates have low uncertainty and the visual system estimates v_t^{obj} and $v_t^{pattern}$ quite accurately. When stimuli appear in the periphery of the visual field, position estimates are relatively uncertain. Accordingly, the Bayesian model leans heavily upon its prior bias in favor of object motion, attributing retinal texture motion largely to v_t^{obj} rather than $v_t^{pattern}$. The dynamical assumption $(*)$ then enforces a change in estimated position toward the direction of perceived motion: the MIPS effect. An immediate consequence is that MIPS magnitude should negatively correlate with perceived pattern speed. Kwon, Tadin, and Knill (2015) confirmed this prediction, manipulating positional uncertainty both by blurring the stimulus and by moving its position in the visual field. The model also explains *peripheral slowing*: perceived pattern motion

44 *Michael Rescorla*

becomes slower as the stimulus moves towards the periphery because the prior bias favoring object motion over pattern motion dominates.[2]

The object-tracking model has ten free parameters, reflecting detailed assumptions about sensory noise and environmental dynamics. Kwon, Tadin, and Knill (2015) used the MIPS stimulus to fit the free parameters to experimental data for individual subjects. The results matched the data quite well. Remarkably, the results also matched data for several additional motion illusions. Videos of these illusions are available online.[3] I highly recommend that you watch all the videos. The key point here is that parameters derived from video 1 yield extremely accurate predictions for videos 2–6. A single model *with a single set of parameters derived from video 1* accommodates the data for all 6 videos. This provides strong support for the object-tracking model. It shows that the model has the unifying power we expect from good explanations.

Over the past century, researchers have explored many alternative frameworks for explaining perception. The alternative frameworks are not nearly as explanatorily powerful as Bayesian perceptual psychology. That is why the Bayesian paradigm dominates contemporary scientific research into perception.

3. Beyond Perception

Inspired by the success of Bayesian perceptual psychology, cognitive scientists have offered Bayesian models for many other psychological domains, including the domains listed in Section 1 and many others besides.

Outside perceptual psychology, the most impressive Bayesian models lie within *sensorimotor psychology*: the study of how we control our bodies to achieve our goals. Suppose I resolve to lift some cup to my mouth. For me to achieve this goal, my motor system must estimate the cup's size, location, and shape, along with the current configuration of my motor organs. The motor system deploys these estimates to select motor commands that promote my goal. On a Bayesian approach, motor commands are selected through expected utility maximization. The utility function rewards achievement of my goal (e.g., lifting the cup to my mouth) and penalizes energetic expenditure. Expectations are computed relative to current credences, which are sequentially updated based upon sensory input and efference copy of motor commands. Models of this kind have proved explanatorily successful (Todorov and Jordan, 2002; Wolpert, 2007; Wolpert and Landy, 2012; Rescorla, 2016).

Beyond perception and motor control, matters become less straightforward. In my opinion, other areas of Bayesian cognitive science do not match Bayesian perceptual psychology and Bayesian sensorimotor psychology in explanatory power. However, Bayesian models in some other areas have been fairly successful. A good example is Bayesian modeling of intuitive physics (Battaglia, Hamrock, and Tennenbaum, 2013).

Bayesian models successfully predict intuitive physical judgments in a range of scenarios, such as judgments about whether a pile of objects will collapse. Sanborn, Masinghka, and Griffiths (2013) show that the Bayesian approach compares favorably with rival non-Bayesian models of intuitive physics.

Like most scientific research programs, Bayesian cognitive science varies in its achievements. Some Bayesian models are highly explanatory, others less so. We must evaluate individual models on a case-by-case basis.

4. Goals and Methods of Bayesian Cognitive Science

In a widely discussed critique of Bayesian cognitive science, Jones and Love (2011, p. 170) write: 'the primary goal of much Bayesian cognitive modeling has been to demonstrate that human behavior in some task is rational with respect to a particular choice of Bayesian model.' They coin the name *Bayesian fundamentalism* for this research agenda. They offer a series of arguments against Bayesian fundamentalism.

Jones and Love's critique has elicited numerous rejoinders (e.g., Chater et al., 2011). The rejoinders amply demonstrate that few if any practicing scientists endorse Bayesian fundamentalism. Jones and Love are attacking a strawman position. Bayesian cognitive scientists do not aim to show that all or most mental processing conforms to Bayesian norms. They aim to construct well-confirmed explanations of mental and behavioral outcomes. They regard idealized Bayesian modeling as a good starting point for constructing such explanations. Ultimately, one must test each Bayesian model against the data. In some cases, actual performance may deviate slightly or dramatically from the model.

More explicitly, Bayesian cognitive scientists pursue the following methodology when studying a psychological task:

(i) *Use Bayesian decision theory to articulate a normative model of the task.* The model describes how an idealized Bayesian system would execute the task. In general, the model will contain various free parameters. For example, the Bayesian object-tracking model contains ten free parameters.

(ii) *Fit the normative model as well as possible to the data by specifying its free parameters.* Kwon, Tadin, and Knill (2015) fit the object-tracking model to the data from video 1 by specifying all free parameters.

(iii) *Examine how well the model with all details specified fits actual performance.* The object-tracking model with free parameters specified was an excellent fit for the data for video 1 and also for the additional videos 2–6.

The core methodology is to articulate a normative model and then fit any free parameters to the experimental data. The model serves as a

46 *Michael Rescorla*

benchmark. The goal is to evaluate how well actual psychological processing conforms to the benchmark. Human performance often, although not always, conforms quite well.

This norms-based methodology implicitly presupposes some degree of baseline approximate conformity to Bayesian norms. If mental activity never remotely conformed to Bayesian norms, or if it approximately conformed only in exceptional circumstances, then constructing idealized Bayesian models would not be a good use of scientific resources. Thus, Bayesian cognitive science enshrines a *methodological* commitment to some baseline level of approximate conformity.[4] Researchers who pursue Bayesian modeling presuppose that at least some mental processes at least approximately conform to Bayesian norms. Clearly, that methodological commitment falls far short of Bayesian fundamentalism as defined by Jones and Love. One can adopt (i)–(iii) as a fruitful methodology without aiming to establish that all, many, or any mental processes conform to Bayesian norms.

The norms-based methodology has been amply vindicated over the past few decades. It has produced successful explanations for numerous mental phenomena, especially perceptual and motor phenomena.

The norms-based methodology does not necessitate *doctrinal* commitment to any putative law or generalization along the following lines:

- Perceptual activity approximately conforms to Bayesian norms, *ceteris paribus.*
- More perceptual processes approximately conform to Bayesian norms than do not.
- Mental activity approximately conforms to Bayesian norms, *ceteris paribus.*
- More mental processes approximately conform to Bayesian norms than do not.

For example, Bayesian perceptual models do not contain, presuppose, or entail any doctrine to the effect that most perceptual processes approximately conform to Bayesian norms. A methodological presupposition of baseline conformity underlies how Bayesian perceptual psychologists *search* for successful models, but no such presupposition figures in the resulting models. No theory espoused by Bayesian perceptual psychologists asserts baseline conformity to Bayesian norms as part of its content. An analogous diagnosis applies to other areas of Bayesian cognitive science. The science supplies Bayesian models of specific mental phenomena, not general pronouncements about the scope of Bayesian modeling. One can hold that certain mental processes approximately conform to Bayesian norms while conceding that *other* mental processes, perhaps *many other* mental processes, dramatically violate Bayesian norms.

The norms-based methodology raises several questions. Why has the methodology proved so successful? Are there *a priori* reasons to expect that the methodology would succeed, or did things simply turn out that way? Why might the methodology prove more successful when applied to some psychological domains (e.g., perception) than others (e.g., high-level reasoning)? In what way, if any, do evolutionary or developmental pressures impel certain psychological systems to conform at least approximately to Bayesian norms? These questions deserve sustained investigation. They connect with topics of longstanding philosophical interest, such as the relation between psychological description and normative evaluation (Davidson, 1980). There is room here for productive interchange between science and philosophy. Unfortunately, overemphasis on strawman positions such as Bayesian fundamentalism has tended to derail recent discussion. More fruitful inquiry should begin by accurately gauging the methodological and doctrinal commitments of Bayesian cognitive science.

5. Implementing Bayesian inference

Bayesian models typically prescind from neural implementation details. The models posit *credal states* (assignments of subjective probabilities to hypotheses) and *credal transitions* (mental transitions among credal states). They do not say how the brain encodes credal states. Nor do they identify neural processes or mental computations that underlie credal transitions. A major research program in contemporary neuroscience aims to illuminate the neural basis of Bayesian inference (Pouget et al., 2013). This research program has generated several interesting proposals about how neural tissue might implement credal states and transitions, but so far no proposal has emerged as well-confirmed.

Although we do not know how the brain implements credal states and transitions, we know quite a lot about possible ways that possible physical systems can implement credal states and transitions. As I will now discuss, Bayesian cognitive science draws upon this knowledge to refine the norms-based methodology presented in Section 4.

In principle, there are many different ways that a physical system can implement credal states. Here are three possible implementation strategies:

- *Explicit enumeration of probabilities.* A physical system can explicitly enumerate the credence assigned to each hypothesis. This implementation scheme is not feasible when the hypothesis space is infinite.
- *Parametric encoding of a probability distribution.* For example, a physical system can encode a Gaussian distribution by recording the distribution's mean and its variance. A parametric encoding scheme is only feasible for probability distributions, such as Gaussians, that are encodable through finitely many parameters. Most probability distributions are not finitely encodable.

48   *Michael Rescorla*

- *Sampling.* Imagine a physical system that draws finitely many *samples* from the hypothesis space. For any hypothesis h, there is an objective probability $q(h)$ that the system will draw h. Call $q(h)$ a *sampling probability*. As several researchers have proposed (Fiser et al., 2010; Icard, 2016; Sanborn and Chater, 2016), sampling probabilities can serve as subjective probabilities. Drawing hypotheses with a certain objective probability is one way of assigning credences to them. The system can implicitly encode a probability distribution via sampling probabilities.[5]

Parametric and sampling encodings both figure prominently in scientific applications of the Bayesian framework, such as within robotics (Thrun, Burgard, and Fox, 2006).

One might ask why these diverse physical implementations all count as credal states. What do the implementations have in common, such that they count as ways of attaching subjective probabilities to hypotheses? Answering that question would require answering a deep question: what is it to attach a subjective probability to a hypothesis? Unfortunately, no one knows the answer to the deep question. A large literature addresses the nature of credal states (Erikkson and Hájek, 2007), but the literature has yielded disappointing results.[6] Any good answer to the deep question must take as a starting point that there are diverse ways to instantiate credal states, including parametric and sampling encodings. All neuroscientific research into neural implementation of Bayesian inference begins from this starting point.

When studying how the brain implements credal states and transitions, we must grapple with the *intractability* of Bayesian computation (Kwisthout, Wareham, and van Rooij, 2011). A computation is *tractable* if it can be implemented by a physical system with limited memory and computing time.[7] In certain special cases, computing the posterior from the priors is a tractable task. For example, if the prior probability and the prior likelihood are Gaussian, then the posterior will also be Gaussian, and its mean and variance are easily computable. In general, though, computing the posterior from the priors is an intractable task. Consider again Bayes's Theorem:

$$p(h \mid e) = \eta \, p(h) \, p(e \mid h).$$

Multiplying together $p(h)$ and $p(e \mid h)$ is easy. But computing the normalizing constant η requires summation (or integration) over the hypothesis space, which is in general an intractable task. Expected utility calculations are also in general intractable. The intractability of Bayesian computation poses a significant problem for Bayesian cognitive science because the brain can only implement tractable computations.

Bayesians across a range of disciplines have intensively studied how a physical system with limited computational resources can *approximately* execute intractable Bayesian computations. Computer scientists, engineers, and statisticians offer various schemes for approximating idealized Bayesian computations in tractable fashion. Cognitive scientists enlist these schemes to construct psychological models (Sanborn, 2017). The approximation schemes employed within Bayesian cognitive science generally fall into two main categories:

- *Variational algorithms* approximate the posterior using a probability distribution drawn from a nicely behaved family (e.g., Gaussian distributions). The basic idea is to pick the distribution from this family that is 'closest' to the actual posterior. Picking the 'closest' distribution from a nicely behaved family is often a much more tractable task than computing the actual posterior. The literature offers various measures for 'closeness' of probability distributions.
- *Sampling algorithms* approximate the posterior by drawing finitely many samples from the hypothesis space. Rather than compute the actual posterior, the system responds to new evidence by altering its sampling probabilities in accord with the sampling algorithm. The new sampling probabilities serve as the system's new subjective probabilities.

Variational and sampling approximations both feature credal transitions that violate Conditionalization but that approximately satisfy it:

- *Variational approximation.* Suppose that a system begins with prior $p(h)$ and that the ideal Bayesian response to input e is to compute a posterior $p(h \mid e)$. Suppose that the system instead computes some probability distribution $q(h)$ drawn from a 'nice' family of distributions, such as Gaussians. By updating credences to $q(h)$ rather than $p(h \mid e)$, the system violates Conditionalization. However, when the variational approximation algorithm is well-chosen, $q(h)$ will be quite 'close' to $p(h \mid e)$.
- *Sampling approximation.* Suppose that the system begins with prior $p(h)$ and then responds to input e by instantiating a sampling probability $q(h)$ over the hypothesis space, as dictated by some sampling algorithm. $q(h)$ serves as the new credence assigned to hypothesis h. By updating credences to $q(h)$ rather than $p(h \mid e)$, the system violates Conditionalization. However, when the sampling algorithm is well-chosen, $q(h)$ will approximate $p(h \mid e)$. More precisely, the objective probability $q(h)$ that the system samples h becomes (roughly) proportional to $p(h \mid e)$ as the number of samples increases. In that sense, the approximation asymptotically approaches the posterior as the number of samples approaches infinity.

50 *Michael Rescorla*

In both cases, credal transitions roughly conform to Conditionalization. The result is a new credal state that approximately, although not exactly, matches the posterior. This new credal state can inform subsequent approximate Bayesian computation, including both inference and decision-making. For example, in the case of sampling algorithms, the system can approximate expected utility maximization by computing over the samples rather than the actual posterior.

Bayesian cognitive scientists deploy variational and sampling approximation schemes to study the mind. They thereby emend the norms-based methodology (i)–(iii) isolated in Section 4. They begin with a normative model of the psychological task, and they supplement the model with a second model that tractably approximates it. They then try to fit the second model to the data as well as possible by fixing any free parameters. The goal is to evaluate how well actual human performance conforms to the tractable approximation (Griffiths, Vul, and Sanborn, 2012).

This revised methodology has achieved notable successes. Sampling algorithms look especially promising (Sanborn and Chater, 2016).[8] To illustrate, consider *binocular rivalry*. When conflicting images are presented to the two eyes, the usual result is that the percept toggles between the images. Gershman, Vul, and Tenenbaum (2012) suggest that binocular rivalry results from a sampling approximation to Bayesian inference. Their main idea is that the perceptual system estimates whether stimulation of some retinal patch reflects distal conditions or whether it should be discarded as an outlier (e.g., it should be discarded if the retinal patch is damaged, or if an occluder blocks that portion of one's visual field). They delineate a computationally intractable Bayesian model that estimates distal conditions via an outlier estimation process. They also present a sampling approximation to the intractable model. According to the sampling approximation, the perceptual system draws hypotheses with objective probability approximately proportional to the posterior. When the two eyes receive conflicting images, multiple hypotheses have relatively high posterior probability. As a result, the percept fluctuates even though retinal stimulation does not change. Gershman, Vul, and Tenenbaum show that their model can explain a variety of phenomena, such as the distribution of time intervals between perceptual switches. The model, which is much more explanatorily powerful than alternative models of binocular rivalry, nicely illustrates the potential payoff from approximation schemes for idealized Bayesian inference.

6. Objections to Bayesian modeling

Bayesian cognitive science has elicited many objections. This section addresses some popular objections, focusing especially on their force against Bayesian perceptual psychology.

A Realist Perspective 51

6.1. Violation of Bayesian norms

A persistent criticism of Bayesian modeling is that human subjects often violate Bayesian norms. Over a series of enormously influential publications, Kahneman and Tversky argued that personal-level reasoning routinely flouts the probability calculus axioms and that personal-level decision-making routinely flouts expected utility maximization (e.g., Kahneman and Tversky, 1979; Tversky and Kahneman, 1983). Some researchers hold that *subpersonal* mental activity also routinely violates Bayesian norms. For example, Morales et al. (2015) present experimental evidence that perceptual processing can violate Conditionalization when the perceiver does not fully attend to the stimulus. Colombo, Elkin, and Hartmann (forthcoming) and Rahnev and Denison (2018) adduce further perceptual phenomena that they deem anti-Bayesian.[9]

I respond that Bayesian cognitive science does not regard Bayesian norms as anything like universal psychological laws. The goal is not to establish that all mental processes conform to Bayesian norms. The goal is to investigate the extent to which various mental processes conform to Bayesian norms and, in cases where they closely conform, to construct good explanations on that basis. Bayesian cognitive scientists can happily say that some mental processes conform to Bayesian norms while others do not. Bayesian perceptual psychologists can happily say that some perceptual processes conform to Bayesian norms while others do not.

Of course, if it turned out that no mental activity conformed even approximately to Bayesian norms, then Bayesian modeling of the mind would not be an empirically fruitful enterprise. However, many mental processes conform quite well. This is especially true of perception, where human performance closely approximates the Bayesian ideal across a wide range of circumstances (Shen and Ma, 2016).

In some cases, allegations that a mental phenomenon violates Bayesian norms have turned out to be ill-founded. Consider the *size-weight illusion*: when you lift two objects of equal weight but different size, the smaller object seems larger. At first, the size-weight illusion looks like an anti-Bayesian effect because it flouts a prior expectation that larger objects are heavier. Colombo, Elkin, and Hartmann (forthcoming) and Rahnev and Denison (2018) cite the illusion as evidence against a Bayesian approach to perception. But Peters, Ma, and Shams (2016) show that the illusion naturally arises from a Bayesian model that estimates relative *densities*. As this example illustrates, the Bayesian framework has repeatedly shown itself flexible enough to accommodate apparent anomalies. By adopting a sufficiently sophisticated Bayesian model, it often turns out to be possible for Bayesians to accommodate perceptual phenomena that initially look anti-Bayesian (Wei and Stocker, 2015). In similar fashion, many of the perceptual phenomena catalogued by Rahnev and

52   *Michael Rescorla*

Denison (2018) may eventually prove explicable by sufficiently sophisticated Bayesian models (Stocker, 2018).[10]

Even when a mental process dramatically violates Bayesian norms, Bayesian modeling may shed light upon it (Griffiths, Vul, and Sanborn, 2012). In many cases, we can explain anti-Bayesian phenomena by pursuing the emended methodology sketched in Section 5: construct an idealized Bayesian model along with a tractable approximation to the idealized Bayesian model; evaluate how well the tractable approximation fits actual human performance. For example, human cognition often exhibits *order effects*: the order in which evidence is received impacts judgment. Order effects violate Bayesian norms. Nevertheless, Sanborn, Griffiths, and Navarro (2010) use a sampling approximation model to explain order effects arising in categorization. Similarly, Levy, Reali, and Griffiths (2009) use a sampling approximation model to explain non-ideal parsing of 'garden path' syntactic structures. In both examples, and in many others, the idealized Bayesian model figures crucially as a basis for the tractable approximation model and a benchmark against which we can compare human performance. Human performance deviates from the benchmark due to limited computational resources.

6.2. Falsifiability

Many critics complain that the Bayesian framework is vacuous or unfalsifiable (Bowers and Davis, 2012; Glymour, 2011). The framework allows us to postulate any priors we like, so one may greet an apparently anti-Bayesian phenomenon by insisting that suitably different priors would accommodate the phenomenon. This immunity to falsification may seem highly suspect. As Anderson, O'Vari, and Barth (2011, p. 495) put it: 'The set of Bayesian models is infinite; at most, only a particular combination of priors, likelihoods, and utility functions can be rejected. This renders the perception as Bayesian inference claim untestable at best, and to the extent that it is always possible to find some combination of priors, likelihood, and utility that can generate any data set, it becomes meaningless.'

I reply that worries about falsifiability rest upon a problematic conception of scientific theory choice. Kuhn (1962) argues convincingly that mature scientific theorizing usually operates within a *paradigm*, such as heliocentric astronomy or evolution by natural selection. The paradigm includes commitments so general or abstract that they resist direct empirical test. For example, Newton's three laws taken on their own have little if any empirical content. They are not 'testable' or 'falsifiable.' Only when one supplements them with additional principles, such as the law of universal gravitation, does experimental testing become possible. Scientists accept a scientific paradigm not because they have directly tested it but rather because it has proved strikingly successful in explaining certain phenomena. Scientists then develop the paradigm so as to bring it into better contact with data. In many cases, the paradigm eventually proves able to explain anomalies that it initially struggled to accommodate (e.g., it took sixty years for Newtonian physics to explain the observed motion of the moon's apogee). If enough recalcitrant anomalies accumulate, then scientists may ultimately replace the paradigm with a new one – as when physicists replaced Newtonian physics with relativity theory.

The progress of Bayesian cognitive science fits the foregoing Kuhnian template. Researchers work within the framework sketched in Sections 4–5. They accept the framework because it has achieved striking explanatory successes (e.g., the motion estimation model). They develop the framework by constructing models of specific mental phenomena, including apparently anti-Bayesian phenomena such as the size-weight illusion. The individual models are empirically tested. The framework itself is not amenable to direct empirical testing (Griffiths et al., 2012), any more than Newton's laws are amenable to direct empirical testing. If enough recalcitrant anomalies accumulate, another framework may ultimately prove more attractive.[11] So far, the Bayesian program has fared quite well in handling apparent anomalies.

Worries about falsifiability are particularly inapt as applied to Bayesian cognitive science, whose core commitments are methodological rather than doctrinal. The core methodology is to assess how well mental activity conforms to Bayesian norms. The science does *not* incorporate general laws to the effect that all or most mental activity is Bayesian. In particular, Bayesian perceptual psychology does not incorporate any general law to the effect that all perceptual processing is unconscious Bayesian inference. The science only incorporates a methodological commitment to constructing and testing Bayesian models of mental activity. This commitment is not the sort of thing that one can 'test' through direct confrontation with empirical evidence. The only meaningful 'test' of the commitment is whether it produces explanatorily fruitful individual models. To date, it has passed that test most impressively.

6.3. Ad Hoc Priors

Another worry about Bayesian modeling is that priors are chosen in ad hoc fashion (Glymour, 2011; Jones and Love, 2011). The Bayesian framework allows us to select any priors we please. The extreme flexibility makes Bayesian modeling look to some critics more like an exercise in curve-fitting than a source of genuine explanations.

This complaint may apply to some Bayesian modeling, but it does not apply to Bayesian perceptual psychology. In typical Bayesian perceptual models, the general form of the priors is well-motivated by environmental statistics or established psychophysics. That general form usually suffices for qualitatively accurate predictions. Of course, quantitative accuracy requires curve-fitting. However, parameters fit to one task often generalize

54 *Michael Rescorla*

to other tasks. In the object-tracking model, for example, parameters fit to individual performance for video 1 also match performance for videos 2–6. I submit that Bayesian perceptual psychology offers genuine explanations, not just *ad hoc* redescriptions of the data. Similar points apply to Bayesian sensorimotor psychology and at least some other areas of Bayesian cognitive science.

6.4. Where Do Priors and Hypotheses Come From?

A common criticism of Bayesian models is that they *postulate* priors without explaining how the priors arise (Orlandi, 2014, p. 91). A related criticism is that Bayesian models postulate a hypothesis space over which priors are defined, rather than explaining how the hypothesis space is chosen (Orlandi, 2014, p. 91; Orlandi, 2016).

Both criticisms conflate *incomplete* theories with *unexplanatory* theories. Explanation must begin somewhere. 19th century chemists explained numerous properties of molecules by postulating that atoms form chemical bonds, but they did not know how chemical bonds arise. Darwin explained speciation and the observed fossil record by postulating evolution through natural selection, but the mechanisms underlying heredity remained mysterious to him. In each case, the explanation was incomplete and widely recognized as such. In each case, the incompleteness served as an impetus for future research. In each case, further developments helped fill the explanatory gap. In each case, the incomplete theory already offered powerful explanations. The same goes for Bayesian cognitive science. A Bayesian model presupposes priors and a hypothesis space, so its explanations are incomplete. Future research should try to fill the gap. Even in its present incomplete state, the Bayesian framework already offers powerful explanations of many psychological phenomena.

Orlandi (2016, p. 335) writes: 'If we are seeking to explain how we derive a single percept from underdetermined stimuli, then we cannot leave aside the question of how the hypothesis space is limited. This would amount to trading the original mystery with a new, similar mystery.' In most cases, it not so mysterious why a given hypothesis space is operative. In the object-tracking model, for example, the perceptual system seeks to estimate three variables: x_t (position), v_t^{obj} (translational velocity), and $v_t^{pattern}$ (pattern motion). Accordingly, it employs a hypothesis space composed of all possible values for x_t, v_t^{obj}, and $v_t^{pattern}$. No other hypothesis space would be as appropriate, given the estimation task in which the perceptual system is engaged. One might ask why the perceptual system engages in that particular estimation task. One might also ask how the perceptual system is able to represent x_t, v_t^{obj}, and $v_t^{pattern}$ in the first place. These are interesting questions. Answering them would require significant progress within both philosophy and psychology regarding the phylogeny, ontogeny, and metaphysics of perceptual representation. Even absent such progress, the Bayesian model taken on its own already illuminates perceptual object-tracking. It isolates crucial explanantia (the priors) and specifies how they causally influence estimation of x_t, v_t^{obj}, and $v_t^{pattern}$.

6.5. Mechanisms

Bayesian models do not say how the brain encodes priors. They do not identify neural processes or mental computations that underlie (approximate) Bayesian inference. Thus, Bayesian modeling does not address the mechanisms through which the brain implements credal states and transitions. Some critics argue on that basis that Bayesian models do not provide good explanations (Jones and Love, 2011; Herschbach and Bechtel, 2011).

This criticism assumes that good explanations must reveal mechanisms that produce the explanandum. Scientific practice offers numerous counterexamples: successful scientific explanations that are not remotely mechanistic (Rescorla, 2018). For example, the ideal gas law helps us explain the pressure exerted by a gas upon a container by isolating causally relevant factors (volume, number of moles of the gas, and temperature) and describing in systematic terms how those factors causally influence temperature. The ideal gas law does not specify underlying physical mechanisms, yet even so it is explanatory. It provides a *non-mechanistic causal explanation* of temperature. Similarly, a Bayesian perceptual model isolates causally relevant factors (the priors) and describes in systematic terms how they influence the percept. The model does not specify underlying neural mechanisms through which the priors influence the percept. Nevertheless, it is explanatory. It provides a *non-mechanistic causal explanation* of perceptual estimation (Rescorla, 2018).[12]

I acknowledge that mechanistic details often *improve* a scientific explanation. For example, statistical mechanics improves upon the ideal gas law by describing a gas in mechanistic terms as a collection of tiny interacting particles. Cognitive scientists hope to improve Bayesian modeling by identifying neural implementation mechanisms for credal states and transitions (Pouget et al., 2013). A satisfying theory of neural implementation mechanisms would doubtless enhance the explanatory power of non-mechanistic Bayesian models. Even lacking mechanistic details, many non-mechanistic Bayesian models are already well-confirmed and highly explanatory.

7. Realism Versus Instrumentalism About Bayesian Cognitive Science

I have argued that many Bayesian models yield satisfying explanations. I will now argue that we should regard these models as approximately

56 Michael Rescorla

true. Thus, I will be defending a realist perspective on Bayesian cognitive science. This section introduces realism along with a competing instrumentalist approach. Section 8 critiques some prominent anti-realist arguments. Section 9 highlights key explanatory advantages that realism offers over instrumentalism.

I presuppose a broadly *scientific realist* viewpoint. Scientific realism has been a central topic within philosophy of science for decades, coming in many versions with many arguments pro and con (Chakravartty, 2017). The intuitive idea behind most versions is that explanatory success is a *prima facie* guide to truth or approximate truth. Scientific realists recommend some kind of positive attitude towards the approximate truth of explanatorily successful scientific theories. My discussion will not hinge upon how exactly one formulates scientific realism.

Scientific realism entails that, when a Bayesian model of a mental process is explanatorily successful, we have reason to regard the model as approximately true. Approximate truth of the model requires that there exist credal states roughly like those described by the model and that mental activity transit between those states roughly as described by the model. For example, a Bayesian perceptual model posits credal states that causally interact with one another and with sensory inputs, yielding perceptual estimates. The Bayesian motion estimation model posits three credal states: a prior probability, a prior likelihood, and a posterior. The Bayesian object-tracking model posits a sequence of credal states $p(x_t, v_t^{obj}, v_t^{pattern} \mid e_1, e_2, \ldots, e_t)$, computed in response to sequential sensory input. These two models are explanatorily successful, and they invoke credal states and transitions in an essential way. Assuming a scientific realist viewpoint, we have strong reason to believe that the models are approximately true. Thus, we have strong reason to believe that motion estimation and object-tracking deploy credal states that interact in approximate accord with Bayesian norms.

My realism is a realism about specific Bayesian models. Realists about Bayesian cognitive science do not undertake a commitment to endorsing all Bayesian models of the mind, any more than scientific realists undertake a commitment to endorsing all scientific theories. One must examine the details of a particular Bayesian model to see whether the model is well-confirmed. One must evaluate how it compares with rival models, whether its predictive successes are attributable entirely to curve-fitting, and so on. When a model passes successfully through this confirmatory crucible, we have reason to accept it as at least approximately true. Some but not all Bayesian models pass the test.

My realist perspective extends straightforwardly to psychological models that approximate idealized Bayesian inference through tractable computations. When such a model is explanatorily powerful, we have reason to regard it as at least approximately true. For example, the empirical success of the binocular rivalry model provides good reason to believe that perception instantiates computations at least roughly like those posited by the model.

A realist approach to Bayesian cognitive science contrasts with an *instrumentalist* approach, on which Bayesian models are predictively useful devices that do not accurately depict psychological reality. Colombo and Seriès (2012, p. 714) endorse instrumentalism: 'Bayesian models should be understood as no more than toolboxes for making predictions and systematizing data.' Block (2018, p. 6) agrees: 'the best attitude towards the Bayesian formalism is an "as if" or instrumentalist attitude.' Block focuses on perception. He urges that, even when the perceptual system transits from proximal input to percept *as if* executing a Bayesian inference, we should not conclude that it *actually* executes a Bayesian inference. Orlandi (2014) also develops a broadly instrumentalist view of Bayesian perceptual psychology. She says that, when perceptual psychologists talk about 'priors,' we should not interpret this talk too literally. We should not posit causally efficacious credal states. We should instead view priors as 'biases' or 'simple constraints' that are 'wired' into the perceptual system (pp. 82–83).

In my opinion, instrumentalism about Bayesian cognitive science is no more plausible than instrumentalism regarding physics, chemistry, biology, or any other successful science. Just as the explanatory success of physics provides evidence for gravity, or the explanatory success of chemistry provides evidence for the chemical bond, or the explanatory success of biology provides evidence for evolution by natural selection, so does the explanatory success of Bayesian cognitive science provide evidence for credal states and transitions across a range of psychological domains. In particular, the striking explanatory success of Bayesian perceptual psychology provides strong evidence for subpersonal credal states figuring in perception. The rest of the chapter defends this realist viewpoint.[13]

8. Arguments Against Realism

The literature offers numerous arguments against realism regarding Bayesian cognitive science. Many arguments, including those critiqued in Section 6, question the scientific value of Bayesian modeling. Other arguments, some of which I will now address, concede that Bayesian cognitive science has scientific value but deny that we should accept Bayesian models as even approximately true.

8.1. Idealization and Approximate Truth

Colombo and Seriès (2012) motivate instrumentalism by observing that Bayesian models often incorporate false idealizing assumptions.

58 Michael Rescorla

For example, the Bayesian motion estimation model posits Gaussian priors. Gaussian priors are convenient because they enable us to derive an elegant closed-form expression for the posterior. However, there is strong evidence that the velocity prior has 'heavier tails' than a Gaussian (Stocker and Simoncelli, 2006). More generally, Bayesian cognitive scientists often select a prior for mathematical convenience rather than psychological realism. If a Bayesian model avowedly incorporates false idealizing assumptions, how can we construe the model as literally true?

To evaluate this argument, note first that false idealization assumptions are pervasive throughout science. The real world is complex. When modeling it, scientists deliberately introduce simplifying distortions so as to achieve mathematical or analytic tractability. A physicist might assume a frictionless plane; a population geneticist might assume an infinitely large population; and so on. Successful theories routinely incorporate idealizing assumptions known to be false or even impossible. McMullin (1985) calls these assumptions *Galilean idealizations*. Scientists introduce Galilean idealizations quite self-consciously, hoping that future research will yield more accurate models. To use Weisberg's (2007) example: quantum chemistry at first gave only highly approximate descriptions of wave functions for virtually all molecules, but with time it gave much more accurate descriptions. Scientific disciplines often take idealized models as a starting point and then gradually produce more accurate models by eliminating or reducing Galilean idealization.

Scientific realists accommodate Galilean idealization by invoking *approximate truth*. A scientific theory that incorporates false idealizing assumptions is not true, but it may be approximately true. When a theory is explanatorily successful, realists hold that we have *prima facie* reason to believe that it is approximately although not perhaps literally true. Subsequent research aims to discover a more accurate theory.

The same goes for Bayesian cognitive science. When a Bayesian model incorrectly postulates a Gaussian prior, this is (and is typically advertised as) a deliberate distortion introduced to simplify calculation and analysis. A model that incorporates an incorrect prior cannot be literally true. If the model exhibits striking empirical success, then we have strong reason to believe that it is approximately true. Scientists can improve upon the model by describing the actual prior more accurately, as Stocker and Simoncelli (2006) did for the velocity prior.[14] A similar progression has transpired within Bayesian modeling of *sensory cue combination*, which initially postulated idealized Gaussian priors and subsequently identified less idealized priors (Trommershäuser, Körding, and Landy, 2011; Rescorla, forthcoming). Thus, scientific realists can accommodate Galilean idealization within Bayesian perceptual psychology in the same way that they accommodate Galilean idealization within other scientific disciplines.

A Realist Perspective   59

One might challenge the realist appeal to approximate truth. No one has ever explained in general, satisfying terms what it is for a theory to be 'approximately true.' However, this worry seems no more troublesome for Bayesian cognitive science than for any other science. I submit that Galilean idealization poses no greater a challenge to realists about Bayesian cognitive science than it does to scientific realists more generally. As already noted, the present chapter assumes a broadly scientific realist viewpoint.

8.2. Explicit Enumeration of Credences?

Block (2018) critiques realism about Bayesian perceptual psychology. He discusses a version of realism on which 'priors and likelihoods (and utilities) . . . are represented explicitly in perceptual systems' (p. 8). Block notes that there are many ways to implement or approximately implement a Bayesian model besides explicit enumeration of probabilities. He mentions sampling as one alternative implementation strategy. He says that we have no reason to favor an explicit encoding scheme over a sampling implementation. He concludes that we should adopt an instrumentalist rather than a realist construal of Bayesian perceptual psychology.

I agree with Block that we have no reason to postulate explicit enumeration of probabilities by the perceptual system. In most perceptual tasks, the distal variable being estimated has infinitely many possible values. The hypothesis space is infinite, so explicit enumeration of credences is not an option. It is unlikely that explicit enumeration of probabilities plays an important role in perception or in any almost any other psychological domain.[15]

I dispute Block's suggestion that these observations undermine a realist construal of Bayesian modeling. Realists about Bayesian perceptual psychology claim that the perceptual system instantiates credal states and that, in certain cases, transitions among those states conform approximately to Bayesian norms. Realists do *not* claim that the perceptual system explicitly enumerates credences. Realism allows that the perceptual system may employ a parametric encoding, a sampling encoding, or some other encoding. In rejecting explicit enumeration of credences, Block is not rejecting realism.[16]

In one passage, Block hints that genuine Bayesian inference requires explicit enumeration of probabilities. He writes (p. 7):

What would show that something that deserves to be called Bayesian inference actually occurs in perception? In the most straightforward implementation, there would have to be perceptual representations of prior probabilities for alternative hypotheses, perceptual

60 Michael Rescorla

representations of likelihoods and some process that involves something that could be described as multiplication of these values.

The 'most straightforward implementation' emphasized by Block plays virtually no role in scientific applications of Bayesian decision theory because virtually all scientific applications feature an infinite hypothesis space. A physical system can execute Bayesian inferences even though it does not employ anything resembling Block's 'most straightforward implementation.' When priors are Gaussian, for example, the system can conform to Conditionalization by updating the mean and variance of the probability distribution. Such a system does not explicitly enumerate probabilities, let alone multiply probabilities together.

Block's discussion rests upon an overly narrow conception of what it is for a physical system to instantiate credal states. The discussion saddles realists with an implausible commitment (explicit enumeration of credences) that they do not and should not accept.

8.3. Approximate Bayesian Inference

Block claims that computational intractability poses a challenge to realism about Bayesian modeling (p. 8): 'A major problem with realist theories in which Bayesian inference literally takes place in the brain is that the kind of Bayesian computations that would have to be done are known to be computationally intractable. . . . So, any realist version of Bayesianism will have to tell us what exactly is supposed to be involved in the computations.'

I disagree. Realists about a scientific theory need not specify exactly how the theory applies to specific cases. Realists about evolution by natural selection are not obliged to say how exactly a given species evolved. Realists about Bayesian cognitive science are not obliged to say how exactly a given mental process approximately implements Bayesian computation. In each case, it is scientific progress to discover as many details as possible. Even absent the desired progress, one can maintain a well-justified realist attitude towards the theory's key elements. One need not know how exactly an organism evolved through natural selection to believe with strong justification that it did so. One need not know exactly how the perceptual system approximately implements Bayesian inference to believe with strong justification that it does so.

Still, it may seem that any appeal to *approximate* Bayesian inference blurs the border between realism and instrumentalism, perhaps even draining realism of all content. If mental activity implements a tractable approximation rather than an idealized Bayesian model, then in what sense does the activity count as Bayesian? Once realists concede that mental activity violates Bayesian norms, what distinguishes their position from the instrumentalist view that mental activity proceeds *as if* it executes Bayesian inferences? In Block's words (2018, p. 8): '[W]hat is the difference between approximate implementation of Bayesian inference and behaving roughly as if Bayesian inference is being implemented . . . ? Until this question is answered, the jury is out on the dispute between realist and anti-realist views.'

I respond that there is a huge difference between systems that approximately implement Bayesian inference and systems that merely behave as if they do. A system of the former type instantiates credal states that interact in rough conformity to Bayesian norms. A system of the latter type may simulate a system of the former type, but it does not instantiate credal states that interact in approximate accord with Bayesian norms. For example, Maloney and Mamassian (2009) note that a physical system can simulate certain simple Bayesian perceptual inferences by using a look-up table, without executing anything like a mental transition among credal states. The system merely looks up what perceptual estimate it should output in response to a given sensory input. Such a system does not approximately implement a Bayesian inference. It does not even instantiate credal states.

Any Bayesian model describes a mapping from inputs to outputs. For example, a Bayesian perceptual model describes a mapping from proximal sensory inputs to perceptual estimates.[17] A Bayesian model posits credal states that mediate the mapping from inputs to outputs. The simplest models posit three mediating credal states:

the prior probability $p(h)$
the prior likelihood $p(e \mid h)$
a credal state $q(h)$ that results from the prior probability, the prior likelihood, and input e.

In an idealized Bayesian model, $q(h)$ is the posterior $p(h \mid e)$. In an approximation model, $q(h)$ may only approximate $p(h \mid e)$. From a realist perspective, the credal states $p(h)$, $p(e \mid h)$, and $q(h)$ are genuine mental states that causally impact the transition from inputs into outputs. The two priors combined with input e cause credal state $q(h)$, which in turn causes a 'decision,' such as selection of a privileged hypothesis $\hat{h}$ (in the case of perceptual estimation) or selection of a motor command (in the case of motor control). Thus, input-output mappings are mediated by a causal structure that conforms approximately to Bayesian norms. Some Bayesian models, such as the object-tracking model, describe a richer causal structure that embeds additional credal states.

Instrumentalists are neutral about the causal structure that mediates between inputs and outputs. From an instrumentalist perspective, input-output mappings might just as well be mediated by a look-up table. So realists are far more committal than instrumentalists about the mental processes that mediate between inputs and outputs.

62 *Michael Rescorla*

The concept of 'approximation' is vague. No doubt there are borderline cases: cases where it is indeterminate whether a system 'approximately implements' Bayesian inference. In practice, most naturally arising cases fall determinately on one or another side of the border. Variational and sampling schemes are clear-cut cases of approximate Bayesian inference. A look-up table is a clear-cut case in which approximate Bayesian inference does not occur. Realists contend that some mental activity falls on the approximate Bayesian inference side of the border. Instrumentalists say that we have no reason to think so. This is substantive and well-defined disagreement, even though it hinges upon a vague concept. Many useful concepts are vague (Williamson, 1994). The vagueness of 'approximation' does not forestall constructive debate between realists and instrumentalists.

8.4. Scientific Practice

Block (2018, p. 8) cites scientific practice to support his instrumentalist construal of Bayesian modeling. He notes that some Bayesian cognitive scientists claim only to be addressing input-output mappings, without any commitment as to the causal structure that mediates between inputs and outputs. These researchers offer a Bayesian model as an ideal solution to a problem faced by the mind, such as estimating distal conditions based on proximal sensory input, or parsing an utterance's syntactic structure, or choosing a motor command that promotes one's goals. The researchers aim to assess how closely humans match the ideal solution, not to discover how humans actually solve the problem. Why should we regard a Bayesian model as approximately true when its own creators decline to do so?

I reply that the dispute between realism and instrumentalism is not about what scientists believe, any more than the dispute between Platonism and nominalism regarding mathematical entities is about what mathematicians believe. The dispute is about what we have *reason* to believe. Some practicing Bayesian cognitive scientists are indeed agnostic about the postulates of their own models, just as some mathematicians are agnostic about whether mathematical entities exist. In neither case does the agnosticism militate against a realist construal. The issue is whether agnosticism is well-grounded, not whether any practitioners partake in it.

In any event, Block neglects important aspects of current scientific practice that fit much better with a realist construal than with an instrumentalist construal. As noted in Section 5, a major strand in current neuroscience is the search for neural mechanisms that approximately implement Bayesian inference. This search presupposes a realist perspective on credal states and transitions. It presupposes that credal states posited by Bayesian models are genuine mental states instantiated by the

A Realist Perspective 63

brain, not just useful fictions. Investigating how priors are realized in the brain would be a fool's errand if there were no priors. Instrumentalists must reject as misguided all ongoing research into neural mechanisms of approximate Bayesian inference.

9. Explanatory Advantages of Realism

I contend that realism offers key explanatory advantages over instrumentalism. I focus on perception, but my arguments generalize to explanatorily successful Bayesian models of non-perceptual domains. I offer two arguments: *the argument from altered priors* and *the argument from iterated inference*.

The argument from altered priors proceeds from the observation that priors can change in response to sensory input. For example, Sotiropoulos, Seitz, and Seriès (2011) investigated whether one can alter the slow motion prior employed during motion estimation. They repeatedly exposed subjects to fast-moving stimuli. In response to this experimental manipulation, the velocity prior shifted so as to favor faster speeds. Motion estimation changed accordingly: the same stimulus looked to be moving faster after the manipulation than it did before the manipulation. As a general matter, one can experimentally manipulate both prior probabilities (Adams, Graf, and Ernst, 2004; Ernst, 2007) and prior likelihoods (Sato and Kording, 2014; Sato, Toyoizumi, and Aihara, 2007; Seydell, Knill, Trommershäuser, 2010) deployed by the perceptual system.[18]

When priors change, there is a change in the mapping from proximal sensory inputs to perceptual estimates. Realists can offer a principled explanation for why the mapping changes as it does. If the perceptual system approximately executes a Bayesian inference based upon prior $p(h)$, then changing the prior from $p(h)$ to $p^*(h)$ will cause approximate execution of a Bayesian inference based upon $p^*(h)$. The original prior $p(h)$ induces one mapping Γ from sensory inputs to perceptual estimates, while the new prior $p^*(h)$ induces a different mapping Γ^*. Realists can describe in systematic terms how different environmental statistics yield different priors and thereby induce different mappings from sensory inputs to perceptual estimates.

Instrumentalists cannot offer nearly so satisfying an explanation. The fact that a system behaves *as if* executing a Bayesian inference from prior $p(h)$ gives no reason expect that any given experimental manipulation would cause the system to behave *as if* executing a Bayesian inference from some other prior $p^*(h)$. From an instrumentalist perspective, there is no reason why a given experimental manipulation should cause mapping Γ^* to replace mapping Γ. Instrumentalists can augment their theory by *stipulating* that the experimental manipulation causes mapping Γ^* to replace mapping Γ. Clearly, though, the augmented theory does not

64   *Michael Rescorla*

explain in a principled way why Γ changes as it does. Similarly, Orlandi can say that the perceptual system is 'wired' one way and then becomes 'wired' a different way in response to changing environmental statistics, but her account yields no principled explanation for why one 'wiring' replaces another (Rescorla, 2015b).

Here we see a stark contrast between realist and instrumentalist construals of Bayesian modeling. From a realist perspective, priors are genuine, causally efficacious mental states. We can say what would happen if we were to hold one mental state fixed while varying another – for instance, if we were to hold the prior likelihood fixed while varying the prior probability. We thereby explain why certain experimental manipulations impact perceptual processing as they do. Instrumentalists cannot offer a comparably satisfying explanation because they deny that the Bayesian model describes genuine mental states that causally influence perceptual processing. Instrumentalists hold that talk about priors is simply a way of summarizing the mapping from proximal inputs to perceptual estimates. Because they invest the Bayesian model with no psychological reality beyond the mapping Γ itself, they have no theoretical resources to explain why certain experimental manipulations change the mapping one way rather than another.

So goes the argument from altered priors. I offered a version of the argument in (Rescorla, 2015a, 2015b). Block responds:

> I find this argument unconvincing because whatever it is about the computations of a system that simulates the effect of represented priors . . . might also be able to simulate the effect of change of priors. Without a comparison of different mechanisms that can accomplish the same goal, the argument for realism is weak.

Block mentions sampling as an example of how a system might 'simulate the effect of change of priors.' However, we saw in Section 8 that sampling is consistent with a realist construal of Bayesian modeling. Sampling algorithms studied in cognitive science do not *simulate* approximate Bayesian inference. They *implement* approximate Bayesian inference. A sampling implementation does not just 'simulate the effect of change of priors.' The system instantiates priors, and those priors can change in response to suitable experimental manipulations, yielding a different mapping from sensory inputs to perceptual estimates. Sampling is an illustration of my argument, not a counterexample to it.

In principle, a system that simulates Bayesian inference from prior $p(h)$ might respond to certain experimental manipulations by simulating Bayesian inference from a new prior $p^*(h)$. But a system that simulates Bayesian inference from prior $p(h)$ need not so respond. Instrumentalists must offer a principled explanation for why the mapping Γ changes as

A Realist Perspective   65

it does. Maybe they will eventually do so. Maybe they will eventually provide a compelling alternative to the realist explanation. However, it is true of virtually *any* explanation that we may eventually discover a compelling alternative explanation. One does not undermine an abductive inference by noting the mere possibility that a compelling alternative explanation may someday emerge.

As an especially vivid illustration of the argument from altered priors, consider an experiment performed by Adams, Graf, and Ernst (2004). The experiment targets perceptual estimation of shape based upon shading cues. In typical humans, shape estimation relies upon a prior probability over possible directions for the light source. The prior assigns a relatively high probability to lighting directions that are overhead and slightly to the left. Adams, Graf, and Ernst (2004) manipulated the light-from-overhead prior by exposing subjects to deviant visual-haptic stimuli indicating a shifted direction for the light source. The prior changed accordingly, inducing an altered mapping from shading cues to shape-estimates. Moreover, the very same experimental manipulation altered performance in a *separate* perceptual task that required subjects to estimate which side of an oriented bar was lighter than the other.

Why does an experimental manipulation in one task (shape estimation) affect performance in a separate task (lightness estimation)? From a realist perspective, the answer is straightforward: both tasks deploy a common light-from-overhead prior; the experimental manipulation affects performance in both tasks by altering that prior. Instrumentalists seem unable to offer a comparably satisfying explanation. From an instrumentalist viewpoint, there is no reason to expect that an experimental manipulation of the mapping from sensory inputs to shape-estimates will *also* change the mapping from sensory inputs to lightness-estimates. For example, imagine a system that simulates Bayesian shape estimation using a look-up table and that simulates Bayesian lightness estimation using a separate look-up table. Let us stipulate that the system can respond to experimental manipulations in a perceptual task by altering the appropriate look-up table: e.g., it responds to deviant stimuli in the shape estimation task by altering the look-up table used for shape estimation. Let us stipulate that the system will change the mapping from shading cues to shape-estimates so as to simulate a change in the light-from-overhead prior. Our stipulations do not entail that the system *also* changes the look-up table used for lightness estimation. There is no principled reason to expect that a change in the look-up table used for shape estimation will correlate with a change in the look-up table used for lightness estimation. More generally, there is no principled reason why a system that simulates a changed prior in the shape estimation task should also simulate a changed prior in the lightness estimation task. Thus, realism offers a satisfying explanation where instrumentalism does not.

66 Michael Rescorla

The argument from iterated inference is similar to the argument from altered priors, but it only applies to a restricted range of Bayesian models. It applies to models, such as the object-tracking model, that postulate sequential Bayesian inferences based upon evolving credal states.

The object-tracking model postulates a sequence of credal states $p(x_t, v_t^{obj}, v_t^{pattern} \mid e_1, e_2, \ldots, e_t)$, yielding perceptual estimates $\hat{x}_t$, $\hat{v}_t^{obj}$, and $\hat{v}_t^{pattern}$. Credal state $p(x_t, v_t^{obj}, v_t^{pattern} \mid e_1, e_2, \ldots, e_t)$ and sensory input e_{t+1} jointly determine the next credal state $p(x_{t+1}, v_{t+1}^{obj}, v_{t+1}^{pattern} \mid e_1, e_2, \ldots, e_{t+1})$. Thus, the model postulates sequential credal states that interact with sensory input to influence perceptual estimation. Each credal state $p(x_t, v_t^{obj}, v_t^{pattern} \mid e_1, e_2, \ldots, e_t)$ induces a mapping Γ_{t+1} from sensory input e_{t+1} to perceptual estimates $\hat{x}_{t+1}$, $\hat{v}_{t+1}^{obj}$, and $\hat{v}_{t+1}^{pattern}$. Intuitively: the system's current credences regarding position and motion determine how it will estimate position and motion based upon the next sensory input it receives. A different credal state $p^*(x_t, v_t^{obj}, v_t^{pattern} \mid e_1, e_2, \ldots, e_t)$ would induce a *different* mapping Γ_{t+1}^*. If we interpret the model realistically, we can explain in a systematic way why mapping Γ_{t+1} rather than mapping Γ_{t+1}^* occurs. We regard the sequence of mappings $\Gamma_1, \Gamma_2, \ldots, \Gamma_t, \ldots$ as resulting from a fixed Bayesian estimator that updates credences based upon sensory inputs $e_1, e_2, \ldots, e_t, \ldots$ We can say that the sequence $\Gamma_1, \Gamma_2, \ldots, \Gamma_t, \ldots$ reflects a sequence of causally relevant credal states governed by a fixed Bayesian dynamics. Instrumentalists offer no comparable explanation. They cannot explain why, when the mapping at t is Γ_t, the mapping at $t+1$ is Γ_{t+1} rather than Γ_{t+1}^*. From an instrumentalist perspective, one sequence of mappings is no more to be expected than any other. Realists can offer a principled explanation for the sequence of mappings. Instrumentalists cannot.

It is not helpful to gloss credal states in terms of biases, constraints, wirings, or other similar locutions. There is of course a sense in which the perceptual system during the object-tracking task is wired one way at t (corresponding to mapping Γ_t) and then becomes wired a different way at $t+1$ (corresponding to mapping Γ_{t+1}). However, the 'wiring' at t reflects a fleeting credal state that occurs at t and loses psychological relevance shortly thereafter. The 'wiring' does not belong to the fixed architecture of perceptual processing. Sequential perceptual estimates $\hat{x}_t$, $\hat{v}_t^{obj}$, and $\hat{v}_t^{pattern}$ derive from an underlying sequence of credal states $p(x_t, v_t^{obj}, v_t^{pattern} \mid e_1, e_2, \ldots, e_t)$. Talk about biases, constraints, and wirings obscures this underlying causal structure. By acknowledging the causal structure, we reap explanatory dividends that appear otherwise unavailable.

The realist arguments I have provided are not decisive. A committed instrumentalist could insist that scientific theories are not in the business of accurate description and that we should construe even the most successful theory as nothing but a useful predictive device. Short of embracing a full-blown instrumentalist stance towards all scientific theorizing, I see little motivation for an instrumentalist construal of Bayesian perceptual psychology.

Although this section has focused on perception, my arguments generalize to other well-confirmed Bayesian models. The argument from altered priors applies whenever priors can change. The argument from iterated inference applies to any Bayesian model that postulates a sequence of inferences based upon evolving credal states – such models are especially common in Bayesian sensorimotor psychology. Taken together, the two arguments show that realism offers notable explanatory advantages over instrumentalism.

10. Conclusion

Helmholtz proposed that unconscious mental processes can resemble familiar conscious activities such as inference and decision-making. Bayesian cognitive science vindicates Helmholtz's proposal through explanatorily powerful, well-confirmed models of perception, motor control, and other domains. Bayesian modeling establishes the existence of subpersonal mental computations that are inaccessible to consciousness yet that share theoretically crucial properties with personal-level credal inference. The computations incorporate transitions among credal states. In some cases, the transitions conform closely to the Bayesian ideal. In other cases, the transitions tractably approximate the intractable Bayesian ideal. How remarkable that the Bayesian paradigm, originally conceived with normative aspirations, has proved such a fertile source of empirical insights!

Acknowledgments

I presented versions of this material at the 2019 Annual Meeting of the Society for Philosophy and Psychology and at a 2019 Workshop on Current Topics in Cognitive Science at Ruhr Universität Bochum. I thank the audience members on both occasions for their helpful feedback. I also thank Steven Gross and Anders Nes for comments that improved the chapter. My research was supported by a fellowship from the National Endowment for the Humanities. Any views, findings, conclusions, or recommendations expressed in this publication do not necessarily reflect those of the National Endowment for the Humanities.

Notes

1. http://movie-usa.glencoesoftware.com/video/10.1073/pnas.1500361112/video-1.
2. For a video of peripheral slowing, modify the URL from note 1 by replacing 'video-1' with 'video-2'.
3. For the additional four videos, modify the URL from note 1 by replacing 'video-1' with 'video-3', 'video-4,' 'video-5', or 'video-6'.
4. In (Rescorla, 2016), I described the methodological commitment as a 'working hypothesis.' That description tallies with the language one finds among

68 *Michael Rescorla*

some practicing Bayesian cognitive scientists (e.g., Stocker, 2018). Overall, though, I think that the phrase 'methodological commitment' more accurately captures how Bayesian cognitive science operates.

5. My formulations here and in my subsequent remarks about sampling require minor emendation when the hypothesis space is continuous, but not in any way that affects the overall thrust.

6. Most discussants tie credal states to personal-level psychological capacities. For example, de Finetti (1937/1980) cites the gambling odds that an agent would accept, while Davidson (1980) explores how an idealized interpreter would measure an agent's credences based upon the agent's linguistically revealed preferences. Both strategies tie credences to sophisticated personal-level activities, such as gambling or linguistic communication. For that reason, they do not directly apply to the credal states studied within most of Bayesian cognitive science. In particular, the credal states postulated by Bayesian perceptual psychology are *subpersonal*. The person cannot access them. They do not serve as fodder for gambling, linguistic communication, or other sophisticated personal-level activities.

7. *Computational complexity theory* studies the distinction between tractable and intractable computation. For discussion of computational complexity theory and its relation to cognitive science, see (van Rooij et al., 2019).

8. In a series of publications (e.g., Friston and Stephan, 2007), Friston and collaborators pursue a version of the variational approximation scheme. Throughout his voluminous writings, Friston provides virtually no serious empirical support for his favored version of the variational scheme. Clark (2015) and Hohwy (2014) enthusiastically promote Friston's approach while neglecting much better confirmed sampling approximations.

9. There is some evidence that the Thompson effect can reverse at high speeds (Thompson, Brooks, and Hammett, 2006): in other words, that fast-moving stimuli can appear to move even faster at low contrast. This reversed Thompson effect is inconsistent with the (Weiss, Simoncelli, and Adelson, 2002) model and with other standard Bayesian models of motion perception. However, the reversed Thompson effect does not replicate very reliably (Sotiropoulos, Seitz, and Seriès, 2014). Moreover, Bayesians could in principle accommodate the effect by suitably altering the prior (Stocker and Simoncelli, 2006). Thus, it is an open question how much of a challenge the reversed Thompson effect poses to Bayesian modeling of perception.

10. Anderson, O'Vari, and Barth (2011) discuss a motion stimulus that causes a percept as of a highly improbable illusory contour. They claim that the contour illusion is anti-Bayesian, on the grounds that a Bayesian perceptual system should not select a highly improbable hypothesis. Colombo, Elkin, and Hartmann (forthcoming) and Rahnev and Denison (2018) concur. However, there are Bayesian models that allow one to select a highly improbable hypothesis, so the contour illusion taken on its own has little force against the Bayesian program (Fleming, 2011). That being said, the illusion is an intriguing one, and it merits closer study by Bayesian perceptual psychologists.

11. Colombo, Elkin, and Hartmann (forthcoming) observe that there are other mathematical frameworks besides Bayesian decision theory for modeling inference and decision-making under uncertainty. They suggest that cognitive scientists should explore these alternative frameworks as theories of mental activity. At present, though, no alternative framework has achieved anything approaching the massive success of the Bayesian framework, especially as applied to perception and motor control. That situation might of

A *Realist Perspective* 69

course change, but current evidence in the perceptual and motor domains strongly favors the Bayesian framework.

12. See (Woodward, 2003, 2017) for general discussion of causal explanation, including non-mechanistic causal explanation.
13. Dennett (1987) develops a broadly instrumentalist approach to psychological explanation. According to Dennett, psychological explanation involves taking the 'intentional stance' towards a subject, without any commitment regarding the subject's actual mental states. Dennett applies his instrumentalist approach both to personal-level and subpersonal psychological explanation. Hornsby (2000) and McDowell (1994) agree with Dennett regarding the subpersonal level, but they favor a more realist approach to the personal level. See (Rescorla, 2016) for critical discussion of Dennett.
14. Sotiropoulos, Seitz, and Seriès (2014) revise the (Stocker and Simoncelli, 2006) model to include a pre-processing step that models speed tuning in the visual cortex. This pre-processing step influences the stimulus measurement that serves as input to Bayesian computation. The resulting model fits experimentally observed interactions between speed and contrast quite well.
15. Orlandi (2016, pp. 334, 336) suggests that the perceptual system must somehow limit the hypothesis space so as to render it finite. I see no need for any such finitary limitation. A physical system can allocate credence over an infinite (indeed, uncountably infinite) hypothesis space. For example, it can parametrically encode a Gaussian distribution. This is how numerous models from Bayesian perceptual psychology work, including the Bayesian object-tracking model. Few models in Bayesian perceptual psychology feature a finite hypothesis space, aside from tinker-toy models deployed for heuristic purposes by introductory expositions.
16. Block attributes to me 'a realist version of Bayesianism in which priors are explicitly represented' (p. 8). I do not endorse the attributed view either in the two papers that he cites, (Rescorla, 2015a, 2015b), or in any other work. Several of my previous writings have extensively discussed sampling implementation of credal states (Rescorla, 2009, 2012).
17. The mapping may be stochastic rather than deterministic. Due to sensory noise, the same proximal input does not yield the same perceptual estimate on each occasion. There are various ways for Bayesian models to capture stochastic variation, such as incorporating a noise term that corrupts expected utility maximization.
18. In (Rescorla, 2015b), I mistakenly claimed that (Beierholm, Quartz, and Shams, 2009) is an example where the prior likelihood changes.

References

Adams, W., Graf, E., & Ernst, M. (2004). Experience Can Change the 'Light-From-Above' Prior. *Nature Neuroscience*, 7, 1057–1058.

Anderson, B., O'Vari, J., & Barth, H. (2011). Non-Bayesian Contour Synthesis. *Current Biology*, 21, 492–496.

Arrow, K. (1971). *Essays on the Theory of Risk-Bearing*. Chicago: Markham.

Ashby, D. (2006). Bayesian Statistics in Medicine: A 25-Year Review. *Statistics in Medicine*, 25, 3589–3631.

Baker, C., & Tenenbaum, J. (2014). Modeling Human Plan Recognition Using Bayesian Theory of Mind. In G. Sukthankar, R. P. Goldman, C. Geib, D.

70 *Michael Rescorla*

Pynadath, & H. Bui (Eds.), *Plan, Activity, and Intent Recognition: Theory and Practice* (pp. 177–204). Waltham: Morgan Kaufmann.

Battaglia, P. W., Hamrick, J. B., & Tenenbaum, J. B. (2013). Simulation as an Engine of Physical Scene Understanding. *Proceedings of the National Academy of Sciences*, 110, 18327–18332.

Beierholm, U., Quartz, S., & Shams, L. (2009). Bayesian Priors Are Encoded Independently from Likelihoods in Human Multisensory Perception. *Journal of Vision*, 9, 1–9.

Berger, J. (1985). *Statistical Decision Theory and Bayesian Analysis*. 2nd Ed. New York: Springer Verlag.

Block, N. (2018). If Perception Is Probabilistic, Why Does It Not Seem Probabilistic? *Philosophical Transactions of the Royal Society B*, 373, 20170341.

Bowers, J., & Davis, C. (2012). Bayesian Just-So Stories in Psychology and Neuroscience. *Psychological Bulletin*, 138, 389–414.

Chakravartty, A. (2017). Scientific Realism. In E. Zalta (Ed.), *The Stanford Encyclopedia of Philosophy* (Summer 2017). https://plato.stanford.edu/archives/sum2017/entries/scientific-realism/.

Chater, N., Goodman, N., Griffiths, T. Kemp, C., Oaksford, M., & Tenenbaum, J. (2011). The Imaginary Fundamentalists: The Unshocking Truth About Bayesian Cognitive Science. *Behavioral and Brain Sciences*, 34, 194–196.

Clark, A. (2015). *Surfing Uncertainty*. Oxford: Oxford University Press.

Colombo, M., Elkin, L., & Hartmann, S. (Forthcoming). Being Realist About Bayes and the Predictive Processing Theory of Mind. *The British Journal for the Philosophy of Science*.

Colombo, M., & Seriès, P. (2012). Bayes on the Brain – on Bayesian Modeling in Neuroscience. *The British Journal for the Philosophy of Science*, 63, 697–723.

Davidson, D. (1980). *Essays on Actions and Events*. Oxford: Clarendon Press.

de Finetti, B. (1937/1980). Foresight. Its logical Laws, Its Subjective Sources. Rpt. In H. E. Kyburg, Jr. & H. E. Smokler (Eds.), *Studies in Subjective Probability* (pp. 94–158). Huntington: Robert E. Krieger.

Dennett, D. (1987). *The Intentional Stance*. Cambridge, MA: MIT Press.

Earman, J. (1992). *Bayes or Bust?* Cambridge, MA: MIT Press.

Erikkson, L., & Hájek, A. (2007). What Are Degrees of Belief? *Studia Logica*, 86, 183–213.

Ernst, M. (2007). Learning to Integrate Arbitrary Signals from Vision and Touch. *Journal of Vision*, 7, 1–14.

Fiser, J., Berkes, P., Orbán, G., & Lengyel, M. (2010). Statistically Optimal Perception and Learning: From Behavior to Neural Representations. *Trends in Cognitive Science*, 14, 119–130.

Fleming, R. (2011). Visual Perception: Bizarre Contours Go Against the Odds. *Current Biology*, 21, R259–261.

Friston, K., & Stephan, K. (2007). Free Energy and the Brain. *Synthese*, 159, 417–458.

Gershman, S., Vul, E., & Tenenbaum, J. (2012). Multistability and Perceptual Inference. *Neural Computation*, 24, 1–24.

Glymour, C. (2011). Osiander's Psychology. *Behavioral and Brain Sciences*, 34, 199–200.

Gopnik, A., Glymour, G., Sobel, D., Schulz, L., & Kushnir, T. (2004). A Theory of Causal Learning in Children: Causal Maps and Bayes Nets. *Psychological Review*, 111, 3–32.

Griffiths, T., Chater, N., Norris, D., & Pouget, A. (2012). How Bayesian Got Their Beliefs (and What Those Beliefs Really Are): Comment on Bowers and Davis (2012). *Psychological Bulletin*, 138, 415–422.

Griffiths, T., Vul, E., & Sanborn, A. (2012). Bridging Levels of Analysis for Probabilistic Cognition. *Current Directions in Psychological Science*, 21, 263–268.

Helmholtz, H. von. (1867). *Handbuch Der Physiologischen Optik*. Leipzig: Voss.

Herschbach, M., & Bechtel, W. (2011). Relating Bayes to Cognitive Mechanisms. *Behavioral and Brain Sciences*, 34, 202–203.

Hohwy, J. (2014). *The Predictive Mind*. Oxford: Oxford University Press.

Hornsby, J. (2000). Personal and Sub-Personal: A Defense of Dennett's Early Distinction. *Philosophical Explorations*, 1, 6–24.

Icard, T. (2016). Sampling Propensity as Subjective Probability. *The Review of Philosophy and Psychology*, 7, 863–903.

Jones, M., & Love, B. (2011). Bayesian Fundamentalism or Enlightenment? On the Explanatory Status and Theoretical Contribution of Bayesian Models of Cognition. *Behavioral and Brain Sciences*, 34, 169–188.

Kahneman, D., & Tversky, A. (1979). Prospect Theory: An Analysis of Decision Under Risk. *Econometrica*, 47, 263–291.

Knill, D., & Richards, W. (Eds.). (1996). *Perception as Bayesian Inference*. Cambridge: Cambridge University Press.

Kuhn, T. (1962). *The Structure of Scientific Revolution*. Chicago: University of Chicago Press.

Kwisthout, J., Wareham, T., & van Rooij, I. (2011). Bayesian Intractability Is Not An Ailment That Approximation Can Cure. *Cognitive Science*, 35, 779–784.

Kwon, O.-S., Tadin, D., & Knill, D. (2015). Unifying Account of Visual Motion and Position Perception. *Proceedings of the National Academy of Sciences*, 112, 8142–8147.

Levy, R., Reali, F., & Griffiths, T. (2009). Modeling the Effects of Memory on Human Online Sentence Processing with Particle Filters. In D. Koller, D. Schuurmans, Y. Bengio, & L. Bottou (Eds.), *Advances In Neural Information Processing Systems*, vol. 21 (pp. 937–944). La Jolla: NIPS Foundation.

Luce, R. D., & Suppes, P. (1965). Preference, Utility, and Subjective Probability. In R. D. Luce, R. Bush, & E. Galanter (Eds.), *Handbook of Mathematical Psychology*, vol. III (pp. 249–410). New York: Wiley.

Madl, T., Franklin, S., Chen, K., Montaldi, D., & Trappl, R. (2014). Bayesian Integration of Information in Hippocampal Place Cells. *PloS One*, 9, E89762.

Maloney, L., & Mamassian, P. (2009). Bayesian Decision Theory as a Model of Human Visual Perception: Testing Bayesian Transfer. *Visual Neuroscience*, 26, 147–155.

McDowell, J. (1994). The Content of Perceptual Experience. *Philosophical Quarterly*, 44, 190–205.

McMullin, E. (1985). Galilean Idealization. *Studies in History and Philosophy of Science Part A*, 16, 247–273.

Morales, J., Solovey, G., Maniscalco, B., Rahnev, D., De Lange, F., & Lau, H. (2015). Low Attention Impairs Optimal Incorporation of Prior Knowledge in Perceptual Decisions. *Attention, Perception, and Psychophysics*, 77, 2021–2036.

Orlandi, N. (2014). *The Innocent Eye: Why Vision Is Not Cognitive Process*. Oxford: Oxford University Press.

72 Michael Rescorla

Orlandi, N. (2016). Bayesian Perception Is Ecological Perception. *Philosophical Topics*, 44, 327–351.

Peters, M., Ma, W. J., & Shams, L. (2016). The Size-Weight Illusion Is Not Anti-Bayesian After All. *PeerJ*, 4, E2124.

Petzschner, F., & Glasauer, S. (2011). Iterative Bayesian Estimation as an Explanation for Range and Regression Effects: A Study on Human Path Integration. *Journal of Neuroscience*, 31, 17220–17229.

Pouget, A., Beck, J., Ma, W. J., & Latham, P. (2013). Probabilistic Brains: Knowns and Unknowns. *Nature Neuroscience*, 16, 1170–1178.

Rahnev, D., & Denisov, R. (2018). Suboptimality in Perceptual Decision Making. *Behavioral and Brain Sciences*, 41, E223.

Ramsey, F. P. (1931). Truth and Probability. In R. B. Braithwaite (Ed.), *The Foundations of Mathematics and Other Logical Essays* (pp. 156–198). London: Routledge and Kegan.

Rescorla, M. (2009). Cognitive Maps and the Language of Thought. *The British Journal for the Philosophy of Science*, 60, 377–407.

Rescorla, M. (2012). How to Integrate Representation Into Computational Modeling, and Why We Should. *The Journal of Cognitive Science*, 13, 1–38.

Rescorla, M. (2015a). Bayesian Perceptual Psychology. In M. Matthen (Ed.), *The Oxford Handbook of the Philosophy of Perception* (pp. 694–716). Oxford: Oxford University Press.

Rescorla, M. (2015b). Review of Nico Orlandi's *The Innocent Eye: Why Vision Is Not a Cognitive Process*. *Notre Dame Philosophical Reviews*, January 2015.

Rescorla, M. (2016). Bayesian Sensorimotor Psychology. *Mind and Language*, 31, 3–36.

Rescorla, M. (2018). An Interventionist Approach to Psychological Explanation. *Synthese*, 195, 1909–1940.

Rescorla, M. (Forthcoming). Perceptual Co-Reference. *Review of Philosophy and Psychology*.

Sanborn, A. (2017). Types of Approximation for Probabilistic Cognition: Sampling and Variational. *Brain and Cognition*, 112, 98–101.

Sanborn, A., & Chater, N. (2016). Bayesian Brains without Probabilities. *Trends in Cognitive Science*, 20, 883–893.

Sanborn, A., Griffiths, T., & Navarro, D. (2010). Rational Approximations to Rational Models: Alternative Algorithms for Category Learning. *Psychological Review*, 117, 1144–1167.

Sanborn, A., Masinghka, J., & Griffiths, T. (2013). Reconciling Intuitive Physics and Newtonian Mechanics for Colliding Objects. *Psychological Review*, 120, 411–437.

Sato, Y., & Kording, K. (2014). How Much to Trust the Senses: Likelihood Learning. *Journal of Vision*, 14, 1–13.

Sato, Y., Toyoizumi, T., & Aihara, K. (2007). Bayesian Inference Explains Perception of Unity and Ventriloquism Aftereffect: Identification of Common sources of Audiovisual Stimuli. *Neural Computation*, 19, 3335–3355.

Seydell, A., Knill, D., & Trommershäuser, J. (2010). Adapting Internal Statistical Models for Interpreting Visual Cues to Depth. *Journal of Vision*, 10, 1–27.

Shen, S., & Ma, W. J. (2016). A Detailed Comparison of Optimality and Simplicity in Perceptual Decision-Making. *Psychological Review*, 123, 452–480.

Sotiropoulos, G., Seitz, A., & Seriès, P. (2011). Changing Expectations About Speed Alters Perceived Motion Direction. *Current Biology*, 21, R883–R884.

——. (2014). Contrast Dependency and Prior Expectations in Human Speed Perception. *Vision Research*, 97, 16–23.

Stocker, A. (2018). Credo for Optimality. *Behavioral and Brain Sciences*, 41, e244.

Stocker, A., & Simoncelli, E. (2006). Noise Characteristics and Prior Expectations in Human Visual Speed Perception. *Nature Neuroscience*, 4, 578–585.

Thompson, P. (1982). Perceived Rate of Movement Depends on Stimulus Contrast. *Vision Research*, 22, 377–380.

Thompson, P., Brooks, K., & Hammett, S. (2006). Speed Can Go Up as well as Down at Low Contrast: Implications for Models of Motion Perception. *Vision Research*, 46, 782–786.

Thrun, S., Burgard, W., & Fox, D. (2006). *Probabilistic Robotics*. Cambridge, MA: MIT Press.

Todorov, E., & Jordan, M. (2002). Optimal Feedback Control as a Theory of Motor Coordination. *Nature Neuroscience*, 5, 1226–1235.

Trommershäuser, J., Körding, K., & Landy, M. (Eds.). (2011). *Sensory Cue Integration*. Oxford: Oxford University Press.

Trotta, R. (2008). Bayes in the Sky: Bayesian Inference and Model Selection in Cosmology. *Contemporary Physics*, 49, 71–104.

Tversky, A., & Kahneman, D. (1983). Extension Versus Intuitive Reasoning: The Conjunction Fallacy in Probability Judgment. *Psychological Review*, 90, 293–315.

van Rooij, I., Blokpoel, M., Kwisthout, J., & Wareham, T. (2019). *Cognition and Intractability*. Cambridge: Cambridge University Press.

Wei, X.-X., & Stocker, A. (2015). A Bayesian Observer Model Constrained by Efficient Coding Can Explain 'anti-Bayesian' Percepts. *Nature Neuroscience*, 18, 1509–1517.

Weisberg, M. (2007). Three Kinds of Idealization. *The Journal of Philosophy*, 104, 639–659.

Weiss, Y., Simoncelli, E., & Adelson, E. (2002). Motion Illusions as Optimal Percepts. *Nature Neuroscience*, 5, 598–604.

Williamson, T. (1994). *Vagueness*. New York: Routledge.

Wolpert, D. (2007). Probabilistic Models in Human Sensorimotor Control. *Human Movement Science*, 26, 511–524.

Wolpert, D., & Landy, M. (2012). Motor Control Is Decision-Making. *Current Opinion in Neurobiology*, 22, 1–8.

Woodward, J. (2003). *Making Things Happen*. Oxford: Oxford University Press.

Woodward, J. (2017). Explanation in Neurobiology: An Interventionist Perspective. In D. Kaplan (Ed.), *Explanation and Integration in the Mind and Brain Sciences* (pp. 70–100). Oxford: Oxford University Press.

3 The Role of Unconscious Inference in Models of Delusion Formation

Federico Bongiorno and Lisa Bortolotti

1. Introduction

Delusions are a commonly observed symptom in people with a wide range of psychiatric disorders, including schizophrenia, dementia, schizoaffective disorder, bipolar disorder, and major depression. In the latest version of the American Psychiatric Association's diagnostic manual (DSM-V), delusion is defined as, 'a false belief based on incorrect inference about external reality that is firmly held despite what almost everyone else believes and despite what constitutes incontrovertible an obvious proof of evidence of the contrary' (APA, 2013, p. 819).

As delusions are understood in DSM-V, they are based on inference. In this chapter, we focus on the role that inference plays in delusion formation. Brendan Maher was the first to suggest that the formation of delusions involve inferential transition – although he denies that the inference from which delusions arise is *faulty* (Maher, 1992; Maher, 1999). Maher defends a view known as *explanationism* (Maher, 1974; Stone and Young, 1997), according to which delusions are hypotheses adopted to explain anomalous perceptual experiences and arrived at by inferential reasoning that is neither biased nor otherwise deficient (Maher, 1974, p. 180). In essence, delusions for Maher are the product of normal reasoning processes brought to bear on some experiential aberration. This means that the pathological nature of the delusion does not lie in the person's inferential reasoning, but in the experience that generates it. An alternative to explanationism is the *endorsement theory*, according to which the delusional belief is an acknowledgement that the anomalous experience is veridical and no inference from experience to belief is required (Pacherie, Green, and Bayne, 2006; Bayne and Pacherie, 2004a).

Over a number of years, Max Coltheart and colleagues (e.g., Coltheart, 2005; Coltheart, 2007; Davies and Coltheart, 2000; Coltheart, Langdon, and McKay, 2007, 2011) advocated a *two-factor theory of delusions*. The theory is primarily in the business of explaining monothematic delusions (i.e., delusions whose content is restricted to a single theme) of neuropsychological origin. The guiding idea is that there are two contributing factors to delusion formation. The first is an impairment that effects the production of abnormal data, the explanation of which is supposed to furnish the content of the delusion.[1] The second is an impairment in the mechanism responsible for belief evaluation, which is supposed to explain why the person with the delusion is willing to maintain unlikely explanations for the abnormal data. Coltheart and colleagues postulate a second factor because they think that the presence of abnormal data is not sufficient for the formation of the delusion. It is tempting to think that the notion of a second factor (construed as an impairment in belief evaluation) is inconsistent with Maher's contention that delusions are formed through unimpaired or unbiased inferential processes applied to abnormal experiences. And indeed, the two-factor theory has been interpreted in the literature as an alternative to Maher's brand of explanationism. However, Max Coltheart, Peter Menzies and John Sutton have offered a Bayesian account of abductive inference (henceforth *the Coltheart model*) that vindicates Maher's basic contention that the inference leading to the adoption of the delusional belief is not faulty (Coltheart, Menzies, and Sutton, 2010). The Coltheart model has been developed with specific reference to the Capgras delusion, the belief that a person or persons dear to the deluded individual have been replaced by identical or nearly identical imposters (Capgras and Reboul-Lachaux, 1923). Specifically, the proposal is that in Capgras unconscious abductive reasoning is used to infer from the abnormal data to the delusional hypothesis – which is the hypothesis that best explains the data. In the Coltheart model the inference involved in the formation of the delusion is Bayesian rational and does not involve a reasoning impairment, though a reasoning impairment is postulated to explain the maintenance of the delusional belief in the face of counterevidence.

In the last decade, several theorists have pointed to the use of Bayesian framework for modelling delusional inference, with the debate revolving around the number of factors necessary for delusion formation, and the similarities and differences between the available models (see, e.g., Coltheart, 2010; McKay, 2012; Bortolotti and Miyazono, 2015; Miyazono, Bortolotti, and Broome, 2015). In this chapter, we want to focus on the implications of the rise of Bayesian models of delusion formation for the debate between explanationist and endorsement theorists on the role of inference, taking the Coltheart model as the sample model throughout. To the extent that it conceptualizes delusions as hypotheses explaining abnormal data, the Coltheart model has been presented as a new version of explanationism. However, we argue that the centerpiece of the Coltheart model – the notion that the delusion is arrived at through unconscious Bayesian-style abductive inference – is no less compatible with the rival account of explanationism, the endorsement theory. If that is correct, the presence of such an inference in the process of delusion formation is not sufficient to discriminate between explanationism and endorsement theory.

76 *Federico Bongiorno and Lisa Bortolotti*

Here is the plan. In Section 2, we pay special attention to the claim that the formation of the Capgras delusion occurs as a consequence of an unconscious Bayesian-style abductive inference and that the data the delusional hypothesis is invoked to explain is not consciously experienced. In Section 3, we elaborate on the differences between explanationism and the endorsement theory and discuss their advantages and disadvantages. In Section 4, we describe two ways of incorporating Bayesian-style abductive inference into the explanationist framework. In Section 5, we show that Bayesian-style abductive inference can also be incorporated into the endorsement framework. In Section 6, we conclude that the Coltheart model should not be described as explanationist because it is couched in terms that are equally compatible with the endorsement theory.

2. The Coltheart Model

2.1. *Preliminaries*

One way to illustrate the Maher approach to delusion is by reference to a model of Capgras advanced by Hayden Ellis and Andrew Young in the nineties. It is widely agreed that familiar face recognition is correlated with an increased activity in the autonomic nervous system that can be measured by changes in skin conductance. The proposal is that in the Capgras delusion a neuropsychological anomaly disrupts the connection between a person's face recognition system and the autonomic nervous system, such that the person with Capgras fails to show differential autonomic responses to familiar compared to unfamiliar faces (Ellis and Young, 1990).

Findings of reduced skin conductance in people with Capgras have confirmed this proposal, making it likely that the formation of the delusion is at least partly explained by a lack of responsiveness in the autonomic nervous system (Hirstein and Ramachandran, 1997; Ellis et al., 1997; Ellis et al., 2000; Brighetti et al., 2007). Conceivably, such a lack of autonomic responsiveness in the presence of a visually familiar face could give rise to anomalous experience, such as an experience of a certain person being unfamiliar or different in some way.

In Maher's view, the hypothesis that one's wife has been replaced by an impostor is a rational response to, or a plausible explanation of, the anomalous experience that is devised to explain. That is, one plausible explanation for the experience of a person who looks like one's mother but feels unfamiliar is that she is not really one's mother, but an impostor. As we will see in more detail in the sections that follow, the Coltheart model vindicates Maher's central idea that the Capgras delusion is a rational explanation for the lack of normal autonomic response to a familiar face, but it differs from Maher in two important respects.

The first difference concerns the role of conscious, person-level processes in the formation of the delusion. Unlike Maher, Coltheart and colleagues (2010) maintain that the 'abnormal data' (as they call them) which initially prompt the Impostor Hypothesis are not mental events of which a person is conscious (i.e., experiences). Warrant for this claim is grounded in the idea that since we are not conscious of the processes going on in the autonomic nervous system, a person would not be conscious of a lack of responsiveness in this system. Note, however, that Coltheart and colleagues (2010) do not deny that people with Capgras have abnormal conscious experiences; they simply claim that these experiences follow on the adoption of the delusion, rather than causing the delusion. In the Coltheart model, everything along the chain of cognitive processes that precedes delusion takes place without conscious awareness. The only content that enters consciousness – 'the only delusion-relevant event of which the patient is aware' (Coltheart, Menzies, and Sutton, 2010, p. 264) – is the delusional hypothesis, 'this person looks like my loved one but is an impostor'.

Second, Maher thinks that discrepant familiarity data (i.e., discrepancies between visual and autonomic recognition of familiar faces) are *the only abnormal factor* necessary for the delusion to be formed and maintained, whereas in the Coltheart model this is not sufficient. Suppose we grant that a failure of autonomic response to a loved one's face accounts for why the impostor hypothesis is initially adopted as a belief. We would expect an otherwise healthy person to subsequently reject the belief in the face of new data that disconfirm it (such as the testimony of a doctor or the assurance of family and friends). People with Capgras, however, continue to believe that their loved ones have been replaced by impostors. Why is this so? According to the Coltheart model, there has to be an impairment in belief formation resulting from right hemisphere damage that prevents the person from rejecting the newly formed belief despite evidence against it. Possible support for the additional factor is provided by the comparison with patients with ventromedial frontal damage (VMF). VMF patients also fail to show autonomic discrimination between familiar and unknown faces, but do not develop delusional beliefs about replacement look-alikes and impostors (Tranel, Damasio, and Damasio, 1995). This has been taken to be evidence that Capgras subjects unlike VMF patients must suffer a second impairment.

For our purposes what matters is the role that the Coltheart model assigns to inferential transitions in the aetiology of Capgras delusion. Coltheart and colleagues argue that the delusion initially arises from normal unconscious inferential responses to an abnormal input that is due to the absence of autonomic response to familiar faces. In the following subsections we focus on two issues: first, what the nature of the inference is that leads from this absence of autonomic activity to the initial adoption

78   *Federico Bongiorno and Lisa Bortolotti*

of the delusional belief; and second, to what extent the inference can be said to be rational.

2.2. Abductive Inference

There are two basic assumptions in the Coltheart model, that the Capgras delusion is best construed as the conclusion of an abductive inference (also called inference to the best explanation, see Harman, 1965; Lipton, 2004); and that the model that is best suited to explain abductive inference in the context of delusion formation is the Bayesian account.[2] Motivation for the former assumption comes from the fact that the processes leading to the initial onset of the Capgras delusion cannot be successfully described in terms of deductive or inductive inference. The impostor belief cannot be the outcome of a deductive chain of inference, for that would imply that the replacement of a close relative x by an impostor is logically entailed by the lack of autonomic response to x's face, which is not. Nor is it plausible to suppose that the impostor belief is obtained by inductive generalization, through the observation that events of type B invariably follow upon events of type A. Unlike inductive generalization, the inference that x is an impostor brings about concepts that go beyond the observable data available to one when one encounters x. More plausible is the suggestion that people with Capgras engage in abductive reasoning or inference to the best explanation (henceforth: IBE). Imagine that you are examining a vast array of potential alternative hypothesis for a single body of data. IBE is the process of selecting the hypothesis which, if true, would best explain that data. So, to say that delusional inference is like IBE is to say that it draws on explanatory considerations for an assessment of how likely competing hypotheses are to be true.

2.3. Bayesian Abductive Inference

As Coltheart and colleagues note, 'the crucial mark of the model is that it marries a natural probabilistic account of explanation to the standard Bayesian model of rational belief systems' (2010, p. 271). The probabilistic account of explanation provides a measure of the relative explanatory power of the alternative hypotheses $H_1, H_2 \ldots H_n$ in light of actual data. The degree to which a hypothesis H explains observations O is a function of the probability of O given H. It follows that one hypothesis H_1 is a better explanation of O than rival hypotheses $H_2 \ldots H_n$ just so long as the probability of O is higher under H_1 than under $H_2 \ldots H_n$. For example, in the case of Capgras delusion, the impostor hypothesis explains better the discrepant familiarity data than rival hypotheses just so long as the probability of observing the data is higher under the impostor hypothesis than under the rival hypotheses.

How the probabilistic account of explanation gets combined with the standard Bayesian model of rational belief systems? The Bayesian model describes the rational way to update beliefs as new evidence is gathered (what is called Bayesian inference). An agent's belief system is represented as consisting of subjective probabilities, measures of the degrees of belief that the agent assigns to various hypotheses. A probability function p accords to each hypothesis H a mean value from the interval $[0,1]$ $p(H)$, which quantifies the agent's degree of belief in what H reports. The agent's subjective probabilities are updated over time through a procedure known as conditionalization.

Suppose you want to know the probability that some hypothesis, H, is true (e.g., 'it is about to rain') given some new evidence, O, (e.g., 'the sky is overspread with clouds') you have observed. Conditionalization requires that you change your degree of belief in H so that it is equal to your prior degree of belief in H conditional on O:

$$P_n(H) = P(H \mid O)$$

The expression can be unpacked by Bayes theorem in the following way:

$$P(H|O) = P(H) \cdot \frac{P(O|H)}{P(O)}$$

One can read the equation as: 'The conditional probability $P(H|O)$ (the posterior probability of H given O) is proportional to the product of $P(H)$ (the prior probability of H), $P(O|H)$ (the likelihood of O given H), and $P(O)$ (the prior probability of O)'.

In this equation, the posterior probability $P(H|O)$ is what we are after, the probability that H is true given the evidence O (e.g., the probability of rain given clouds). The likelihood $P(O|H)$ is the probability of attaining the evidence O if H is true (e.g., the probability of there being clouds given that it is raining), or, as per the probabilistic account of explanation, how well H explains the evidence O (i.e., the higher the likelihood, the greater H's explanatory power). The prior probability $P(H)$ represents the probability attributed to H before the evidence O is in (e.g., the probability of rain in general). A hypothesis may well have a high likelihood, but assuming that the prior probability is extremely low, the posterior probability will also be low. The hypothesis that aliens have produced clouds around their spacecraft to hide themselves (H_a) may explain the fact that there are clouds overhead, and therefore have a high likelihood. But since the prior probability is very low, it would be wrong to assign a high posterior probability to H_a (i.e., conclude that H_a is probably true) given that there are clouds overhead.

The remaining term $P(O)$ refers to the prior probability of O before the relevant observation begins (e.g., the probability of there being clouds in general).

Coltheart and colleagues dismiss $P(O)$ as unimportant, for they are less interested in whether evidence supports a hypothesis absolutely than in which of two or more candidate hypotheses the evidence best supports (Coltheart, Menzies, and Sutton, 2010, p. 273). When beliefs about the world can be reduced to a set of two competing hypotheses (H, H_1), Bayes theorem can be used as a normative criterion for selecting the one with the highest posterior probability:

$$\frac{P(\text{H}|\text{O})}{P(\text{H}_1|\text{O})} = \frac{P(\text{H}) \bullet P(\text{O}|\text{H})}{P(\text{H}_1) \bullet P(\text{O}|\text{H}_1)}$$

Put into words, the two-hypothesis formulation of Bayes theorem states that the ratio of the posterior probabilities of H and H_1 (the *posterior* odds) is equal to the ratio of their prior probabilities (the *prior* odds, the second term on the right of the previous equation), multiplied by the ratio of the respective likelihoods of O given H and H_1 (the *likelihood* ratio, the first term on the right of the equation previous equation). The term $P(O)$ no longer figures in the equation because it was cancelled out during multiplication.

We are now in a position to see how the Bayesian model can accommodate an account of IBE. One such account must answer the question of what makes it rational to accept a hypothesis, or favor one hypothesis over others, in light of certain observations, the evidence. The Bayesian model (via Bayes theorem) tells us that it is rational to select the hypothesis which best fits the evidence but weighted by its plausibility independent of (or apart from) the evidence (Hohwy, 2013). That is, the hypothesis with a higher posterior than rival alternatives, or, to put it otherwise, the hypothesis that is better supported by the evidence than rival alternatives are. The central claim is that an abductive inference from the available evidence O to the hypothesis H is rational or justified only insofar as O supports H more strongly than it does any other hypotheses H_n (Coltheart, Menzies, and Sutton, 2010, p. 274). We will now consider the implications of this for understanding the Capgras delusion.

2.4. Bayesian Inference and Delusion Formation

As we said at the onset, the Capgras delusion is formed in the presence of discrepant familiarity data resulting from a disconnection between the facial recognition system and the autonomic nervous system. Imagine a man whose face recognition system has become disconnected from the

Unconscious Inference in Delusion Formation 81

autonomic nervous system as the result of a brain injury when he hit his head during a car accident. Let O stand for the incongruous data presented to him upon encountering his wife for the first time in the hospital after the accident:

> O: lack of autonomic familiarity data to the presence of visual familiarity data.

Suppose our man is considering a set of two mutually exclusive and exhaustive hypotheses to account for O, denoted by H_w and H_i:

> H_w: This woman who visibly resembles my wife and claims to be my wife really is my wife.
> H_i: This woman who visibly resembles my wife and claims to be my wife is an impostor posing as my wife.

After observing O, which hypothesis fares better? From a Bayesian perspective, this question is equivalent to asking whose posterior probability is greater. Bayes rule dictates how we should update some prior probability distribution over a set of hypotheses to provide the posterior probabilities of the hypotheses given the data. Specifically, the formula tells us that the posterior probability of each of our two hypotheses is obtained by multiplying together the likelihood (the probability of seeing O if H_w or H_i were true) and the prior probability (the probability assigned to H_w or H_i before observing O).

Accordingly, the first step towards an answer to the question of which hypothesis is more plausible is to examine whether O is more likely under the wife hypothesis H_w or under the impostor hypothesis H_i (i.e., whether O is better explained by one or the other). In the model, O is 'much more likely' under H_i than H_w, since it would be highly unlikely for our man to observe discrepant familiarity data if the person was in fact his wife (Coltheart, Menzies, and Sutton, 2010, p. 277). So, it is argued that the likelihood ratio (1)

$$\frac{P(O|Hi)}{P(O|Hw)}$$

will be very high. However, as we saw above, in assessing the posterior odds for any pair of hypotheses, we need to ask not only how well they explain the evidence, but also how probable they were (believed to be) in view of the knowledge available prior to taking the evidence into account. Most of us would say that the prior probability of the impostor hypothesis is very low compared with that of the wife hypothesis, since the former is generally plausible, whereas the latter is generally

82 Federico Bongiorno and Lisa Bortolotti

implausible. If this is right, the prior odds of the impostor hypothesis (2) will be very low:

$$\frac{P(Hi)}{P(Hw)}$$

Nevertheless, a fundamental component in the Bayesian comparison of hypotheses is that the ratio of posterior probabilities (3)

$$\frac{P(Hi|O)}{P(Hw|O)}$$

can still favor H_i over H_w even when the prior odds of H_i (2) are relatively low, provided that the likelihood ratio (1), i.e., the relative explanatory power of H_i, is sufficient to overwhelm the prior odds against it. According to the model (Coltheart, Menzies, and Sutton, 2010), this is what happens in Capgras. The impostor hypothesis accounts much better for the discrepant familiarity data than the wife hypothesis, and this offsets its relative low prior probability in calculating the ratio of posterior probabilities.

So, a Bayesian-rational agent (i.e., one who updates their beliefs in accordance with Bayes rule) will infer the belief that the woman who came to visit him in the hospital is an impostor posing as his wife. To this extent, the Coltheart model is consistent with Maher's approach. The adoption of the impostor belief in the wake of discrepant familiarity data is a 'perfectly rational response' (Coltheart, Menzies, and Sutton, 2010, p. 281; McKay, 2012).

2.5. Challenges to the Coltheart Model

Ryan McKay argues that the Coltheart model presupposes an unrealistic estimation of prior probabilities (McKay, 2012). In the model, prior probabilities are expressed as $P(H_w) = 0.99$ and $P(H_i) = 0.01$. According to McKay, the hypothesis of one's wife being replaced by a physically identical impostor 'represents an exceedingly unlikely – almost miraculous – state of affairs' (McKay, 2012, p. 340). For this reason, he thinks the value chosen in the Coltheart model for the prior probability of the impostor hypothesis, $P(H_i) = 0,01$, is far too optimistic. A more realistic distribution of prior probabilities would so strongly favor the wife hypothesis that it could not be so easily outweighed by the likelihood ratio. McKay suggests assigning a prior probability of 0.00027 to $P(H_i)$ and a prior probability of 0.99973 to $P(H_w)$. If we accept McKay's proposed prior probabilities, the posterior probability for the impostor

Unconscious Inference in Delusion Formation   83

hypothesis H_i would be much lower than (only 0.27 of that for) H_w, such that it would irrational to choose H_i over H_w.

The question then arises as to why the person with Capgras adopts the impostor hypothesis as a belief. Why isn't the belief rejected? McKay proposes that this happens because the person updates their probabilities in a way that is heavily biased towards observational adequacy at the expense of conservatism (Stone and Young, 1997). Unbiased updating of probabilities would strike a fair balance between two conflicting demands: forming beliefs that explain the data well (observational adequacy) and forming beliefs that require as little as possible readjustment to the subject's prior beliefs (conservatism). In McKay's view, people with Capgras discount the prior implausibility of the impostor scenario on account of its relative explanatory power, and that is why H_i gets a higher posterior than H_w.

Another challenge to the Coltheart model is that it denies any role to anomalous experience in the etiology of the delusion. As we have already seen, in the Coltheart model the process from the abnormal data to the onset of the delusion is entirely unconscious. In a recent paper, Garry Young challenges this, suggesting that the impostor hypothesis (i.e., 'that must be an impostor masquerading as my wife') co-occurs with an anomalous experience (i.e., a salient sense of unfamiliarity) before being accepted as a belief (Young, 2014; Young, 2008). Young agrees that the impostor hypothesis emerges as a product of an entirely unconscious inference process. However, he thinks that people with Capgras come to believe this hypothesis because it makes probable an experience that is otherwise unexpected: 'the experiential state gives credence to the freshly emerged impostor thought such that the corresponding (delusional) belief is formed to explain the experience' (Young, 2014, p. 94).

On a similar note, Davies and Egan note that even if we are not consciously aware of the activities in the autonomic nervous (e.g., the failure of autonomic response to a spouse's face), it does not follow that there is no conscious experience prior to the formation of the delusional belief (Davies and Egan, 2013). This is because it remains possible that the lack of autonomic response to the sight a spouse's face should generate some kind of anomalous experience, which would in turn serve as a basis for the delusional belief. Specifically, Davies and Egan claim that the delusional belief is adopted as a result of computations being carried out by a perceptual module, where these are understood as processes of Bayesian inference. On their account, the winning hypothesis (i.e., the conclusion of Bayesian inference) gives the experience the content it has (e.g., 'that's actually not my wife'), and the initial adoption of the delusional belief is a prepotent doxastic response to that content (Davies and Egan, 2013, p. 722). Interestingly, the module's probabilities may be incongruous with the actual state of the world (i.e., unrealistic) because modules can draw only on a restricted class of inputs (i.e., are domain-specific).

84 Federico Bongiorno and Lisa Bortolotti

In addition, the module's probabilities may be at odds with what the person knows or believes because modules are informationally encapsulated (i.e., they have little or no access to information at higher levels of processing); and, to this extent, they may be naturally biased against pre-existing beliefs and in favor of likelihoods (Davies and Egan, 2013, p. 714; Fodor, 1983).

3. Explanationist Versus Endorsement Accounts

In this section we describe two distinct varieties of 'empiricist' (i.e., experience-based) approaches to delusions: the explanationist and the endorsement accounts.[3] If experience is to figure in the causal chain leading to delusion formation, then the representational content of the experience may be more or less close to the content of the delusion itself. Proponents of the explanationist account (henceforth EX) claim that the content of the Capgras experience is sparser than the content of the delusion (e.g., 'this woman feels unfamiliar'), and that the delusion arises as a means to explain the anomalous experience (Ellis and Young, 1990; Maher, 2005; Coltheart, 2005). On the other hand, those who advocate an endorsement account (EN) hold that (much of) the content of the delusion is already encoded in the content of experience, and that the delusion simply reports the content of that experience – 'seeing is believing', as is sometimes said (Bayne and Pacherie, 2004a; Pacherie, Green, and Bayne, 2006; Pacherie, 2009).

Endorsement theorists typically take the anomalous experience to be a perceptual state with propositional content, where the content amounts to misidentification. EN breaks down into three components: (1) the person has an experience with the misidentification content 'this woman is not my wife'; (2) the experience is endorsed as veridical, such that the person believes that this woman, who looks like his wife, is not really her; (3) this belief is later developed into the belief that the person's wife has been replaced by an impostor. The content available to be endorsed is the misidentification content, while the impostor belief is just an explanatory hypothesis for the fact that, as the person believes, the woman looks like his wife but is not really her (Davies and Davies, 2009, p. 302; Langdon and Bayne, 2010). Another possibility is that the person's experience already includes the impostor idea as part of its content (see Pacherie, 2009; Bongiorno, 2019 for explorations of this possibility).

EX and EN have complementary strengths and weaknesses. One strength of EN is that it offers a plausible framework for understanding why delusions are held with such high conviction that they outweigh the evidence of testimony. If the conscious perception of the person with Capgras, on looking at a woman's face, is of 'seeing a stranger' (i.e., someone who looks like but is not one's wife), testimony may not suffice to persuade him that the woman is in fact his wife (Langdon and

Connaughton, 2013, p. 29). On this account, the delusional conviction flows directly from perceptual experience. In contrast, explanationist theorists have a harder time explaining where the conviction comes from. Imagine Matt experiences a coarse-grained feeling of unfamiliarity on looking at his wife's face. If Matt's delusional belief is a result of his attempt to explain this, we would expect him to have some awareness of the explanatory reasons for believing it, and hence of what renders it justified. But this clashes with the quality of self-evident truth with which the delusion is usually maintained (Langdon and Bayne, 2015, p. 332).

Another alleged advantage of EN over EX is that it is better suited to explain the content of the delusion itself. The reason is that delusions that have been formed via endorsement processes preserve, or are very strongly constrained by, fine-grained contents of experience. In contrast, the process of content acquisition is more difficult to explain for proponents of EX, since on this account there is no tight connection between experiential contents and belief contents. If all that Matt experiences is a coarse-grained feeling of unfamiliarity towards his wife's face, it is not obvious why he should come to believe that the face seen is that of a stranger. Nor, for that matter, is it clear why he fails to seek out alternative explanations. Indeed, arguably there are more plausible ways for Matt to make sense of why his wife seems subtly different: she is about to break bad news; she is playing a prank on him; she is unhappy in their marriage; he is unhappy in their marriage; he is falling out of love; he is acquired a brain damage, and so on (Gold and Gold, 2014; Langdon and Coltheart, 2000).

What EX is better suited to account for is how the anomalous experience gets its content. Because the content is so sparse, explanationists can simply say that when visual familiarity data occur in the absence of autonomic familiarity data, the discrepancy is reported to consciousness, such that one becomes aware that there is something odd about the perceived person (Coltheart, 2005). Things are more complicated when we come to EN, however. For one thing, if the anomalous experience is to have a rich misidentification content like, 'this woman is not my wife', then there is the question of what properties perception can represent. Specifically, the worry is that endorsement theorists might need to accept a controversial claim in the philosophy of perception, the claim that properties such as being numerically identical with, or distinct from, a certain person are properties that one can directly perceive (Davies and Egan, 2013, p. 715).[4] Furthermore, it remains to be seen how EN is to be squared with the finding suggestive of a lack of response to familiar faces in people with Capgras. For clearly, reduced autonomic arousal in response to a familiar face does not imply that one perceives the face as the face of a stranger.

4. Inference in Explanationism

We have now seen two different ways of developing an account of delusional belief formation, one (EX) according to which the belief arises from an attempt to explain the experience, another (EN) according to which the belief results from an endorsement of the experience. Perhaps the clearest formulation of EX is by Maher: 'a delusion is a hypothesis designed to explain unusual perceptual phenomena and developed though the operation of normal cognitive processes' (Maher, 1974, p. 103). The language Maher uses elsewhere (Maher, 1988, 2005) suggests that he conceives of the person's attempt at explaining the anomalous experience as a personal-level phenomenon. He compares the mechanisms of delusion formation to scientific theory-building (Maher, 2005, p. 142), and he notes that the content of the delusional explanation reflects from the person's scientific, religious and political background, what he calls 'general explanatory systems' (Maher, 1974, p. 103). If that is right, then, according to Maher, the stimulus input of the inference (i.e., anomalous experience), the end product of the process (i.e., delusional hypothesis), and the inferential process itself are all available to consciousness.

But could the explanatory-inferential route to the delusional belief in EX remain unconscious? There appear to be just two options for envisaging how it could. One is to argue that the inference begins from a conscious experience – e.g., the fact that one's wife feels unfamiliar – but is carried out unconsciously. Although the psychological processes leading to the belief are opaque to the person, the belief is susceptible to a personal-level explanation. Indeed, on this story, the person can appeal to the fact that his wife feels unfamiliar to explain why he believes that she is not really his wife. Alternatively, one can argue that the unconscious inference starts from an unconscious input – that is, there is no role for anomalous experience, as in the Coltheart model. On this account, there is no fact at the personal level that grounds the delusional belief.

5. Inference in the Endorsement Theory

5.1. Can Perception Be Inferential?

The fundamental idea of EN is that the person with Capgras perceives the woman in front of him (who is wife) as a stranger. It is tempting to assume that if you are perceiving something, you are not making any inference. However, this is true only if one rules out the possibility that perception itself is inferential. Let us now then consider this possibility, and let us look at the general possibility of unconscious inference, which we have thus far taken for granted. The idea of perceptual inference can be traced back at least as far as to Hermann von Helmholtz (1867) and has been later developed by the work of a number of scholars (see e.g.,

Rock,1983; Barlow, 1990; Gregory, 1997; Rescorla, 2015; Siegel, 2017). Hermann von Helmholtz proposed that some of our visual perceptions result from unconscious inferences in which sensory clues are interpreted to form hypotheses about the distal environment (Helmholtz, 1867). The visual system would make such inferences in compliance with what has nowadays been known as the *likelihood principle*, according to which perception represents the most likely environmental situation given the pattern of sensory stimuli. The rationale for this proposal derives from the attempt to overcome what Tyler Burge has labelled the *underdetermination problem* (Burge, 2010, p. 91). At the core of the problem lies the fact that any given encoding of proximal stimulation underdetermines its possible distal causes. This is to say that the same proximal stimulations are compatible with a variety of different entities in the environment, and therefore with numerous possible perceptual representations. A good example of underdetermination comes from visual illusions. For example, consider the hollow-face illusion (Gregory, 1973). In this illusion, a concave facial mask lighted from below misperceived as being convex. Here the same encoding of proximal stimulation could have been produced by a convex mask with overhead illumination. Then we would have had a veridical perceptual representation of a different distal cause. The same pattern of sensory registration is consistent with either environmental scenario, but only one perceptual state is formed.

Helmholtz's theory of perceptual inference can seemingly account for this and similar cases of underdetermination by relying on the likelihood principle. As we saw, the principle says that the visual system would check sensory cues against implicit assumptions so as to infer the most likely interpretation of those sensory cues. As such, it would seem, it may happen that reliance on implicit assumptions generates biases towards false interpretations engendering misperceptions. In the specific case of the hollow-mask illusion, the source of bias may consist of a two-fold assumption which has been thought to underlie inferences from shading to shape: (1) that there is only one light source; and that (2) the light source is positioned overhead (Ramachandran, 1998). There is, of course, a wider range of perceptual phenomena (e.g., perceptual constancies) that can be purportedly explained by appeal to unconscious inference, but we will not address them here. In the next subsections we will turn to whether perception as unconscious inference can be integrated into EN. We will do so by considering how unconscious inference can produce the content of a perceptual experience.

5.2. *From Bayesian inferences to experience*

Michael Rescorla has identified three questions that any plausible theory of unconscious perceptual inference must satisfactorily answer (Rescorla, 2015, p. 696). These questions are: (1) In what sense does the perceptual

88   *Federico Bongiorno and Lisa Bortolotti*

system carry out inferential tasks? (2) In what sense do implicit assumptions count as premises from which to draw inferential conclusions? (3) In what sense does perceptual inference select the best hypothesis among the available candidates? Currently, the most prominent approach to answering such questions is to treat the perceptual system as executing Bayesian inferences (e.g., Knill and Richards, 1996; Bülthoff and Yuille, 1991; Kersten, Mamassian, and Yuille, 2004).

We saw when discussing the Coltheart model how Bayes theorem can serve as a framework for characterizing inferences that are unconscious and whose conclusions are contents of beliefs. A problem that arises in applying Bayes theorem to perception is that of explaining how Bayesian inference can select one hypothesis to be the content of experience, or in other words, how a Bayesian inference to the effect that P can lead to an experience with content P. For instance, how does the inference of shape from shading result in a perceptual experience of an object's shape? A further difficulty lurks in the question of what kind of content perceptual experiences have. Advocates of a conservative view (e.g., Tye, 1995; Price, 2009; Brogaard, 2013) claim that perceptual experience is restricted to representing basic properties that are straightforwardly available to sensory transducers, such as spatial and chromatic ones. Other scholars (e.g., Siegel, 2006, 2010; Bayne, 2009) adopt a more liberal view, which grants that perceptual experience represents a wide array of high-level properties, including natural kinds but also perhaps causal interactions and highly specific subordinate-level categories.

Bayesian formulations of perceptual inference differ depending on which of these views one takes. If one takes the conservative view, then perceptual inferences process only low-level information, that is, information about color, size, shape, motion, and so on. In such a context, what needs explaining is how perceptual unconscious inferences determine low-level perceptual states like seeing yellow. To illustrate, consider the case where an achromatic grey picture of a banana looks yellow (Hansen et al., 2006). From a Bayesian perspective, this misperception can be interpreted as caused by an overreliance on one's prior expectations as to what bananas look like. Indeed, the likelihood that there is a grey banana in front of one may be overridden by one's belief that bananas are yellow, yielding the inference that the banana is yellow, and thus the experience as of there being a yellow banana.

On the other hand, if one accepts the view that high-level and categorical content features in perceptual phenomenology, presumably one will also take unconscious inference to have high-level effect on phenomenal content, namely, an influence on the perceptual categorization of an object as an object of a certain kind. Bayesian theories of this second kind will thus have the additional task of describing how inferences underwrite one's ability to perceptually represent objects in respect of high-level categories. Consider the following case of a high-level property representation, where the property represented is that of being a snake. Imagine walking down a busy street in London and you seem to see a snake wriggling across the ground. What you are really seeing is a coil of rope and yet it looks to you as if a snake is there. A Bayesian interpretation of this example would look somewhat as follows. The prior probability of there being a snake in central London would seem comparatively too low for the likelihood ratio in favor of the snake hypothesis to override it. Yet your prior belief that the zoo is around the corner paired with your fear of snakes may lead you to favour the snake hypothesis over the rope one, with the result that the snake hypothesis is selected to be the content of experience.

5.3. Inference and Endorsement

Let us now return to our original question, namely, whether EN can be characterized in terms of unconscious perceptual inference. Recall that EN is based on the intuition that an anomalous experience plays a prominent role in the etiology of the delusion. Also, recall that on the endorsement account the anomalous experience has the same, or nearly the same content as the delusion. That is to say, for the delusional belief to be that one's wife has been replaced by an impostor, one must at a minimum have an experience with the content that the woman one is looking at is not one's wife. This view can be developed in an inferential framework only if one assumes that perceptual inferences have a high-level effect on phenomenal content, in the sense sketched above; and that a Bayesian framework provides a systematic means to accommodate perceptual inference within the context of delusion formation.

We saw that one alleged advantage of EN over EX is that EN posits no (or little) gap between the content of the experience and the content of the resulting delusion. So if the endorsement theorist wants to avoid leaving the gap open, they are committed to the claim that relatives are perceived by the person with Capgras delusion as being numerically distinct from themselves. This calls forth a rather liberal conception of perceptual content according to which properties like numerical identity and distinctness are represented in perceptual experience (cf. Wilkinson, 2016; Bongiorno, 2019). It follows that if such a content is brought about by perceptual inferences, those inferences ought to have a high-level influence on perceptual phenomenology. This means, for example, that the hypotheses generated through perceptual inferences should not be thought of being merely about the physical qualities of a person's face (e.g., shape from shading and pigmentation values), but also as being about the identity of the visually presented person, such as whether the person is numerically distinct from, or identical to, one's wife (Davies and Egan, 2013).

90   *Federico Bongiorno and Lisa Bortolotti*

Can a Bayesian framework accommodate perceptual inference within the context of delusion formation? There are grounds for thinking that the perceptual system operates through unconscious inferences that conform to Bayes theorem. We noted above that the *raison d'etre* behind the inferential account of perception is to explain how the perceptual system draws on proximal stimuli to yield hypotheses as to what in the environment is causing them. We further noted that the registrations of the proximal stimuli underdetermine their possible distal causes. This suggests that the perceptual system must conduct probabilistic assessments to select one distal cause over others. A number of studies have shown that this is often done by computing posterior distributions in accordance with Bayes theorem (see for instance, Knill and Richards, 1996; Mamassian, Landy, and Maloney, 2002; Kersten and Yuille, 2003; Kersten, Mamassian, and Yuille, 2004). These considerations put together make it at least probable that if perceptual inference plays a role in Capgras delusion, then it can be accommodated within the Bayesian paradigm.

We have already made reference to Davies and Egan's suggestion that Bayesian probability distribution over absent autonomic activation in people with Capgras should be understood as the operation of a perceptual module (Davies and Egan, 2013). To our knowledge, this represents the only attempt so far to conceptualize EN in terms of the Bayesian framework of perceptual inference. In a previous work, Davies and colleagues proposed to describe the route from anomalous experience to delusional belief as a prepotent doxastic response to the experience (Davies et al., 2001). After the initial adoption, the delusion would be maintained due to the person's inability to refrain from accepting the experience as true. We take it that Davies and Egan's suggestion is to be interpreted as a corollary to this earlier proposal. Assuming that the delusion arises as a prepotent doxastic response to some perceptual experience, how does this experience come about? Davies and Egan's approach to answering this question appeals to Bayesian inference. In this sense, their approach is equivalent to the Coltheart model, the obvious difference being that the outcome of the inference is the content of a conscious perception.

Here too, we have a cluster of hypotheses, all of which reflect a possible identity of the visually presented person. Each hypothesis is assigned a certain subjective probability prior to updating on the new evidence. The prior distribution is then updated to reflect the new evidence provided by the facial appearance of the visually presented person, a person whose face looks identical to the face of the wife. After this first updating, the posterior probability of the person being the wife is higher than the probability of her being a stranger. At this stage, argue Davies and Egan, the perceptual module formulates predictions as to the level of autonomic activation that would be present if either hypothesis was true. The prediction derived from the wife hypothesis is that there will be a high level of activation, whereas the prediction from the stranger hypothesis is that there will be little or none autonomic activity. If those predictions are obtained by Bayesian conditionalization, then it would seem that the likelihood ratio between the two hypotheses conditional to the absence of autonomic activity will favor the stranger hypothesis over the wife hypothesis. The preferred hypothesis, in turn, will be appointed to be the content of experience, such that the person who in fact is the wife will be experienced as another individual (Davies and Egan, 2013, pp. 713–714).

On these grounds, Davies and Egan arrive at the conclusion that the explanationist and endorsement options are both compatible with the possibility of Bayesian inference being involved in the onset of the Capgras delusion (Davies and Egan, 2013, p. 712). Our discussion has offered further reasons to support this conclusion. We saw that inferences that are unconsciously performed can produce conscious perception and determine its content. We also saw that Bayes theorem offers a perspicuous framework for characterizing perceptual inference. All the endorsement theorist needs to argue is that the delusional belief is an endorsement of the anomalous experience. We take it that an experience is endorsed if one forms a belief that P based on an experience that has P as its content (Siegel, 2017, p. 107). So, as long as there can be inferred experiences (viz. experiences whose content P is determined by the outcome of an inference that P), there is no principled basis to deny compatibility between EN and the idea that delusions arise from inferences about the world. All of that being said, the notion of EN being implemented in terms of perceptual inference is far from unproblematic. Though it is widely accepted that unconscious processes of Bayesian inference determine how things are perceived to be, it is controversial whether such things can be perceived as strangers, let alone imposters. In other words, it is one thing to say that unconscious inferences may be a factor behind misperceiving a grey banana as yellow; it is another thing to say that they can prompt one to misperceive their wife as numerically distinct from herself (e.g., Bongiorno, 2019).

6. Lessons From the Coltheart Model

So, does the Coltheart model embody a version of explanationism? Three features of the model are most relevant to answering the question. First, Coltheart and colleagues think that the *misidentification* content 'this woman here present is a stranger' (or the *impostor* content 'this woman here present is a stranger impersonating my wife') enters into consciousness through a process of Bayesian inference on the basis of abnormal unconscious data. Second, this process is itself assumed to happen at an unconscious level. Finally, by implication, there is no causal antecedent of the delusion that can be consciously experienced.

92 *Federico Bongiorno and Lisa Bortolotti*

It may seem obvious that the Coltheart model is not an endorsement theory, since it disavows any role for conscious experience prior to delusion formation. Indeed, several theorists are confident that the Coltheart model yields a modern version of explanationism. For example, Young assures us that the Coltheart model 'is explanationist because the process of Bayesian-style abductive inference is used to select the best hypothesis from those available to explain abnormal data O' (Young, 2014, p. 92; see also Parrott, 2019). However, we suspect that this confidence is misplaced. As we have claimed, the Coltheart model and EN are alike with respect to role of inference in the processes of hypothesis generation. In both cases, inference is invoked as a means of selecting from competing hypotheses the one that best explains discrepant familiarity data. However, if both EN and EX as empiricist accounts rely on there being a conscious experience which is causally antecedent to the adoption of the delusional belief, the Coltheart model does not fit neatly into either because in the model the phenomenon to be explained does not qualify as conscious experience.

Another consideration favoring this conclusion is that the Coltheart model shares some elements with 'rationalist' accounts such as John Campbell's that are neither explanationist nor endorsement accounts. The thrust of Campbell's account is that delusion formation 'is a matter of top-down disturbance in some fundamental beliefs of the subject which may subsequently affect experiences and actions' (Campbell, 2001, p. 89). What does this mean? First, delusions do not originate in experience, but are a direct result of neurobiological alterations in the brain. Second, any experience that the subject reports are a consequence rather than cause of the delusion. The Coltheart model shares the latter feature, as the delusional belief is the first delusion-related event of which the person is conscious.

One must be careful not to overstate what these considerations show. They do not show that the Coltheart model is consistent with Campbell's rationalism. If the cause of a delusion is crudely organic, as Campbell suggests, then the delusion cannot be seen as the product of an inferential process, let alone a Bayesian rational one. What they do show, however, is that some of the implications of the Coltheart model tally with rationalism better than any version of empiricism. This causes further doubt about the Coltheart model being an instance of explanationism.

7. Conclusions and Implications

The idea that delusions are acquired through inferential processes is not new. But there has been little attempt to explain how exactly this may work and what the role of conscious and unconscious inference is in influential models of delusion formation. One notable exception is the Coltheart model, which is a detailed proposal about how delusions arise via a process of probabilistic Bayesian inference. Although the Coltheart model itself does not seem to share the typical features of either explanationism or the endorsement theory, we have argued that the role of Bayesian inference in delusion formation is compatible with both endorsement and explanationist accounts of delusions.

If the rival accounts are alike in this respect, that is, they allow for Bayesian inference to be involved in the process of delusion formation, how should they be distinguished? We know that they both presuppose the existence of a grounding relationship between conscious experience and the resulting delusion. So, we can reasonably consider EN and EX to differ in terms of *where* the inferential transitions responsible for the delusion are positioned in relation to the experience (Langdon and Bayne, 2010). For EN theorists, the key inferential transitions yield perceptual experiences, whereas EX theorists cast them as processes that operate only after the experiences.

Notes

1. As we shall see later in this chapter, Coltheart has recently used the term 'abnormal data' instead of 'abnormal experience' to avoid commitment to the idea that the abnormalities which prompt delusional hypotheses are always consciously accessible.
2. Davies and Egan (2013) have raised doubts whether the notion of Bayesian inference can be adequately captured in terms of abductive inference (or inference to the best explanation). They argue that all the relevant theoretical considerations made by the Coltheart model could be achieved equally well by replacing its talk of Bayesian *abductive* inference by the talk of Bayesian inference *per se* (p. 696). Since our only concern here is to outline the Coltheart model, we do not take stand on this matter.
3. The distinction between 'explanationist' *versus* 'endorsement' options has been so phrased by Bayne and Pacherie (2004a). Others have drawn the same distinction using different terminology. See Davies and Coltheart (2000), Fine, Craigie, and Gold (2005), Aimola Davies and Davies (2009), Langdon and Bayne (2010), and Turner and Coltheart (2010).
4. See Hawley and MacPherson eds. (2011) for several different views of perceptual content.

References

American Psychiatric Association (2013). *Diagnostic and Statistical Manual of Mental Disorders* (DSM-V). Washington DC: American Psychiatric Press.

Barlow, H. B. (1990). Conditions for Versatile Learning. Helmholtz's Unconscious Inference, and the Task of Perception. *Vision Research*, 30, 1561–1571.

Bayne, T. (2009). Perception and the Reach of Phenomenal Content. *Philosophical Quarterly* 59(236), 385–404.

Bayne, T., & Pacherie, E. (2004a). Bottom-Up or Top-Down? Campbell's Rationalist Account of Monothematic Delusions. *Philosophy, Psychiatry, & Psychology*, 11, 1–11.

94 *Federico Bongiorno and Lisa Bortolotti*

Bayne, T., & Pacherie, E. (2004b). Experience, Belief, and the Interpretive Fold. *Philosophy, Psychiatry, & Psychology*, 11, 81–86.

Bongiorno, F. (2019). Is the Capgras Delusion an Endorsement of Experience? *Mind and Language*.

Bortolotti, L., & Miyazono, K. (2015). Recent Work on the Nature and the Development of Delusions. *Philosophy Compass* 10(9), 636–645.

Brighetti, G., Bonifacci, P., Borlimi, R., & Ottaviani, C. (2007). Far from the Heart Far from the Eye: Evidence from the Capgras Delusion. *Cognitive Neuropsychiatry*, 12, 189–197.

Brogaard, B. (2013). Do we Perceive Natural Kind Properties? *Philosophical Studies*, 162(1), 35–42.

Bülthoff, H. H., & Yuille, A. L. (1991). Bayesian Models for Seeing Shapes and Depth. *Comments of Theoretical Biology*, 2(4), 283–314.

Burge, T. (2010). *Origins of Objectivity*. Oxford: Oxford University Press.

Campbell, J. (2001). Rationality, Meaning, and the Analysis of Delusion. *Philosophy, Psychiatry, & Psychology*, 8(2–3), 89–100.

Capgras, J., & Reboul-Lachaux, J. (1923). L'illusion des 'Sosies' Dans un Délire Dystématisé Chronique. *Bulletin de la Societé Clinique de Médicine Mentale*, 11, 6–16.

Coltheart, M. (2005). Conscious Experience and Delusional Belief. *Philosophy, Psychiatry, & Psychology*, 12(2), 153–157.

Coltheart, M. (2007). The 33rd Sir Frederick Barlett Lecture: Cognitive Neuropsychiatry and Delusional Belief. *The Quarterly Journal of Experimental Psychology*, 60(8), 1041–1062.

Coltheart, M., Langdon, R., & McKay, R. (2011). Delusional Belief. *Annual Review of Psychology*, 62, 271–298.

Coltheart, M., Menzies, P., & Sutton, J. (2010). Abductive Inference and Delusional Belief. *Cognitive Neuropsychiatry*, 15(1–2–3), 261–287.

Davies, A., & Davies, M. (2009). Explaining Pathologies of Belief. In M. Broome & L. Bortolotti (Eds.), *Psychiatry as Cognitive Neuroscience* (pp. 285–323). Oxford: Oxford University Press.

Davies, M., & Coltheart, M. (2000). Introduction: Pathologies of Belief. In M. Coltheart & M. Davies (Eds.), *Pathologies of Belief* (pp. 1–46). Oxford: Blackwell.

Davies, M., Coltheart, M., Langdon, R. & Breen, N. (2001). Monothematic delusions: towards a two-factor account. *Philosophy, Psychiatry, & Psychology*, 8(2/3), 133–158.

Davies, M., & Egan, A. (2013). Delusion: Cognitive Approaches – Bayesian Inference and Compartmentalization. In K. W. M. Fulford, M. Davies, R. G. T. Gipps, G. Graham, J. Z. Sadler, G. Stanghellini, & T. Thornton (Eds.), *The Oxford Handbook of Philosophy and Psychiatry* (pp. 689–727). Oxford: Oxford University Press.

Ellis, H. D., Lewis, M. B., Moselhy, H. F., & Young, A. W. (2000). Automatic without Autonomic Responses to Familiar Faces: Differential Components of Covert Face Recognition in a Case of Capgras Delusion. *Cognitive Neuropsychiatry*, 5, 255–269.

Ellis, H. D., & Young, A. W. (1990). Accounting for Delusional Misidentifications. *British Journal of Psychiatry*, 157, 239–248.

Ellis, H. D. Young, A. W., Quayle, A. H., & De Pauw, K. W. (1997). Reduced Autonomic Responses to Face in Capgras Delusion. *Proceedings of the Royal Society, London B: Biological Sciences*, 264, 1085–1092.

Fine, C., Craigie, J., & Gold, I. (2005). Damned If You Do, Damned If You Don't: The Impasse in Cognitive Accounts of the Capgras Delusion. *Philosophy, Psychiatry, & Psychology*, 12, 143–151.

Fodor, J. A. (1983). *The Modularity of Mind*, Cambridge, MA: MIT Press.

Gold, J., & Gold, I. (2014). *Suspicious Minds: How Culture Shapes Madness*. New York: Free Press.

Gregory, R. L. (1973). The Confounded Eye. In R. L. Gregory & E. H. Gombrich (Eds.), *Illusion in Nature and Art* (pp. 49–95). London: Duckworth.

Gregory, R. L. (1997). Knowledge in Perception and Illusion. *Philosophical Transactions of the Royal Society of London B*, 352, 1121–1127.

Hansen, T., Gegenfurtner, K., Olkkonen, M., & Walter, S. (2006). Memory Modulates Color Experience. *Nature Neuroscience*, 9(11), 1367–1368.

Harman, G. (1965). The Inference to the Best Explanation. *Philosophical Review*, 74, 88–95.

Hawley, K. & MacPherson, F. (Eds.) (2011). *The admissible contents of experience*. Malden, MA: Wiley-Blackwell.

Helmholtz, H. von. (1867). *Handbuch der Physiologischen Optik*. Leipzig: Voss.

Hirstein, W., & Ramachandran, V. S. (1997). Capgras Syndrome: A Novel Probe for Understanding the Neural Representation of the Identity and Familiarity of Persons, *Proceedings of the Royal Society of London B: Biological Sciences*, 264, 437–444.

Hohwy, J. (2013). *The Predictive Mind*. Oxford: Oxford University Press.

Kersten, D., Mamassian, P., & Yuille, A. (2004). Object Perception as Bayesian Inference. *Annual Review of Psychology*, 55, 271–304.

Kersten, D., & Yuille, A. L. (2003). Bayesian Models of Object Perception. *Current Opinion in Neurobiology*, 13(2), 150–158.

Knill, D., & Richards, W. (Eds.). (1996). *Perception as Bayesian Inference*. Cambridge: Cambridge University Press.

Langdon, R., & Bayne, T. (2010). Delusion and Confabulation: Mistakes of Perceiving, Remembering and Believing. *Cognitive Neuropsychiatry*, 15, 319–345.

Langdon, R., & Coltheart, M. (2000). The Cognitive Neuropsychology of Delusions. *Mind & Language*, 15, 184–218.

Langdon, R. & Connaughton, R. (2013). The neuropsychology of belief formation. In F. Kreuger & J. Grafman (Eds.), *The neural basis of human belief systems* (pp. 19–42). Hove; New York, NY: Taylor and Francis.

Lipton, P. (2004). *Inference to the Best Explanation*. London: Routledge.

Maher, B. A. (1974). Delusional Thinking and Perceptual Disorder. *Journal of Individual Psychology*, 30, 98–113.

Maher, B. A. (1988). Anomalous Experience and Delusional Thinking: The Logic of Explanations. In T. F. Oltmanns & B. A. Maher (Eds.), *Delusional Beliefs* (pp. 15–33). Chichester: John Wiley and Sons.

Maher, B. A. (1992). Delusions: Contemporary Etiological Hypotheses. *Psychiatric Annals*, 22, 260.

Maher, B. A. (1999). Anomalous Experience in Everyday Life: Its Significance for Psychopathology. *The Monist*, 82(4), 547–570.

Maher, B. A. (2005). Delusional Thinking and Cognitive Disorder. *Integrative Physiological & Behavioural Science*, 40, 136–146.

Mamassian, P., Landy, M., & Maloney, L. (2002). Bayesian Modelling of Visual Perception. In P. N. Rao, B. A. Olshausen, & M. S. Lewicki (Eds.), *Probabilistic Models of the Brain* (pp. 13–60). Cambridge, MA: MIT Press.

McKay, R. (2012). Delusional Inference. *Mind & Language*, 27, 330–355.

Miyazono, K., Bortolotti, L., & Broome, M. (2015). Prediction-Error and Two-Factor Theories of Delusion Formation: Competitors or Allies? In N. Galbraith (ed.), *Aberrant Beliefs and Reasoning*. London: Psychology Press.

Pacherie, E. (2009). Perception, Emotions and Delusions: Revisiting the Capgras Delusion. In T. Bayne & J. Fernandez (Eds.), *Delusions and Self-Deception* (pp. 107–126). Hove: Psychology Press.

Pacherie, E., Green, M., & Bayne, T. (2006). Phenomenology and Delusions: Who Put the 'Alien' in Alien Control? *Consciousness and Cognition*, 15(3), 566–577.

Parrott, M. (2019). Delusional Predictions and Explanations. *British Journal for the Philosophy of Science*.

Price, R. (2009). Aspect-Switching and Visual Phenomenal Character. *Philosophical Quarterly*, 59(236), 508–518.

Ramachandran, V. S., & Blakeslee, S. (1998). *Phantoms in the Brain: Human Nature and the Architecture of the Mind*. London: Fourth Estate.

Rescorla, M. (2015). Bayesian Perceptual Psychology. In M. Matthen (Ed.), *The Oxford Handbook of the Philosophy of Perception* (pp. 694–716). Oxford: Oxford University Press.

Rock, I. (1983). *The Logic of Perception*. Cambridge, MA: MIT Press.

Siegel, S. (2006). Which Properties are Represented in Perception? In T. Gendler Szabo & J. Hawthorne (Eds.), *Perceptual Experience* (pp. 481–503). Oxford: Oxford University Press.

Siegel, S. (2010). *The Contents of Visual Experience*. New York: Oxford University Press.

Siegel, S. (2017). *The Rationality of Perception*. New York: Oxford University Press.

Stone, T., & Young, A. W. (1997). Delusions and Brain Injury: The Philosophy and Psychology of Belief. *Mind and Language*, 12, 327–364.

Tranel, D., Damasio, H., & Damasio, A. R. (1995). Double Dissociation Between Overt and Covert Recognition. *Journal of Cognitive Neuroscience*, 7, 425–432.

Turner, M., & Coltheart, M. (2010). Confabulation and Delusion: A Common Monitoring Framework. *Cognitive Neuropsychiatry*, 15, 346–376.

Tye, M. (1995). *Ten Problems of Consciousness*. Cambridge, MA: MIT Press.

Wilkinson, S. (2016). A Mental File Approach to Delusional Misidentification. *Review of Philosophy and Psychology*, 7, 389–404.

Young, G. (2008). Capgras Delusion: An Interactionist Model. *Consciousness and Cognition*, 17, 863–876.

Young, G. (2014). Amending the Revisionist Model of the Capgras Delusion: A Further Argument for the Role of Patient Experience in the Delusional Belief Formation. *Avant: Trends in Interdisciplinary Studies* (3): 89–112.

Part II

Inference in Speech Comprehension

4 Seeing and Hearing Meanings

A Non-Inferential Approach to Speech Comprehension

Berit Brogaard

1. Introduction

When I tell my dog James to sit, most of the time he sits. When I tell him to stay, most of the time he stays. When I tell him to come, most of the time he comes. When I say 'good boy!', he wags his tail. A loud 'stop it!' when he barks at inappropriate times usually makes him stop barking. Does James understand the commands 'sit', 'stay' and 'come'? Does he understand that 'Good boy!' conveys that he is being good? Does he understand that 'Stop it!' conveys that he is engaging in bad behavior? Judging from the reliability of his behavioral responses to my commands and words of praise or criticism, he does indeed understand these phrases on some level. But what is the nature of this type of understanding?

It may be thought that dogs come to understand commands, praise, and criticism by engaging in instrumental reasoning that take the form of a conscious or consciously accessible inference. We will probably never know for sure whether they do. But it seems unlikely (Millikan, 2006). Certainly, prior to James' behavioral responses to the command 'come', James is not in the business of performing a practical inference that has any semblance of the following piece of reasoning: 'My owner said 'come.' When she says 'come' she wants me to run to where she is. I want to satisfy her desires. So, it is in my best interest to run to where she is'. Although it is difficult to know exactly how sophisticated non-human animal minds are, it is almost certain that James did not perform a conscious or consciously accessible inference of this sort.[1] But if he did not, in what sense does he understand the phrases to which he responds?

There is a simple and an initially plausible answer to this question: Dogs and other sophisticated non-human animals are capable of perceiving the distinct sound patterns of the phrases that people use with them. The distinct sound patterns trigger specific behavioral responses, as predicted by the phenomena of classical as well as operant conditioning (Rescorla, 1988; Bouton, 2016). So, understanding in dogs and other sophisticated non-human animals amounts to no more than a sensory detection of sounds and associative learning via classical or operant conditioning. No mystery here. Or so the envisaged explanation goes. When I want James to sit, I use the word 'sit'. Usually he responds by sitting. But I could have trained him differently. Instead of using the word 'sit' I could have used a hand signal, a whistle, a clicker or a flute and received the same result. James could easily have been trained to perform the intended behavior using any kind of audible sound device.

Compare the case of speech 'comprehension' in domestic dogs to that of speech comprehension in neurotypical children who have learned to respond to common phrases and sentences in English. Consider this case. During dinner I notice that my daughter has finished all her French fries but has barely touched her vegetables or chicken. I request that she eat at least some of what is left on her plate. There are a number of distinct ways in which she can satisfy my request. She can eat everything left on her plate, all of her vegetables but no chicken, all of her chicken but none of the vegetables, some but not all of her vegetables, some but not all of her chicken, or some of the chicken and some of the vegetables. Although my daughter must carry out one of the actions in order to satisfy my request, she has a choice as to which of the six possible actions she chooses to perform. She might even put some conscious thought into the options before she decides what to do. However, she likely does not *need* to perform any conscious or consciously accessible inference in order for her to understand what I want her to do.

Despite the fact that children can grasp what is said to them without engaging in inference, their level of understanding seems notably different from what we find in domestic dogs. When I make the request 'Please eat at least some of what is left on your plate!', my daughter most likely doesn't satisfy my request as a result of classical or operant conditioning. That is, she does not merely respond to an experience of a particular pattern of sounds. But if she does not, then how is she capable of understanding what I am saying?

In this chapter I will argue that we typically comprehend speech by sensorily experiencing meanings and without having to rely on conscious, or consciously accessible, inferences.[2] Call this view 'the non-inferential view of speech comprehension'. The meaning experienced may or may not be a meaning the speaker intended to convey or a meaning she successfully conveyed to someone else. When it is not, what is experienced is – with some exceptions – a case of misperception.[3] Misperceiving what a speaker intended to convey or successfully conveyed need not result in miscommunication, however. For example, it may appear to me that you said 'Do you have any *beer*?' when in reality you said 'Do you have anything to drink *here*?'. If my grasping the meaning of 'Do you have any beer?' is a case of perception, it is a case of misperception. However, it needn't be a case of miscommunication – at least not if communication is miscommunication only insofar as it leads to practical misunderstanding. If I nod and go to the fridge and bring you a beer, you may be perfectly happy. No further questions asked.

The non-inferential view is a view about the nature of understanding. As such, it need not be combined with any particular epistemological theory. As I have argued in previous work (Brogaard, 2016), however, the non-inferential view is particularly attractive when combined with phenomenal dogmatism – the view that phenomenal seemings (or experiences) can confer immediate prima facie justification on belief (Brogaard, 2016, 2017). Here I will defend the non-inferential view on epistemically neutral grounds. That is, I will provide a number of considerations in favor of the non-inferential view that are independent of whether or not one accepts phenomenal dogmatism.

The plan for the chapter is as follows. In Section 2 I specify what I mean by the term 'inference' and look at the types of valid or otherwise legitimate inferences speakers typically make. In Section 3 I look closer at what it means to say that a meaning property is presented in experience. In Section 4 I provide my main arguments for thinking that we frequently perceive apparently conveyed meanings.

2. Linguistic Inferences

Before examining what exactly it means to say that a meaning property is presented in sensory experience and defending the view that they are sometimes thus presented, let's have a closer look at the nature of linguistic inference. Before saying something about *linguistic* inference, however, we need to be clear on what an inference is.

One might suggest that an inference is a process during which a system transitions from the informational content of a state (e.g., a computational, mental or neurological state) to the informational content of another – in accordance with a particular rule set.[4] This definition is clearly too broad. It allows us to truly say of an unconscious machine that it makes inferences as long as it computes information. It also classifies many brain computations that intuitively are not inferences as inferences. Here is an example of a process that is not consciously accessible yet would count as an inference on the broad definition of 'inference' (for discussion, see Brogaard, 2011a). When you reach to and grasp your coffee mug, you automatically fold your fingers in a particular way that fits the handle of the mug. This folding of your fingers is also known as 'the hand aperture'. Your brain calculates the hand aperture it assumes will fit the mug. But there is no way you could reproduce these calculations on a conscious level. The process takes place below the level of conscious awareness and is inaccessible to consciousness. The calculation of the correct hand aperture does not involve *you* making inferences about how to bend your fingers.

102 Berit Brogaard

'Inference', as the phrase ought to be used, refers to processes performed by entities that at least sometimes are (phenomenally) conscious in the sense of having (phenomenally) conscious mental states (Valaris, 2017).[5] If a transitioning from the content of one mental state or dispositional structure to the content of another is inaccessible to consciousness, then the process takes place only on a subpersonal level and hence does not count as an inference.

Following Daniel Dennett (1969:93), the distinction between the personal level and subpersonal level is grounded in distinct kinds of explanations one can provide for why people behave the way they do. The distinction is that between 'the explanatory level of people and their sensations and activities and the subpersonal level of brains and events in the nervous system' (196, p. 93). Personal level explanations are distinctive kinds of explanation for persons:

> When we've said that a person's in pain, that she knows which bit of her hurts and that this is what's made her react in a certain way, we've said all that there is to say within the scope of the personal vocabulary. . . . If we look for alternative modes of explanation, we must abandon the explanatory level of people and their sensations and activities and turn to the sub-personal level of brains and events in the nervous system.
>
> (1969, p. 93)

Although personal-level explanations may refer to arational mental states like pain, they can also refer to mental states, such as 'needs, desires, intentions, and beliefs', that can be evaluated in terms of rationality, (Dennett, 1969, p. 164). Subpersonal-level explanations, on the other hand, are not concerned with normative properties such as that of being rational; they merely make reference to causal relations and mechanisms.

Inference is a type of process that contributes to making behavior intelligible in terms of norms of rationality. For example, I might make the following inference. 'Otávio turned off the air conditioning in the seminar room. When Otávio turns off the air conditioning, he is cold. Hence, Otávio is cold'. Since the process of transitioning from the content of a mental state or dispositional structure that is inaccessible to consciousness to the content of another (perhaps in accordance with a particular rule set) does not and cannot make behavior intelligible in terms of norms of rationality, these types of processes do not count as inferences.

To recap: 'inference', as the phrase ought to be used, refers to a process of transitioning from the content of one personal-level state to the content of another personal-level state (perhaps in accordance with a particular rule-set). Because unconscious machines do not make computations that transition from the content of a personal-level state to the content of another, they do not make inferences. This definition of 'inference' restricts inferences to those that are either explicit (i.e., the subject is consciously aware of making them) or consciously accessible (i.e., the subject could – under different psychological or environmental conditions of the sort that can obtain in this world – have been aware of making them). This definition leaves out 'inferences' that are subpersonal and therefore not consciously accessible. It also rules out that cognitive penetration – the phenomenon according to which the content of a cognitive state is semantically impacting the content of a sensory experience – is a case of inference, even if it could be likened to inference (Brogaard and Chomanski, 2015). This is because cognitive penetration, as commonly conceived, is not a process accessible to consciousness. It occurs at a subpersonal level. Although it has been argued that cognitive penetration can result in a downgrade of the justificatory status of experiences, the subject would not ordinarily be able to tell whether an experience has been cognitively penetrated (Siegel, 2017; Chudnoff, 2018).

Turning now to linguistic inference, a linguistic inference made by a listener or addressee, then, is a conscious or unconscious (but consciously accessible) process that transitions from the content of one mental state about what was conveyed to the content of another state concerning what was conveyed – in accordance with a particular rule set. When linguistic inferences are valid, the rule set is derived from principles governing inductive or deductive inferences or inferences to the best explanation.

Paul Grice (1975) suggested that when rational agents engage in conversation, all participants in the conversation stand to gain if they all adhere to a super-maxim known as 'the cooperative principle' as well as four sub-maxims:

> *The cooperative principle (super-maxim):* Make your contribution as is required, when it is required, by the conversation in which you are engaged.
> *Quality:* Contribute only what you know to be true. Do not say false things. Do not say things for which you lack evidence.
> *Quantity:* Make your contribution as informative as is required. Do not say more than is required.
> *Relation:* (Relevance): Make your contribution relevant.
> *Manner:* (i) Avoid obscurity; (ii) avoid ambiguity; (iii) be brief; (iv) be orderly.

Grice cites four types of cases in which a conversationalist fails to adhere to the maxims:

(1) *Violation*: A speaker may violate a maxim without making it explicit that she is doing so, for instance, by lying or providing misleading information.

104   *Berit Brogaard*

(2) *Opting out*: A speaker may opt out of the conversation by explicitly saying or signaling that she refuses to be cooperative, for instance, by giving the speaker the silent treatment.

(3) *Flouting*: A speaker may flout a maxim. The speaker still adheres to the cooperative principle but she is blatantly violating a maxim to achieve a particular communicative effect.

(4) *Clash*: If two maxims cannot both be satisfied, the speaker is then forced to choose between the two, thus violating a maxim but only because there is no way not to do so.

Grice thought of apparently conveyed meanings as derived from inferences that presume that the speaker knows the conversational maxims. He calls these derived meanings 'conversational implicatures'.

In some cases, conversational implicatures are derived on the assumption that the speaker adheres by all maxims. Consider the following case. Jill points to a group of people at a function she is attending and informs Jack that her friend is the one with glasses. Jack looks at the group and spots a person without glasses, a person with glasses, and a person with a hat and glasses. He assumes that Jill is cooperative and hence is providing all information needed in order for him to unequivocally identify her friend. According to the Gricean model, Jack then infers that if Jill's friend had been the one with both hat and glasses, Jill would have mentioned the hat in addition to the glasses (see Figure 4.1). Since she didn't mention the hat, and since she is cooperative, the friend must be the person with glasses but no hat.

In other cases, implicatures are derived by an inference from a presumed violation of a maxim. Consider the following discourse fragment:

Jill: I am upset because this student of mine keeps complaining about the grade I gave him in my logic class and now his mother has gotten involved too. She has been calling me three times to try to get me to change his grade.

Jack [sarcastically]:   Yeah, UM students are so independent.

The implicature here is that UM students are not very independent. Here is how Jill might infer this implicature from what Jack said. Jill presupposes that Jack is obeying the cooperative principle. But Jack blatantly violated the maxim of Quality by saying something that he believes to be false. He has done nothing to make Jill think he accidentally violated the maxim. So Jack must be attempting to convey a claim that is different from but related to the one that he semantically expressed. Since he said what he believes is false, he must be attempting to convey that UM students are *not* very independent.

Figure 4.1 Gricean Implicature

The speaker points to a group of people at a function and states that her friend is the one with glasses. The listener looks at the group and spots one person without glasses, one person with glasses and one person with a hat and glasses. He assumes that the speaker is cooperative and hence is providing all relevant information for identifying her friend. According to the Gricean model, he then infers that if the friend was the one with both hat and glasses, the speaker would have mentioned the hat in addition to the glasses. Since she didn't mention the hat, and since she is cooperative, her friend must be the person with glasses but no hat.

Grice's own description of his notion of conversational implicature makes it clear that he thinks conversational implicatures are derived inferentially rather than at a subpersonal level:

> I am now in a position to characterize the notion of conversational implicature. A man who, by (in, when) saying (or making as if to say) that p has implicated that q, may be said to have conversationally implicated that q, PROVIDED THAT (1) he is to be presumed to be observing the conversational maxims, or at least the cooperative principle; (2) the supposition that he is aware that, or thinks that, q is required in order to make his saying or making as if to say p (or doing so in THOSE terms) consistent with this presumption; and

(3) the speaker thinks (and would expect the hearer to think that the speaker thinks) that it is within the competence of the hearer to work out, or grasp intuitively, that the supposition mentioned in (2) IS required.

(Grice, 1975, pp. 49–50)

Note that Grice here assumes that the listener is aware of, or thinks about, what is required in order for an utterance to satisfy the conversational maxims or the cooperative principle. This view strongly suggests the inferential view, at least with respect to conversational implicature. In the following section, I will provide a number of considerations against an inferential view of speech comprehension.

3. Experiencing Apparently Conveyed Meanings

If the non-inferential view of speech comprehension is correct, then we sometimes experience apparently conveyed meanings, i.e., meanings that appear to us to be conveyed by the speaker who is addressing us (see, however, O'Callaghan, 2011). Consider this case: Jack informs Jill that the rain stopped. Assuming Jill has an accurate experience of the meaning conveyed by Jack's utterance, the meaning *the rain stopped* is presented in Jill's auditory experience. Because Jill believes Jack is a reliable witness, she comes to believe that the rain stopped.

Contrast this with the following case: Jill already believes it is raining. But she looks out the window and sees a sunny sky. Jill forms the belief that that the rain stopped on the basis of her visual experience of the sunny sky, without ever reflecting on the reliability of her visual system.

The two cases differ in how easily Jill forms the belief that the rain stopped. Of course, Jill may not trust her senses, and this may block the formation of belief. But it is safe to say that neurotypical individuals ordinarily are more likely to form belief on the basis of what they visually experience than on the basis of what they hear others say. One belief Jill is very likely to form on the basis of hearing Jack utter 'the rain stopped', however, is the belief that *Jack said that* the rain stopped. So, if Jill auditorily perceives the meaning *the rain stopped* but she comes to believe that Jack said that the rain stopped, then there is an asymmetry between experiencing what is apparently conveyed and forming a belief about what is apparently conveyed on the basis of hearing the utterance.

But what is the difference between a visual experience as of, say, a sunny sky and an auditory experience of, say, the meaning *it's sunny*? The most natural answer to this question is that these meanings are experienced in different ways. A visual experience represents its content under a visual manner of representation (Chalmers, 2004). A tactile experience represents its content under a tactile manner of representation (e.g., the roundness of a ball is represented differently visually and tactually).

Seeing and Hearing Meanings 107

Likewise, it is safe to assume that an auditory experience of an apparently conveyed meaning will be represented under its own manner of representation – a manner of representation that is different from the visual manner, the tactile manner, etc.

Now it is tempting to think of the perception of meanings as something that occurs only when a sentence is expressed verbally or in ordinary writing. But I do not want to restrict the term 'apparently conveyed meaning' in this way. If speech comprehension can be a perceptual process, then a person fluent in braille can probably touch meanings. Perceiving what appears to be conveyed by a sequence of signs in American Sign Language is a way of seeing meanings that are not necessarily written down. There are also a plethora of linguistic and non-linguistic *signals* that convey meanings, for instance: emojis – or the corresponding behavior (e.g., thumbs up) or facial expressions (e.g., surprise), punctuation and intonation (e.g., 'Mary went to the store' versus 'Mary went to the store?'), demonstrations (e.g., pointing to or gazing at something), linguistic conventions (e.g., replying 'good' to 'how are you?', uttered by a relative stranger, even if you are not good.), back channeling (e.g., replying with 'mhm,' 'uhuh,' 'sure,' 'OMG,' 'No kidding' to indicate that you are listening and/or are still interested in the content of the conversation).

As these cases demonstrate, understanding what a person means often relies on what is also known as 'mind reading' (Carruthers et al., 1996). Mind reading is the grasping of what a person appears to be thinking, feeling, or intending to do. If mind reading requires actually possessing a theory and making inferences about what people think, feel and intend, then the *non-inferential* view may be false. However, even advocates of the so-called 'theory theory', which takes us to rely on folk psychology when reading other people's minds, denies that mind-reading is typically inferential (Gopnik, 2003, 2012). In any event, the purposes of the rest of the chapter, I will assume that an inferential view of mind-reading is incorrect.

A further remark of clarification about the experience of meanings is in order here. There is a vast body of literature discussing how presuppositions in conversational contexts can influence meaning (see e.g., Stalnaker, 1973). For instance, if it is presupposed in the conversational context that bank robbers are more likely than police officers to wear masks, then an utterance of the discourse fragment in (1) means something entirely different from what it means in conversational contexts where police officers are more likely than bank robbers to wear masks (the example is borrowed from Pettit, 2010; see also Stanley, 2005):

(1) The police officer caught the bank robber. He was wearing a mask.

It may be thought that the context dependence of conveyed meanings is in direct opposition to the non-inferential view. This, however, is not

108 Berit Brogaard

so (Brogaard, 2016b). The presupposed fact (or alleged fact) that bank robbers wear masks is information 'stored' in what is known as 'semantic memory' (memory of facts and apparent facts, such as the fact that Obama was the 44th President of the United States).

If semantic memory is distributed across the neocortex, as some argue (Price, Bonner, and Grossman, 2015), then semantic memory may influence perceptual processing via top-down influences. There is a long-standing debate about whether top-down influences on sensory perception constitute cognitive penetration (Pylyshyn, 1999; Firestone and Scholl, 2016). The outcome of this debate does not matter for our purposes here. Even if the distributed semantic memory model is correct, (implicitly) retrieved (reassembled) semantic memory may still be able to influence the experience of apparently conveyed meaning. Such top-down influences, however, would not be inferences for the same reason that cognitive penetration is not an inference.

Another possibility is that semantic memory makes an imprint on the mechanisms of the language center via a phenomenon known as 'perceptual learning' (Brogaard, 2016b). Perceptual learning, unlike other forms of learning, can be defined as 'experience-induced changes in the way perceivers pick up information' (Kellman and Garrigan, 2009) or as extracting perceptual information that was previously unused (Gibson and Gibson, 1955). In perceptual learning, semantic information indirectly influences the content of experiences but it does so by altering the mechanisms for computing experiences. In perceptual learning, our sensory system is transformed in a way that affects how things appear to us.

If speech comprehension is a result of top-down influences on perception or a kind of perceptual learning where semantic memory alters the neural processing in the language center, then the fact that speech comprehension depends heavily on context is perfectly consistent with the non-inferential view (Brogaard, 2016b).

A question here arises: if meaning properties are presented in experience, what is the nature of these properties? Meaning properties are a type of high-level property like artificial kind properties (e.g., *being a house, being a table* or *a being laptop*) or emotional properties (e.g., *being angry, being afraid* or *being surprised*). We can take the high-level properties that are presented in experience to be the result of an instantiation of particular configurations of lower-level properties (e.g., *being watery* or *looking like a zebra*). Call high-level properties of this kind 'Gestalt properties' (Brogaard, 2018).[6] To see what the nature of Gestalt properties is, consider the image of the three squares in Figure 4.2.[7]

The three figures are all perceived as possessing the Gestalt property of looking square. But none of the configurations of lower-level properties that we visually detect suffices for squareness to be present in our perceptual experience. In the first figure the property of looking square presented in our experience is a result of us visually detecting a solid black

Figure 4.2 The Gestalt Property of Looking Square

The three figures all possess the property of looking square, but that property is not metaphysically determined by any of the low-level properties of the figures.

mass. In the second figure the property of looking a square presented in experience is a result of us visually detecting a particular configuration of dots. In the third figure the property of looking square presented is the result of us visually detecting a particular configuration of line segments.

The relationship between the Gestalt property presented in experience and the low-level properties visually detected is not one of metaphysical entailment but rather one of causation. To capture the relation of causality, let's exploit Mackie's (1965) famous INUS condition. 'INUS' stands for 'an insufficient but necessary part of a condition which is itself unnecessary but sufficient for the result'. For example, an electrical short-circuit may cause a fire but the short-circuit is not necessary for the fire to occur. The fire could have been the result of arson rather than a short circuit. Nor is the short-circuit sufficient for the fire to occur. If there is no oxidizing agent, a short-circuit does not result in a fire. The occurrence of the short circuit is a necessary member of a set of conditions that is itself unnecessary but sufficient for the fire. Other members of that set include the presence of oxygen, the presence of flammable material, the absence of flooding, etc.

Now, we can take Gestalt properties presented in experience to be caused by sets of sensorily processed INUS conditions (e.g., configurations of dots or line segments). These sets of sensorily processed configurations of low-level properties (together with other INUS conditions) are sufficient but not necessary for the Gestalt property to be presented in the resulting sensory experience. For example, in the case of looking angry, sensory processing of the properties that are universally characteristic of an angry face (together with other INUS conditions), is sufficient but not necessary for the property of being angry to be presented in the resulting sensory experience of anger.

The meaning properties that are presented in experience, I want to suggest, are Gestalt properties. For the case of auditory perception,

110   *Berit Brogaard*

the meaning properties presented in experience are caused by auditory information – for instance, information taken in from the external environment or information possessed from birth or acquired through past perception or testimony. This pre-existing information must either affect sensory processing through feedback mechanisms or be the result of altered computational mechanisms in sensory areas. Sensorily processed information sufficient for meaning properties to be presented in experience may include information about:

- The sound properties produced by the utterance
- The grammatical structure of language
- Consciously accessible or inaccessible semantic memory such as knowledge of the semantic meaning of lexical items, pragmatic principles, and cultural habits
- The identity of the speaker
- Conversation preceding the utterance

Possession of this experienced or stored information (that influences the processing of perceptual contents) is sufficient but not necessary for particular meaning properties to be presented in experience. It is not necessary because different chunks of information can result in the same meaning property being experientially presented. For instance, exposure to utterances of 'Homo sapiens evolved 200,000 years ago' and 'Human beings evolved 200,000 years ago' may result in experiences that represent different sound properties but the same meaning properties.

4. Theoretical and Empirical Considerations in Favor of the Non-Inferential View

There are several considerations in favor of the non-inferential view of speech comprehension: empirical as well as theoretical. Each of these considerations merely indicates that apparently conveyed meanings can be sensorily perceived. Together, however, they make a decent case for the non-inferential view.

4.1. Neuroanatomical Evidence

There is broad consensus that speech comprehension is closely tied to processing in Wernicke's area, sitting in the superior temporal gyrus close to the auditory cortex, usually on the left side of the brain (sometimes on the right) (Bogen and Bogen, 1976).[8] Being located in a lower region of the brain, Wernicke's area may be considered a sensory area for language comprehension, neuroanatomically speaking.

The hypothesis that Wernicke's area is central to language comprehension does not rule out that many other areas of the brain are also involved in speech comprehension. As noted earlier, one theory of semantic memory is that semantic memory is distributed across the entire neocortex (outer layer) of the brain. Since semantic memory is a strong influence on speech comprehension, the entire brain may be dedicated to the understanding of language.

But even on this theory, meaning processing may take place primarily in Wernicke's area in the temporal lobe – subsequent to feedback entry from other brain regions. If this is indeed the case, then brain regions often correlated with inferential processes (such as the prefrontal cortex) do not play a direct role in the neural processes involved in speech comprehension.

One of the things we cannot rule out on the basis of neuroanatomical evidence is that the brain regions in the left temporal lobe (together with parts of the frontal lobe) – constituting the so-called 'language center' – are a neural substrate for *linguistic* inference. It could be that linguistic inference and other types of inference have anatomically distinct neural correlates.

4.2. Semantic Satiation

Semantic satiation (also known as 'semantic saturation' and 'semantic adaptation') is a phenomenon in which a repeated phrase may lose its meaning for the listener. Leon Jakobovits James, who coined the term in his dissertation in 1962, found that repeating a phrase prior to completing a task depending on its meaning resulted in response inaccuracy or a delayed response time (James, 1962).

Semantic satiation is a special case of stimulus satiation (which is also sometimes called 'sensory adaptation'; see Block, 2014; Nes, 2016). Stimulus satiation is different from habituation, a method in behavioral therapy that seeks to eliminate an emotional response to a particular stimulus by repeating exposure to the stimulus (Glanzer, 1953). This is a slow process that likely has a different neural mechanism from the fast process of stimulus satiation.

Stimulus satiation is generally believed to be a sensory phenomenon that involves a change in the responsiveness of the sensory system to a repeated or constant stimulus (Glanzer, 1953). If you put your hand on a textured pillow, you will initially feel the texture on the palm of your hand. But it only takes a few seconds before the intensity of the feeling of the texture subsides. What happens is that the neurons that process tactile experience provide a significant response at first but the neural response of the sensory neurons then slowly diminishes.

Stimulus satiation occurs in all sensory modalities. If you live right next to the runways of an airport, you will quickly cease to hear the noise of the departing planes. Your visitors, on the other hand, will initially get startled by the loudness of the engines. Likewise, if your house

112   *Berit Brogaard*

smells of old garbage or cigarette smoke, your olfactory sensory system will quickly adapt to the smell to the point where you no longer notice it.

The dominant hypothesis concerning the mechanism underlying stimulus satiation is that the transmission from the thalamus to the sensory cortical brain regions decreases with constant exposure, leading to a partial or full closure of the gateway in the thalamus that is responsible for blocking irrelevant information from entering cortical areas of the brain while letting relevant information enter. Information that doesn't enter the cortical areas of the brain will not generate any conscious mental states.

The phenomenon Leon Jakobovits James (1962) identified when he coined the term 'semantic satiation' is that we have a similar tendency to quickly adapt to repeated phrases, quickly tuning out on what they mean. The phenomenon of semantic satiation is another indicator that meanings typically are sensorily comprehended rather than being the result of an inferential process.[9]

4.3. Stroop Effect

Another piece of evidence for the non-inferential view comes from the standard Stroop effect (Stroop, 1935). The Stroop effect, in its classical form, is interference found when attention-grabbing word meanings interfere with the naming of the ink color the words are printed in. It typically takes longer to name the ink color when it does not match the word meaning. We are also more prone to mistakes when the ink color is contrary to the color depicted by the word. For example, if the word 'red' is printed in the ink color green, then it is harder to name the color than if it had been printed in red (or black).

A common explanation of this effect is that because grasping the meaning of color words is far more automatized than color naming, the meaning of the color word captures our attention and thereby distracts us from the color naming task we were supposed to carry out (see e.g., Brown, Gore, and Carr, 2002).

On a widely received view, this kind of attentional bias can be explained by the fact that the processing of meaning in sensory cortical brain regions interferes in a feedforward fashion with the intellectual naming task in the prefrontal cortex (Brown, Gore, and Carr, 2002). The effect thus appears to indicate that the grasp of meanings occurs automatically as a result of sensory processing, which points to the non-inferential view of meaning comprehension.

4.4. Pop Out Effect

A further piece of evidence in favor of the non-inferential view comes from a variation on a standard visual search paradigm. Visual search paradigms can be used to test whether visual detection of a target item

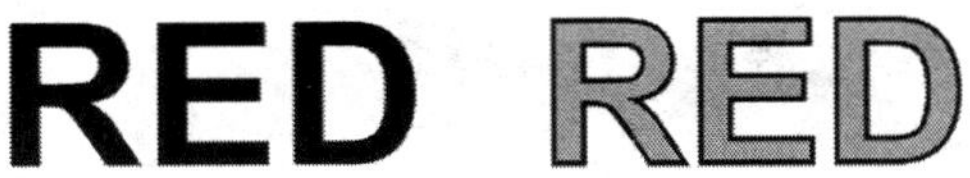

RED RED

Figure 4.3 Stroop Effect

The word 'red' is here displayed in the color black (left) and the word 'green' is displayed as the color gray (right). It takes longer for subjects to name the color of the ink when the word is printed in a color that differs from the color designated by the word than when it is printed in black or the same color as the color designated.

occurs early on in the visual system. If a target captures our attention, the visual detection of the target is thought to be processed early on in the visual system.

A visual search test that consists of words or pseudowords can likewise serve as a test of whether we sensorily experience meanings. In visual search paradigms of this kind, subjects are exposed to an array containing a meaningful word (the target) and meaningless variations on that word (the distractors).

If comprehension of apparently conveyed meanings is a sensory phenomenon, then we should expect the target item to capture attention bottom-up either prior to, or simultaneously with us, becoming aware of the target (Beck, 1966; Treisman, 1982). When attention is automatically drawn to a target, strenuous efforts is unnecessary for the identification of the target. Thus, identification of the target should be highly efficient (i.e., fast and accurate). This is also known as a 'pop-out effect'. If, on the other hand, experience of conveyed meaning requires systematic search and systematically applied top-down attention, then the target word should not capture attention bottom-up and the identification process should be less efficient (slower and less accurate).

A pop-out effect in visual search paradigms thus suggests that a property of the target item is sensorily presented in the early visual system. So if a visual search for a real word (the target) among pseudowords (the distractors) yields a pop-out effect, then this indicates that the apparently conveyed meanings is presented in visual experience.

This is indeed what we find. When subjects are shown an array of a meaningful word (the target) and meaningless variations on that word (the distractors), the meaningful word pops out and immediately grabs their attention (Brogaard, 2017) (Figure 4.4).[10]

When subjects are presented with a target word that may appear to be meaningful ('phonetele'), a pop-out effect can be observed but the average response time is radically decreased compared to the response time in the experimental case (Figure 4.5).

Finally, when subjects are asked to search for a pseudoword within an array of other pseudowords, there is no pop-out effect (Figure 4.6).

phleteone	enlehpoet	telephone
ohleetenp	tlhepeone	eelehonpt
honetelep	letenepho	eeetlponh

Figure 4.4 Experimental Case

The word 'telephone' pops out in an array of words and pseudowords. This test indicates that grasping meanings or at least meaningfulness is a sensory phenomenon.

phleteone	enlehpoet	tlhepeone
ohleetenp	tlhepeone	phonetele
honetelep	letenepho	eeetlponh

Figure 4.5 First Control Case

The word 'phonetele' hidden in an array of meaningless pseudowords yields only a weak pop-out effect.

phleteone	enlehpoet	ophntleee
ohleetenp	tlhepeone	eelehonpt
honetelep	letenepho	eeetlponh

Figure 4.6 Second Control Case

When the array consists of pseudowords and no meaningful or quasi-meaningful words, there is no pop-out effect.

It should be noted that the experimental paradigm used here doesn't aim at showing directly that we perceive word meanings but rather whether the property of being meaningful is presented in experience. However, there is good reason to think that the ability to perceptually determine meaningfulness normally depends on the ability to perceptually identify particular meanings. For example, in order to experience 'telephone' as meaningful, you would likely need to have implicit knowledge of the semantic meaning of 'telephone'. If this is so, however, then the pop-out effects indicate that apparently conveyed meanings are presented in sensory experience.

This suggestion yields an empirically testable prediction: we should expect to find that we are capable of quickly and accurately detecting a target word that belongs to one domain, say, the domain of sea animals (e.g., 'Nemo'. – 'fish' – 'squid') when hidden among distractor words (matched in length, frequency, level of abstraction, prototypicality, etc.) that derive from a rather different domain, say that of land animals or

Seeing and Hearing Meanings 115

mammals (e.g., 'Elmo', 'Lilo', 'Dora', 'Bart', 'Hulk'. – 'bear', 'goat', 'wolf', 'lion', 'mule' – 'camel', 'zebra', 'tiger', 'horse', 'panda').

One limitation of the present data, but not the research paradigm as such, is that they do not eliminate the possibility that we would get the same effect with any familiar string of letters, including nonsensical words, like 'mimsy'.

4.5. Immediacy, Automaticity, and Amodal Completion

The non-inferential view gains further support from the speed and automaticity of language comprehension. Average college students can read about 255 words per minute, which would be an impossible feat if they were to slow down and make inferences about what the writer intended to convey (Christianson, Luke, and Ferreira, 2010; Ferreira, Bailey, and Ferraro, 2002; Swets et al., 2008).

The speed and automaticity of language comprehension may be due in part to our ability to amodally complete partially perceived meanings. Suppose you see the following sentences in a newspaper that contains some ink stains:

(2) (a) Plus spacious 1554 sq. ft. home with large lot, family room with fireplace and huge ███ for entertaining and enjoying the views.
  (b) Local guitarist Jon Henninger announced yesterday that the track features Henninger on guitar and Henninger's band mate Eric Lyday on ███.
  (c) Charlie's hiccups were cured through the use of carbon ███ xide.
  (d) Recipe ingredients: 3 cups chopped tomatoes, 1/2 cup chopped green bell pepper. 1 cup diced onion, 2 tablespoons chopped fresh ███. 2 tablespoons fresh lime juice.

We naturally fill in 'deck' or 'terrace' in 2(a), 'drums' or another word designating a musical instrument in 2(b), 'carbon dioxide' in 2(c) and 'cilantro' or some other edible ingredient in 2(d). However, errors have a tendency to creep in in unfortunate ways. The original version of 2(a) is shown in Figure 4.7.

The original version of 2(b) contained a typing error, which the Illinois newspaper *The Morning Sentinel* later announced: 'Due to a typing error, Saturday's story on local artist Jon Henninger mistakenly reported that Henninger's band mate, Eric Lyday, was on drugs. The story should have read Lyday was on drums'.

2(c) too contains a spelling error – in this case one that potentially could lead people to kill themselves instead of curing their hiccups (Figure 4.8).

The original version of the recipe in 2(d) recommended adding two tablespoons of cement. A correction was later issued: 'Recipe correction: in a recipe for salsa published recently, one of the ingredients was

116 Berit Brogaard

Figure 4.7 Unfortunate Typo: Newspaper Advertisement for Real Estate

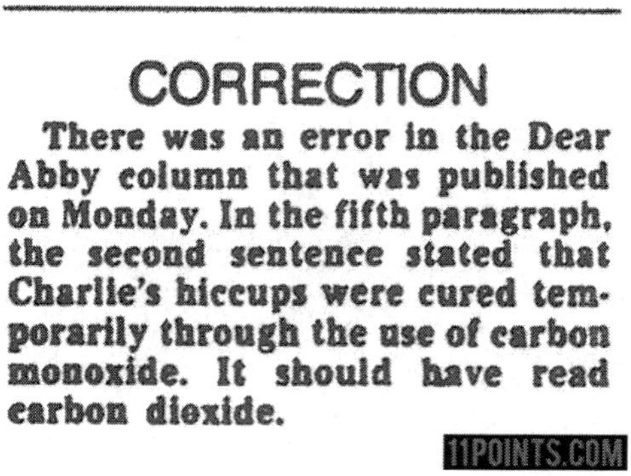

Figure 4.8 Unfortunate Typo: Correction of Unfortunate Typo on Website

misstated due to an error. The correct ingredient is 'two tablespoons of cilantro' instead of 'two tablespoons of cement'.

While the envisaged ink stains force us to fill in words in the cases in (2), this 'good-enough' approach naturally employed here is, in fact, the normal way we comprehend language, even when there are no occluders. We usually process only part of what we read or hear and fill in the rest through top-down processing or amodal completion (Christianson, Luke, and Ferreira, 2010; Ferreira, Bailey, and Ferraro, 2002; Swets et al., 2008).

Seeing and Hearing Meanings 117

The speed and automaticity of language comprehension suggests that the processes involved in grasping conveyed meaning are not typically personal-level processes. Hence, they are not typically the result of inferences but are more likely to be the result of processes akin to the sensory processes involved in producing low-level sensory mental states.

4.6. Evidence Insensitivity

Perceptual experiences can be appropriate or inappropriate but they are not assessable for rationality – as I am using the term in this chapter. Granted, if the perceptual view of emotions is correct, then emotions can be said to be rational or irrational only to the extent that perceptual experiences can be said to be rational or irrational (Brogaard and Chudnoff, 2016).[11]

But experiences are not assessable for rationality in the sense in which, say, beliefs are. To a first approximation, a rational belief is a belief that is based on good reasons and does not stand in opposition to other beliefs indicating that it may be inaccurate. For instance, if I see water pouring down outside the window, this may give me a good reason to believe that it is raining. If, however, I also believe that the water is due to a new sprinkler system that has been installed on the rooftop, then that second belief defeats my belief that it is raining. In that case, my belief that it is raining is not rational. It may be prima facie justified. But the justification is defeated by my second belief.

Unlike beliefs, sensory experiences retain their prima-facie justifying power in light of evidence that they may be inaccurate. They are relatively informationally encapsulated (Fodor, 1983). For example, in the case of amodal completion, partially occluded figures are not perceived as the fragments of the foregrounded figures but as hidden behind or covered by the occluder (Figure 4.9).

In the case of vision, the process of amodal completion proceeds in accordance with its own rules, viz. intra-perceptual principles, or 'organizing principles of vision', that modulate early visual processes (Pylyshyn, 1999; Fodor, 1983; Raftopoulos, 2001).[12] These intra-perceptual principles are not rational principles, such as maximum likelihood or semantic coherence. The visual system employs them to compensate for the inherent ambiguity of proximal stimuli. In Figure 4.9, for example, the proximity of the regular octagons to the occluded figure should make it more likely that the occluded figure is also a regular octagon. But the principles of amodal completion work according to their own algorithms and the occluded object is not experienced as a regular octagon.

In recent work, Susanna Siegel (2017) has argued that perceptual experience can be epistemically downgraded. Here is one of her examples. Jill fears that John is angry at her. This causes her to experience his neutral face as an angry face. Hence, her experience is epistemically downgraded,

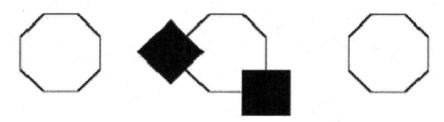

Figure 4.9 Kanizsa Amodal Completion
Despite the flanking cases of octagons, the occluded figure is not seen as a regular octagon.
Source: Pylyshyn 1999

according to Siegel. In her view, 'both perceptual experience and the processes by which they arise can be rational or irrational' (2007, p. 15).

I am not going to dispute this hypothesis here (for a counterargument, see Chudnoff, this volume; Brogaard, 2019). Even if it's true, this does not challenge Pylyshyn's (1999) claim that intra-perceptual principles are not rational principles.

The question that remains is whether our (apparent) comprehension of what is said is immune to defeaters in the same way as uncontroversial cases of sensory experience. It appears that they are. If I hear John ask me whether Brian has remembered to pick up beer for the bachelor party in Miami, but I subsequently learn that he actually asked whether Brian had remembered to pick up headgear for the bachelor party, I may come to believe that I was wrong about what I heard but the auditory appearance of what I initially heard appears to be immune to this belief.

Here is a further consideration in favor of this thesis. This is intended to be analogous to Pylyshyn's (1999) octagon case. Imagine you are talking to one of your frenemies Ben. I hear you say 'leave me alone'. I am likely going to get the impression that you intended to convey to Ben that he should leave you alone. Suppose, however, that several other people in your group start crying out loud: 'Please don't leave me alone in this god forsaken place'. In this case, the appearance of you having said 'leave me alone' may well be immune to the possibility that you said something that is partially occluded but similar to what others in your group were saying (i.e., 'please [. . .] leave me alone [. . .]').

We can easily conjure up other examples of the same kind. Suppose I hear you say to your friends Jill and Jack 'I have not had breakfast' and it comes to seem to me that you are informing them that you have not had breakfast on the day in question. But I then hear Jack exclaim: 'Two weeks! That's nothing. Susan and I have not had breakfast together since she started her new job with the MPD'. If I know I only heard a fragment of what you and your friends were talking about, the possibility that you said something to the effect that you had not had breakfast with such-and-such a person for two week now ought to cast doubt on what I initially thought you said. But in spite of the fact that there is reason to doubt my initial appearance of what you said, that appearance is likely to stick with me.

It seems plausible then that apparently conveyed meanings are immune to defeat in the same way that uncontroversial cases of visual experience are. Since this kind of evidence insensitivity is a mark of uncontroversial cases of visual experience, the intuition that appearances of conveyed meanings can also be immune to defeat provides some support for thinking that appearances of conveyed meanings are sensory in nature.

5. Perception or Type-1 Reasoning?

In this chapter I have provided psychological and philosophical considerations in favor of a non-inferential view of speech comprehension. On this view, speech comprehension need not require personal-level inferences on the part of the hearer.

Let me end the chapter by pointing to a limitation of my argument. The argument does not show that we can auditorily (or visually or tactually) experience the meanings that it would seem that the author or speaker was intending to convey. Indeed, the findings reviewed in this chapter are compatible with the idea that a hearer (or reader or viewer) comes to understand what the speaker (or writer) apparently intended to convey by employing type-1 cognitive processes that make use of semantic associations and heuristics rather than, say, probability theory or logic.

The hypothesis that cognitive processing can be divided into two types is a postulate of dual-processing theory. According to this view, there are two distinct ways in which we make decisions or come to conclusions in daily life. Type-1 cognitive processes are fast and rely on semantic associations and heuristics ('rules of thumb'), whereas type-2 processes are slow and rely on careful reflection and inference (Tversky and Kahneman, 1973, 1983; Samuelson and Church, 2014; Roberts and West, 2015). If indeed we often rely on type-1 cognitive processes in order to understand speech, then it's possible that grasping what a speaker appears to want to communicate is neither inferential nor perceptual. But it is also possible that at least some of the fast and automatic type-1 processes are in fact perceptual processes.

To see this, consider judgments of personality in thin-slicing conditions (i.e., conditions in which you are only exposed to a person or a still-photo of the person for a very brief period of time). It is widely agreed in cognitive science that these types of judgment rely on type-1 cognitive processing (Gigerenzer, 2007). However, there are independent grounds for thinking that the processes that support personality judgments in these conditions are the exact same processes that produce perceptual appearances (Brogaard, 2016a).

120 Berit Brogaard

Likewise, it remains a possibility that if we rely on type-1 cognitive processes in trying to understand language, these processes give rise to perceptual appearances. This is a topic I hope to deal with on a future occasion.[13]

Notes

1. There may, of course, be other forms of instrumental reasoning that non-human animals do engage in. See e.g., Camp and Shupe (2018).
2. Note that the non-inferential view does not imply that we never rely on inferences when engaging in speech comprehension. When the speaker intentions are not immediately clear to the addressee, the addressee may engage in an inference before forming a belief about what the speaker might possibly have intended to convey. The non-inferential view is thus consistent with the occasional reliance on inference in order to derive the meaning of what the speaker intended to convey. Consider the following case. Marianne is a foreigner with very little familiarity with the meaning of slurs in English. She does not automatically grasp their meanings. One day Marianne accidentally bumps into a stranger Jennifer. This makes Jennifer angry and she screams: 'Bitch!' We can imagine that Marianne, who is not very familiar with the meaning of slurs in English, engages in the following inference on a conscious level: ' 'Bitch' literally means a female fox but there is no good reason to think the angry lady thinks I am female fox. So, she was probably using the term in its derogatory sense, thereby conveying to me that I have some negative traits that caused me to intentionally bump into her in order to harm her'.
3. The exceptions I have in mind include cases in which the speaker intends to convey that p but actually conveys that q, or fails to convey anything at all. While visiting Spain I ask someone where I can buy some groceries. Or so I think. What I actually asked, using the Spanish word 'groserias', was where I could buy some vulgarities. In this case, what I intended to convey is not what native speakers hear me say. Arguably, in cases like this, what is conveyed is what the naive speakers think I convey. In that case, the perceptions of the native speakers are not misperceptions.
4. Note that the rules need not specify valid inferences, as a rule set could be any set of rules. For example, the rules that govern transitions between neurological states might be computational in a non-standard sense (see Piccinini and Bahar, 2013). The rules that govern transitions between mental states are probably psychological laws of a kind that rules out mere associative transitions, such as the associative transition from 'doctor' to 'nurse'.
5. Markos Valaris (2017) is primarily interested in reasoning, but his notion of reasoning is closely related to the notion of 'inference' in the narrow sense (in the wide sense, any rule-based transition between quantities of information can count as an inference; in the wide sense, my MacBook Pro is capable of making inferences).
6. Gestalt properties are different from high-level properties that constitute the essence of a thing, for instance, *being H_2O, having tiger-DNA* or *being made of this or that piece of clay.*
7. This is just an analogy. I will remain neutral on the issue of whether shape-like properties can reasonably be considered high-level properties.
8. The location of Wernicke's area remains controversial.

9. Anders Nes (2016) also invokes semantic satiation and the kinship of the latter with sensory adaptation to suggest that utterance comprehension has an important similarity, in this respect, to perceptual processes.
10. Pilot study, Brogaard Lab for Multisensory Research.
11. On the perceptual view, emotions are bodily sensations produced in response to value objects (e.g., fearfulness of tiger) (Brogaard and Chudnoff, 2016). Bodily sensations (or bodily feelings–also known as 'interoception') have not traditionally been construed as sensory experiences. However, one might argue that the modality that produces bodily feelings just is a sensory modality closely related to proprioception, our sense of balance (the vestibular system) and nociception (pain and spice perception), which arguably are *sensory* modalities unlike intuition and introspection (Macpherson, 2011; Schwenkler, 2013; Briscoe, 2016).
12. These principles are akin to what Helmholtz called 'unconscious inferences' (Gordon, 2004), what Gregory (1968) calls 'hypotheses', or what Bayesians call 'implicit assumptions' (Rescorla, 2015). See also Brogaard (2011b).
13. For helpful comments on previous versions of this paper, I am grateful to an anonymous reviewer for this volume, Tim Bayne, Jake Beck, Ned Block, Elijah Chudnoff, Jack Lyons, Fiona Macpherson, Mike Martin, Michelle Montague, Anders Nes, Pär Sundström, Charles Travis, Sebastian Watzl, and audiences at Humboldt University, Kirschberg, Miami, NYU, and the 2017 Meeting of the SPP.

References

Beck, J. (1966). Effect of Orientation and of Shape Similarity on Perceptual Grouping. *Perception and Psychophysics*, 1, 300–302.

Block, N. (2014). Seeing-As in the Light of Vision Science. *Philosophy and Phenomenological Research*, 89(1), 560–572.

Bogen, J. E., & Bogen, G. M. (1976). Wernicke's Region – Where Is It? *Annals of the New York Academy of Sciences*, 280, 834–843.

Bouton, M. E. (2016). *Learning and Behavior: A Contemporary Synthesis*. 2nd Ed. Sunderland, MA: Sinauer.

Briscoe, R. E. (2016). Multisensory Processing and Perceptual Consciousness: Part I. *Philosophy Compass*, 11(2), 121–133.

Brogaard, B. (2011a). Conscious Vision for Action vs. Unconscious Vision for Action. Cognitive Science, 35, 1076–1104.

Brogaard, B. (2011b). Are There Unconscious Perceptual Processes?, *Consciousness and Cognition*, 20(2), 449–463.

Brogaard, B. (2016a). Perceptual Appearances of Personality. *Philosophical Topics*, a supplement to *Nous*, 44(2), 83–103.

Brogaard, B. (2016b). In Defense of Hearing Meanings. *Synthese*. First Online: 06 August 2016, 195(7), 2967–2983.

Brogaard, B. (2017). The Publicity of Meaning and the Perceptual Approach to Speech Perception. *Protosociology*, 34.

Brogaard, B. (2018). *Seeing & Saying*. New York: Oxford University Press.

Brogaard, B. (2019). Bias-Driven Attention, Cognitive Penetration and Epistemic Downgrading. In Christoph Limbeck & Friedrich Stadler (Eds.), *Philosophy of Perception and Observation*. De Gruyter: Publications of the Austrian Ludwig Wittgenstein Society.

122 *Berit Brogaard*

Brogaard, B., & Chomanski, B. (2015). Cognitive Penetrability and High-Level Properties in Perception: Unrelated Phenomena? *Pacific Philosophical Quarterly*, 96, 469–486.

Brogaard, B., & Chudnoff, E (2016). Against Emotional Dogmatism. *Philosophical Issues*, a supplement to *Nous*, 26(1), 59–77.

Brown, T. L., Gore, C. L., & Carr, T. H. (2002). Visual Attention and Word Recognition in Stroop Color Naming: Is Word Recognition 'Automatic'? *Journal of Experimental Psychology: General*, 131, 220–240.

Camp, E., & Shupe, E. (2018). Instrumental Reasoning in Nonhuman Animals. In K. Andrews & J. Beck (Eds.), *The Routledge Handbook of Philosophy of Animal Minds*. Oxford: Routledge, 100–108.

Carruthers, P., & Smith, P. K. (Eds.). (1996). *Theories of Theories of Mind*. Cambridge: Cambridge University Press.

Chalmers, D. (2004). The Representational Character of Experience. In B. Leiter (Ed.), *The Future for Philosophy*. Oxford: Oxford University Press, 153–181.

Christianson, K., Luke, S. G., & Ferreira, F. (2010). Effects on Plausibility on Structural Priming. *Journal of Experimental Psychology: Learning, Memory, and Cognition*, 36, 538–544.

Chudnoff, E. (2018). Epistemic Elitism and Other Minds. *Philosophy and Phenomenological Research*, 96(2), 276–298.

Chudnoff, E. (this volume). Experience and Epistemic Structure: Can Cognitive Penetration Result in Epistemic Downgrade? In T. Chan & A. Nes (Eds.), *Inference and Consciousness*.

Dennett, D. C. (1969). *Content and Consciousness*. London: Routledge & Kegan Paul.

Ferreira, F., Bailey, K. G. D., & Ferraro, V. (2002). Good-Enough Representations in Language Comprehension. *Current Directions in Psychological Science*, 11, 11–15.

Firestone, C., & B. J. Scholl (2016). Cognition Does Not Affect Perception: Evaluating the Evidence for 'Top-Down' Effects. *Behavioral and Brain Sciences*, 39, e229. doi: 10.1017/S0140525X15000965. Epub 2015 Jul 20.

Fodor, J. (1983). *The Modularity of Mind*. Cambridge, MA: MIT Press.

Gibson, J. J., & Gibson, E. J. (1955). Perceptual Learning: Differentiation or Enrichment? *Psychological Review*, 62, 32–41.

Gigerenzer, G. (2007). *Gut Feelings: The Intelligence of the Unconscious*. New York: Penguin Group.

Glanzer, M. (1953). Stimulus Satiation: An Explanation of Spontaneous Alternation and Related Phenomena. *Psychological Review*, 60(4), 257–268.

Gopnik, A. (2003). The Theory as an Alternative to the Innateness Hypothesis. In L. Antony & N. Hornstein (Eds.), *Chomsky and His Critics*. Oxford: Blackwells. Retrieved 2013–04–26.

Gopnik, A. (2012). Reconstructing Constructivism: Causal Models, Bayesian Learning Mechanisms, and the Theory. *American Psychological Association*, 138, 1085–1108.

Gordon, I. E. (2004). *Theories of Visual Perception*. 3rd Ed. Hove: Psychology Press.

Gregory, R. L. (1968). *Visual Illusions, Image, Object, and Illusion*. Readings from Scientific American. San Francisco: W. H. Freeman and Company.

Grice, H. P. (1975). Logic and Conversation. In P. Cole & J. Morgan (Eds.), *Syntax and Semantics*, vol.3. Cambridge, MA: Academic Press.

James, L. J. (1962). Effects of Repeated Stimulation on Cognitive Aspects of Behavior: Some Experiments on the Phenomenon of Semantic Satiation. Doctoral Dissertation, April 1962.

Kellman, P. J., & Garrigan, P. (2009). Perceptual Learning and Human Expertise. *Physics of Life Reviews*, 6(2), 53–84.

Mackie, J. L. (1965). Causes and Conditions. *American Philosophical Quarterly*, 2(4), 245–264.

Macpherson, F. (Ed.) (2011). *The Senses: Classic and Contemporary Philosophical Perspectives*. Oxford: Oxford University Press.

Millikan, R. (2006). Styles of Rationality. In S. L. Hurley & M. Nudds (Eds.), *Rational Animals?* (pp. 117–126). Oxford: Oxford University Press.

Nes, A. (2016). On What We Experience When We Hear People Speak. *Phenomenology and Mind*, 10, 58–85.

O'Callaghan, C. (2011). Against Hearing Meanings. *The Philosophical Quarterly*, 61(245), 783–807.

Pettit, D. (2010). On the Epistemology and Psychology of Speech Comprehension. *The Baltic International Yearbook of Cognition, Logic and Communication*: Meaning, Understanding and Knowledge pages, 5, 1–43.

Piccinini, G., & Bahar, S. (2013). Neural Computation and the Computational Theory of Cognition. *Cognitive Science*, 37(3), 453–488.

Price, A. R., Bonner, M. F., & Grossman, M. (2015). Semantic Memory: Cognitive and Neuroanatomical Perspectives. In Arthur W. Toga (Ed.), *Brain Mapping: An Encyclopedic Reference*, vol. 3 (pp. 529–536). Elsevier: Academic Press.

Pylyshyn, Z. W. (1999). Is Vision Continuous with Cognition? The Case for Cognitive Impenetrability of Visual Perception. *Behavioral and Brain Sciences*, 22, 341–423.

Raftopoulos, A. (2001). Is Perception Informationally Encapsulated? The Issue of the Theory-Ladenness of Perception. *Cognitive Science*, 25, 423–451.

Rescorla, M. (2015). Bayesian Perceptual Psychology. In Mohan Matthen (Ed.), *The Oxford Handbook of the Philosophy of Perception* (pp. 694–716). New York: Oxford University Press.

Rescorla, R. A. (1988). Pavlovian Conditioning – It's Not What You Think It Is. *American Psychologist*, 43, 151–160.

Roberts, R. C., & West, R. (2015). Natural Epistemic Defects and Corrective Virtues. *Synthese*, 192(8), 2557–2576.

Samuelson, P. L., & Church, I. M. (2014). When Cognition Turns Vicious: Heuristics and Biases in Light of Virtue Epistemology. *Philosophical Psychology*, 28(8), 1095–1113.

Schwenkler, J. (2013). The Objects of Bodily Awareness. *Philosophical Studies*, 162(2), 465–472.

Siegel, S. (2017). *The Rationality of Perception*. Oxford: Oxford University Press.

Stalnaker, R. (1973). Presuppositions. *The Journal of Philosophical Logic*, 2, 447–457.

Stanley, J. (2005). Hornsby on the Phenomenology of Speech. *The Aristotelian Society* Supplementary, 79, 131–146.

124 Berit Brogaard

Stroop, J. R. (1935). Studies of Interference in Serial Verbal Reactions. *Journal of Experimental Psychology*, 18(6), 643–662.

Swets, B., Desmet, T., Clifton, C. Jr., & Ferreira, F. (2008). Underspecification of Syntactic Ambiguities: Evidence from Self-Paced Reading. *Memory & Cognition*, 36, 201–216.

Treisman, A. (1982). Perceptual Grouping and Attention in Visual Search for Features and for Objects. *Journal of Experimental Psychology: Human Perception and Performance*, 8(2), 194–214.

Tversky, A., & Kahneman, D. (1973). Availability: A Heuristic for Judging Frequency and Probability. *Cognitive Psychology*, 5, 207–232.

Tversky, A., & Kahneman, D. (1983). Extensional versus Intuitive Reasoning: The Conjunction Fallacy in Probability Judgment. *Psychological Review*, 90(4), 293–315.

Valaris, M. (2017). What Reasoning Might Be. *Synthese*, 194(6), 2007–2024.

5 Metacognition and Inferential Accounts of Communication

Nicholas Allott

1. Introduction

This chapter aims to show that metacognitive processes of monitoring and control play a role in utterance interpretation, even when the process is smooth, automatic, and unreflective. More precisely, I argue that unconscious monitoring and control – what Joelle Proust (2013) has referred to as 'procedural metacognition' and Shea et al. (2014) 'system 1' metacognition – is a central feature of utterance interpretation. I support my claim with theoretical arguments and evidence from two empirical paradigms.

This is intended as a step towards understanding how utterance interpretation can both be an inferential achievement (Grice, 1989; Wilson and Sperber, 2012), and a largely subliminal, automatic process, phenomenologically very different from full-blown reasoning. In the terms of dual-processing accounts of cognition (Sloman, 1996; Stanovich and West, 1998; Evans, 2003; Evans and Frankish, 2009), utterance interpretation resembles 'system 2' reasoning in some respects: the inferences are generally warranted, and apparently unencapsulated. But in normal, smooth communication, they are typically quick and seemingly effortless, thus in this respect more akin to paradigmatic unconscious, 'system 1' inferences. A good theory of utterance interpretation should shed light on this tension and in my view this will require an account of the role played by unconscious, automatic feedback mechanisms, for reasons I explain in Section 2.

Feedback here is understood in terms of processes that monitor and control other processes, and monitoring and control are the essential ingredients of what has become known as *metacognition*.[1] Metacognition, often loosely characterized as 'thinking about thinking', has been studied in several separate literatures in psychology over several decades which have recently attracted attention from philosophers. I briefly describe one classic experimental paradigm in Section 2.3.

Several lines of research suggest that metacognitive feedback often shapes behavior unconsciously (Kentridge and Heywood, 2000; Spehn and Reder, 2000; Paynter, Reder, and Kieffaber, 2009; Shea et al., 2014).

126 *Nicholas Allott*

This view may have a paradoxical air if one sees metacognition as bringing first-order thought processes to second-order awareness by metarepresenting them. However Proust has forcefully argued that metacognition does not require metarepresentation, and that the basic form of metacognition is what she terms *procedural* metacognition (Proust, 2013). That is, there are mental processes that are dedicated to monitoring and controlling other mental processes without representing them, or at the least without representing them as such. Crucially for my purposes here, it is plausible that much of this procedural metacognition is unconscious. Dedicated subpersonal metacognitive processes track how 'first-order' mental processes are doing in their tasks, so that subsequent processing can be guided by that performance, even when there is no awareness at the personal level that anything like this is happening.

Shea et al. (2014) also argue that unconscious metacognition exists, although unlike Proust they define metacognition as representational. They argue for a distinction between system 1 metacognition, which is unconscious and is dedicated to the control of processes within one agent, and system 2 metacognition, which brings properties of processes to conscious awareness so that this information can be shared with con-specifics.

What is important for current purposes is that on either of these views, it is likely that many processes that have not been regarded as metacognitive because they lack conscious metacognitive phenomenology will turn out to involve metacognition.[2] Here I argue that this includes normal, smooth utterance interpretation.

Various rival accounts of utterance interpretation are current in linguistic pragmatics. The most prominent share two central assumptions: i) that utterance interpretation is a type of inference to the best explanation about certain intentions of the speaker; and ii) that it is performed by, or according to, a specialized heuristic or heuristics.

Paul Grice's well-known work on meaning (Grice, 1957) and on conversation (Grice, 1975; Grice, 1978) suggested an inferential model of communication (Sperber and Wilson, 1986, pp. 21ff.). This was a major shift from most previous views of communication, which focused on the role of language seen as a code for transmitting thoughts.

In a pure coding/decoding model, communication is simply the transmission of a meaning – the message – by encoding it in language or some other code. The idea is that the transmitter encodes and transmits the message as a linguistic signal, which the receiver then decodes. There is some truth to this. Language *is* a code in the sense that the relationship between word-types and what they mean is (mostly) arbitrary. So linguistic parsing is indeed a form of decoding.

However, it is now well-established that what a speaker conveys by an utterance ('speaker meaning' in the prevailing terminology) is not determined by the linguistic material that she utters. The inferential model accounts for this by treating the parsed linguistic form of each utterance as merely an input to the hearer's inference about what the speaker meant by uttering it. The inference in question is from some observed behavior (an utterance) to an explanation for that behavior in terms of the speaker's intentions to convey something (the speaker's meaning). This inference may draw on the linguistic and extra-linguistic context and on personal and cultural background knowledge. On all these points, the major tendencies in linguistic pragmatics and philosophy of language are in agreement – that is, Griceans such as Kent Bach, neo-Griceans such as Levinson, and relevance theorists (who are best understood as post-Griceans) such as Sperber and Wilson.[3] A second key assumption, shared by neo-Griceans and relevance theorists, is that the process can be seen as the operation of a heuristic or heuristics. (Sperber and Wilson, 1986, p. 45; Levinson, 2000, pp. 30ff.) This chapter's thesis is a claim about properties of this utterance interpretation heuristic (or suite of heuristics): namely that it involves subliminal metacognition.

There are two prongs to my argument. One, dealt with later in Section 2, is that very general considerations about processing suggest that utterance interpretation must be steered by feedback of this sort. This line of argumentation depends on some general assumptions about mental computation and heuristics and on framing utterance interpretation as inference performed by a heuristic, which I motivate briefly; I cannot mount here a full-dress defense of inferential pragmatics or of basic assumptions about the computational character of mental processes.

The other prong of the argument is provided by two sets of experimental results that I discuss in Section 3. I argue that they show that tacit feedback occurs in utterance interpretation. The way I proceed is to set out some ways that subliminal metacognition could work in communication and then present the empirical results. These suggest that there is subliminal metacognition in i) suppression of activated word senses; ii) slowing of reading speed when there are problems integrating the interpretation of an utterance with the model of the context.

I also discuss whether these effects could be accounted for without postulating metacognition. Here I consider Recanati's bottom-up accessibility-driven account of recovery of what is said, which is an attempt to show that this component of speaker's meaning can be arrived at without abductive inference. I argue that his account is non-metacognitive and also highly implausible.

This discussion raises the question of how claims about low-level properties of a heuristic are relevant to questions about what kind of task the heuristic performs, and I make some tentative suggestions, appealing to David Marr's distinction between different levels of explanation in cognitive science.

2. Theoretical Discussion

The inferential processing involved in utterance processing is not in general full-blown reasoning or reflective inference, thus differing from what at least some philosophers mean when they use the word 'inference'. In his recent paper on inference, Paul Boghossian writes:

> By 'inference' I mean reasoning with beliefs. Specifically, I mean the sort of 'reasoned change in view' . . . in which you start off with some beliefs and then, after a process of reasoning, end up either adding some new beliefs, or giving up some old beliefs, or both.
>
> (Boghossian, 2014, p. 2)

He adds:

> I am interested in reasoning that is person-level, conscious and voluntary, not sub-personal, sub-conscious and automatic, although I shall not also assume that it is effortful and demanding.
>
> (Boghossian, 2014, pp. 2–3)

Utterance interpretation differs from this in that it is typically involuntary and subconscious: we do not have any choice about whether we perform it, and we are not occurrently aware of doing so, only of its result.[4] At least, that is so for cases where everything goes smoothly, which I will be focusing on for two reasons.

The first reason is that I take that to be the normal case. What we seem to be aware of typically is that the speaker is stating p and/or implying q, promising to do r and so forth. The speech sounds and words that are uttered are also available to awareness, although not – at the personal level – represented in the detail, or with the structure that they are parsed to have by subpersonal processes.

We are typically *not* aware of having to infer what the speaker meant from the sounds she made, although this must be happening, since the input to the process is a stream of speech sounds, and a) the sound stream does not possess either linguistic or speaker meaning intrinsically, and b) one sound stream typically corresponds to many possible linguistic meanings and an open-ended number of speaker meanings.

We generally interpret utterances without noticing that we have (for example, and *inter alia*) assigned reference to indexicals, chosen senses for ambiguous expressions and reconstructed what was meant by the use of degree adjectives and possessives. For example, a utterance of the sentence in (1a) might be an assertion of something like the proposition in (1b), and in the right context that proposition could and generally would be arrived at without the hearer noticing that there was inferential work involved.

(1a) Mary: His book is too long.
(1b) The book that John wrote is too long for Mary to expect her students to read.

My second reason for focusing on utterance interpretation that is phenomenologically effortless is that it is a harder case for the view that I am arguing for. It would be no great surprise to find metacognition involved in reflective, voluntary, phenomenologically effortful utterance interpretation. It is much less obvious that it plays a central role in normal, smooth utterance interpretation. That is therefore the more interesting claim.

A distinction that is relevant here is between what Sperber and Mercier call *intuitive* and *reflective* inference.[5] The latter is processing whose purpose is to provide a person with (consciously available) reasons, in which, '[y]ou are paying conscious attention to the relationship between argument and claim, or premises and intended conclusions' (Sperber and Mercier, 2012, p. 375).

Utterance interpretation does not in general involve reflective inference, so understood. Hearers are arguably *able* to become aware of the way that their conclusions about speaker meaning are supported by what the speaker uttered, but such inferential links are not something that hearers typically attend to or become aware of.

One might wonder what is left of the notion of 'inference' once awareness and reflection have been stripped away. I suggest that utterance interpretation is inferential in approximately (and at least) the following sense:

> An inference, as the term is used in psychology, is a process that, given some input information, reliably yields as output further information that is likely to be true if the input information is.
>
> (Sperber and Mercier, 2012, p. 371)

In sum, utterance interpretation is one type of (mostly) involuntary 'change in view', a process that adds beliefs about utterance content by drawing warranted, but non-demonstrative, conclusions from the input.

2.1. Utterance Interpretation Seems Ill-structured

Utterance interpretation, like other inference to the best explanation, is *prima facie* an ill-structured problem. That is, very roughly, it is a problem for whose solution there is apparently no failsafe algorithm (Simon and Newell, 1958; Simon, 1973; Sperber and Wilson, 1986, p. 45; Simon,

130 *Nicholas Allott*

1997, p. 128; Allott, 2008). I would argue that it is ill-structured in at least two ways.

The first applies to abductive inference in general. It is unclear what information is relevant, so it is hard to see how an algorithm could decide with certainty what information to consult: in computational terms, the search-space is indefinitely large. This is what Jerry Fodor calls *isotropy*, and it is one reason that he has argued that there is no theory of central cognition (Fodor, 1983; see also Allott, 2019, on this argument applied to pragmatic theory). Just about anything could turn out to be relevant in inference to the best explanation. Drawings of rabbits on ancient pots may provide evidence about the astrophysics of supernovae, to take a well-known example (Robbins and Westmoreland, 1991; Antony, 2003).

Pragmatic inferences are responsive in principle to just about any information (Sperber and Wilson, 1996), as illustrated by examples like those in (2):

(2a) John was arrested by a policeman yesterday; he had just stolen a wallet. (Recanati, 1993, p. 265)
(2b) John was arrested by a policeman yesterday; he had needed one more arrest to qualify for an end-of-year bonus.
(2c) John was arrested by a policeman yesterday; he had just taken a bribe.

The examples in (2) illustrate the intricate dependence on world knowledge of the assignment of referents to indexicals. The hearer will probably take 'he' to be anaphoric on 'John' in (2a) and on 'a policeman' in (2b). The assignment of reference to 'he' in (2c) could go either way, depending on the hearer's estimate of the relative honesty of John and the local police force. Disambiguation, enrichment, implicatures etc. are similarly sensitive to non-linguistic information.

The other way in which utterance interpretation (like much other abductive inference[6]) seems ill-structured, but which is hardly discussed in the pragmatics literature, is that there is apparently no simple test to show that a putative solution is the right one (Allott, 2008, pp. 179–180). Suppose that at some stage in the process, the hearer's pragmatic faculty has somehow generated a candidate interpretation of an utterance. How can it tell that this is the right interpretation, or at least the best one that it can generate? Here, one should compare with a well-structured problem like solving an equation in two variables, where once you have a putative solution it is simple to check whether it really is one: simply plug the hypothesized values of x and y into the equation and if the two sides come out equal then you have found a solution.

Elsewhere I have suggested that there are several properties that we should expect to be possessed by utterance interpretation given that it is a process that deals rapidly with an ill-structured problem (Allott, 2008,

Metacognition and Communication   131

ch. 5). Here I focus on just one: subliminal monitoring and control, or 'procedural metacognition'.

2.2. Metacognition and Communication

I think that we can distinguish at least three levels at which there may be monitoring and control in communication. My concern in this chapter is with only one of them: monitoring and feedback internal to the hearer in normal, smooth utterance interpretation.

This needs to be distinguished from monitoring that disrupts smooth processing, taking the hearer into a qualitatively different, occurrently conscious, somewhat reflective process, which feels effortful. Robyn Carston (2010) has argued that there are two different 'routes or modes of processing' in metaphor understanding, one of which is 'rapid' and 'local', the second being 'more global [and] reflective' (Carston, 2010, p. 295). This is plausibly true of utterance interpretation more generally, and intuitively, the more conscious, reflective process comes into play in various situations that roughly divide into two types:

a)   Where there is more to unpack than one would normally get out of an utterance, e.g., in reading a rich text such as a Henry James novel, or when one notices a pun or a *double lecture*.
b)   Where what the speaker wanted to communicate is not well packaged from the hearer's point of view, as for example, when you notice that the speaker used a wrong word or infelicitous expression. Conscious effort may then be required to arrive at even one plausible interpretation.

My concern in this chapter is to show that there is metacognition even in cases where this sort of thing does not happen. My thesis amounts to the claim that the presence of monitoring and control does not entail that we are concerned with occurrently conscious metacognition.

It is also important to distinguish between the kind of metacognition that this chapter focusses on and monitoring of the hearer's comprehension performed by the speaker. Speaker monitoring of hearer comprehension is an aspect of what Proust refers to as 'conversational metacognition', which she defines as 'the set of abilities that allow [a. . .] speaker to make available to others and to receive from them specific markers concerning his/her 'conversing adequacy' (Proust, 2008, pp. 329–330).

Speakers gauge whether hearers are paying attention to them, particularly in the normal case of face-to-face conversation, by monitoring facial expression, gaze direction and various forms of feedback such as nodding, saying 'Mm hmm', 'I see' etc. This leads them to send signals about their level of commitment to what they are saying, their wanting to 'hold the floor' or to let the other person have a turn at speaking and so on (Clark

132   *Nicholas Allott*

and Wilkes-Gibbs, 1986; Clark, 1994; Fox Tree and Clark, 1997; Clark and Fox Tree, 2002; Clark and Krych, 2004; Allott, 2016, pp. 501–503).

Such monitoring and feedback is surely metacognitive. It also appears to be ubiquitous in face-to-face conversation. However, it cannot be essential to verbal communication, given that this can occur in situations where such feedback is not possible, as in answerphone messages as well as almost all written communication. Here I am concerned instead with metacognition that is internal to the addressee of an utterance, which I argue is central to utterance comprehension.

2.3. Metacognition and Awareness

It is necessary to illustrate in a little more detail what psychologists mean by 'metacognition'. In one common experimental paradigm for investigating metacognition, subjects are presented with a series of tasks under time pressure and can choose at each trial either to perform the task or to opt out of it. The task might be to assign a stimulus correctly to one of two previously learned categories, for instance, to say if a presented visual array is 'sparse' or 'dense'. The crucial finding is that people opt out preferentially from tasks they are less good at: in this case stimuli that are close to the boundary between the categorizations.

This metacognitive ability is often accompanied by so-called noetic feelings, which one might think of as feelings that could be informally glossed as *this task is easy/difficult*, or *I know/don't know the answer to this one*. (Note that I do not mean by these glosses to commit myself to the claim that noetic feelings have conceptual content). Now it is very often assumed in work on metacognition that these noetic feelings are causes of (or at least causally implicated in) the behavior that paradigmatic metacognition tasks investigate.[7] It is essential for my thesis, though, that internal feedback does not always or necessarily come with such feelings; there is some fully subliminal monitoring and control.

As noted earlier, there has been some discussion of this question in the metacognition literature. One obvious logical possibility is that in some or all cases where there are noetic feelings they are epiphenomenal: the feelings and the performance are both due to the metacognitive mechanisms, but the causal path to performance does not or need not go via the feelings. Asher Koriat argues that '[s]ubjective experience is based on an interpretation and attribution of one's own behavior, so that it *follows* rather than precedes controlled processes' (Koriat, 2007, p. 315).

Whatever the truth about cases where noetic feelings are present, I agree with Kentridge and Heywood when they write:

> There is nothing inherent in metacognitive regulation that demands consciousness. Metacognitive and executive processes serve to select and deploy methods for dealing with events and to assess the utility

of those methods. The presence of a self-referential loop, a system which assesses its own performance and adapts accordingly, might tempt us to infer that such processes necessarily elicit awareness. Feedback loops are ubiquitous in biology and, of themselves, do not seem to be grounds for invoking consciousness.

(Kentridge and Heywood, 2000, p. 308)

There is some empirical evidence that in utterance interpretation, monitoring and control is separate from reportable awareness of difficulty and anomaly, which I discuss in Section 3. First, though, I set out the case that theoretical considerations imply that utterance interpretation requires this sort of monitoring and control.

2.4. Theory-Driven Argument for Subliminal Metacognition

It seems a virtual conceptual necessity to see interpretation of verbal utterances as a suite of processes that construct an representation of utterance meaning on the basis of speech sounds. Like other pragmatic theorists, I assume that this processing can be factored into two parts:

I) A linguistic front-end which a) segments the stream of sound into phonemes and morphemes and b) assigns a syntactic structure to the utterance (parsing);
II) A conceptually distinct process or processes, 'pragmatic inference', which takes this linguistic material as input and arrives at utterance content.

Pragmatic inference is described here as (merely) 'conceptually' separate from linguistic parsing because it is widely assumed that in practice there are interactions between parsing and pragmatics, including 'top down' effects. One such is *suppression*, which I discuss in Section 3.1.

As discussed earlier, utterance interpretation is typically fast and automatic. Therefore, given very general assumptions about costs of computation, it seems reasonable to assume that there is limited information search (to use a term from the literature on simple heuristics: e.g., Todd and Gigerenzer, 2000, pp. 729–730): a great deal of information that might be relevant is not processed and not even recalled from memory.

A further reasonable assumption is that the system is not calculating for each item of information that could be processed whether it would be worth considering. That approach, called 'optimization under constraints', will often be more computationally expensive. In general, to calculate for each piece of information whether it is worth processing and to what depth is 'a more complex . . . procedure that includes the basic decision problem plus the problem how many costly resources to allocate to that original problem.' (Vriend, 1996, p. 278. See also Todd and Gigerenzer, 2000, pp. 729–730; Allott, 2008, pp. 170–172.)

Such considerations strongly suggest that there is a kind of metacognition that 'opts out' from lines of thought that are not progressing well, and opts in to just one or a few lines of thought that seem more promising. This would (on average) steer pragmatic processing towards recall and processing of information that would be cognitively worthwhile, and towards processing it in ways that would be profitable. Given the speed and seamless phenomenology of (much) utterance interpretation this metacognition must normally operate below the level of consciousness.

This kind of model is fundamental to relevance theoretic pragmatics, although as far as I am aware the term 'metacognition' has not been used in this literature until now. One of relevance theory's fundamental aims is 'to describe how the mind assesses its own achievements and efforts from the inside, and decides as a result to pursue its efforts or reallocate them in different directions' (Sperber and Wilson, 1986, p. 130; see also Sperber and Wilson, 1996; Sperber and Wilson, 2002; Allott, 2008). Something similar is implicit in the use of the term 'heuristic' in neo-Gricean pragmatics (Levinson, 2000, pp. 30ff.), although there has been less attention in that tradition to the details of cognitively realistic theories of utterance interpretation.

3. Types of Monitoring and Control in Utterance Interpretation

In this section I give empirical evidence that two types of monitoring and control, *suppression* and *guided resource allocation*, do indeed take place. One way that monitoring and control could feature in utterance interpretation is suppression of senses. That is, when an interpretation is beginning to be favored, rival candidates are actively demoted. I discuss evidence for this in Section 3.1.

A second way is preferential allocation of resources guided by monitoring of the success or failure of the ongoing interpretation process. An obvious possibility is that more effort and time is put into interpretation when no overall interpretation is successfully reached. There is considerable evidence for this, and some evidence for it happening subliminally, as I discuss in Section 3.2.

3.1. Metacognition and Suppression of Word Senses

There is evidence that suppression of unintended senses of words occurs in utterance interpretation. In this section I first explain the phenomenon and then present evidence that suggests that such sense suppression is an unconscious metacognitive process.[8]

It is known that word-senses and core meaning features of words are activated regardless of whether the sense/feature coheres with the context. This is known as 'priming' and is seen in experiments on the effect

Metacognition and Communication 135

of utterances of ambiguous words and metaphors. Classic examples are in (3) and (4):

(3) The man found several bugs in his room.
(4) My lawyer is a shark.

Hearing (3), both senses of the word – *covert listening device* and *small invertebrate* – are activated, as we know from experiments which test how fast participants are to respond with *word* or *non-word* to related words such as 'spy' and 'ant'. Crucially, both are primed even in contexts where only one sense of 'bug' is plausible (Meyer and Schvaneveldt, 1971; Schvaneveldt and Meyer, 1973). Similarly, the example in (4) is a metaphorical use of 'shark', but it is known that core features are activated, e.g., in this case <FISH>, even when they are incompatible with the metaphorical reading.

It is also known that activation of a word-sense or feature is typically followed by decay of that sense. This can be shown by probing at different times after the initial activation. The priming effects that indicate activation gradually decrease. But it has been shown that the drop-off in activation is faster than in normal decay for both the non-target sense in disambiguation cases and the feature that clashes with the correct interpretation in metaphor. This is standardly interpreted by researchers in this field as *suppression* of the unrelated feature or word sense (Neely, 1976; Tanenhaus, Leiman, and Seidenberg, 1979), as the following summary of the literature describes:

> The results of these experiments showed an early activation of target words related to both meanings of the homonym, which was interpreted in terms of an automatic, exhaustive process of spreading activation of associates. However, the activation of the contextually inappropriate meaning dropped as early as 200–300 ms from the offset of the ambiguous word. This pattern of results was interpreted as showing active suppression of the irrelevant reading of the ambiguity, given that passive decay should take considerably longer.
> (Rubio Fernández, 2007, pp. 353–354)

It is important to see that while we can probe this activation and suppression in cases of ambiguity and metaphor, it probably occurs in all utterance interpretation, and perhaps in thought more generally. Some evidence comes from work on schizophrenia. Schizophrenic patients 'often jump from one subject to another based on the sounds or associations of words they have uttered' (Covington et al., 2005, p. 87). This has been linked to excessive priming or impaired control of priming (Kuperberg, 2010, pp. 582–3). Such problems with priming may also be connected with the loss of control of the train of thought which is a

136 *Nicholas Allott*

primary symptom of schizophrenia: patients with thought-disorder have been found to have increased priming relative to non-schizophrenic controls (Pomarol-Clotet et al., 2008). To the extent that these problems are due to lack of control of activations of senses they support the claim that such control is a feature of normal language processing and perhaps of thought more generally.

Priming and suppression of senses are certainly not conscious processes, neither occurrently nor in the sense of being available. This is obvious introspectively: we only know that this sort of thing is going on because of the experimental evidence. Moreover both the activation and the suppression are too fast to be under conscious control:

> since controlled, attentional processes take 400–500 ms to operate . . . although the meaning selection process must be context-sensitive (unlike the early spreading activation phase), it operates in an almost automatic way. . . . This would explain why hearers are usually unaware of having encountered a homonym in a disambiguating context.
>
> (Rubio Fernández, 2007, p. 353)

Suppression of a sense seems metacognitive. Why think so? The argument is that we know that there is a natural outcome: decay. We assume that is what would happen in the absence of control. When we see suppression rather than decay, this is therefore a sign of control. What is more, the control seems to be directed by monitoring of the way that the process is going, since it is unintended senses that are being shut down.

A possible objection is that the experimental results could be accounted for by a suppression process that operates automatically once a sense is selected. But I think that this objection is misconceived because such a process would be metacognitive. It would involve monitoring and control, in this sense: there would have to be sensitivity to the success of the first-order process (monitoring) and then as a result, changes to the first-order process (control).

A second possible objection is more cogent. A critic could argue that what those in the field call 'suppression' is actually a bottom-up effect of context (perhaps acting via activation of concepts) interacting with the activation effects caused by the words in the target sentence. The idea is that the activations caused by words happen first, followed by an inhibition from context. On this view the accelerated decay of activation in cases of poor fit with context could be accounted for without any need to postulate monitoring and control.

This is very much like the view François Recanati has advocated as an explanation of pragmatic 'garden-path' effects. These (which are a theoretical possibility rather than a well-established phenomenon) are cases where the first interpretation constructed is not the one ultimately accepted (Recanati, 2004, pp. 32ff.). Suppose a speaker uses the word 'bank' in a context in which the financial-institution sense is highly accessible, but where only interpreting the word as *river bank* makes sense. It is plausible that an interpretation containing the financial sense is constructed and then rejected or superseded. If so, this is a pragmatic garden path. Dan Sperber argued that such cases would show that interpretation is not driven only by accessibility of senses: the most accessible interpretation can be rejected if it leads to an overall interpretation that is unsatisfactory. Recanati's reply is that such cases could be accounted for solely in terms of accessibility, if we assume (e.g.,) that lexical priming is faster than activation from the context: then an initial interpretation could be superseded by a competitor that simply takes longer to emerge, and there is no need to postulate any top-down evaluation of the interpretations.

This line of argument raises some difficult questions which I return to in Section 4. Here I offer two responses. First, such an opponent would be asking us to believe in miracles. That is, he would be asking us to accept that in successful communication all the activations (from the words in the utterance, plus features of the context) always happen to add up to making the speaker's intended meaning the most accessible one. One can see how this might sometimes work out, but why should we think it always does? It is worth noting that even Recanati makes that claim only about recovery of what is said, and not about other pragmatic processing such as arriving at implicatures. My second response is to agree with Kentridge and Heywood's point, quoted in Section 2.3. Given that feedback loops are ubiquitous in biology we should expect to find that mental processes exist to keep track of the success or otherwise of other mental processes and to shut down unnecessary activation (ultimately, that is, to save energy).

3.2. Metacognition and Resource Allocation

There are further empirical findings that lend support to the claim that there is subliminal feedback in utterance interpretation. They come from a series of experiments that aimed to probe two abilities in development and their relation to each other: sensitivity to textual anomaly indexed by reading time and conscious awareness of comprehension difficulties (Harris et al., 1981). There were two groups of participants, aged eight and eleven years old respectively.

In the experiment the participant reveals a short story line by line as she reads it silently to herself. There are two conditions, which only differ in which of two titles is presented as the first line. In each condition, one line of the text is anomalous, but there is nothing intrinsically odd about that line. The anomaly is purely a result of encountering that line in the context of the title, as the following example materials demonstrate. The

138 *Nicholas Allott*

anomalous line in the first scenario is labelled (i) while the one labelled (ii) fits the context, and vice versa in the second scenario. This design allows the two conditions to be compared in order to control for all effects on reading time other than the anomaly.

Title 1: Together on the boat

Title 2: The toy boat

Charles has a sailing boat.
He shows it to his friend.
'Do you like it?' asks Charles.
'Please don't drop it'. (i)
The two boys climb aboard. (ii)
The little boat is now rolling on the water.
The wind is blowing in the sails.
Then the boat is off the shore.
(Harris et al., 1981, p. 216)

There are two crucial findings. First, both eight-year-olds and eleven-year-olds read the anomalous line more slowly than the appropriate line in all stories, with no statistically significant difference between the two groups in this respect. This indicates that, as expected, both groups were affected by textual anomaly, and in fact were affected to an indistinguishable degree. Secondly, eight-year-olds were significantly less good at picking out the problem line when asked to identify it after reading the whole text, and when successful were also slower to identify it. The authors say that this 'suggest[s] that they had not 'registered' it during their initial reading of the story.' (Harris et al., 1981, p. 219), and that if they found it at all, they typically did so by re-reading the text (which they had in front of them at this stage).

The obvious objection that the eight-year-olds' difficulty might be due to memory limitations was made less plausible by a second run in which participants were also tested for recall of the lines, including the problematic line. No significant difference was found between the age groups. Therefore the authors conclude that the eight-year-olds' poorer ability to pick out the problem line was not well explained in terms of their having lost track of which line was problematic after having noticed the anomaly during their initial reading of the story.

This experiment indicates that the time (and presumably effort) put into utterance interpretation was modulated in response to the anomaly in both age groups, and that the ability to modulate processing in this way does not depend on conscious awareness of the anomaly. However, a possible objection is that the increased reading time does not show

Metacognition and Communication 139

that there is any second-order monitoring and control of the first-order comprehension process. Rather, it may be that reading takes longer in the anomalous cases because they are harder to understand.

Here is my response to this objection. Consider why it takes longer to read the anomalous line. The explanation, I suggest, is that the anomaly is detected at some level, and more resources (including, at least, longer time) are devoted to processing. Recall that the anomalous line is not anomalous in itself, but only against a particular context. If the anomaly were not detected at any level, why should the participant read more slowly? Participants could just read through the sentences at normal speed, understanding each sentence, but not integrating the meanings of the sentences at any higher level. Note that this is not a purely theoretical possibility: there is some evidence that younger (six-year-old) participants do just this (Markman, 1977). They may understand the individual words and sentences but apparently do not try to build a consistent mental model for the text as a whole.

Harris et al. conclude that

> for the age period under consideration [between 8 and 11 years old], there is evidence that the improvement in comprehension monitoring can be attributed to changes in the capacity to notice or interpret internally generated signals, rather than to any differential frequency in the generation of those signals.
>
> (Harris et al., 1981, p. 219)

That is, for both the eight-year-olds and the eleven-year-olds there was internal monitoring for anomaly in the process of 'constructive interpretation', and this monitoring resulted in changes to the first-order process (i.e. control). However, only in the eleven-year-olds did it reliably give rise to something that was available to conscious recall and report. This is evidence for subliminal metacognition in utterance interpretation in eight-year-olds.

What, if anything, can we conclude about the eleven-year-olds and about mature utterance interpretation? Earlier in this chapter I suggested that performance and noetic feelings may have a common causal basis without noetic feelings being causally responsible for spontaneous performance. Given that eight-year-olds and eleven-year-olds slow down to the same degree when they encounter anomaly, these experiments suggest that the noetic feelings that the eleven-year-olds have some access to are not what drives their spontaneous reading performance. In other words, subliminal monitoring and control takes place during utterance interpretation for everyone above a certain age, modulating reading speed. Some ability to consciously 'dip into' the internal signal stream develops with age.

140 Nicholas Allott

4. Metacognition and Inference

I have already mentioned that there has been a theoretical challenge to the view that there is assessment and consequent reallocation of effort in utterance interpretation, at least for non-implicated utterance content. François Recanati has claimed that recovery of what is said, including disambiguation, reference assignment to indexicals and pragmatic enrichment, is a brute-causal, non-inferential process (Recanati, 2004, ch. 2). My interest in that view here is that the non-inferential picture that Recanati suggests for part of utterance interpretation is also a non-metacognitive one (although Recanati does not use this term).

There is general agreement that senses of words and potential referents of indexicals have accessibilities: that is, they are easier or harder to bring to mind. As noted earlier, accessibility is known to be affected by recent use of a word-sense ('priming'). It also correlates with how frequent the word-sense is in usage. Now, as briefly sketched in Section 3.1, Recanati has proposed that accessibilities in context determine the explicit utterance content reached (in normal, smooth communication).

Consider again the examples in (2). There is general agreement that there are certain 'frames' that are associated with lexical items and made accessible by tokenings of them, for instance, that 'arrest' comes with a frame that has 'slots' for an arrester, an arrestee, a crime and so forth. Here is how Recanati explains the selection of John as referent for 'he' in (2a):

> John is the subject of 'was arrested' and therefore occupies the role of the person being arrested; now that role is linked to the role of the person doing the stealing, in some relevant frame. Because of this link, the representation of the referent of 'he' as the person doing the stealing contributes some activation to the representation of the person being arrested and therefore raises the accessibility of John *qua* occupier of this role. John thus becomes the most accessible candidate.'
>
> (Recanati, 2004, p. 31)

Recanati's claim is that such combinations of frames and accessibility factors do the job, except of course in cases where the hearer fails to recover the intended interpretation. (Equally, we should exclude cases where there is conscious reasoning about what is said).

As noted, Recanati's concern was to develop a non-inferential account of the recovery of explicit utterance content/what is said (in contrast to recovery of implicatures that he views as inferential). In my view it is also, and connectedly, a metacognition-free account of interpretation of what is said. In other words, as I understand it, Recanati is ruling out monitoring and control. This is because his account is purely bottom-up,

Metacognition and Communication   141

and bottom-up accounts are in a certain sense 'blind': the output of such a process is determined by the inputs (albeit perhaps in complex ways). This is in contrast to a process governed by metacognitive feedback, where the output of the first-order process is monitored and the first-order process may be affected in a top-down way by the monitoring process.

Recanati sketches a way of simulating effects which seem top-down, such as an influence from the general context on the sense of a word that is chosen as the intended sense. What is crucial is that in his view these arise only through activations caused by features of the input: the priming of word senses, mental frames and so on. His account rules out any kind of genuinely top-down evaluation process that gauges how well things are going and 'decides as a result to pursue its efforts or reallocate them in different directions' to quote Sperber and Wilson again.

This is brought out in Recanati's reply to a criticism from Dan Sperber. Here's the criticism:

> Sometimes the first interpretation that comes to mind (the most accessible one) turns out not to be satisfactory and forces the hearer to backtrack. According to Sperber, the possibility of such garden-path effects shows that success, for a candidate semantic value, cannot be equated with sheer accessibility.
>
> (Recanati, 2004, p. 32)

As discussed earlier, Recanati's response is that such garden-path effects can be understood as due to accessibility shifts during processing: e.g., lexical priming from other words in the immediate linguistic context might rapidly make one sense of an ambiguous word highly activated, but then other activation from the broader context might kick in, so that a different sense ends up most highly activated. Presumably the sense that is most highly activated at some cut-off time after the utterance is the sense that 'wins', that is, the one that features in the hearer's representation of what is said.

I have discussed the exchange here because it illustrates that Recanati, unlike Sperber and Wilson, takes monitoring and control to be outside of his framework. What is more, there seems to be a more general claim implicit in the argument, namely that purely bottom-up processing cannot amount to abductive inference. I am also inclined to endorse this claim, although I draw the opposite conclusion from it about the character of the processes involved in utterance interpretation.

4.1. Inference, Metacognition, and Marr's Levels

The claim that purely bottom-up processing cannot amount to abductive inference raises the general question of how, and indeed whether, facts about

142   Nicholas Allott

whether a process involves monitoring and control or 'metacognition' relate to whether that process interpretation is inferential. Here I think that it is helpful to consider the well-known distinction between different levels of description for cognitive processes, as suggested by David Marr (1982).

Marr proposed three levels of description: the functional or computational, the algorithmic, and the hardware level. A functional account is concerned with questions such as 'What is the goal of the computation, why is it appropriate, and what is the logic of the strategy by which it can be carried out?'(Marr, 1982, p. 25). The algorithmic (or 'representational') level is concerned with questions about how the computational account can be implemented. In particular, what is the representation for the input and output, and what is the algorithm for the transformation between them? Finally, at the hardware level, which I won't be considering here, one can ask how the representation and algorithm are realized physically.

For example, at the functional level a cash register (Marr, 1982, p. 22ff.) is (among other things) an adding machine. At the algorithmic level we want to know what format its input has to be in and what is the format of the output it produces and how the computation is performed: in decimal or in binary, for example. If it can do multiplication, we want to know whether it uses look-up tables of some sort, or performs repeated addition, or something else.

Now consider the pragmatic faculty i.e. whatever suite of abilities is responsible for spontaneous interpretation of utterances. The question about whether it performs inference is at the functional level. As noted earlier, the consensus view is that the task that it performs is inferring the best explanation for an utterance in terms of the speaker's communicative intentions.

Recanati's claims about spreading activation delivering a representation of what is said are at the algorithmic level. He does not postulate a specific algorithm, but rather a characterization of the kind of processes involved: use of the word 'police' activates a certain set of assumptions to various degrees, use of the word 'arrest' activates a certain frame which has the roles <*arrester, arrestee, crime*>, and similarly for other words.

How, then, is this relevant to the computational-level description as inference to the best explanation? In particular, one wants to know what it is about Recanati's spreading activation model that rules out that the correct computational level description is inferential. Why shouldn't we instead see Recanati's description as a hypothesis about how inference is performed?

That is a difficult question, and I do not pretend to have a fully satisfactory answer. Here are sketches of two possible ones. The first is that what is going on in a purely accessibility-driven system is all non-propositional or sub-propositional, so it could not connect input and output together in warrant-preserving ways. One can compare here i) spreading activation which raises the accessibility of certain nodes in a network with

ii) warrant- or truth-preserving transitions between mental representations with propositional content (e.g., in a Language of Thought).

I think that there is another reason why a Recanati-type model cannot be an implementation of inference, or at least not of abductive inference. Purely bottom-up processes without monitoring and control have no way of evaluating how well the output coheres with the input.

There is no known failsafe algorithm that, given any observation or fact, computes the best explanation for it. For this reason, in previous work I have argued that inference to the best explanation must in general be implemented as trial and error search (with various other properties): there is no alternative but to generate a trial solution and then evaluate it somehow. But in this chapter I have instead suggested that what is important is a process that has monitoring and control which checks on progress and steers processing towards better solutions. (I now think that trial and error search is a sub-category of such processes). My point here is that without some kind of steering it would be a miracle if the output happened to be the best explanation for, and warranted by, the input. Miracles may happen occasionally, but if an account relies on their occurring routinely it is defective.

5. Concluding Remarks

In utterance interpretation, any information may be relevant, but very little information can actually be processed. Therefore, I have argued on theory-driven grounds that an account of the psychology of utterance interpretation needs to explain how processing is steered towards promising lines of inquiry and away from others. There must be metacognition: monitoring and control of the first-order processes involved. Given that utterance interpretation is normally phenomenologically 'seamless' and 'effortless', it follows that there must be subliminal metacognition, which I have compared with Proust's 'procedural metacognition' and Shea et al.'s 'system 1 metacognition'.

I have discussed two distinct experimental bodies of literature that back up this theoretical claim. The first is a considerable body of work that shows that activated word senses are suppressed when they are not needed as part of the final interpretation. The second is a study that found that time taken to read is modulated in response to contextual anomaly even in younger participants who lack consciousness of the anomaly in question.

Finally, I have tried to sketch out an explanation of how my claim that utterance interpretation involves metacognition is related to the view that utterance interpretation is inferential, appealing here to Marr's levels of description. The claim about metacognition is at the algorithmic level, while the view that a process is inferential is a functional-level claim, but facts at one level may have consequences on the other.

144   *Nicholas Allott*

Utterance interpretation is not the only abductive inference task that we typically perform rapidly and without apparent effort. If it is right (following Proust and Shea et al.) that metacognitive processes can be unconscious and perhaps also non-metarepresentational, and the model I suggest of utterance interpretation is on the right lines, then a broader upshot suggests itself, namely that we can better understand how abductive inferences in general (not just ones implicated in utterance interpretation) can combine informational unencapsulation with speed, automaticity, and little awareness of execution.[9]

Notes

1. I don't claim to have a watertight definition of 'feedback'. The *Oxford Shorter Dictionary* offers the following reasonable characterisation: 'the modification or control of a process or system by its results or effects'. I would only add that in this paper I am concerned with effects on a mental system that come from other mental systems that are sensitive to what the first system is doing.
2. As noted by Glenn Carruthers (2013).
3. Thus, for example: 'The coded signal, even if it is unambiguous, is only a piece of evidence about the communicator's intentions, and has to be used inferentially and in a context' (Sperber and Wilson, 1986, p. 170); and 'even if what a speaker means consists precisely in the semantic content of the sentence he utters, this still has to be inferred.' (Bach, 2006, p. 24).
4. It is also worth noting that utterance interpretation is apparently a process that only *adds* beliefs, not one that may add some and subtract others. The hearer starts with a belief that the speaker has uttered certain linguistic material, in a certain way, in a certain context, and, if all goes well, ends up with beliefs about what the speaker intended to convey by her utterance, e.g., what she stated and what she implicated. Of course, what the speaker conveys may contradict a previous belief of the hearer's, and the hearer may end up dropping that belief as a result of the utterance. (The speaker might state or implicate that the cat is on the mat and the hearer may thereby learn that the cat is on the mat and not, as he supposed, elsewhere.) But this is arguably 'downstream' of the utterance interpretation process proper.
5. N.B. it is not entirely clear whether in Sperber and Mercier's terminology, 'intuitive inference' is simply a positive name for non-reflective inference, given that they also say that intuitive inferences are carried out by domain-specific mechanisms, but do not make it clear whether this is part of their definition or an empirical claim.
6. As Anders Nes points out (pc), one reason for this is that there will often be clashes between explanatory virtues such as simplicity, degree of fit with observation, and conservativeness and it often will not be clear how to weigh them against each other.
7. Asher Koriat writes: 'Students of metacognition not only place a heavy emphasis on subjective experience but also assume that subjective feelings, such as the feeling of knowing, are not mere epiphenomena, but actually exert a causal role on information processing and behavior' (2007, p. 293; see also pp. 315–316).
8. The claim that sense suppression is unconsciously metacognitive has previously been made in the context of schizophrenia (Carruthers, 2013), in a

suggestion that brings together the idea that deficits in metacognition abilities are a central factor in schizophrenia (Bob et al., 2016) with the finding that 'studies of word recall in schizophrenia generally point toward impaired control of spreading activation' (Covington et al., 2005). See also what follows in the main text.

9. Thanks are due to Anders Nes for pressing me to be explicit about how there is an upshot for our understanding of other abductive inference processes.

References

Allott, N. (2008). *Pragmatics and Rationality*. PhD thesis, University of London.

Allott, N. (2016). Misunderstandings in Verbal Communication. In A. Rocci & L. de Saussure (Eds.), *Verbal Communication* (pp. 485–507). Berlin: Walter De Gruyter.

Allott, N. (2019). Scientific Tractability and Relevance Theory. In K. Scott, R. Carston, & B. Clark (Eds.), *Relevance: Pragmatics and Interpretation* (pp. 29–41). Cambridge: Cambridge University Press.

Antony, L. (2003). Rabbit-Pots and Supernovas: On the Relevance of Psychological Data to Linguistic Theory. In A. Barber (Ed.), *Epistemology of Language* (pp. 47–68). Oxford: Oxford University Press.

Bach, K. (2006). The top 10 Misconceptions About Implicature. In B. J. Birner & G. L. Ward (Eds.), *Drawing the Boundaries of Meaning: Neo-Gricean Studies in Pragmatics and Semantics in Honor of Laurence R. Horn* (pp. 21–30). Amsterdam: John Benjamins.

Bob, P., Pec, O., Mishara, A. L., Touskova, T., & Lysaker, P. H. (2016). Conscious Brain, Metacognition and Schizophrenia. *International Journal of Psychophysiology*, 105, 1–8.

Boghossian, P. (2014). What Is Inference? *Philosophical Studies*, 169, 1–18.

Carruthers, G. (2013). Review of *Foundations of Metacognition, 2012*. In Michael J. Beran, Johannes Brandl, Josef Perner, & Joëlle Proust (Eds.), *Notre Dame Philosophical Reviews*, 2013, January 22.

Carston, R. (2010). XIII-Metaphor: Ad Hoc Concepts, Literal Meaning and Mental Images. *Proceedings of the Aristotelian Society (Hardback)*, 110(3pt), 295–321.

Clark, H. H. (1994). Managing Problems in Speaking. *Speech Communication*, 15(3–4), 243–250.

Clark, H. H., & Fox Tree, J. E. (2002). Using *uh* and *um* in Spontaneous Speaking. *Cognition*, 84(1), 73–111.

Clark, H. H., & Krych, M. A. (2004). Speaking While Monitoring Addressees for Understanding. *Journal of Memory and Language*, 50(1), 62–81.

Clark, H. H., & Wilkes-Gibbs, D. (1986). Referring as a Collaborative Process. *Cognition*, 22(1), 1–39.

Covington, M. A., He, C., Brown, C., Naçi, L., McClain, J. T., Fjordbak, B. S. et al. (2005). Schizophrenia and the Structure of Language: The Linguist's View. *Schizophrenia Research*, 77(1), 85–98.

Evans, J. S. B. T. (2003). In Two Minds: Dual-Process Accounts of Reasoning. *Trends in Cognitive Science*, 7(10), 454–459.

Evans, J. S. B. T., & Frankish, K. (Eds.). (2009). *In Two Minds: Dual Processes and Beyond*. Oxford: Oxford University Press.

146   *Nicholas Allott*

Fodor, J. A. (1983). *The Modularity of Mind: An Essay on Faculty Psychology*. Cambridge, MA: MIT Press.

Fox Tree, J. E., & Clark, H. H. (1997). Pronouncing 'the' as 'thee' to Signal Problems in Speaking. *Cognition*, 62(2), 151–167.

Grice, P. (1957). Meaning. *The Philosophical Review*, 66, 377–388.

Grice, P. (1975). Logic and Conversation. In P. Cole & J. Morgan (Eds.), *Syntax & Semantics 3: Speech Acts* (pp. 41–58). New York: Academic Press.

Grice, P. (1978). Further Notes on Logic and Conversation. In P. Cole (Ed.), *Pragmatics* (pp. 113–127). New York: Academic Press.

Grice, P. (1989). *Studies in the Way of Words*. Cambridge, MA: Harvard University Press.

Harris, P. L., Kruithof, A., Terwogt, M. M., & Visser, T. (1981). Children's Detection and Awareness of Textual Anomaly. *Journal of Experimental Child Psychology*, 31(2), 212–230.

Kentridge, R. W., & Heywood, C. A. (2000). Metacognition and Awareness. *Consciousness and Cognition*, 9, 308–312.

Koriat, A. (2007). Metacognition and Consciousness. In P. D. Zelazo, M. Moscovitch, & E. Thompson (Eds.), *The Cambridge Handbook of Consciousness* (pp. 289–326). Cambridge: Cambridge University Press.

Kuperberg, G. R. (2010). Language in Schizophrenia Part 1: An Introduction. *Language and Linguistics Compass*, I(8), 576–589.

Levinson, S. C. (2000). *Presumptive Meanings: The Theory of Generalized Conversational Implicature*. Cambridge, MA: MIT Press.

Markman, E. M. (1977). Realizing That You Don't Understand: A Preliminary Investigation. *Child Development*, 48(3), 986–992.

Marr, D. (1982). *Vision: A Computational Investigation Into the Human Representation and Processing of Visual Information*. San Francisco: Freeman.

Meyer, D. E., & Schvaneveldt, R. W. (1971). Facilitation in Recognizing Pairs of Words: Evidence of a Dependence Between Retrieval Operations. *Journal of Experimental Psychology*, 90(2), 227–234.

Neely, J. H. (1976). Semantic Priming and Retrieval from Lexical Memory: Evidence for Facilitatory and Inhibitory Processes. *Memory & Cognition*, 4(5), 648–654.

Paynter, C. A., Reder, L. M., & Kieffaber, P. D. (2009). Knowing We Know Before We Know: ERP Correlates of Initial Feeling-of-Knowing. *Neuropsychologia*, 47(3), 796–803.

Pomarol-Clotet, E., Oh, T. M., Laws, K. R., & McKenna, P. J. (2008). Semantic Priming in Schizophrenia: Systematic Review and Meta-Analysis. *British Journal of Psychiatry*, 192(2), 92–97.

Proust, J. (2008). Conversational Metacognition. In I. Wachsmuth, M. Lenzen, & G. Knoblich (Eds.), *Embodied Communication in Humans and Machines* (pp. 329–356). Oxford: Oxford University Press.

Proust, J. (2013). *The Philosophy of Metacognition*. Oxford: Blackwell.

Recanati, F. (1993). *Direct Reference : From Language to Thought*. Oxford: Blackwell.

Recanati, F. (2004). *Literal Meaning*. Cambridge: Cambridge University Press.

Robbins, R. R., & Westmoreland, R. B. (1991). Astronomical Imagery and Numbers in Mimbres Pottery. *Astronomy Quarterly*, 8(2), 65–88.

Rubio Fernández, P. (2007). Suppression in Metaphor Interpretation. *Journal of Semantics*, 24(4), 345–371.

Schvaneveldt, R. W., & Meyer, D. E. (1973). Retrieval and Comparison Processes in Semantic Memory. In S. Kornblum (Ed.), *Attention and Performance IV* (pp. 395–409). New York: Academic Press.

Shea, N., Boldt, A., Bang, D., Yeung, N., Heyes, C., & Frith, C. D. (2014). Supra-Personal Cognitive Control and Metacognition. *Trends in Cognitive Sciences*, 18(4), 186–193.

Simon, H. A. (1973). The Structure of Ill Structured Problems. *Artificial Intelligence*, 4(3–4), 181–201.

Simon, H. A. (1997). *Administrative Behavior: A Study of Decision-Making Processes in Administrative Organizations*. 4th Ed. New York: Free Press.

Simon, H. A., & Newell, A. (1958). Heuristic Problem Solving. *Operations Research*, 6(1), 1–10.

Sloman, S. A. (1996). The Empirical Case for Two Systems of Reasoning. *Psychological Bulletin*, 119(1), 3–22.

Spehn, M. K., & Reder, L. M. (2000). The Unconscious Feeling of Knowing: a Commentary on Koriat's Paper. *Consciousness & Cognition*, 9, 187–192.

Sperber, D., & Mercier, H. (2012). Reasoning as a Social Competence. In H. Landemore & J. Elster (Eds.), *Collective Wisdom: Principles and Mechanisms* (pp. 368–392). Cambridge: Cambridge University Press.

Sperber, D., & Wilson, D. (1986). *Relevance: Communication and Cognition*. 2nd Ed. 1995. Oxford: Blackwell.

Sperber, D., & Wilson, D. (1996). Fodor's Frame Problem and Relevance Theory (reply to Chiappe & Kukla). *Behavioral and Brain Sciences*, 19(3), 530–532.

Sperber, D., & Wilson, D. (2002). Pragmatics, Modularity and Mind-Reading. *Mind & Language*, 17(1&2), 3–23.

Stanovich, K. E., & West, R. F. (1998). Individual Differences in Framing and Conjunction Effects. *Thinking & Reasoning*, 4(4), 289–317.

Tanenhaus, M. K., Leiman, J. M., & Seidenberg, M. S. (1979). Evidence for Multiple Stages in the Processing of Ambiguous Words in Syntactic Contexts. *Journal of Verbal Learning and Verbal Behavior*, 18(4), 427–440.

Todd, P. M., & Gigerenzer, G. (2000). Précis of 'Simple Heuristics That Make Us Smart'. *Behavioral & Brain Sciences*, 23(5), 727–741; discussion 742.

Vriend, N. J. (1996). Rational Behavior and Economic Theory. *Journal of Economic Behavior and Organization*, 29(2), 263–285.

Wilson, D., & Sperber, D. (2012). *Meaning and Relevance*. Cambridge: Cambridge University Press.

Part III

Inference, Structure, and Generality

6 Non-Inferential Transitions
Imagery and Association

Jake Quilty-Dunn and Eric Mandelbaum

1. Kinds of Thinking

Thinking is not one kind of thing. The various forms of thinking studied in psychology include navigating with mental maps (Tolman, 1948; Camp, 2007; Rescorla, 2009), scanning and rotating iconic mental images (Shepard and Metzler, 1971; Kosslyn, Ball, and Reiser, 1978), sampling from a probability distribution (any Bayesian), detecting probable kin (Lieberman, Tooby, and Cosmides, 2007), making moral judgments (Mikhail, 2011), and doing simple arithmetic (Dehaene, 2011). Getting from thought A to thought B sometimes takes the form of a deductive, logical argument (Braine and O'Brien, 1998), but sometimes does not. One can think without utilizing full thoughts, for example. A thought like DONALD TRUMP IS THE PRESIDENT may lead you to think SOMEONE IS THE PRESIDENT; but, depending on your temperament, it might lead you simply to contemplate the abyss, which may just amount to thinking about the abyss as such and nothing more (that is, merely tokening the concept THE ABYSS).

A completed theory of thinking should exhibit full generality, capturing thought in all its various forms. One part of this theory concerns logical inferential transitions like the move from IT IS RAINING and IF IT IS RAINING THEN THE GAME IS CANCELLED to THE GAME IS CANCELLED. With respect to inference proper, we think there is something special about constituent structure. Inferential transitions occur between thoughts based on rules that are built into the architecture of the mind and specify types of constituent structure (such as *If [P] and [IF P THEN Q] then [Q]*). We've argued elsewhere for this view of inference (Quilty-Dunn and Mandelbaum, 2018). Inference isn't everything, however, and may indeed account for a small part of our mental lives. In this article we intend to account for types of transitions that look to be inference-like but, according to our account, aren't genuine inferences. We'll also consider the structure of association in more detail, which sheds light not only on associative transitions but also on their rule-governed foils, both inferential and non-inferential. Providing an adequate, coherent theory of thinking requires

152   *Jake Quilty-Dunn and Eric Mandelbaum*

that we give an account of all these transitions. We aim to undertake this project, thereby providing a short (and surely incomplete) taxonomy of types of mental transitions here.

2. Content-Specificity and Inference

Let's start with a quick overview of our theory. The fundamental case of inference, what we termed BITs (for Bare Inferential Transitions) was characterized as follows:

> The transition from state A to state B is inferential if (i) A and B are discursive, (ii) some rule is built into the architecture such that A satisfies its antecedent in virtue of A's constituent structure and B satisfies its consequent in virtue of B's constituent structure (*modulo* logical constants), and (iii) there is no intervening factor responsible for the transition from A to B.
> (Quilty-Dunn and Mandelbaum, 2018, p. 539)[1]

Discursivity is central to this definition. This was, in part, to separate out two very different kinds of mental transition: associations and inferences. We'll say more about the difference between association and inference later in the chapter. But one might wonder, aren't there mental representations that are not discursive? For instance, perhaps representations in perception (Carey, 2009; Burge, 2010; Block, 2014; Fodor, 2008) or mental imagery (Kosslyn, 1994) are iconic. Is it merely definitional that movements among them couldn't be inferential? We'll now look at how these kinds of transitions relate to inference.

Sentences and pictures have different sorts of structures. A sentence like 'This is a blue square' involves discrete constituents that pick out an individual object ('This'), a color ('blue') and a shape ('square'). A picture of a blue square doesn't have this sort of structure – parts of the picture correspond to parts of the square (i.e., icons are *structure-preserving*), and the same part of the representation that picks out the object simultaneously represents its color and shape (i.e., icons are *holistic*). Icons thus lack the constituent structure distinctive of discursive representations, which tend to be neither structure-preserving nor holistic (Kosslyn, 1980; Fodor, 2007). We'll assume for the sake of argument that there are mental representations that are iconic in this sense, and that they're used online in perception as well as offline in mental imagery (Quilty-Dunn, forthcoming).

Icons figure in computations. They can be mentally rotated, such that the time needed to identify a match between two objects at different orientations increases as a function of increases in the difference in orientation (Shepard and Metzler, 1971). Icons can serve as inputs to categorization,[2] particularly via attentional selection of a subset of their contents (Sperling, 1960; Lamme, 2003). They can be scanned, such that sequentially retrieving information from spatially disparate parts of icons takes more time (due to more intermediating steps) as a function of the represented distance (Kosslyn, Ball, and Reiser, 1978). They also doubtless serve diverse functions only dimly glimpsed by cognitive science at present, such as their role in structuring long-term memory (Paivio, 1969).

Our present question is this: Do any of the computations that range over mental icons constitute inferences? And if not, what are they like? Certainly in the Helmholtzian sense in which low-level perceptual computations constitute inferences, icons can be inputs to, outputs of, and brought to bear on inferences in perception. But if inference proper is limited to BITs, then icons may not be able to function in inferences. There is a very loose sense of 'inference' that ranges over any transition between states that solves an underdetermination problem (i.e., where the content of the output goes beyond the content of the input in some way). It is doubtful that much of interest can be said about the broad category that will also shed light on the particular type of transition involved in moving from the beliefs that p and if p then q to the belief that q. We don't deny that inference can occur unconsciously (on the contrary, it usually does) or that inferential transitions can range over 'subpersonal' representations. We also don't deny that genuinely inferential transitions may occur in perceptual systems; we simply regard this as an empirical question, whereas the broad Helmholtzian notion of inference would make it trivially true that they do. Our approach is to take it that inference is a natural psychological kind of mental transition with paradigm cases (e.g., modus ponens) and explore whether instances of that kind occur in non-paradigm cases. One relevant difference between transitions in early vision and modus ponens inferences over beliefs is a difference in representational format. We turn now to transitions between icons that appear at first glance to be inference-like.

While some transitions involving icons don't seem at all like inferences – mental rotation, for example, might be useful in reasoning but seems qualitatively different than, say, *modus ponens* – others might. For example, some perceptual process might transition from an icon that encodes the color of an object and an icon that encodes the shape of an object to an icon that encodes the color and shape of the object. This kind of transition might be an instance of what Anne Treisman calls 'feature integration' (Treisman and Gelade, 1980 – though see Clark, 2004 for a non-iconic model). It also resembles conjunction introduction, that is, the transition from P and Q to P AND Q.[3] For present purposes, we're agnostic about whether this kind of process occurs (see Green and Quilty-Dunn, forthcoming for reasons to doubt the hypothesis that object-based feature integration is iconic). Supposing it does, however, should it count as an inference?

There is a quick argument that, presupposing the BIT view of inference, establishes a firm negative answer. BITs require rules to be built into the architecture that specify types of constituent structure. Icons lack constituent structure; therefore they fall outside of the scope of rules that specify types of constituent structure; therefore they cannot figure in BITs. Presupposing that something is an inference if it is a BIT, icons therefore cannot figure in inferences.

Though this argument is, by our lights, sound, it fails to engage with the intuition that iconic transformations can implement paradigmatically inferential rules like conjunction introduction. If transitions between icons can in fact implement conjunction introduction, then any view that entails that iconic transformations are invariably non-inferential would seem at best to lack full generality and at worst to be arbitrary and false. We'll now consider some more principled reasons (i.e., ones that don't presuppose that something is an inference if it's a BIT) to think that icons cannot implement conjunction introduction.

We understand the term 'inference' to refer to a subset of the truth-preserving computations in the mind; that wider class excludes some processes, like associative transitions, but includes virtually all properly rule-governed ones. What marks out inference as we understand it from other sorts of rule-governed, truth-preserving computations is that inferences obey some *logic*. That is, the rules that govern them are logical rules, and they preserve truth in virtue of their form. That's not to say that the rules of human inference are identical to any logic taught in philosophy courses. We suppose mental logic is idiosyncratic to humans (and possibly phylogenetically related ancestor species), partly for empirical reasons (Braine and O'Brien, 1998) and partly for *a priori* ones (Kripke, 1982).[4] What makes a rule logical is its formal character, i.e., that it abstracts away from all content except for the contents of logical operators like conjunction, disjunction, negation, and conditionals.

Their formal character allows logical rules to be relatively sparse in number and general in application. You don't need one inference rule to conclude from THE WEATHER IS BAD and IF THE WEATHER IS BAD THEN THE GAME IS CANCELLED that THE GAME IS CANCELLED and another to conclude from THE APPLE IS WAX and IF THE APPLE IS WAX THEN THE APPLE IS INEDIBLE that THE APPLE IS INEDIBLE. *Modus ponens* (as well as its psychofunctional equivalents – see note 4) is sufficient to generate the conclusion in both cases. The fact that rules of mental logic apply also to syntactically well-formed thoughts that are semantically inane such as 'If there's a 3 then there's an 8' (Reverberi et al., 2012) and valid inferences that have unbelievable conclusions like 'The feather is heavy' (Handley, Newstead, and Trippas, 2011) provides reason to think that those rules are formal and therefore sparse and general.

What allows logical rules to be formal is that they specify types of structures that can be satisfied by representations. Suppose *If [F(x)] and*

[IF F(X) THEN G(X)] then [G(X)] is an inferential rule. Since THE WEATHER IS BAD and THE APPLE IS WAX both instantiate the structure F(X), they can both function as premises in an inference governed by that rule. Satisfying the structural specifications of a rule is independent of the particular semantic values of (non-logical) constituents of the representation, so rules that only specify structural properties of representations are *ipso facto* formal rules.

Now we can go back to the case of an iconic transition that resembles conjunction introduction. We should note that since icons don't have constituent structures, they don't have constituents that function as logical operators (e.g., that express conjunction). But instead of harping on that point, we want to argue for the more interesting thesis that icons can't be governed by formal rules even independently of their inability to incorporate explicit logical operators.

The fact that icons lack constituent structures precludes them from satisfying structural specifications of logical rules. An iconic representation of a red square doesn't have separate constituents corresponding to redness and squareness, which means it doesn't share a constituent with an iconic representation of a red triangle. In that case, a red icon and a square icon cannot be combined into a complex red square icon; rather some rule has to map from the color and shape properties encoded in separate icons to a holistic icon that encodes both color and shape. A rule that says *If [F(x)] and [G(x)] then [F(x) & G(x)]* can't accomplish this task, since there is no constituent of the form F(x) in common between either of the input icons and the output icon.

This is not to deny that there can be rules that specify aspects of icons that allow for combination of contents. For example, a rule of the form *If [red*] and [square*] then [red square*]* can accomplish combination.[5] We also don't intend to deny that there can be rules that specify more abstract aspects of icons, such as *If [color*] and [shape*] then [color shape*]*, which ranges over all colors and shapes.[6] But neither of these rules is identical to a formal rule such as conjunction introduction; they concern the combinations of features at different levels of abstraction.

The basic problem is that representations that don't have constituent structures will be governed by rules that are *content-specific*, in that they specify the identities of particular representations.[7] Consider rules that only range over syntactically atomic representations, e.g., *If A and B then C*. If this rule were not content-specific, then tokening any two representations would cause the tokening of any third representation with no limitations – i.e., thinking CAT and DOG would cause you to token any other atomic representation you can. For rules that govern atomic representations to be psychologically plausible, they have to specify particular representations. And in that case, they can't be formal rules and therefore can't govern inferences.

The case of icons is more complicated, however, since icons are not atomic. Icons break down into parts that correspond to parts of what they represent, and moreover each part encodes multiple features separately. A red icon with no shape information and a red square icon don't have a *constituent* in common, but they do have something in common – if we denied this fact, then there would be an explosion of primitives whereby every possible arrangement of features is a primitive icon that has nothing in common with any other icon.

What allows parts of icons to express multiple features at once is that they instantiate multiple properties at once, each of which corresponds to a property of what's represented. A part of a photograph might be red and square, and these properties of the part might correspond to the redness and squareness of what's represented. Another part might be red and triangular, corresponding to the redness and triangularity of what's represented. Since these parts are both red, they have a property (and content) in common. In this case the properties of parts are the properties of what's represented, which is surely not the case for mental icons. But what matters is that parts of mental icons have vehicular properties (i.e., properties of the representation itself, the 'vehicle' of what content it carries) like red* and square* that enable them to express redness and squareness. How these vehicular properties should be individuated and how the compositionality of parts of icons should be modeled is an extraordinarily thorny issue we won't tackle here (for discussion see Quilty-Dunn, 2017). What's important for present purposes is that nothing about lacking constituent structure *per se* precludes a representation from combining features systematically, as long as it doesn't do so by means of composing discrete constituents (which the properties of redness, squareness, redness*, and squareness* are plainly not).

All this entails that icons can be compositional without having constituent structure, so there's no explosion of representational primitives. But the fact that icons compose features holistically (i.e., by means of properties of a single part rather than combining parts) means that their limited form of compositionality cannot be computationally exploited the same way the compositionality of discursive representations can. If a shape* value, an orientation* value and a location* value all hold of a given part of an icon, then accessing the shape* value requires accessing the orientation* and location* values as well. This means that a computational extraction of shape from an icon requires non-trivial work to differentiate the shape feature from its specific orientation, location, and any other holistically bound properties.

This *a priori* computational difficulty in extracting a single property from an icon has been noted by philosophers (Dretske, 1981; Haugeland, 1998; Fodor, 2003). It also makes sense of some of the most famous psychological effects involving icons. Take mental rotation. It's because the shape and orientation of the object are represented by the same parts of

Non-Inferential Transitions   157

the mental image that you can't immediately compare the shape of two objects at different orientations to see if they're identical. Instead, the orientation needs to match as well – that is, you have to mentally rotate the image of object B until its orientation* matches the orientation* of object A, and then see whether the simultaneously accessed shape* values concur as well.

The upshot of this discussion is that while icons can compose features without an explosion of representational primitives, the holistic manner in which they do so entails that computational processes have to access features in combination rather than individually. A consequence of this is that the rules governing those processes have to specify particular combinations without breaking them down into their primitive elements. Thus the rule that moves from a red* square* icon to a square* icon cannot simply be of the form *If AB then B*. A rule of that sort requires that B can be directly extracted from the complex AB, and the holisticity of icons simply precludes that sort of operation. An individual property can be extracted from an icon only by virtue of some (presumably highly complicated) intermediating process; the extraction cannot be a primitive computational operation. Not so for discursive representations: COW can be extracted directly from BROWN COW because it is a discrete constituent in its own right.

This moral applies in the other direction as well. There can be rules for composing discursive representations of the form *If [P] and [Q] then [P AND Q]* because P AND Q has P and Q as discrete constituents and ties them together via a conjunction operator. But this rule cannot hold over icons, since the computational process can't differentially specify the elements of the iconic counterpart of P AND Q (e.g., red* square*). Thus the feature integration process of taking a red* icon and a square* icon and delivering a red* square* icon cannot be a genuine instance of conjunction introduction but must instead implement some content-specific rule that maps red* and square* to red* square* under that specific description.

Note that while we've managed to avoid an explosion of primitive representational contents, we have run headlong into a mess of primitive computational rules. This would worry us if it weren't antecedently plausible. But as far as we can tell, perceptual psychology is up to its ears in massively complicated and proprietary algorithms – e.g., there's little reason to think that the computational rules implemented in deriving 3D shape on the basis of texture gradients are used for chromatic color constancy, or for anything else in the mind for that matter.

The content-specificity of rules for transforming icons also makes sense of an otherwise puzzling aspect of the mental imagery literature. Recall that the fact that orientation* and shape* have to be accessed together explains why you can't immediately compare the shapes of two objects represented at two different orientations. This means there needs to be some process that matches orientation* in order to match (or discriminate) shape*. But why does this process need to take longer the more intermediating orientation values there are – i.e., why does it have to be mental *rotation*? If the image of object A is at orientation-0* (i.e., perfectly upright) and the image of object B is at orientation-60* (i.e., at about two o'clock), why does the process that delivers an image of B at orientation-0* have to access the orientations* between 0* and 60*? The fact that shape* is bound up with orientation* doesn't by itself predict this result, since there could be a process that allows you to transform the orientation to whatever value you want. But this process doesn't underwrite the actual effect, since the effect is that reaction time increases as a linear function of the difference in orientation, and this strongly implies that the process represents the intermediating orientation values (otherwise what else would explain the linear increase?). If we suppose that rules for transforming icons are not content-specific, there's no principled explanation on offer for why the process can't immediately bridge any two orientation* values via some rule that abstracts away from specific values.

Now suppose that the rules for transforming icons *are* invariably content-specific. In that case, to go directly from orientation-60* to orientation-0* would require a specific rule for those specific orientations. Likewise for every combination of orientation* values, presenting an unwieldy computational burden. It would be relatively tractable, however, for there to be a content-specific rule for every specific orientation that simply delivers the adjacent orientation values. Thus the process could move from orientation-60* to orientation-59* via a content-specific rule and likewise for each pair between 60* and 0*. The content-specificity of rules governing iconic transformations thus explains the mental rotation results.

To sum up this section: inferences are governed by logical rules; logical rules are formal; formal rules specify structures independently of content; transitions between icons are governed by content-specific rules; so transitions between icons cannot be inferences.[8] We thus reject the claim that inferences occur in early vision not because we deny that early perceptual processes involve literal transformations over explicitly represented content in line with explicitly stored information but rather because the most plausible format for (many) such early representations precludes them from entering into inferential transitions. This applies to any transition featuring an icon as an input or output, even if the other representation being transitioned to (or from) is discursive.

So, for example, categorization on the basis of iconic inputs can't be a species of inference. There must be some content-specific rules that map types of icons to types of discursive representations. This point fits naturally with so-called 'template-based' or 'view-based' theories of categorization, on which categorization processes match stored unstructured viewpoint-dependent representations (which look to us to be icons) to inputs to see whether to apply a category (Ullman, 1996; Edelman and Intrator, 2001). On alternative 'structural description' models (Biederman, 1987; Green, 2017) categorization processes instead convert iconic inputs into discursive representations that specify abstract structural features; if the incoming structural description accords with the stored description for some category, then the category is applied.[9] While the process of deploying a category on the basis of a structural description may be inferential – since both the category and the description are discursive, the transition may be governed by a formal rule – the part of the process that transforms an iconic input into a structural description must be content-specific. While on some theories icons play no role at any stage of perception (Pylyshyn, 2003), we assume that icons can at least occasionally function as inputs to categorization, which entails that categorization is not (or at least not always) a form of inference.

We're using 'icon' to refer to the pure icons that arguably figure in perception and mental imagery. There may be other sorts of icon-ish formats in the mind such as cognitive maps used for navigation. Rescorla (2009) argues that transitions involving maps only resemble logical inferences, and should instead be modeled differently due to their lack of explicit logical operators. We're happy to grant this distinction. However, we also think maps have constituent structures (Camp, 2007; Blumson, 2015), and that they are thus discursive representations that consist of an iconic representation of a spatial terrain combined with other constituents of various possible formats (including markers that may themselves be discursive or iconic). It's thus possible on our account that iconic-discursive hybrids like maps could figure in transitions in virtue of rules that specify their constituent structures, and thus count as genuine inferences despite lacking logical operators.

3. The Structure of Association

Transitions involving icons are interesting because they appear to be not quite inferential while also being clearly distinct from association. Association is a useful contrast with both inferential and many non-inferential processes because association is, in some deep way, *dumb*. Though we think a process such as mental rotation isn't strictly speaking an inferential one, for example, it nonetheless manifests complex computational intelligence.

We think it instructive to dwell on the nature of association, perhaps the most basic type of mental transition. Though the notion of association has a long and storied history (see, e.g., Mandelbaum, 2015, 2016), we think that previous analyses may have moved too quickly, and that the basics of the theory of association could use a reappraisal.

The term 'association' covers at least three different processes: associative learning, associative structures, and associative transitions. Associative learning refers to a paradigm in which one learns . . . something. What exactly is learned is part of the debate. One can put it neutrally by saying that one learns contingencies about the world, but a further question pertains to the structure of these acquired contingencies. Pure associationists (e.g., John Locke, David Hume, Ivan Pavlov, Anthony Dickinson, Cecilia Heyes) think what is acquired in an associative learning paradigm is an associative structure – a pair of mental representations that are structured associatively.[10] But what does 'structured associatively' and its cognates ('instantiating an associative relation') amount to? Association is supposed to be the most basic relation that two mental representations can bear to one another. For example, Dickinson (1980, p. 85) describes association as 'an excitatory link which has no other property than that of transmitting excitation from one event representation to another.' Such a link is supposed to be maximally simple in that it is a brute connection between representations (one which is merely excitatory, not inhibitory).

The structures formed through association needn't be simple. It is reasonable to suppose that the semantic network of concepts in each person's mind is an enormous reticulated structure consisting of thousands of concepts linked together at varying associative strengths. What makes association dumb is thus not its simplicity, but rather its insensitivity to rational considerations. If you're simultaneously presented with a picture of Trump next to a picture of Rosa Luxemburg two hundred times, then you'll form an association between Trump and Luxemburg. Your knowledge of the fact that Trump and Luxemburg bear no sort of resemblance and have virtually no relation to each other won't prevent you from thinking LUXEMBURG when you think TRUMP. The only way to weaken the association would be through an extinction paradigm, that is, to see pictures of Trump without pictures of Luxemburg and vice versa.

One can therefore take an operationalized approach to the distinction between associative and non-associative transitions: the former can only be changed through extinction (and counter-conditioning) paradigms while the latter may be changeable in other ways, or not at all. This approach can be useful (Mandelbaum, 2015; Quilty-Dunn and Mandelbaum, 2018), but it isn't fully philosophically satisfying. Operationalism is an unacceptably superficial metaphysics of mind. *Pace* verificationists, operationalizations should be used as measures of underlying mental states and processes, not as specifications of their nature.

So, what is the nature of association? Associative transitions between mental states are mediated by a stored associative structure that links those mental states. A familiar point from centuries of rationalist critique of associationism is that an associative link does not have a propositional structure. Specifically, association is never sufficient for predication. Thinking SUGAR and SWEET is not sufficient for thinking SUGAR IS SWEET. Thinking the full propositional thought requires some kind of

Non-Inferential Transitions   161

semantically exploitable ordering, such that the meaning of SWEET is predicated of the meaning of SUGAR and not (necessarily) vice versa (Kant, 1781; Fodor, 2003). The predicative relation between constituents of propositional structures is thus asymmetric.

As noted, the argument that associative links don't suffice for propositional structure is quite well known. But the deeper point is that as classically understood, associative links don't merely have a non-propositional structure – they simply have no internal structure to speak of. An associative link is just the propensity of two representations to be activated together. It follows that, at least ideally, associative links are *symmetric*. That is, if A and B are associated, then (*ceteris paribus*!) activating either will cause the activation of its associate.

The symmetry condition on association leads to a problem, however, since most links between mental representations are not in fact symmetric. Thinking ULTERIOR leads to thinking MOTIVE quicker than thinking MOTIVE leads to thinking ULTERIOR. Some asymmetries can be explained away by differences in the other links between representations. Suppose that ULTERIOR is linked to very few concepts and MOTIVE is linked to many more, and suppose that the strength of associative spreading activation is a function not only of the strength of the link between two representations but also of the total number of linked concepts that have to be activated. In that case, the excitation off MOTIVE will be more diffuse than that stemming from ULTERIOR.

Another tool for explaining away associative asymmetry would be averting to inhibitory links. Such links would be outside the purview of association proper, however, and would thus be seen as extra performance constraints from an outside system affecting the true underlying nature of association. Of course, differential linkage and inhibitory relations are by no means ad hoc posits – they are independently plausible parameters of theory construction for the mind.[11]

However, it seems that the asymmetry of association cannot fully be explained by appeal to linkage and inhibition. For one thing, there's no reason to think that MOTIVE actually *inhibits* ULTERIOR simply because it does not activate it to as high a level as ULTERIOR activates MOTIVE. Moreover, the fact that MOTIVE has more independent links doesn't seem like the only possible source of the asymmetry. It's plausible that the fact that the association is based in repeatedly hearing the phrase 'ulterior motive' (where 'ulterior' always precedes 'motive' and rarely or never vice versa) is responsible for ULTERIOR activating MOTIVE faster (or to a higher activation level) than MOTIVE activates ULTERIOR. It seems plausible, furthermore, that this would hold even if they had the same number of links to other concepts (e.g., SALT and PEPPER may have roughly the same number of links to other concepts but there may be an asymmetry due to the fact that people hear 'salt and pepper' much more often than 'pepper and salt').

162 *Jake Quilty-Dunn and Eric Mandelbaum*

The plausibility of this sort of asymmetry creates a serious problem for the idea that association is a bare propensity for two mental states to be tokened together. Instead, there needs to be an ordering of the relation between the two representations, such that the link from SALT to PEPPER has a different strength than the link between PEPPER and SALT. In which case we see two options: 1) reject the empirical hypothesis that human beings actually harbor associative structures, or 2) augment the notion of association.

According to option 1, it turns out as a matter of fact that nothing, or nearly nothing, in the mind instantiates the bare relation posited by classical associationism. Though we are not associationists, we've happily granted that associations exist (Mandelbaum, 2016; Quilty-Dunn and Mandelbaum, 2018). But other critics of associationism such as Jan De Houwer and colleagues (De Houwer, 2009; Mitchell, De Houwer, and Lovibond, 2009) and C.R. Gallistel and colleagues (Gallistel, 1990; Gallistel and King, 2009) have argued that even the associationist's favorite examples of learning (e.g., conditioning paradigms, learning in simple animals like insects, etc.) involve the acquisition of propositionally structured representations. De Houwer and colleagues hold that controlled reasoning is always needed to learn contingencies and that learning is never the consequence of mere automatic excitatory and inhibitory links. If asymmetry in structures like the one between ULTERIOR and MOTIVE are internal to the structure itself, then there may be reason to follow De Houwer down the path of rejecting associationism *in toto*.

However, denying the existence of associative links is probably an overreaction to asymmetry. For one thing, many associationists in the early stages of psychology explicitly thought of associative links as unidirectional (Thorndike [1932] referred to associative 'polarity'; see also Rescorla, 1967). Indeed, early associationists puzzled over the existence of 'backward association,' i.e., the fact that presenting *a* before *b* led not only to a link from *a* to *b* but also from *b* to *a* (Cason, 1924; see also Ebbinghaus, 1885). Thus some associationists see asymmetry as a consequence of rather than a problem for associationism.

Furthermore, we suspect that the strong line taken by De Houwer and others is tied to learning; but learning is not the only form of evidence for the psychological reality of association. Lexical priming provides an independent source of evidence. Reading the word 'doctor' will speed recognition of the word 'nurse' (Meyer and Schvaneveldt, 1971) and reading 'bug' will speed recognition of both 'insect' and 'microphone' independently of contextual disambiguation (i.e., reading 'Ants are bugs' still activates MICROPHONE – Swinney, 1979). We have no idea how to propositionally model the link between DOCTOR and NURSE. Do you have to believe that doctors are nurses? Or that doctors often appear next to nurses? Aside from being blatantly *ad hoc*, these hypotheses commit to empirical predictions about which representations mediate semantic

Non-Inferential Transitions   163

priming that we strongly suspect wouldn't be borne out by the data. Instead, by far the most parsimonious explanation of (some forms of) semantic priming simply posits associative links between concepts and spreading activation that decreases in strength as it metastasizes (Anderson, 1983). These links can be understood as genuinely associative in that they are modulable through conditioning and that they are insensitive to rational evidence (as is clear in the BUG → MICROPHONE case).

Assuming association is worth saving, then if asymmetry is to be countenanced, perhaps the notion of association as the bare propensity of two representations to be co-activated ought to be augmented in some way. The most extreme reaction would be to simply throw out the idea of bare associative links and construe association as fundamentally structured. This reaction would alienate the spirit if not the letter of classical associationism – though some early associationists posited asymmetry, they never specified how the supposedly structure-free character of association allows for it. Not only have associationists described association as an unstructured pairing of representations, but this lack of structure also plays a key role in the motivation for associationism. A core part of the appeal of associationism is its ontological simplicity, and its parsimonious ontology derives from the simplicity of the associative relation itself. Building structure into the basic associative relation thus drives a wedge between the theory of association and its aboriginal motivating idea.[12]

Moreover, supposing associations to be asymmetric creates a corresponding problem, viz., the problem of 'backward association.' It is generally true that even presentation orders that clearly favor a particular direction (A→B) will generate not only the desired 'forward' link but also a 'backward' link in the other direction, B→A (Asch and Ebenholtz, 1962; Hogan and Zentall, 1977). If association is asymmetric, then it's totally unclear why backward association would develop. Thus associationists who scrambled to appeal to independent factors to explain backward association (Cason, 1924; Storms, 1958).

Another reaction is to construe associative links as consisting of two layers. One is an unordered pairing of representations (i.e., the basic associative relation), and another is an ordered pairing with some strength. Thus if ULTERIOR and MOTIVE are truly associated, then activating either will guarantee the activation of the other; this is the bare associative link. However, while the bare associative link might guarantee whether or not a representation is activated (i.e., in a binary fashion), it might be silent on the *degree* of activation. The degree of activation might be modulated by a separate structure that specifies both direction and strength (e.g., ULTERIOR→MOTIVE, 0.8; MOTIVE→ULTERIOR, 0.2).

A significant theoretical cost of complicating associative structures in this way is that the structure of the transition from ULTERIOR to MOTIVE ends up being partially rule-governed, where the rule is something like *If ULTERIOR is activated, then activate MOTIVE to 0.8*. Nonetheless, this sort of transition could still be different from other rule-governed transitions in the following ways: (a) it's modulable through (and only through) conditioning; (b) it is blind to compositional structure and logical form (e.g., activating THAT IS NOT A BROWN COW will initiate all links that hold for both BROWN and COW); and (c) it is not truth preserving (e.g., if it's true that the table has salt on it, it may be false that it has pepper on it, but the associative transition proceeds anyway even if it has the kind of asymmetric structure on offer). This layered view faces a more significant problem in that it's not clear what explanatory work remains to be done by the bare symmetrical associative link.

We've been exploring these options in the hope of mapping out the logical space. But it is not in fact obvious that asymmetries like those we have discussed are to be explained by appeal to association. In cases like the relation between ULTERIOR and MOTIVE, there is a complex concept ULTERIOR MOTIVE with a corresponding complex linguistic representation (viz., 'ulterior motive'), both of which have an ordering in which ULTERIOR/'ulterior' comes before MOTIVE/'motive' – and similarly for 'salt and pepper' and other cases. It may be that some non-associative structure or rule facilitates the activation of the complex conceptual/ linguistic structure upon the activation of its primary constituent (viz., ULTERIOR/'ulterior') but not its secondary one (viz., MOTIVE/'motive'). In that case, ULTERIOR will cause the activation of MOTIVE both through the bare associative link between them and through activating ULTERIOR MOTIVE (and this transition may itself go through ULTERIOR activating 'ulterior', which activates 'ulterior motive', which activates ULTERIOR MOTIVE). But MOTIVE can only activate ULTERIOR through the bare associative link (which may have its own modulable strength as long as it's not unidirectional).

This difference would explain the asymmetry in activation strength and yet be wholly extrinsic to the association between ULTERIOR and MOTIVE, thus allowing us to avoid either discarding or complicating the associative relation itself. It does come at the cost of saying that presentation order facilitates the acquisition of non-associative structures (like ULTERIOR MOTIVE and 'ulterior motive') as well as associative links – but there's a wealth of evidence for that conclusion anyway (Mandelbaum, 2015, 2016), and it's particularly plausible in the case of complex linguistic constructions (the acquisition of which associationism is notoriously ill-equipped to explain). Linguistic structure is known to mediate the acquisition of associative links as well. For example, presenting two words together in a syntactically well-formed sentence forms a stronger automatic associative connection than presenting them in an ill-formed sentence; this effect can't be reduced to mere increased attention and cognitive resources but rather arises from the syntactic structure itself (Prior and Bentin, 2008; and of course any instantiations of mere syntactic structures have their own associative effects).

Non-Inferential Transitions 165

Moreover, Asch and Ebenholtz (1962) rather plausibly argued that asymmetry arising from order of presentation was an effect of availability for recall, that is, not because of any asymmetry in the associative link itself:

> When the task is that of paired-associate learning (or the learning of a set of *a-b* pairs), it is customary to require of S that he recall (i.e., anticipate) the *b* term (or the 'response' member of the pair), whereas the *a* term (or the 'stimulus') must be recognized and at best recited out loud. The test of backward association requires S for the first time to anticipate the *a* terms; since he has not had the opportunity to anticipate them previously, it would seem plausible that these items are less available to recall. Thus the study of backward association has not equated the conditions of availability, and often availability has systematically favored forward over backward recall.
>
> (Asch and Ebenholtz, 1962, p. 139)

Availability for recall is a performance constraint that is highly context dependent. For example, if you spent yesterday thinking DOG over and over, then today you will tend to be better at recall tasks that involve dogs. This fact about availability for recall is independent of any associations DOG may have or acquire. Thus if you induce an association by repeatedly presenting the word 'dog' with 'New Jersey', then it will be easier to recall 'dog' upon reading 'New Jersey' than vice versa, but this fact is to be explained by differences in availability that are wholly extrinsic to the associative link itself (i.e., the fact that you happened to spend yesterday repeatedly activating DOG). Likewise, order of presentation may simply structure the availability of recall, causing a symmetrical associative link to manifest in asymmetric capacities for recall.

We can thus preserve the psychological reality of association as a bare symmetric relation as long as we posit multiple different interacting structures – some associative, some not – to explain the phenomena favored by associationists. Even semantic priming will turn out to be more than the activation of associative links. But viable forms of associationism are always replete with such complications. For example, while some forms of semantic priming seem purely associative (e.g., doctor – nurse), others are structured, such as priming that goes by way of superordinate – subordinate category structure (e.g., cousin – nephew) (Perea and Rosa, 2002; see McNamara, 2004 for a useful overview). As one would expect if one were positing distinct structures, these are dissociable: patients who display symptoms of Alzheimer's disease preserve purely associative lexical priming but lose priming that goes by way of category structure (Glosser et al., 1998).

The history of associationism is an object lesson in appending epicycles to an overly simple theory (as can be seen in, for example, stipulations

166 *Jake Quilty-Dunn and Eric Mandelbaum*

made by Rescorla and Wagner [1972] in their famous model of associative learning). The continuing legitimacy of the notion of association as articulated in the earliest stages of psychology depends on these epicycles being mostly extrinsic to the associative relation itself; the associative relation should be complicated as minimally as possible and only as a last resort. We've noted a fundamental problem in asymmetric activation strengths, and outlined a number of possible explanations. The most likely outcome is that all these explanations are at least partially true and work in tandem: association is a bare propensity of coactivation but is also rarer than it's often thought to be, many classically associative phenomena are in fact undergirded by some non-associative as well as associative structures, and performance constraints like recall availability exert a significant impact on behavior.[13] Simplicity in the associative relation must be compensated for by complexity in other structures and conditions of acquisition. Human learning and memory are complicated, byzantine even, and that fact has to surface somewhere eventually.

4. Conclusion

The mind is not simply a logical inference-making machine. We've outlined a number of non-inferential transitions, including iconic transformations, content-specific rules in central modules, and associations. This partial taxonomy leaves out a great deal of important mental processes (Bayesian processing being a glaring example, see Mandelbaum, 2019). But it is intended to add some detail to a fuzzy sketch of how the mind might be structured and thereby provide some systematicity to our understanding of human psychology.[14]

Notes

1. We also distinguished BITs from RITs (*rich inferential transitions*), a fuller notion of inference in which the subject is also disposed to endorse the transition.
2. We assume that categorization involves the application of a discursive concept to a perceived item (Mandelbaum, 2017); if that's wrong and the outputs of categorization can be icons as well (a possible interpretation of Prinz, 2002), then the computational role of icons is yet richer.
3. The case might better be modeled by introducing conjunction in the predicate terms, i.e., from X IS F and X IS G to X IS F AND G (though importantly not for Treisman, since feature integration *a la* Treisman and Gelade (1980) requires the introduction of a new object). We'll generally ignore this distinction.
4. As we've argued (Quilty-Dunn and Mandelbaum, 2018), we don't see Kripkenstein as threatening to the psychological reality of rules as long as one grants a competence/performance distinction sufficiently robust to distinguish failure of conformity to a psychologically real rule (like *plus*) from conformity to a weird rule (like *quus*). And Kripke's insistence that the rule-following argument doesn't assume behavioristic limitations on mental architecture (1982, 14–15) seems to us to allow for such a distinction.

But we accept the Kripkensteinian point that the functional properties of finite systems like human brains cannot distinguish rules with infinite scope, such as *modus ponens*, from weird rules that are, for such finite systems, extensionally equivalent, such as *modus schmonens* (which is equivalent to *modus ponens* except for conjunctions so large they cannot be thought by a human being in any possible world). Our account entails that all extensionally equivalent rules that describe 100% of transitions made in worlds where human beings think without performance errors are built into the architecture. Since these rules will thereby be truth-preservationally equivalent for propositions thinkable by humans, we don't see this entailment of our view as skeptical in any deeply worrying sense. Thus *modus ponens* and *modus schmonens* have equal psychological reality and human inference preserves truth no more or less than we pre-theoretically thought it did.

5. We use asterisks to denote aspects of icons.

6. We're trying to be as non-committal as possible about what causes these features to be integrated; it might be that they're represented at the same location (in which case the rules should be enriched to reflect sameness of location) or simply that they're attended together.

7. Note that content-specificity in this sense is compatible with being formal in a different, computational sense, i.e., that computation operates over symbols in virtue of their internal symbolic features and not what they actually represent out in the world (Fodor, 1980). Here we mean that a rule that pertains only to the concept DOG is content-specific because it doesn't pertain to CAT despite DOG and CAT being structurally equivalent; it is compatible with this notion of content-specificity that the rule is 'solipsistic', i.e., that it specifies the symbol DOG in a way that is completely blind to what DOG represents.

8. We've discussed elsewhere some inference forms like semantic entailment (e.g., X IS RED to X IS COLORED) and probabilistic reasoning (Quilty-Dunn and Mandelbaum, 2018). The former seem to us to be genuinely inferential only when mediated by explicit knowledge of the connection (e.g., IF X IS RED THAN X IS COLORED) and therefore logical. The latter can be straightforwardly accommodated in our sort of framework (see, e.g., Goodman et al., 2015). A third form of inference is abduction, or 'inference to the best explanation' (Harman, 1965). Abduction strikes us as a mess, one that has not been successfully captured by *any* extant theory and probably involves a maelstrom of different processes including task-relevant memory search, formulation of analogies, and probably some purely associative spreading activation and properly logical inferences. We put these forms of reasoning aside here.

9. Biederman's theory is couched in terms of 'geons,' which are representations of types of cylindrical shapes of varying lengths, orientations, etc. Geons might look to be icons, especially when diagrammed (e.g., Prinz, 2002, p. 140ff), but they are nothing more than descriptions, explicitly analogized to sentences by proponents of structural-description theories (e.g., Hummel, 2013, p. 34).

10. N.b.: according to this way of cutting up the pie Skinner and Watson do not, strictly speaking, count as associationists because neither believes in mental representations; a fortiori they don't believe in associative links between mental representations and anything else. However, Skinner and Watson did think that associative learning causes the acquisition of an associative link between stimulus and response. In any case, given the demise of behaviorism we'll describe association from a mentalistic point of view.

11. For example, activating one of a pair of homonyms (e.g., [river] bank), will inhibit the activation of the other homonym (e.g., [savings] bank) Pylkkänen, Llinás, and Murphy (2006); Macgregor, Bouwsema, and Klepousniotou (2015).

12. It's perhaps puzzling why any associationist would ever have insisted on asymmetry given its tension with the idea that association is unstructured. But it's important to keep in mind the co-development of behaviorism and associationist models in the early twentieth century. Since many doubted the existence of representations, let alone associative links between representations, the one form of associative link that all associationists could agree on was the link from stimulus to response. And the notion of associative symmetry in stimulus-response associations makes little sense – being confronted with a ringing bell may associatively cause you to salivate, but salivation tends not to cause bells to ring. We thus suspect that behaviorist (and, more generally, operationalist) influence – not to mention the bare empirical fact that there are asymmetric transitions – caused some early associationists to regard association as asymmetric without seeing how uneasily that fits with their claim that association is unstructured.

13. What kind of 'bare propensity' is association? It's simply that there is no deeper psychological explanation for the propensity of the representations to be co-activated. Contiguity, resemblance and the like may serve to acquire the association, but once the association is acquired, the functional relation between the two is primitive from the standpoint of psychology. Activation spreading, for example, is not the sort of effect that is explicable in other psychological terms; instead, there are nodes in a network and levels of activation that spread associatively throughout the network. Why is it that activating one of a pair of nodes directly linked to each other will cause the other to activate? There is simply no psychological-level story to tell. Whatever story there is to tell will be told in the vocabulary of sub-psychological reality (such as neuroscience, or whatever intermediate computational levels may connect neural activation to full-blown psychological functioning). None of this entails that the associative activation can't be modulated – associative links, by being primitive at the psychological level, are not therefore immutable rules built into the architecture. Counterconditioning and extinction can still suffice to modulate associative links. Thus associative links can have a characteristic functional role (viz., being so modulable) while nonetheless inhabiting a lower ontological level than inference and other properly psychological-level phenomena. Thanks to Anders Nes for the concerns that prompted these reflections.

14. Eric Mandelbaum's work on this paper was made possible in part by a major grant from the National Endowment of the Humanities. For Jake Quilty-Dunn: This project has received funding from the European Research Council (ERC) under the European Union's Horizon 2020 research and innovation programme under grant agreement No 681422.

References

Anderson, J. R. (1983). A Spreading Activation Theory of Memory. *Journal of Verbal Learning and Verbal Behavior*, 22(3), 261–295.

Asch, S. E., & Ebenholtz, S. M. (1962). The Principle of Associative Symmetry. *Proceedings of The American Philosophical Society*, 106(2), 135–163.

Biederman, I. (1987). Recognition-by-Components: A Theory of Human Image Understanding. *Psychological Review*, 94(2), 115–147.

Block, N. (2014). Seeing-As in the Light of Vision Science. *Philosophy and Phenomenological Research*, 89(3), 560–572.

Blumson, B. (2015). Mental Maps. *Philosophy and Phenomenological Research*, 85(2), 413–434.

Non-Inferential Transitions 169

Braine, M. D., & O'Brien, D. P. (Eds.). (1998). *Mental Logic*. Mahwaw, NJ: Psychology Press.

Burge, T. (2010). *Origins of Objectivity*. Oxford: Oxford University Press.

Camp, E. (2007). Thinking With Maps. *Philosophical Perspectives*, 21(1), 145–182.

Carey, S. (2009). *The Origin of Concepts*. Oxford: Oxford University Press.

Cason, H. (1924). The Concept of Backward Association. *The American Journal of Psychology*, 35(2), 217–221.

De Houwer, J. (2009). The Propositional Approach to Associative Learning as an Alternative for Association Formation Models. *Learning & Behavior*, 37(1), 1–20.

Dehaene, S. (2011). *The Number Sense: How the Mind Creates Mathematics*. New York: Oxford University Press.

Dretske, F. (1981). *Knowledge and the Flow of Information*. Cambridge, MA: MIT Press.

Ebbinghaus, H. (1885). *Memory: A Contribution to Experimental Psychology*. H. A. Ruger & C. E. Bussenius (trans.), 1913. New York: Teacher's College, Columbia University.

Edelman, S., & Intrator, N. (2001). A Productive, Systematic Framework for the Representation of Visual Structure. In T. K. Leen, T. G. Dietterich, & V. Tresp (Eds.), *Advances in Neural Information Processing Systems 13* (pp. 10–16). Cambridge, MA: MIT Press.

Fodor, J. A. (1980). Methodological Solipsism Considered as a Research Strategy in Cognitive Psychology. *Behavioral and Brain Sciences*, 3(1), 63–73.

Fodor, J. A. (2003). *Hume Variations*. Oxford: Oxford University Press.

Fodor, J. A. (2008). *LOT 2: The Language of Thought Revisited*. Oxford: Oxford University Press.

Gallistel, C. R. (1990). *The Organization of Learning*. Cambridge, MA: MIT Press.

Gallistel, C. R., & King, A. P. (2009). *Memory and the Computational Brain: Why Cognitive Science Will Transform Neuroscience*. West Sussex: Wiley-Blackwell.

Glosser, G., Friedman, R. B., Grugan, P. K., Lee, J. H., & Grossman, M. (1998). Lexical Semantic and Associative Priming in Alzheimer's Disease. *Neuropsychology*, 12(2), 218–224.

Green, E. J. (2017). On the Perception of Structure. *Noûs*, 53(3), 564–592. doi: 10.1111/nous.12207.

Green, E. J., & Quilty-Dunn, J. (Forthcoming). What Is an Object File? *British Journal for the Philosophy of Science*.

Handley, S. J., Newstead, S. E., & Trippas, D. (2011). Logic, Beliefs, and Instruction: A Test of the Default Interventionist Account of Belief Bias. *Journal of Experimental Psychology: Learning, Memory, and Cognition*, 37(1), 28–43.

Haugeland, J. (1998). Representational Genera. In His *Having Thought: Essays in the Metaphysics of Mind*. Cambridge, MA: Harvard University Press, 171–206.

Hogan, D. E., & Zentall, T. R. (1977). Backward Associations in the Pigeon. *The American Journal of Psychology*, 90(1), 3–15.

Hummel, J. E. (2013). Object Recognition. In D. Reisburg (Ed.), *Oxford Handbook of Cognitive Psychology* (Oxford: Oxford University Press), 32–46.

Kosslyn, S. M. (1980). *Image and Mind*. Cambridge, MA: Harvard University Press.

Kosslyn, S. M. (1994). *Image and Brain*. Cambridge, MA: MIT Press.

Kosslyn, S. M., Ball, T. M., & Reiser, B. J. (1978). Visual Images Preserve Metric Spatial Information: Evidence from Studies of Image Scanning. *Journal of Experimental Psychology: Human Perception and Performance*, 4(1), 47–60.

Kripke, S. A. (1982). *Wittgenstein on Rules and Private Language: An Elementary Exposition*. Cambridge, MA: Harvard University Press.

Lamme, V. A. (2003). Why Visual Attention and Awareness Are Different. *Trends in Cognitive Sciences*, 7(1), 12–18.

Lieberman, D., Tooby, J., & Cosmides, L. (2007). The Architecture of Human Kin Detection. *Nature*, 445(7129), 727–731.

MacGregor, L. J., Bouwsema, J., & Klepousniotou, E. (2015). Sustained Meaning Activation for Polysemous But Not Homonymous Words: Evidence from EEG. *Neuropsychologia*, 68, 126–138.

Mandelbaum, E. (2015). *Associationist Theories of Thought*. The Stanford Encyclopedia of Philosophy.

Mandelbaum, E. (2016). Attitude, Inference, Association: On the Propositional Structure of Implicit Bias. *Noûs*, 50(3), 629–658.

Mandelbaum, E. (2019). Troubles with Bayesianism: An Introduction to the Psychological Immune System. *Mind & Language*, 34(2): 141–157.

McNamara, T. P. (2004). *Semantic Priming: Perspectives from Memory and Word Recognition*. New York: Taylor & Francis Group.

Meyer, D. E., & Schvaneveldt, R. W. (1971). Facilitation in Recognizing Pairs of Words: Evidence of a Dependence Between Retrieval Operations. *Journal of Experimental Psychology*, 90(2), 227–234.

Mikhail, J. (2011). *Elements of Moral Cognition: Rawls' Linguistic Analogy and the Cognitive Science of Moral and Legal Judgment*. New York: Cambridge University Press.

Mitchell, C. J., De Houwer, J., & Lovibond, P. F. (2009). The Propositional Nature of Human Associative Learning. *Behavioral and Brain Sciences*, 32(2), 183–198.

Paivio, A. (1969). Mental Imagery in Associative Learning and Memory. *Psychological Review*, 76(3), 241–263.

Perea, M., & Rosa, E. (2002). The Effects of Associative and Semantic Priming in the Lexical Decision Task. *Psychological Research*, 66(3), 180–194.

Prinz, J. J. (2002). *Furnishing the Mind: Concepts and Their Perceptual Basis*. Cambridge, MA: MIT Press.

Prior, A., & Bentin, S. (2008). Word Associations are Formed Incidentally During Sentential Semantic Integration. *Acta Psychologica*, 127(1), 57–71.

Pylkkänen, L., Llinás, R., & Murphy, G. L. (2006). The Representation of Polysemy: MEG Evidence. *Journal of Cognitive Neuroscience*, 18(1), 97–109.

Pylyshyn, Z. W. (2003). *Seeing and Visualizing: It's Not What You Think*. Cambridge, MA: MIT Press.

Quilty-Dunn, J. (2017). *Syntax and Semantics of Perceptual Representation*. Doctoral dissertation, City University of New York.

Quilty-Dunn, J. (Forthcoming). Perceptual Pluralism. *Noûs*. https://doi.org/10.1111/nous.12285.

Quilty-Dunn, J., & Mandelbaum, E. (2018). Inferential Transitions. *Australasian Journal of Philosophy*, 96(3), 532–547.

Rescorla, M. (2009). Cognitive Maps and the Language of Thought. *The British Journal for the Philosophy of Science*, 60(2), 377–407.

Rescorla, R. A. (1967). Pavlovian Conditioning and Its Proper Control Procedures. *Psychological Review*, 74(1), 71–80.

Rescorla, R. A., & Wagner, A. R. (1972). A Theory of Pavlovian Conditioning: Variations in the Effectiveness of Reinforcement and Non-Reinforcement. In A. H. Black & W. F. Prokasy (Eds.), *Classical Conditioning II: Current Research and Theory*. New York: Appleton-Century-Crofts, 64–99.

Reverberi, C., Pischedda, D., Burigo, M., & Cherubini, P. (2012). Deduction without Awareness. *Acta Psychologica*, 139(1), 244–253.

Shepard, R. N., & Metzler, J. (1971). Mental Rotation of Three-Dimensional Objects. *Science*, 171(3972), 701–703.

Sperling, G. (1960). The Information Available in Brief Visual Presentations. *Psychological Monographs: General and Applied*, 74(11), 1–29.

Storms, L. H. (1958). Apparent Backward Association: A Situational Effect. *Journal of Experimental Psychology*, 55(4), 390–395.

Swinney, D. A. (1979). Lexical Access During Sentence Comprehension: (Re)consideration of Context Effects. *Journal of Verbal Learning and Verbal Behavior*, 18(6), 645–659.

Thorndike, E. L. (1932). *The Fundamentals of Learning*. New York: Teachers College Bureau of Publications.

Tolman, E. C. (1948). Cognitive Maps in Rats and Men. *Psychological Review*, 55(4), 189–208.

Treisman, A. M., & Gelade, G. (1980). A Feature-integration Theory of Attention. *Cognitive Psychology*, 12(1), 97–136.

Ullman, S. (1996). *High-Level Vision: Object Recognition and Visual Cognition*. Cambridge, MA: MIT Press.

7 Knowledge of Logical Generality and the Possibility of Deductive Reasoning

Corine Besson

1. Introduction

A central task for the philosophy of logic is to articulate what logical knowledge consists in, and in particular what knowledge of basic logical principles, such as Modus Ponens, consists in. One aspect of this task is to account for how we make use of such knowledge in reasoning: how our knowledge of the principle of Modus Ponens, for instance, can be *employed* in reasoning.[1]

One way to approach this task is *epistemological*. It concerns the questions of whether and how we can know logical principles or be justified in using those principles in reasoning. Another is *psychological*. It concerns the questions of what form logical knowledge has to take, what kind of state it has to be, so that it can be employed in reasoning.

There are many difficulties surrounding answering both the epistemological and the psychological questions, notably related to threats of regress and circularity. For instance, concerning the epistemological question, some philosophers worry that no non-circular justification of basic logical principles can be given, since the very basic logical principles requiring justification will be needed to provide it.[2] Worries also revolve around so-called 'Carroll's Regress',[3] some of which concern psychological questions. The Regress seem to suggest that knowing a principle of reasoning such as Modus Ponens cannot require having a belief about that principle – e.g., a belief that P, together with if P then Q, entails Q; for that would not be the kind of state that can explain how we can reason using it. Thus suppose that you believe that it is day and that if it is day, then it is light. From this, you are licensed to believe that it is light. If you also had to believe Modus Ponens to draw this conclusion – the very principle that you are using in your reasoning – it would seem that you would have to add this belief to your original set of premises. This would mean that you would then need to believe a new principle that licenses you to draw a conclusion from this new set of premises, and so on and so forth; you could never draw a conclusion from a set of premises.

Logical Generality and Deductive Reasoning   173

In light of Carroll's Regress – to avoid the infinite proliferation of premises to a given conclusion – many have suggested that *cognitivism* about logic cannot provide the right answer to the psychological question of what form logical knowledge has to take so that it can be employed in reasoning. According to *logical cognitivism*, knowing a basic logical principle is having propositional knowledge of that principle – where this requires that it is explicitly or consciously represented in the minds of speakers (e.g., as a belief). Non-cognitivism about basic logical principles has become a widespread strategy to avoid the threat of Carroll's Regress, whereby knowing such principles is either non-propositional or non-consciously represented in the minds of speakers.[4]

In this chapter, I focus on a specific type of circularity threat to a cognitivist account of knowledge of basic logical principles, in connection with psychological questions.[5] This threat has to do with the fact that such principles are *general principles* and in ordinary reasoning we are typically using *particular* cases or *applied* instances of them. Thus, you might think that to reason from the beliefs that it is day and that if it is day, then it is light, to the belief that it is light, you have to know that the latter follows from the former. And you might think that this has to be an application of your knowledge of a general fact – that Modus Ponens is valid – to this *particular* fact of implication. There is a worry of circularity looming here, in that applying a general principle to a particular instance might itself be a sample of reasoning that requires applying that very general principle. This worry is the topic of this chapter, which I label the 'general/particular circularity threat'.

More precisely, we can state the general principle of Modus Ponens as a schema as follows:

(MP): P; if P, then Q ⊨ Q.[6]

Here the letters are schematic letters, devices of generality, roughly expressing the fact that no matter which argument of the same form you substitute for it (through uniform substitution of the schematic letters), this argument is valid. The semantic turnstile '⊨' is a formal representation of 'entails' or 'therefore', here really only used for convenience. A particular instance of (MP) is the following:

(i)–(iii): (i) It is day; (ii) If it is day, it is light ⊨ (iii) It is light.

The general/particular circularity threat revolves around psychological questions such as: how might someone recognize the particular argument (i)–(iii) as an instance of the general pattern (MP) and apply the latter to the former? What form would knowledge (MP) have to have for this recognition to be possible? Is this recognition required to appreciate the validity of the particular argument? Or can this appreciation be arrived

174 *Corine Besson*

at in a different way? Would this appreciation require doing some logical reasoning? If so, would this bit of reasoning lead to circularity? And if so, what would that mean for the notion that we employ (MP) in reasoning? What is the significance of the worry that recognizing (i)–(iii) as an instance of (MP) requires you to reason according to (MP)?

In this chapter, I present two recent versions of the general/particular circularity threat:[7] one offered by Romina Padro (2015) as the 'Carroll-Kripke Adoption problem'; the other offered by Paul Boghossian (2003) as 'Carrollian Circularity'. Both authors acknowledge that they are not really articulating versions of Carroll's Regress, sketched earlier, since Carroll's concerns are not with the general character of logical principles. The threats have nonetheless a Carrollian character, since they suggest that it is impossible to draw conclusions from premises by applying basic logical principles. Also, both versions are meant to speak against cognitivism, the view that we have propositional knowledge of basic logical principles. The first aim of the chapter is to argue against both versions of the threat, indeed against the very way in which they are formulated. Its second aim is to show that we need not take someone who engages in the reasoning (i)–(iii) to be applying a general principle such as (MP) in the way suggested by the setting of the general/particular circularity threat.

The chapter is organized as follows. Section 2 sketches Padro's Carroll-Kripke version (Section 2.1) and Boghossian's version (Section 2.2) of the general/particular circularity threat, and (Section 2.3) offers some initial discussion. Section 3 argues against both versions: Section 3.1 shows that they both wrongly rely on employment of the principle of Universal Instantiation to explain deductive reasoning; Section 3.2 shows that this rests on an implausible account of the role of general principles in deductive reasoning; and Section 3.3 shows how the general/particular circularity threat can be defused.

2. The Circularities

2.1. *Padro's Carroll-Kripke Adoption Problem*

The first version of the general/particular circularity threat is what Romina Padro labels the 'Carroll-Kripke Adoption Problem' or '(AP)'. (AP) is based on a reconstruction of some of Saul Kripke's unpublished work that Padro cites and describes in her (2015, 2016). Here is the problem as she states it (2015, pp. 41–42):

> (AP): certain basic logical principles cannot be adopted because, if a subject already infers in accordance with them, no adoption is needed, and if the subject does not infer in accordance with them, no adoption is possible.

Logical Generality and Deductive Reasoning 175

(AP) is meant to be a challenge to answering psychological questions concerning what form logical knowledge has to take so as to be applicable in reasoning.[8]

Let us have a look at the key moving part of Padro's reconstruction of (AP). According to her, adoption is a two-phase process (Padro, 2015, p. 31ff, 2016, p. 74):

(1) Learning the general logical principle;
(2) Applying it to particular instances/using it in particular cases.

(AP) arises in connecting up the two phases. To illustrate, Padro uses the example of the principle of Universal Instantiation (UI) that governs the elimination of the universal quantifier, according to which if all objects satisfy a condition F, a particular arbitrary one does too. Schematically:

(UI): $\forall xFx \vDash Fa$.

Thus, suppose that you believe that everything is extended. You have never used (UI) and you learn (UI) in its general form – you complete phase (1). I then ask you whether you also believe that atom A is extended ('A' is the name we have given to a fundamental particle we have hypothesized). The problem seems to be that for you to reason from your belief that everything is extended to A is extended, you would have to *instantiate in two ways*: you would have to infer the particular application from the general principle (UI); and then instantiate from 'Everything is extended' to 'A is extended'. That is, before applying (UI) to your particular reasoning in phase (2), you would have to apply (UI) to reason from (UI) to an instance of (UI). This means that you cannot complete phase (2), cannot adopt (UI) and cannot answer my question: any adoption of (UI) presupposes applying (UI); that is, presupposes having adopted (UI).[9]

Let me reconstruct the argument, as I see it. You complete phase (1) by learning the general principle (UI) and Padro reckons you need two applications of (UI) to complete phase (2) – perhaps as follows:

(UI_1): Everything is extended $\vDash$ A is extended.
(UI_2): $(\forall xFx \vDash Fa) \vDash$ (Everything is extended $\vDash$ A is extended).

Padro's contention is that an application of (UI_1) requires an application of (UI_2), which she construes as an application of (UI) – a contention which I will question in Section 3.1. This is problematic if your application of (UI_1) is going to partly constitute adopting (UI) for the first time. Schematically, the situation is this:

(I) Everything is extended	Initial belief
(II) $\forall xFx \vDash Fa$	(UI)/Adoption phase (1)
Is A extended?	
(III) Everything is extended $\vDash$ A is extended	(II), (UI_2)
(IV) A is extended	(I), (III) (MP)[10]

You never get to apply (UI_1); for any application of it presupposes an application of (UI_2). Moreover, as Padro stresses, it appears that (MP) too would be required to adopt (UI) – to reach step (IV). She concludes that we need both (UI) and (MP) to adopt (UI), that (UI) cannot be adopted, and that step (IV) cannot be reached.

To see the matter more clearly, let us run (AP) for (MP) and for Conjunction Elimination (&E), a principle not in play in setting up (AP).

Consider (MP) first. Suppose that you have never reasoned according to (MP) and suppose that you learn (MP) in its general form – you complete phase (1). Suppose also that you believe (i) and (iii). Someone then asks you whether you also believe (iii) or are willing to reason to (iii). For you to reason to (iii), you would have to see your reasoning as an instance of (MP) and then apply (MP) to the particular bit of reasoning you are considering (phase (2)). To complete phase (2) you need to apply (MP) to the particular case (i)–(iii). The problem here is that to do so, you have to see that (i)–(iii) is an instance of (MP) and it would seem that this requires what Padro takes to be an application of (UI):

(UI_{MP}): (P; if P, then Q $\vDash$ Q) $\vDash$ (It is day; if it is day, it is light $\vDash$ it is light

So the situation seems to be this:

(V) It is day; if it is day it is light	Initial beliefs (i) and (ii)
(VI) P; if P, then Q $\vDash$ Q	(MP)/Adoption phase (1)
Is it light?	
(VII) It is day; if it is day, it is light $\vDash$ it is light	(VI), (UI_{MP})
(VIII) It is light	(V), (VII) (MP)

Adopting (MP) presupposes (UI), which, as we have seen, Padro argues cannot be adopted. It also involves an application of (MP). However this is clearly less problematic given how Padro describes phase (2) of adoption, which requires applying the adopted principle to a particular case; this is precisely what happens in step (VIII).

Finally, let us briefly run the adoption template for conjunction elimination (&E):

(IX) It is day & it is light	Initial beliefs
(X) P & Q ⊨ P	(&E)/Adoption phase (1)
Is it day?	
(XI) It is day & it is light ⊨ it is day	(X), $(UI_{\&E})$
(XII) It is day	(IX), (XII) (MP)

Again, to adopt (&E), you need (UI) and (MP).

Padro, who focuses chiefly on the case of adopting (UI), concludes from her argument that *certain* basic logical principles such as (MP) or (UI) cannot be adopted – since adopting them presupposes their application. Indeed (UI) and (MP) are for her the cornerstones of (AP). However, it appears that a stronger conclusion should be drawn, given her setting: if (UI) and (MP) cannot be adopted, *no* basic logical principle can be adopted, as the case of (&E) illustrates. It also seems that the problems raised by (UI) and (MP) are different, contrary to what Padro suggests.[11]

Given her construal of adoption, she is committed to saying that if (UI) could be adopted, (MP) could be adopted. Thus consider (V)–(VIII) again. Supposing that (UI) has been adopted, (MP) could be adopted since phase (2) requires that you apply the very principle that you are adopting. In general, it seems that if you can reach step (VII), you have seen (i)–(iii) as an instance of (MP). If so, you can use (MP) in reasoning and reach (VIII). If you can reach steps (III), (VII) and (XI) of the arguments given earlier, you can complete Padro's phase (2) for adopting the relevant principles. The problem is that she thinks that (UI) is required prior to reaching any of them. It thus seems that (UI) is the cornerstone of (AP), as I will discuss further in Section 3.1.

In light of (AP), Padro argues that we should reject cognitivist accounts of knowledge of basic logical principles, which require these principles to be adoptable in terms of phases (1) and (2). Rather, we should take these principles not to be adoptable. While she does not settle for an account, she is sympathetic to accounts along the lines of non-propositional knowing how (2015, p. 196), or skills; or else the view that there is no real cognitive achievement underpinning our inferential practices but simply kinds of 'habit or instinct, or a process resulting from a mechanism that cannot itself count as a state of knowledge' (2015, p. 209). I do not review the various options she considers here, as my discussion is confined to the very the set-up of (AP) and in particular its use of (UI).

2.2. Boghossian's Carrollian Circularity

Paul Boghossian (2003) offers a version of the general/particular circularity threat directed at 'Simple Inferential Internalism', a foundationalist internalist

178   *Corine Besson*

account of knowing basic logical principles, which is clearly cognitivist. It states the following condition (C) for an agent being justified to believe a conclusion of a valid argument such as (i)–(iii) on the basis of its premises:

> (C) [A subject] S is able to know by reflection alone that his premises provide him with a good reason for believing the conclusion.
> (Boghossian, 2003, p. 229)

According to Boghossian's account of Simple Inferential Internalism, being justified in reasoning according to Modus Ponens, for instance, requires knowing that Modus Ponens is valid, which can be done 'by reflection alone'. How might S be in a position to know 'by reflection alone that p and 'p $\rightarrow$ q' imply q?' (2003, p. 229). Boghossian considers Laurence BonJour's way of articulating how one might have such direct, non-inferential, cognitive access to such logical facts in terms of rational insight:

> When I carefully and reflectively consider the . . . inference . . . in question, I am able simply to see or grasp or apprehend . . . that the conclusion of the inference must be true if the premises are true. Such a rational insight, as I have chosen to call it, does not seem to depend on any particular sort of criterion or any further discursive or ratiocinative process, but is instead direct and immediate.
> (Bonjour, 1998, pp. 106–107, cited in Boghossian, 2003, p. 230)

Boghossian goes on to raise many objections to this version of Simple Inferential Internalism. The key one, and the one that concerns us here, he labels 'Carrollian Circularity'. Here is how the argument goes. His initial claim is that:

> For obvious reasons, it's not plausible to think of this capacity for rational insight as operating on individual inferences one by one, generating for each of them the insight that if its premises are true, then so is its conclusion.
> (Boghossian, 2003, p. 232)

This means for Boghossian that rational insight operates on 'wholly general' principles (2003, p. 232) such as:

(MPP) For all p, q: Necessarily: If both p and 'p $\rightarrow$ q', then q.[12]

Bu then it seems that a 'fatal' circularity looms:

To bring knowledge [of (MPP)] to bear on the justifiability of that inference will, it would seem, *require the thinker first to establish its relevance to that inference*, by reasoning as follows:

Logical Generality and Deductive Reasoning 179

[XIII] Any inference of the form (MPP) is valid.
[XIV] This particular inference, from (i) and (ii) to (iii) is of (MPP) form.
Therefore,
[XV] This particular inference from (i) and (ii) to (iii) is valid.

Rational insight, we are conceding, gets us as far as the general propositional knowledge that all arguments of MPP form are valid. However, *to bring this knowledge to bear* on the justifiability of any particular inference will require the thinker to be able justifiably to infer the validity of that particular inference from the validity of all arguments of MPP form. And this will require him to be able to reason according to MPP justifiably.

Now, however a fatal circularity looms. To infer from (i) and (ii) to (iii) justifiably, I must be able justifiably to believe that the inference from (i) and (ii) to (iii) is valid. To be able justifiably to believe that this inference is valid, I must be able justifiably to infer that it is valid from the general proposition that all inferences of its form are valid. To be able justifiably to infer that it is valid from the general proposition that all inferences of its form are valid, I must be able justifiably to infer according to MPP. So, on the picture on offer, my inference from (i) and (ii) to (iii) will count as justifying only if I am already able to infer according to MPP justifiably. *The very ability we are trying to explicate is presupposed by the internalist account on offer.* (2003, pp. 233–234; my emphasis)[13]

For Boghossian the problem is two-fold: first, knowing that (i)–(iii) is valid comes out as inferential, with (MPP) as a premise, when the advertised account was meant to be non-inferential;[14] second, the relevant inference requires an application of (MPP) itself: to apply (MPP) to (i)–(iii), we need first to apply it to [XIII]–[XV]. Because of this, we have a 'fatal' circularity.

Boghossian (2014) restates the same general/particular circularity threat (although here he calls it a 'regress') against his own view, that reasoning from (i) and (ii) to (iii) is a matter of *following a rule*: i.e. applying a general rule such as (MPP) that one accepts. The threat arises, again, if we give an internalist account of following a rule. The kind of internalist account he considers, 'the intentional view of rule-following', is clearly cognitivist as it requires one to have an explicit representation of the principles one follows, for instance, as a belief or propositional knowledge. This view has an 'Inference Problem':

[M]y actively applying a rule can only be understood as a matter of my grasping what the rule requires, forming a view to the effect that its trigger conditions are satisfied, and drawing the conclusion

180 *Corine Besson*

that I must now perform the act required by its consequent. In other words, on the intentional view of rule-following, rule-following requires inference. [S]o, now we face a problem. On the one hand, we have the Intentional View of rule-following, according to which applying a rule always involves inference. On the other hand, we have the Rule-Following picture of inference according to which inference is always a form of rule-following.

(Boghossian, 2014, p. 13)

Boghossian thinks that we need the intentional notion of rule-following to account for what he calls 'Taking Condition', which he takes to be a platitude about basic logical reasoning:

(Taking Condition): Inferring necessarily involves the thinker *taking* his premises to support his conclusion and drawing his conclusion *because* of that fact.

(Boghossian, 2014, p. 5; his emphasis)

For him, any view that does away with intentionality cannot explain the guiding aspect of logical principles captured by Taking Condition (2012, p. 15). For instance, the view that knowledge of rules is intentional but subpersonal, thus not consciously accessible to the thinker, is rejected for failing to underwrite the rational character of inferring. (2014, p. 16). But given that the intentional view is in fact open to Carrollian Circularity, just like the rational insight account, it has to be rejected nonetheless. This means that while reasoning is 'essentially' rule-following (2012, p. 17), it has to be understood as a kind of *primitive state*, that does not afford analysis – where that state somehow displays the relevant intentionality and guiding character required by Taking Condition. Boghossian thus rejects cognitivism while hoping that we can still make sense of rule-following as a sort of *sui generis* cognitive personal state.

2.3. Interpretation

Before moving to objections to both Padro and Boghossian's versions of the general/particular circularity threat, I here clarify how exactly I think they should be interpreted as versions of the same argument. Consider again the Carrollian Circularity argument given in Boghossian (2003, pp. 233–234) cited in Section 2.2. He claims that argument [XII]–[VX]'s key problem is that it requires an application of (MPP). But notice that [XII]–[XV] is an argument in Universal Modus Ponens, which requires an application not only of (MPP) but also of (UI), as follows:

(XVI)	Any inference: if it is of the form (MPP), it is valid.	Rational Insight
(XVII)	If (i)–(iii) is of the form (MPP), it is valid	(XVI), (UI)
(XVIII)	(i)–(iii) is of the form (MPP)	Assumption
(XIX)	(i)–(iii) is valid	(XVII), (XVIII), (MPP)

Boghossian's problem then becomes that, on the internalist picture considered, to be justified in reasoning from (i) to (iii) you must believe that the reasoning (i)–(iii) is valid. But you can only have this belief through reasoning from (XVI) to (XIX) – from a general belief about the validity of (MPP) to a particular one about the validity of (i)–(iii); a reasoning that requires applying both (UI) and (MP). It thus appears that Boghossian's Carrollian Circularity, just like Padro's (AP), crucially involves (UI).

The conclusion that Boghossian draws from his argument is that Carrollian Circularity is 'fatal'. The question is why exactly. Notice first that Boghossian endorses a kind of rule circular account of the justification of logical principles (see Boghossian, 2000, 2001). So the fatal circularity must be different from that of circularity of justification. The answer becomes clearer if we fix our attention on the passages I emphasized in the long quote of Section 2.2 from his (2003, pp. 233–234), especially the last sentence: 'The very *ability we are trying to explicate is presupposed* by the internalist account on offer'.

The problem is that we are presupposing the possession of an ability the very possession of which we are trying to account for. It thus appears that the fatal circularity really concerns the fact that a subject has to already be able reason according to (MPP) when trying to apply (MPP) in reasoning. And that worry makes sense only if we are trying to 'explicate' how one might be able to reason according to (MPP) in the first place. That is to say, the argument (XVI)–(XIX) is problematic if we think of it as an argument a subject would have to go through as part of acquiring the ability to reason according to Modus Ponens. A subject could not do so because the very abilities they would thus be endowed with would be presupposed. Understood like this, Boghossian presents us with a problem akin to (AP): what it takes to possess (MPP) already requires one to employ (MPP), and indeed (UI).[15]

One last important interpretative point concerns Boghossian's contention that rational insight, taken to operate on general proposition, delivers step (XVI). While I do not think that he is wedded to this formulation, (XVI) strikes me as excessively complicated; fully spelt out, it says that: Any inference: if it is of the form (for all p, q: Necessarily: If both p and 'p → q', then q), it is valid. For one thing, (MPP) is not a statement of an argument but of a necessarily true conditional. This would require the rational insight not to be about general inference forms but about logical

182   *Corine Besson*

truths, something that is at odds with BonJour's formulation and indeed Boghossian's own intentions. To that extent, (MP) represent more closely what the insight might be about, namely a fact of entailment.

One might feel that schemas are not apt to represent knowledge of (MP) and (UI): first, schematic letters lack referents and thus seem contentless; second, schemas are metalinguistic.[16] For our purposes, we can use schemas informally and not fix on a specific interpretation of their meanings: thus, a schema, such as (MP), could be thought of as a collection of arguments with a certain form, where knowing a schema is, for each of its instances, recognizing that it is valid; or a schema could be thought of as a recipe telling you what expressions you are allowed to substitute for the schematic letters, where, e.g., knowing (MP), is knowing that you are allowed certain types of substitutions for the schematic letters. Further questions concern whether entailment should really be expressed with '⊨' and whether, for instance (MP) should be expressed as a normative rule expressed using 'ought' or as an imperative.

While important, these questions of how to state Modus Ponens do not matter to the substance of my criticism of the general/particular circularity threat. That threat seems to arise for any view that states that reasoning in a particular case is following a general principle – naturally stated using some kind of device of generality, such as quantification over the sentences or propositions of a language. However, these questions may matter to how we take the threat to relate to the issue of cognitivism. For instance, if we frame (AP) for the case of Modus Ponens, in terms of the imperative 'from P, and if P, then Q, conclude Q!', then from the fact that this imperative cannot be adopted, we cannot conclude anything much about cognitivism as I have formulated it, since imperatives are not propositions. However, while the issue would have to be framed in different terms, (AP) could still be taken to threaten the specific aspect of cognitivism as I have spelt it out, according to which these imperatives are explicitly represented by the thinkers using Modus Ponens in reasoning.

With these caveats in place, I will conduct my discussion of the general/particular circularity threat using (MP) and treat it as a threat to cognitivism, and will take Boghossian's argument to be adequately reformulated as follows:

(XVI*)	P; if P, then Q ⊨ Q	Rational Insight[17]
(XVII*)	If (i)–(iii) is an instance of (MP), (i); (ii) ⊨ (iii)	Assumption
(XVIII*)	(i)–(iii) is an instance of (MP)	(XVI*) (UI)
(XIX*)	(i); (ii) ⊨ (iii)	(XVII*), (XVIII*), (MP)

This formulation brings Boghossian's argument closer to Padro's, with the relevant principle as the key assumption and as explanatorily prior.

Logical Generality and Deductive Reasoning 183

I will thus focus on (MP), rather than (MPP), which seems a better candidate to help articulate grasp of general logical principles.

3. Logical Generality and Universal Instantiation

A crucial feature of the general/particular circularity threat is the contention that one's application of knowledge of general logical principles in reasoning requires an application of (UI). I start this section by arguing against this contention in two ways. In Section 3.1, I argue against the idea that it is (UI) that is applied; in Section 3.2, I argue that reasoning according to logical principles need not even be exercise of one's general knowledge applied to particular cases; and in Section 3.3, I show that this gives us the resources to block the general/particular circularity threat.

3.1. *Universal Instantiation Versus Substitution*

A feature of the general/particular circularity threat is that to be able to apply (MP) in reasoning we first need to use (UI). Now, with respect to (AP), I argue that what I have labelled (UI_2), (UI_{MP}) and $(UI_{\&E})$ in my reconstruction of Padro's argument should in fact *not* be thought of as applications of (UI). Similarly with respect to Boghossian's Carrollian Circularity, I argue that step (XVIII*) should *not* be thought of as requiring an application of (UI).

Let me start by spelling out clearly how I think we should contrast the generality of the quantifier that figures in (UI) and the generality (UI), (MP) and (&E) insofar as they are schemas: these are two kinds of generality that are involved in two different kinds of transition to different kinds of instance. (UI) contains a universal quantifier that is *prima facie* unrestricted. If interpreted objectually, as is natural to do, the quantifier ranges over absolutely everything (over uncountably many objects).[18] Thus an unrestricted application of (UI) takes us from a claim about all objects whatsoever to a claim about a particular one, as illustrated in (UI_1):[19]

(UI_1) Everything is extended $\models$ A is extended

The generality of schemas is different. It is restricted in that the generality of schematic letters is limited to (the countable set of) formulas or sentences of a given language. Accepting (UI), (MP) and (&E) is respectively accepting the validity of any argument with the same form, that is, of each of their respective *substitution instances*. The crucial feature of substitution instances is that they are of the *same form* as the formulas that they are instances of. But within (UI) we do not transition from one formula having a given form to another having the same one. Thus, in (UI_1) the formulas on the right-hand and left-hand side of '$\models$' have

184 *Corine Besson*

different forms, whereas in (UI₂), where we are going from one formula to its substitution instance, the formulas on the right-hand and left-hand side of '⊨' have the same form. That is, (UI₂), unlike (UI₁) cannot be seen as an application of (UI) and neither can (UI_{MP}) and (UI_{&E}).

With this in mind, consider again (AP) in connection with adopting (UI). Suppose that you believe that everything is extended and conclude that A is extended as a result of applying (UI₁). This is a genuine application of (UI): that takes you from a universally quantified statement to a particular one. As just emphasized, the transition from (UI) to (UI₂) itself is different: the latter is a substitution instance of the former. Crucially, the transition from (UI) to (UI₁) does not require any detachment of a conclusion from a premise and arguably does not constitute an inferential transition, requiring reasoning from premises to conclusion.

Indeed, logicians tend not to think of substitution as an inferential step governed by the basic logical principle of a logical system, but rather as a non-inferential transition governed by meta-principles of that logical system. So-called 'substitution rules' specify how general logical principles should be interpreted – what the forms they have really mean – rather than being further principles alongside them. For instance, they tell you about which substitutions are permitted in a general form such as (MP): you can substitute the argument (i)–(iii) but you cannot substitute the argument 'It is light; if it is day, it is light; therefore: it is day'. Rather than logical principles, substitutions are thus taken to be kinds of syntactico-semantic transitions and substitution rules are taken to codify what kinds of syntactico-semantic transitions can occur for a given schema or pattern.[20]

These considerations about how to think of substitution, as opposed to universal instantiation, naturally lend themselves to the following picture. What it is to recognize instances of a pattern, or to appreciate that two patterns have the same form, is simply to apply a cognitive capacity that enables us to recognize two (simple enough) forms or patterns as the same – as having the same kind of syntactico-semantic features. It is natural to think that this capacity also enables us to see that two sentences share the same semantic structure or are composed in the same way: for instance, to see that while they have different meanings, 'Brutus killed Caesar' and 'Oswald killed Kennedy' have the same semantic structure.[21] It might thus be the same competence that enables us to process compositionality and substitution, and perhaps other structural phenomena.[22] It is also natural to think that this capacity is not an inferential capacity but a kind of direct cognitive capacity: there does not seem to be an inference involved in my recognition that 'Brutus killed Caesar' and 'Oswald killed Kennedy' share a form', just as there seems to be none involved in my recognition that (i)–(iii) and (MP) share a form.

If the transition from a general pattern to a substitution instance is *not* an inferential transition, at least not inferential in the sense of

Logical Generality and Deductive Reasoning 185

deriving a conclusion from a set of premises using a basic logical principle, but essentially an application of our capacity to recognize patterns, this again means that it is not an application of (UI). It is thus wrong to characterize the transition as was done in Section 2.1, in the set-up of (AP). We should think of the transitions I labelled (UI_2), (UI_{MP}) and $(UI_{\&E})$, *neither* as inferences using (UI) *nor* as transitions characterizable in terms of '$\vDash$'. Rather they are exercises of our capacity to recognize patterns as the same.

These considerations about how (AP) should not be set up in terms of (UI_2), (UI_{MP}) and $(UI_{\&E})$ equally apply to my expansion (XVI*)–(XIX*) of Boghossian's argument (XIII)–(XV) in Section 2.3. We should not think of step (XVIII*) as requiring an application of (UI) but as an exercise of our non-inferential capacity to apprehend patterns as the same. If this is the case, we are some way towards addressing the general/particular circularity threat in its contention that we are *reasoning* from general principles to particular applications: we are not reasoning if we are directly apprehending that instances share patterns with general principles.

3.2. The Alleged Priority of the General Over the Particular

The general/particular circularity threat requires the psychological direction of explanation to go from grasping a general logical principle to grasping its substitution instances. This issue is perspicuous in the sharp division between the two phases (AP). It is also perspicuous in Boghossian's Carrollian Regress, where one has to reason from (MP) to one of its substitution instances (see again his argument [XIII]–[XV] and my reconstruction in [XVI]–[XIX*]). I now argue that while we may be able to apprehend general principles, this need not occur prior to reasoning with their substitution instances.

3.2.1. The Epistemological Perspective

Let us briefly consider the issue from the perspective of the epistemological question of justification. In this respect, it is far from clear that it is the general pattern that justifies its substitution instances, and not vice-versa, or indeed a mix of the two. Indeed this was the point famously made by Nelson Goodman in his 'New Riddle of Induction':

> Principles of deductive inference are justified by their conformity with accepted deductive practice. Their validity depends upon accordance with the particular deductive inferences we actually make and sanction. If a rule yields unacceptable inferences we drop it as invalid. Justification of general rules thus derives from judgments rejecting or accepting particular deductive inferences.
>
> (Goodman, 1954, pp. 63–64)

186   Corine Besson

According to Goodman, justification between substitution instances and general principles is largely circular but the circle is a virtuous one that enables us to reach 'agreement' between the two. My aim is not to promote the method of reflective equilibrium or forms of coherentism as a way of justifying logical principles.[23] It is simply to emphasize that justification of basic logical principles need not concern general forms rather than substitution instances. Indeed, there does not seem to be a genuinely interesting epistemological question to be raised concerning the justification of the general principle prior to the justification of its substitution instances.[24]

A congenial argument is given by Graham Priest (2016), who argues that what counts as evidence for a given logic or set of logical principles might be chiefly our intuitions about the validity of inferences *in the vernacular*. This evidence is 'soft' and can be can be 'overturned by a strong theory, especially if there is an independent explanation of why our intuition is mistaken' (2016, p. 42).[25] But the intuitions that yield it are still more reliable than intuitions about general patterns of inference: given that it is difficult to foresee all the possible instances of that pattern, it is harder to justify a general pattern than it is to justify a given instance. It is easier to see that (iii) follows from (i) and (ii), or that (iii) couldn't be false if (i) and (ii) were true, than it is to see that any instance of (MP) whatsoever is valid or that the pattern could not ever be invalidated.[26]

Thus intuitions about the vernacular can be taken to wear the justificatory trousers and Priest in my mind correctly suggests that it may be 'best to think of our views about forms of inference as low-level theoretical generalizations formed by some kind of induction'.[27] Or we might also think of them as inferences to the best explanation. Such generalizations need not be as sophisticated conceptually or as general as (MP). They might be along the following lines: 'arguments that are like (i)–(iii) seem correct'; or 'arguments of the same kind as (i)–(iii) are good'; where the notions of *being like* or *being of the same kind*, as well as the measures of goodness and correctness, can be left relatively unspecified just like the sort of generality so attributed. There thus seems to be room for some kind of recognition of generality and validity that falls short of recognition of principles such as (MP) and that is posterior to the recognition of the validity of particular instances.

3.2.2. *The Psychological Perspective*

When it comes to psychological questions concerning what form logical knowledge has to take to underwrite the possibility of reasoning, similar considerations hold as those offered in the context of justification. There seems to be no compelling reason to think that ordinary thinkers need to grasp general logical principles prior to/in order to grasp their vernacular substitution instances. If anything like the justificatory processes

Logical Generality and Deductive Reasoning   187

described by Goodman and Priest occur, we need to be able to reason with instances, not just as a by-product of reasoning with general principles. We equally need to be able to adopt general principles on the basis of, or as a by-product of, reasoning with its substitution instances (which would not initially be conceptualized as such).

With this in mind let me go back to the general/particular circularity threat as it applies to internalism, and to rational insight in particular. It is useful to note here that these worries concerning the relation of the general to the particular in the psychology of reasoning are not new. For instance, John Cook Wilson and Bertrand Russell both offer a kind of rational insight view of how logical facts are apprehended. Cook Wilson suggests that the psychological direction of apprehension has to go from the instance to the general principle:

> The validity of the general rule of inference can only be apprehended in a particular inference. If we could not see the truth directly in the particular inference, we should never get the general rule at all. Thus, it is impossible to deduce the particular inference from the general rule.
> (Cook Wilson, 1926, §237, p. 445).

Russell makes a similar point in (1903, §45), attributing it to Bradley (1883):

> The fact is, of course, that any implication [i.e. relation between particular premises and a particular conclusion] warranted by a rule of inference [i.e. general principle] does actually hold, and is not merely implied by the rule. [T]he fact that our rule does imply the said implication, if introduced at all, *must be simply perceived*, and is not guaranteed by any formal deduction; *and often it is just as easy and consequently just as legitimate, to perceive immediately the implication in question as to perceive that it is implied by one or more of the rules of inference.*
>
> (My emphasis)

Thus both Cook Wilson and Russell suggest that recognizing an argument such as (i)–(iii) as valid need not be mediated by the recognition of a general pattern: it is 'immediate', indeed 'perceived' (Russell).

With this in mind let us go back to Section 2.2, where I quoted Boghossian quoting BonJour's characterization of rational insight. Looking at the context in which BonJour offers this characterization, it is clear that he takes it to be crucial to his view that rational insight operates on particular propositions – not the general patterns they may or may not be instances of – such as: 'nothing is red all over and green all over at the same time', 'if Alice is taller than Jeanne and Jeanne is taller than Clara, then Alice is taller than Clara', 'two plus three equals five' or inferring

188   *Corine Besson*

the 'conclusion that David ate the last piece of cake from the premises, first, that either David ate the last piece of cake or else Jennifer ate it and, second, that Jennifer did not eat it' (see 1997, pp. 100–106). Of the last example, he writes: 'if I understand the three propositions involved, I will be able to see or grasp or apprehend directly and immediately that the indicated conclusion follows from the indicated premises. [I]t is obvious, of course, that I might appeal in this case to a formal rule of inference, namely the rule of disjunctive syllogism. But there is no reason to think that any such appeal is required in order for my acceptance of the inference as valid to be epistemically justified'. (1997, p. 106).

So there seems to be a long tradition of taking rational insight to apply directly to particular propositions/arguments and taking the formal principles to be secondary in the order of apprehension and justification of such propositions/arguments. This is completely at odds with Boghossian's contention that (see again his quote from 2003, p. 232 in Section 1.2.) it is obvious that rational insight cannot operate on individual arguments such as (i)–(iii).

So where does this contention come from? My sense is that the requirement that rational insight has to operate on general patterns arises from the following sorts of consideration. To have a rational insight into the truth/validity of the relevant proposition/inference, you need to *understand* these propositions/inferences. But understanding these requires that you grasp general principles because these principles in some way spell out the concepts or the meanings that are involved in these propositions/ inferences. For instance, Boghossian (1996) argues that the meanings of the logical constants, such as the conditional 'if, then', 'everything' and 'and', is given by their introduction and elimination rules – e.g., the meaning of 'if, then' is given by Modus Ponens and Conditional Proof. If so, grasping Modus Ponens, in its generality, is required for understanding 'if, then'. On that picture, any insight into the validity of a piece of reasoning such as (i)–(iii) is derivative from an insight into the validity of a principle such as (MP): there is no understanding what is going in (i)–(iii), what the sentences that compose (i)–(iii) really mean, without grasping (MP).

This is not the place to argue against this account, which makes it a condition on understanding logical constants such as 'if, then', that one follows a logical principle such as (MP) in reasoning. Let me just make three quick points. First, this view faces serious challenges[28] and there are of course alternative accounts, which do not construe understanding the connection between (i) and (iii) as requiring grasp of (MP); because, for instance, they simply take 'if, then' to be a truth-function. Second, this view need not be part of the internalist/rational insight package. It is typically part of another package that conceives of reasoning as rule-following and rule-following as constitutive of understanding certain types of proposition/inference. Third, this package is not only open to the general/ particular circularity threat, but it also does not capture a natural way

Logical Generality and Deductive Reasoning 189

to understand the epistemology and psychology of reasoning according to logical principles, according to which we generalize (from particular facts of entailment to general ones) rather than instantiate (from general facts to particular ones). It is indeed worth stressing that the transition, sketched in Section 3.2.1, from particular facts to general ones, through low-level generalizations, gives us the resources to show how relatively untrained thinkers may be granted knowledge or proto-knowledge of basic logical principles while falling short of appreciation of the conceptual complexities associated with grasping something like (MP) or (UI).

3.3. Reasoning Without Generality

Let us consider again the general/particular circularity threat in light of the arguments of Sections 3.1 and 3.2. Consider first Padro's Adoption Problem (AP) in connection with (UI) – as summarized in argument (I)–(IV). Suppose again that you do not know (UI) and that you believe that everything is extended. Suppose also that you are asked whether A is extended. The following story, radically different from Padro's, can be coherently told: once you consider this question, it strikes you that the fact that everything is extended entails that A is extended, and so you are happy to reason from the fact that everything is extended to the fact that A is extended. Your reasoning need not go through the recognition of a general logical principle, it can be direct.

Of course this does not (yet) constitute adopting (UI) nor does it constitute knowing (UI). This is merely reasoning with an instance of (UI) and what is known is simply that : that everything is extended entails that A is extended. But what is crucial is that this reasoning – the fact that it can occur – requires neither phase (1) – adopting the general principle (UI) – nor an application of (UI), with its consequent application of (MP). Thus it does not require steps (II) and (III) of that argument. It proceeds from (I) to (V) – from premise to conclusion – through a direct apprehension of the validity of a particular inference.

To further adopt (UI) would require first to engage in the sorts of low-level generalizations mentioned in Section 3.2.1 – some kind of generalization across instances. How? Here we can draw on our discussion of substitution instances and pattern recognition of Section 3.1. What underpins these generalizations is our capacity to recognize patterns as the same: this capacity underpins the mechanism of generalization and helps explain how we may feel justified in generalizing from our apprehension of particular instances to fully general principles such as (UI). That is to say, recognizing that two instances share a form is non-inferential, recognizing that (UI) is a substitution instance of (UI_1) is non-inferential, but *arriving at* the general form for the first time is a product of inference – namely of generalization. Thus, on this picture, insofar as we may wish to speak of phases in adopting a logical principle, Padro's phases (1) and

190   *Corine Besson*

(2) are to be reversed. On this picture, there is a lot of reasoning that is in fact reasoning with instances of (UI) that proceed not from from the recognition that (UI) is valid to its application in reasoning but directly from apprehending instances as valid. Rather, (UI) is a by-product of generalizations underpinned by a capacity for pattern-recognition.

The same considerations offered here for (UI) hold of the issue of the adoption of (MP) and argument (V)–(VII) and of (&E) in argument (IX)–(XII). Concerning (MP), I can directly apprehend that (iii) follows from (i) and (ii). I do not need first to adopt (MP) and then to apply it in my reasoning. I can apprehend that the inference is valid directly. And then I can generalize over this insight. Such generalizations are underpinned by grasp of similarity. This may eventually yield full grasp and knowledge of (MP).

Finally, we can apply these considerations to Boghossian's Carrollian Circularity and argument (XVI*)–(XIX*). Rational insight can be an insight into the fact that (i) and (ii) entail (iii) – the recognition of that entailment need not proceed from an insight into (MP) first, from which the validity of (i)–(iii) is then inferred through the use of (UI) and (MP).

4. Closing Discussion: Internalism, Rule-Following, and Cognitivism

The general/particular circularity threat rests on faulty assumptions concerning both the relation between general principles and their instances and how we apprehend and justify general patterns and their instances. Where does this leave us with regard to internalism, rule-following and cognitivism?

Concerning internalism, and rational insight in particular, there is room for the view that rational insight provides justification for directly apprehended individual substitution instances in the vernacular as a ground for apprehension of general patterns of inference. This is at odds with Padro's and Boghossian's order of explanation. But my suggested order is both epistemologically and psychologically compelling and also avoids the general/particular circularity threat. Of course I have not here offered a defense of rational insight or internalism more generally, but merely suggested ways of developing them in a way that blocks a key objection – the general/particular circularity threat.[29]

Concerning rule-following, the view sketched here is not compatible with *characterizing* reasoning deductively as following logical rules in reasoning. In the closing remarks of his (2014), Boghossian suggests the following possibility as a way of addressing the general/particular circularity threat:

'A [p]ossible lesson of the present discussion [of rule-following] concerns the question of the generality of reasons. Particularism, the view that we act out of reasons that are particular rather than general, is

Logical Generality and Deductive Reasoning 191

increasingly influential in many quarters (see Dancy, 2004) for the moral case). The rule-following approach to reasoning would seem to militate against Particularism by claiming that our best prospects for making sense of reasoning sees us as guided by general rules of reasoning. I am not saying that this consideration by itself defeats Particularism in any specific domain, just that it poses a further challenge for it to overcome'.

(Boghossian, 2014, p. 18)

The view advocated here is not a form of particularism about reasoning. It does not spring from a kind of skepticism about there being valid principles such as (MP). For instance, it can assume that there are such general principles and also, as is commonly thought, that the kind of generality they display speaks to the essence of logic: logic is concerned with the most general truths and the most general facts of entailment. The view can moreover appeal to these general facts as grounds for the validity of their particular instances: to the metaphysical question of why (i)–(iii) is valid, we may well reply that this is because (MP) is valid. Crucial to the view is that this need not reflect a justificatory and psychological order. The general patterns need not come first in accounts of why I am justified in reasoning to (iii) from (i) and (ii) and of what it is for me to appreciate or know that (i) and (ii) entail (iii). The view can thus avoid both the pitfalls of rule-following (general/particular circularity threat) and of particularism (skepticism about general patterns).[30]

The proposed view can also vindicate Taking Condition of Section 2.2,[31] which is meant to capture the idea that reasoning is a rational activity. Indeed, Taking Condition is a principle about particular inferences, such as (i)–(iii). It thus can be satisfied by someone who, rather than applying a general rule, simply sees that this particular set of premises entails this particular conclusion and draws the conclusion for this reason.

Finally, concerning cognitivism, it should be clear by now that the view suggested is compatible with cognitivism. Cognitivism was meant to be the target of the general/particular circularity threat. This threat has been defused: we do not believe general principles first, that we then try to apply to instances in the vernacular through a hopelessly circular argument. We may thus know *that* the argument from (i) to (iii) is valid, know *that* (MP) is valid, and indeed know *that* that the former is a substitution instance of the latter. The combination of these beliefs leads to a general/particular circularity threat only when they are put in a certain explanatory order in accounting for our capacity for deductive reasoning. Obviously this is only a local defense of cognitivism since, as I suggested in the introduction, there are many more regresses and circularity threats, Carrollian or otherwise, for it to overcome.[32]

192 *Corine Besson*

Notes

1. I take reasoning (and, interchangeably, inferring) to be a kind of conscious intentional action. I also take the basic logical principles - principles not derived using other principles - to be those of classical logic, but nothing hangs on this.
2. See Boghossian (2000) for a review/discussion.
3. See Lewis Carroll (1895).
4. This line of thought goes back to Ryle (1945–1946) and his claim that knowing basic logical principles is (non-propositional) knowing how. I do not review here ways in which we may articulate the contrast between cognitivism and non-cognitivism within debates over the nature of knowledge how. See Besson (2018, 2019) for a discussion of non-cognitivist ways of addressing Carroll's Regress.
5. I will thus set aside epistemological questions and presuppose that the basic principles of logic can be known.
6. There are various ways of stating Modus Ponens and the other logical principles discussed in this paper: with propositional variables rather than schematic letters, as a normative principle rather than a fact of implication, as a more precisely stated symbolic principle rather than the informal one offered here, and so on. I will comment on this issue in Section 2.3 and emphasize that the argument of the paper does not rest on any particular formulation.
7. As I highlight in Section 3.2.2, discussions of this issue go as far back as Francis Bradley (1883).
8. According to Padro, one of Kripke's targets with (AP) is Quine's use of Carroll's Regress in the context of his attack on (Carnapian) conventionalism about logic (see Quine, 1936, p. 121). I will not focus on Quinean issues and whether either conventionalism, or Quine's further views on logic, can escape (AP). See Padro (2015, Ch.5) for discussion of such issues.
9. Kripke illustrates how (AP) arises for (UI) using the example: 'All ravens are black. Therefore: this raven is black' (see Padro, 2015, n.49). Since 'All ravens are black' is typically paraphrased as a universally quantified *conditional* statement, I prefer the example in the text, which is simpler.
10. Strictly speaking, this is not an application of (MP) – I take advantage here of the connection between an implication and its corresponding conditional. For simplicity, and in keeping with the literature reviewed here, I will use (MP) loosely in this way.
11. Her suggestion also seems to be at odds with Kripke's take on (AP): 'Kripke said in passing that UI is a nicer example, though he didn't say why and is now not sure about what he had in mind. Perhaps UI could be thought to be more basic, since MPP as a generally stated principle needs the inference pattern of universal instantiation to be of use: without it we wouldn't be able to conclude that a particular instance is a case of MPP. But this doesn't seem right, since UI also seems to require MPP'. (Padro, 2015, p. 39). I agree that (UI) is a 'nicer example' in that it holds the key to the adoption problem, but that might not be what Kripke had in mind.
12. Boghossian formulates Modus Ponens differently – using universally quantified variables for propositions, rather than schematic letters. He labels it (MPP) which I keep to distinguish from mine his formulation of what is essentially the same principle. I discuss his formulation in Section 2.3.
13. Boghossian uses a different instance of Modus Ponens and a different numbering for his argument. For convenience, I have harmonized with the example and numbering used so far.
14. Strictly speaking this charge does not apply: given that he construes rational insight as only applying to (MPP), it is no objection that justification for (i)-(iii) comes out as inferential. I do not pursue this here.

Logical Generality and Deductive Reasoning   193

15. These considerations apply equally to Boghossian's argument in (2014, p. 13) quoted in Section 2.2. There is nothing fatal in us having to grasp what the rule requires, form a view to the effect that its trigger conditions are satisfied, and draw the conclusion that we must now perform the act required by its consequent in order to apply a rule in reasoning. This seems fatal only as an explication of the very ability to do so.

16. For instance, Russell calls a schema a 'mere shell, an empty receptacle for meaning, not something already significant'. (1919, p. 157)

17. If (XVI*) were, like (XVI), stated as a conditional, it would say that: Any inference, if it is of the form P; if P, then Q ⊨ Q, it is valid. But stating that P; if P, then Q ⊨ Q is just stating that any inference of this form is valid; so (XVI*) would start looking a lot like: P → P.

18. There are debates over the coherence of absolute generality – of the notion that we can quantify over absolutely everything – mostly concerning the threats of paradoxes, especially Russell's Paradox. See Rayo and Uzquiano (2006) for a survey.

19. How exactly to interpret (UI) is a complicated matter, where a lot depends on how we interpret the individual constants. I cannot review here all the possible semantic interpretations that may be given of the individual constants (as schematic letters, as expressions which make arbitrary reference to objects, as expressions which refer to arbitrary objects, as expressions which indicate objects arbitrarily, as quantifiers of sorts, etc.). See Fine (1986) for an excellent discussion, and also Besson (2014).

20. There is little written about the status of substitution. Frege makes abundant use of substitution in his *Begriffsschrift* (1879) and it is clear that he does not think of it as an inferential step. Since then it seems to have become common not to think of substitution as an inferential step and to think of substitution rules as kinds of meta-rule of a logical system. See Lemmon (1965, p. 53ff.) and Corcoran and Hamid (2016).

21. See Cohnitz and Nicolai (ms) for a similar suggestion.

22. José Zalabardo (2011, pp. 130–131) offers a very interesting general proposal about how such types of capacities might work and be knowledge conducive. He takes us to be able to develop a kind of general non-inferential cognitive ability for 'feature or pattern recognition', that enables us to (fallibly) recognize generics such as 'colors, shapes, human faces, voices, accents, melodies, chord progressions, pictorial styles, grape varieties, grammatical sentences, friendly strangers, dangerous situations. . . . ' and of course valid inferences. While I do not have the space to discuss the proposal, it could be taken to offer a systematization of the picture sketched here.

23. Notice that this kind of circularity in justification is different from that which Boghossian is endorsing as justification for basic logical principles (see again Section 2.2). Goodman's has to do with the relation of general principles to its (vernacular) substitution instances. Boghossian's has to do with his project of justifying basic logical principles in terms of their relation to the meanings of the logical constants. See for instance his (1996).

24. However see my (2014) for a discussion of how certain types of existence assumptions and existential commitments may require us to treat the epistemology of vernacular substitution instances differently from that of general principles.

25. What Priest means here is that those intuitions may be overturned by our best theory about, say, the Liar Paradox, which might mean that certain inferences we find obvious are in fact not valid.

26. Indeed counterexamples or challenges have been offered to pretty much every standard basic logical principle. See for instance Putnam (1969), McGee (1985), Priest (1987), and Dummett (1993).

27. Priest (2016, p. 44). Priest writes these remarks in the different context of his defense of anti-exceptionalism about logic: the view that logic is not exceptional in its methods for justifying logical theories – it operates in much the same way as scientific disciplines.
28. Notoriously from Williamson (2003) and (2007).
29. Philosophers who appeal to rational insight typically want to underwrite the fact that logic is a priori – while Cook Wilson and Russell are not concerned with this issue, this is certainly the case for BonJour. This is in principle compatible with the rational insights operating on substitution instances in the vernacular, rather than on general patterns directly. Similarly, low-level generalisations over instances might well be taken to operate on a priori propositions, which could pave the way for the justification for general patterns such as (MP) that is consistent with their apriority.
30. One might wonder here how these considerations relate to Wittgenstein's famous discussion of rule-following in the *Philosophical Investigations* (1953, p. 185ff) offered as a criticism of the view that we (explicitly) know abstract general rules. On the view suggested here there is reasoning without rule-following; so trivially there can be indeterminacy about which rule is being followed in a particular case and trivially our reasoning behaviour in a particular case is consistent with any number of rules being followed. Following a rule on this view would be a by-product of reasoning with instances and not the result of simply grasping an abstract and general rule. There are issues to be addressed about which generalisations are right – which logical principles are the correct ones – and how we might be justified in thinking they are. This is a topic for another paper. But given that we are not presupposing that a rule has to be explicitly known prior to reasoning according to it, the view is not susceptible to Wittgenstein's criticism.
31. I am not here endorsing Taking Condition – simply pointing out its compatibility with the view offered here. See for instance McHugh and Way (2016) for criticisms of it.
32. Acknowledgements: Thanks to Bartłomiej Czajka, Julien Dutant, Anandi Hattiangadi, Bruno Jacinto, Carlo Nicolai, Gilad Nir, and Manish Oza for helpful comments/discussions on the topic of this paper. Thanks also to the audiences at the Formal Methods Seminar KCL and at the Munich LMU Centre for Mathematical Philosophy for great discussions. Special thanks to Anders Nes for extremely useful comments on the penultimate draft of this paper. This research was funded by the Bank of Sweden (for the Research Project: The Foundations of Epistemic Normativity (grant number P17–0487:1)) to whom I am very grateful.

References

Besson, Corine (2014). A Note on Logical Truth. *Logique et Analyse*, 57(227), 309–331.

Besson, Corine (2018). Norms, Reasons and Reasoning: A Guide Through Lewis Carroll's Regress Argument. In Daniel Star (Ed.), *The Oxford Handbook of Reasons and Normativity*. Oxford: Oxford University Press, 504–528.

Besson, Corine (2019). Logical Expressivism and Carroll's Regress. Philosophy, 86, 35–62.

Boghossian, Paul (1996). Analyticity Reconsidered. *Noûs*, 30, 360–391.

Boghossian, Paul (2000). Knowledge of Logic. In P. Boghossian & C. Peacocke (Eds.), *New Essays on the A Priori*. Oxford: Oxford University Press, 229–254.

Boghossian, Paul (2001). How Are Objective Epistemic Reasons Possible?. *Philosophical Studies*, 106, 1–40.

Boghossian, Paul (2003). Blind Reasoning. *Proceedings of the Aristotelian Society*, Supplementary Volume, 77, 225–248.

Boghossian, Paul (2014). What Is Inference?. *Philosophical Studies*, 169, 1–18.

BonJour, Laurence (1998). *In Defence of Pure Reason*. Cambridge: Cambridge University Press.

Bradley, Francis H. (1883). *The Principles of Logic*. Oxford: Oxford University Press.

Carroll, Lewis (1895). What the Tortoise Said to Achilles. *Mind*, 4, 278–280.

Cohnitz, Daniel, & Nicolai, Carlo. (ms). *How to Adopt a Logic*.

Cook Wilson, John (1926). *Statement and Inference*. Oxford: Clarendon Press.

Corcoran, John, & Hamid, Idris Samawi (2016). Schema. In Edward N. Zalta (Ed.), *The Stanford Encyclopedia of Philosophy*, <https://plato.stanford.edu/archives/fall2016/entries/schema/>.

Dummett, Michael (1993). *The Logical Basis of Metaphysics*. Cambridge, MA: Harvard University Press.

Fine, Kit. (1986). *Reasoning with Arbitrary Objects*. Oxford: Blackwell, Aristotelian Society Series.

Frege, Gottlob (1879). Begriffsschrift, Eine der Arithmetischen Nachgebildete Formelsprache des Reinen Denkens. Translated as Concept Script, a Formal Language of Pure Thought Modelled Upon That of Arithmetic, *S. by Bauer-Mengelberg*. In J. vanHeijenoort (Ed.), *From Frege to Gödel: A Source Book in Mathematical Logic, 1879–1931* (1967). Cambridge, MA: Harvard University Press.

Goodman, Nelson (1954). *Fact Fiction and Forecast*. Atlantic Highlands, NJ: The Athlone Press.

Lemmon, E. John (1965). *Beginning Logic*. London: Chapman & Hall.

McGee, V. (1985). A Counterexample to Modus Ponens. *The Journal of Philosophy*, 82(9), 462–471.

McHugh, Conor, & Way, Jonathan (2016). Against the Taking Condition. *Philosophical Issues*, 26(1), 314–331.

Nir, Gilad. (ms). *On Russell's Account of Inference*.

Padro, Romina (2015). What the Tortoise Said to Kripke: The Adoption Problem and the Epistemology of Logic. *CUNY Academic Works*. https://academicworks.cuny.edu/gc_etds/603

Padro, Romina (2016). Interview in the *Reasoner*, 10(9).

Priest, Graham (1987). *In Contradiction: A Study of the Transconsistent*. The Hague: Martinus Nijhoff. 2nd (extended) Ed. Oxford: Oxford University Press, 2006.

Priest, Graham (2016). Logical Disputes and the A Priori. *Logique et Analyse*, 59, 347–366.

Putnam, Hilary (1969). Is Logic Empirical?. In R. Cohen & M. Wartofsky (Eds.), *Boston Studies in the Philosophy of Science*, vol. 5 (pp. 216–241). Dordrecht: Reidel.

Quine, W. V. O. (1936). Truth by Convention. In O. H. Lee (Ed.), *Philosophical Essays for Alfred North Whitehead*. New York: Longmans, Green and Co., 90–124.

Rayo, Augustín, & Uzquiano, Gabriel (2006). Introduction. In Augustín Rayo & Gabriel Uzquiano (Eds.), *Absolute Generality*. Oxford: Oxford University Press.

196 *Corine Besson*

Russell, Bertrand (1903). *The Principles of Mathematics*. Cambridge: Cambridge University Press.

Russell, Bertrand (1919). *Introduction to Mathematical Philosophy*. London: George Allen and Unwin.

Ryle, Gilbert (1945–1946). Knowing How and Knowing That. *Proceedings of the Aristotelian Society*, 46 Reprinted in (1971) *Collected Papers*, vol. 2 (pp. 212–225). London: Hutchinson.

Williamson, Timothy (2003). Blind Reasoning. *Aristotelian Society Supplementary Volume*, 77(1), 249–293.

Williamson, Timothy (2007). *The Philosophy of Philosophy*, Oxford: Blackwell.

Wittgenstein, Ludwig (1953). *Philosophical Investigations*. G. E. M. Anscombe & R. Rhees (Eds.), G. E. M. Anscombe (trans.). Oxford: Blackwell.

Zalabardo, José (2011). Boghossian on Inferential Knowledge. *Analytic Philosophy*, 52, 124–139.

Part IV
Conscious Non-Demonstrative Inference

8 Fore- and Background in Conscious Non-Demonstrative Inference

Anders Nes

1. Introduction

Philosophical discussion of conscious, personal-level inference has often focused on simple deductions, with only a small handful of premises, like modus ponens.[1] Consciousness has, in this context, often been left as something of a global heading of the relevant inferences. Specifically, such questions as whether the different premises, or the conclusion, differently manifest in consciousness, or whether different notions, forms, or gradations of consciousness are apt for their respective characterization, have not been much explored. When philosophical discussion of inference has turned to unconscious cognition, the focus has often been on quite different, subpersonal processes. For example, it has been discussed whether the alleged unconscious inferences posited by some vision scientists to explain even low-level vision can qualify as genuine inferences.[2] In these cases, none of the premises and, in some cases, not even the conclusion of the alleged inferences would be consciously entertained or even available to consciousness. In this chapter, I will look at a class of inferences that seem to fall somewhere between simple explicit deductions and subpersonal inferential processes on dimensions relevant to consciousness, viz. at certain non-demonstrative inferences. These are personal-level. They proceed from a consciously noticed fact, or apparent fact, to a similarly entertained conclusion. Yet they seem also to be sensitive to a rich stock of background information, not all of which seems to be consciously present in quite the same way as certain more explicitly noted or considered elements of the thinker's overall perspective. These inferences suggest that consciousness can vary, in potentially interesting ways, across the body of assumptions from which a given conclusion is drawn

The relevant sort of inferences may, I will assume, be exemplified by such cases as:

> *Getting Irony* You overhear someone, known to be heading to a work retreat, casually remark that the evening will be spectacular. You are initially surprised, given what you assume to be to on their

agenda, your familiarity, such as it is, with their likings, views, and habits, the likely feelings of her addressees, etc. It dawns on you the intent must have been ironic.

Car Means Home As you approach your house a rainy Tuesday, you see your car parked outside. Drawing on what you know of your partner's travelling habits, use of modes of transportation in different weathers, etc., you infer she is at home.[3]

Joke Getting You are reading a New Yorker cartoon, showing two men at a bar, one of whom, with a flustered, puzzled expression, tells the other 'What I don't, like, get is how she, like, figured out I was, like, having an affair with the, like, babysitter'. Drawing on various knowledge concerning, e.g., the speech mannerisms of young adults, how intimacy may bring imitation, how this might be unself-conscious, the implications of having an affair and being found out, etc., you get what's funny about this joke.[4]

These exemplify, I shall assume, non-demonstrative inference. Thus, Car Means Home is not to be construed as a deduction from two assumptions to the effect that the car is parked outside, and that if the car is parked outside, my partner is at home (or that whenever the car is parked outside, my partner's at home).

The inferences are personal-level. They are attributable to you, not just to subsystems (though subsystems may of course have a role in explaining how and why they were drawn). Relatedly, they are in some sense conscious. You have some awareness of what you are thinking and why. In Getting Irony, for example, you are conscious of the remark as being ironically intended, and as being, probably, so intended since such-and-such activities, awaiting the speaker this evening, clearly would not be considered very exciting, given so-and-so features of the speaker and her addressees, and so forth. It is a familiar point, though, that the ease or readiness with which you can spell out your reasons, filling out the 'such-and-such's, 'so-and-so's, and so forth's, may vary across information you are relying on. In so far as this ease or readiness is an index of the extent to which, or the sense or manner in which, the information figures in consciousness, it raises the question in what ways consciousness extends among it.

That question is raised also by the commonplace distinction between what is at the forefront of one's mind versus what lingers only more towards the back of one's mind. Our examples invite description in these commonplace terms. In Getting Irony, say, it might be towards the fore of your mind that the speaker's work retreats are known heavily to feature Insanely Fun Team Building Activities. You also recall, perhaps a tad more dimly, that the speaker and her addressees have lately voiced appreciation for @NeinQuarterly. Quite a bit further to the back your mind may be found presumptions that begin to approximate to, say, Gricean maxims, such as the idea that that people would not seriously assert what they clearly would not be taken to believe. The latter does not seem to be entertained in the way the just-mentioned points are, even though you, at some level, know it, or something like it, to be true (at least assuming a broadly Gricean, or cognitivist, approach to pragmatics). The presumption would not strike you as an unfamiliar point, or simply as news, were it to be put to you.

More generally, personal-level non-demonstrative inferences seem not uncommonly to rely on a long tail of assumptions, where the latter differ in how salient or available they are. We could say a certain fore-v-background structure – or perhaps several such structures – hold(s) over them. What structures in consciousness do these correspond to?

The next section introduces a distinction between (comparatively simple) Boring and (more complex) Interesting Views of fore-v-background structures. Section 3 gestures at some motivations for Boring Views; Section 4 at reasons for thinking Interesting Views may nevertheless merit exploration. Sections 5 and 6 take stock of some promising resources for an Interesting View, from, respectively, Sebastian Watzl, and Terry Horgan, Matjaž Potrč, and various co-workers. Some remarks of Edmund Husserl's on what he calls the horizons of acts of consciousness are drawn on in Section 7. These remarks suggest, I argue, ways of refining the resources charted in the two preceding sections, in order thereby to overcome some difficulties or limitations noted in those sections. Section 8 finds support for the indicated Husserlian ideas in psychological work on gist or schema representations in perception and memory. That section also notes how a conscious role for gist or schema representations in cognition can be understood in terms of the idea that the phenomenology of thinking exhibits thematic unity (cf. Nes, 2012). Drawing on the picture emerging over Sections 5–8, Section 9 outlines an account of what I dub thematic gist in conscious inference. Section 10 concludes.

2. Two Views of Fore-v-Background Structures

What differences in consciousness do fore-v-background structures in inference correspond to? One might draw a rough and ready distinction between two types of view here.

The first are comparatively simple and boring – tendentiously, I dub them 'Boring'. Views of this sort think fore-v-background structures can be described quite simply by specifying, for the various assumptions relied on, whether they are phenomenally conscious, access conscious, or, alternatively, how easily they can be brought to mind. In somewhat more formal terms, such views may be said to distinguish three backgrounding relations (relations by which an assumption, B, may or may not be backgrounded to another, A, or equivalently A foregrounded to B), and hold that fore-v-background structures can be fully described by describing their instantiation. Assumptions, here, can be considered thought

202 *Anders Nes*

contents, corresponding to what is said by utterances. I will dub the three relations *generic phenomenal*, *access*, and *availability* backgrounding.

An assumption, B, is generically phenomenally backgrounded to another, A, if A is phenomenally conscious but not B. Now, it is disputed in what sense, if any, it is so much as possible for thought contents to figure in phenomenal consciousness.[5] 'Liberals' about cognitive phenomenology hold that thoughts, including their conceptual contents, can be partly constitutive of what things are like psychologically for a subject. 'Conservatives' by contrast limit phenomenal consciousness to lower-level sensory or affective phenomena – impressions or imagery of shapes or colours, bodily sensations, etc. –, denying that thought contents can be partly constitutive of one's overall phenomenal experience. It might be thought that, on a conservative view, no assumption can be generically phenomenally backgrounded to another, since no assumption can be phenomenally conscious. However, conservatives allow assumptions to figure in phenomenal consciousness as it were by proxy, in as much as they can be articulated verbally or can be associated with perceptions or imagery. Thus, a conservative might seek to define a non-vacuous generic phenomenal backgrounding relation, obtaining if A is so articulated or associated but not B. Tricky questions arise here, though. In just what detail, or with what degree of explicitness, need an assumption be elaborated in inner or outer speech to evade the relevant backgrounding? What sorts of association between an assumption and imagery suffice? I shall however have to leave these questions for another occasion, or for conservatives to ponder. The working assumption here will be a liberal view.[6]

An assumption, B, is *access* backgrounded to another, A, if A is subject to access consciousness but not B. Here 'access' is understood in an occurrent and not merely dispositional sense. The assumption is not merely accessible but accessed. There are various ways of spelling out what this involves more precisely. For present purposes, though, we may adopt what Carruthers (2015, p. 48) has described as 'the most widely endorsed notion of access-consciousness', according to which:

> [access] conscious states are ones that are generally, or globally, accessible to an extensive set of other cognitive systems, including those for forming memories, issuing in affective reactions, as well as a variety of systems for inference and decision making.
>
> (Carruthers, 2015, p. 48)

Finally, B is *availability* backgrounded to A to the extent that A is more readily brought to mind than B. This is, to be sure, a vague, multidimensional matter. The readiness for bringing something to mind can, plausibly, vary with the time, or the effort, or the nearness to hand of various apt cues, needed to bring the respective assumption to mind. The notion of 'bringing to mind' could be understood in terms of bringing

Conscious Non-Demonstrative Inference 203

to either phenomenal or to access consciousness. Evidently, then, availability backgrounding could, and ultimately should, be unpacked into several dimensions, which might turn out to vary independently. For the purposes of this chapter, I shall however skate over these complications, resting content with a rough-and-ready notion of how easily a certain assumption is brought to mind.

The three backgrounding relations thus roughly distinguished are likely to be interrelated. In so far as phenomenal and access consciousness go hand in hand, so do the correlative backgrounding relations. Depending on how availability is fleshed out, one or both of generic phenomenal or access backgrounding implies availability backgrounding, though not conversely. Boring Views hold, again, that fore-v-background structures are adequately described just by describing the instantiation of these relations.

The alternative type of views is, in comparison, complex and interesting – tendentiously, I call them 'Interesting'. They allow the three aforementioned backgrounding relations but hold that the story of their instantiation is not the full story of fore-v-background. Different Interesting Views may offer different proposals as to what remains to be said. It might be argued there are backgrounding relations *within* phenomenal consciousness, whereby two assumptions may both be phenomenally conscious, yet unequally 'prominent' or 'salient', where this does not amount simply to a difference in access or availability-to-access. It might be said that access consciousness itself is a graded matter, i.e. that two assumptions might both be accessed, but one more so than the other. Another line of thought here, to be developed in Sections 6 through 9, is that information can be backgrounded by being, as it were, 'nested' or 'condensed' into other, more foregrounded mental states, from which it can then be unspun or decondensed, in characteristic ways.

3. Boring Views

Boring Views are the default option, being simpler. Although rarely explicitly argued for, various dichotomies and associations are suggestive of such views.

As for dichotomies, we have the familiar, two-fold distinction between standing beliefs, more or less easily available to consciousness, and occurrent thoughts or judgements.[7] In so far as we operate merely in terms of this distinction, the status of an assumption in or for consciousness would be specified just by specifying to which of these two classes it belongs. Plausibly, being 'occurrent', in the relevant sense, may understood in terms of either phenomenal or access consciousness. This classification would thus amount to describing relations of generic phenomenal or access backgrounding.

204 *Anders Nes*

As for associations, conscious thought has been equated with, or restricted to, that to which one intellectually attends. Thus, Graham Oddie remarks that 'a belief is occurrent if it is the belief that you are consciously attending to' (Oddie, 2005, p. 240, cited from Crane, 2013). Michael Martin writes:

> In general, whatever we are prepared to call an object of thought – be it the things thought about, what one thinks about them, or the proposition one thinks in thinking these things – we can also take to be an object of attention. Conscious, active thought is simply a mode of attending to the subject matter of such thoughts.
>
> (Martin, 1997, p. 77)

Now, suppose such a view is combined with a view of attention on which attention gets devoted to at most a small number (three or four, say) of objects or chunks of information and where either no difference is posited in how attention gets devoted among these objects or chunks, or, at least, any such difference is not supposed to make for any counterpart difference in consciousness. This suggests a view on which, to specify the role of an assumption in or for consciousness, we need just to specify the following: whether it is among the few things attended to, and thus conscious (phenomenally or with regard to access); or else, how easily attention could be turned to it. That story would be within the genre of Boring Views.

Closely related arguments could be run in terms of the notion of working memory, or kindred notions of short-term memory capacities. The idea would be that thought is conscious (phenomenally or with regard to access) only if it is held in working memory, or maintained in some similar, short-term memory system.[8] Again, such systems are often assumed to have a low capacity limit, being restricted to about three or four chunks of information.[9] Suppose no difference is drawn with regard to how assumptions, activated in this system, figure in consciousness. That would suggest a view on which, to specify the role of an assumption in or for consciousness, we need just to specify whether it is activated in this system, or else how easily it could become so active. That story would, again, be within the genre of Boring Views.

No elaboration or evaluation of these lines of thought will be attempted in this chapter. I will rest content with gesturing towards some (mutually compatible) avenues along which a sympathizer with Interesting Views might seek out a response. First, it could be suggested that the evidence for the capacity limits on attention, or on working memory, only supports the weaker claim that correspondingly low limits apply, at least, to certain comparatively *foregrounded* elements or aspects of conscious thought. The evidence may not yet establish the stronger claim that such low limits apply to conscious thought *tout court*. Second, it might be

Conscious Non-Demonstrative Inference 205

proposed that information might be attended to, or be held in the relevant forms for short-term memory, in different ways, or to different degrees, where some of these differences make for or go along with a difference in how that information figures in consciousness. Section 5 returns to this idea. Thirdly, it could be argued there are certain interesting dynamics of consciousness, whereby information occurs to us in a manner revealing of, or indicative of, its status as partially filling out certain more schematic anticipations. These dynamics may be consistent with consciousness having a low capacity limit at any given moment, yet may be held to constitute an interesting form of backgrounding. Ideas in this territory are developed in Sections 6 through 9. Whether any of these avenues of response, or some others, will ultimately be successful must be left for another occasion. The emphasis of this chapter is on exploring promising resources for an Interesting View, not on defending such views against Boring ones.

4. Interesting Views, Why Bother?

Interesting Views are perhaps interesting, but why think we need the further complexity they bring? A key motivation comes, I think, from two connected reflections. On the one hand, conscious thought might seem to be, on occasion, rather rich its content. On the other, on some such occasions, the various ingredients of the richness might seem not to be grasped or entertained in quite the same way: in particular, they might seem to be unequal with respect to their prominence or salience.

To begin with the first point, concerning richness: it is a familiar observation that it may take quite a few words to spell out what one is thinking in a given situation. Even after having gone to some length attempting to articulate what one is thinking of, how one is thinking of it, etc., one might still have a sense there is more that could be said. One's thinking forms, it seems, a rather inclusive, multifarious, many-angled take on things.

The following passage from John Searle illustrates aspects of this richness:

> Sally looks at Sam and suddenly has a thought in a flash: 'That's it!' If asked to state the thought, she might begin, 'Well, I suddenly realized that for the past eighteen months I have been wasting my time in a relationship with someone who is totally inappropriate for me, that whatever its other merits, my relationship with Sam was founded on a false premise on my part. It suddenly occurred to me that I could never have an enduring relationship with the head of a motor-cycle gang like the Hell's Angels because . . .' And so on.

206 *Anders Nes*

> In such a case the immediate content tends to spill over, to connect with other thoughts that in a sense were part of the content but in a sense were not.
>
> (Searle, 1992, p. 137)

Let's suppose that, among the things Sally soon enough would say to fill out the ellipsis following 'because . . . ', is the thought that Hells Angels are associated with crime – dub this thought 'Crime'. Although Crime is in a sense part of what Sally is thinking, it is, Searle suggest, not entertained in quite the same way – it is not equally 'immediate' – as the first few things Sally is saying, such as, e.g., that she has been wasting eighteen months – dub the latter thought 'Wasting'. This exemplifies the second point, about the apparently unequal prominence or salience among the things of which one is thinking.

It is not clear how such a structure could be captured on Boring Views. We cannot do justice to it just by saying that Crime is availability backgrounded to Wasting. That feature would not distinguish Crime from myriad other thoughts that Sally very easily and quickly can retrieve, such as, say, the thought that her name starts with an 'S', that she lives in London, that London is the capital of the UK, etc. etc. None of the latter are in some sense on Sally's mind here the way Crime may seem to be. Nor can we do justice to the structure by saying that Crime, unlike Wasting, is neither phenomenally nor access conscious. First, it is (or so we shall suggest) at least not clear that Crime *is* entirely unconscious in both these senses. Second, if indeed it were unconscious in these senses, then that status would, again, be shared with myriad other unrelated thoughts not currently on her mind, and so not distinguish Crime from the latter. If, on the other hand, we say Crime is phenomenally and access conscious, nothing has yet been said to distinguish it from, say, Wasting.

Could it be that, whereas Wasting is both phenomenally and access conscious, Crime is one but not the other? Now, Crime does seem to be access conscious, at least on the earlier-cited criterion, formulated by Carruthers. After all, Crime is available to systems for introspection, in as much as it will be among the things Sally reports herself to be thinking. It is available to, and indeed used by, systems of inference. For example, Wasting may be supposed to occur to Sally as an inference drawn, in part, from Crime. Moreover, Crime can partly explain her affective reaction: her present flash of revulsion towards the relationship might issue from, let's say, a new-found, or newly intensified, antipathy towards crime, combined with Crime.[10]

If this is right, it leaves the option that Crime is access but not phenomenally conscious whereas Wasting is both. However, that status on Crime's part would not, arguably, distinguish it from various other ingrained beliefs or pieces of knowledge that seem to qualify as access conscious, in as much as they are regularly in use across several contexts, but seem not be distinctively or specifically relevant in this case. Consider such elementary beliefs as, say, that unsupported heavy objects tend to fall downwards, that one and one is two, that people typically can see what is in front of their open eyes, etc. These beliefs inform inferences, decisions, and emotional reactions in innumerable contexts. We will readily volunteer that we have these beliefs if the question arises. It is at least not clear why they should not qualify as access conscious in Sally's case. Yet they do not seem to concern what is currently flowing through Sally's mind in the way Crime does.

Second, and irrespective of the last point, it might be insisted Crime plays some, even if merely peripheral, role in Sally's experience of thinking – that it has some interesting manifestation in what it is like for her to be thinking as she is at the moment, even before she clearly articulates Crime, fleshing out the lacuna in 'I could never have an enduring relationship with the head of a motor-cycle gang like the Hell's Angels because. . . '. We may contrast Sally here with Sally*. In place of Crime, Sally* harbor thoughts of how Hell's Angels are given to noisy, swaggering pursuits. For Sally*, these thoughts combine with a dawning realization that calm and restful activities appeal so much more to her. Even before Sally* spells this out, the way in which her thoughts of Sam and HA are placed in a context not of crime but of noise and swagger might, arguably, make for a phenomenal difference with Sally. If this is so, it suggests Crime has some phenomenal role for Sally, if only a peripheral one.

These brief reflections are not, it goes without saying, intended to come even close to establishing Interesting Views as true. They are offered only to suggest grounds for thinking such views are at least worth exploring.

5. Attention as a Structure Within Consciousness

William James described the role of attention, or what he variously termed 'interest', in experience in terms of 'foreground' and 'background':

> [T]he moment one thinks of the matter, one sees how false a notion of experience that is which would make it tantamount to the mere presence to the senses of an outward order. . . . Without selective interest, experience is utter chaos. Interest alone gives accent and emphasis, light and shade, background and foreground – intelligible perspective, in a word.
>
> (James, 1890, p. 402, cited from
> Watzl, 2017, p. 183)

James's suggestion here is that inattention is a background *within* consciousness. Besides James, such views of attention and consciousness have been suggested inter alia by Husserl (1913/1983, §92) and Searle (1992, pp. 137–9). I shall here, however, focus on a recent account due

208 *Anders Nes*

to Watzl (2017), on which attention has the role of structuring mind, in general, and consciousness, in particular. Specifically, attention is viewed a process of prioritizing elements in one's mental life – of putting these elements in relations of priority to each other, whereby they together form what Watzl terms a 'priority structure'. The focus of attention corresponds to the content of the mental state with top priority (Watzl, 2017, pp. 70–114). In so far as the mental states prioritized relative to each other are conscious, the priority structure constitutes or entails what Watzl dubs a 'centrality structure'. This is a structure of conscious states related by a phenomenal centrality relation. The latter is the phenomenal counterpart or manifestation of priority relations (Watzl, 2017, pp. 183–210). Conscious states necessarily partake in the process of attention, Watzl argues, in that they necessarily enter into centrality structures. However, they may be relatively peripheral in that structure, their contents being relegated to a position far from the focus of attention (Watzl, 2017, pp. 251–282).

Now, let's say that B is inattentively backgrounded to A if B, like A, is consciously entertained but receives less attention than B and thereby is less prominent in consciousness than A; to put it Watzl's terms, attention renders A more central than B (though both are conscious). I am inclined to think, and will anyhow here assume, that there is such a relation as being inattentively backgrounded, and that it is apt to at least in part illuminate the structure of consciousness in conscious inference.

The question is how far it goes in this respect. As Watzl acknowledges, it does not, as it stands, capture a certain distinction within the less-than-focal aspects of one's state of mind that was stressed by Aron Gurwitsch (1964), and that arguably reflects a structure in conscious thought and inference. Consider Car Means Home. Here, we might suppose, the manifest presence of our car outside, and my concluding thoughts of my partner's being at home are comparatively central in my consciousness. Ideas about her working schedule, preferred methods of transportation in different weathers, likelihood of going out a walk or jog around this time of day, etc. are more peripheral though still, at some level, assumed in the case at hand. We may contrast these ideas with, say, various bodily or agentive experiences of mine as I am walking towards our house: the sense of my feet regularly touching the ground, the slight ache in my legs from walking up the hill, etc. These are also conscious, but not relevant to or bound up with my inference in quite the way my ideas of my partner's movement patterns are. Gurwitsch marked this putative difference by distinguishing my ambulatory sensations as 'marginal awareness' from my ideas of my partner's various habits as a 'thematic field'. Both differ from the 'theme', that is, from what is at the forefront of my awareness or most gripping on my attention. The thematic field, unlike the margin, is however experienced as somehow relevant to the theme. In as much as both thematic field and margin are inattentively backgrounded, that status does not distinguish between them.

One response here would be that there is no systematic difference in conscious character between margin and thematic field. It is just that we believe, or are disposed to believe, that items in the thematic field are relevant in a way in which the margin is not. Alternatively, or in addition: it is just that a certain conscious thought, viz. that of my partner's being at home, causally depends on the thematic field (henceforth simply 'field'), or is dispositionally connected with it (I would, e.g., sooner or later invoke ingredients from the field if pressed to explain my conclusion), in ways in which it does not depend on, or connect with, the margin.

Watzl however does not make this move, and I suspect he is right not to do so. Instead, he proposes to account for the field-v-margin distinction by identifying the field with a certain sub-form of the periphery of one's overall experience, dubbed the 'coloring and sustaining periphery', that is distinguished by a certain causal or counterfactual role vis-à-vis the center. Specifically, a part, Y, of one's overall experience is in the coloring and sustaining periphery of another part, X, if Y is peripheral to X (i.e. X is more central than Y) and the fact that this is so (i) affects the 'appearance properties' of X (this is the 'coloring' aspect) and (ii) sustains the comparatively central status of X, in the sense that, had not Y been peripheral to X, X would be less central to the overall experience (this is the 'sustaining' aspect) (Watzl, 2017, p. 200–1). Here 'appearance properties' are defined as those properties of a phenomenally conscious episode 'that contribute to the way an aspect of the world appears to the subject when she undergoes that episode' (Watzl, 2017, p. 160). Such properties plausibly include the intentional properties of the episode, although they are not necessarily limited to such properties. If we apply this account to Car Means Home, the idea, roughly, would be that the presence in the periphery of my thoughts of my partner's general travelling routines affect how I think or conceive of our car's and my partner's location, and sustain the comparatively central status of my thoughts of the latter things. My bodily sensations of walking up the hill in contrast lack such a role.

I worry, though, that the relevant causal or counterfactual dependence can be gotten by in too diverse ways in order adequately to capture Gurwitsch's distinction. Could it not be that because of more or less ingrained habits, or my general constitution, there are certain trains of thought, let's say about literary matters, that I am only able to pursue, or, at least, more prone to pursue, when comfortably seated? I now enjoy the tactile, proprioceptive, etc. experience as of being comfortably seated. My mind turns to a remark by a certain character in *Madame Bovary*. Bringing to mind, more or less peripherally, various earlier scenes and dialogues, it dawns on me that the remark was ironically intended. This conclusion would not have come to the fore of my mind without the experience of being comfortably seated. Indeed, the conclusion would, arguably, not have come to the fore without the seated-experience being merely peripheral: had the seated-experience been more central, it would have distracted me from ever reaching the conclusion. So the chair-experience would seem to be in the sustaining periphery of the conclusion. Does its presence in the periphery also affect the appearance properties of the more central part of my experience? Arguably, it does, for my central thought of the remark made by the relevant literary character would not have been to the effect that the remark was ironic – an intentional property of the thought, and so an appearance property thereof – had I not been comfortably seated as I am. Nevertheless, that comfortable experience seems merely marginal and no part of the thematic field. Called on to justify my conclusion, or, more loosely, to say what's been on my mind, I would not invoke these cushy feelings but rather my more or less dim recollections about the other passages of the novel.

The underlying problem is that the causal cum dispositional terms in which Watzl aims to separate field from margin seem to be insufficiently tightly linked with the content-dependent connections, of relevance versus non-relevance, that separate the distinct ways in which field and margin stand to the theme.

6. Chromatic Illumination and Looming Potentialities

Not much has been written in recent analytical philosophy on fore-v-background structures in conscious inference; in particular, not much that goes beyond alluding to the distinctions drawn in a Boring View. An exception, apart from Watzl, from this trend is the account of 'chromatic illumination' due to Horgan, Potrč, and various co-workers.[11] I will dub this team 'HPA'. They concentrate on conscious abduction. Adverting to the frame problem in AI, and Jerry Fodor's (1983) discussion of the Quinean and isotropic character of central cognition, they argue the rationality of abductive inference goes hand in hand with its sensitivity to broad ranges of information possessed by the thinker. Typically, they argue, much of this information is implicitly appreciated in drawing the inference. While not being at the forefront of awareness, it still in some sense registers in consciousness. Indeed, it is epistemically vital that it does, HPA argue. Its doing so explains how abductive inference can be rationally grounded from the thinker's point of view in a way that contrasts with, say, the brute seeming rightness of gut feelings.

Adopting a 'coloring' metaphor akin to Watzl's, HPA say background information 'chromatically illuminate' certain, more foregrounded pieces of information. The analogy is that of light sources affecting how a scene appears, without themselves being seen. When HPA proceed to cashing out this metaphor, they stress, first, that chromatically illuminating

Conscious Non-Demonstrative Inference 211

information is not 'explicit', and second, that it is associated with 'looming potentialities'. I shall address these two ideas in turn.

What do HPA intend by the claim that the relevant information is not explicit? One way of understanding 'explicitness' here would be in terms of the personal-level representational format of the relevant information. Thus, it might said that, other things equal, information A is present to one in a more explicit way than information B, if A is verbally articulated, or imagined, or rendered perceptually apparent in greater detail than B is. However, HPA does not have such a personal-level notion of explicitness in mind, but rather one defined by the representational format of the subpersonal processes that, on their view, implement sensitivity to such background information. That information is not explicit, they claim, in that it is not subpersonally represented through the tokening of LOT vehicles or similarly syntactically structured representations. Rather, they suggest it can be regarded as information implicit 'in the weights' of the connections among nodes of neural network (cf. Henderson and Horgan, 2011, p. 224).

However, this conception of the subpersonal systems implementing conscious abduction seems, all by itself, to tell us rather little about how (if at all) implicit information manifests in consciousness. Notoriously, a network can give correct classifications or predictions, given such-and-such inputs, without it being clear, to its designers or to theorists analyzing it, just how it goes about doing it.[12] In such cases, it is far from clear why the information associated with its weights should be any more readily available to an agent for whom the relevant network constitutes parts of her cognitive architecture. To be sure, the burgeoning research on neural networks contain various streams of work on how networks can be structured so as to make the grounds for their classifications (to put it loosely) more apparent.[13] However, the need for some special design here underscores the point that information attributable to the weights in a network system need not, absent special designs, be a readily available matter. This is not to say, of course, that HPA are wrong about the subpersonal architecture, just that the notion of inexplicitness, glossed in these terms, does not seem all that revealing of how the relevant assumptions figure in or for consciousness (a claim with which HPA may well agree).

The second way in which HPA spell out what it is for some background information to chromatically illuminate more foregrounded considerations invokes the suggestive phrase of 'looming potentialities'. Concerning the case of Joke Getting, they write:

> One's appreciation of implicit background information manifests itself experientially, in part, via an aspect of 'looming potentialities' concerning the joke, viz., *a sense that one could*, if suitably prompted by others or by oneself, manifest one's appreciation of

212   *Anders Nes*

such information – in overt linguistic behavior, and/or by explicitly bringing such information to mind in one's conscious thought. One kind of looming potentiality, for example, is *the capacity* to spontaneously arrive at consciously explicit answers to suitable background-probing questions. (Roughly how old is the babysitter? Who is the 'she' who figured out that the guy is having the affair with babysitter? Etc.)

(Horgan and Potrč, 2010, p. 166; my italics)

Here, and elsewhere in HPAs writings, there are pointers towards different interpretations of looming potentialities. On a deflationary construal, they consist in a capacity to use such-and-such information in so-and-so ways, e.g., to answer certain questions. On a more inflationary interpretation, they consist in a *sense of* such a capacity.

The deflationary interpretation seems too deflationary. The capacity to bring information consciously to mind so at so answer questions bearing on that proposition, or on logically related propositions, it is not specific to background information relevant to the foregrounded conclusion at hand. As noted earlier in Section 4, any old proposition known very well and easily recalled meets that condition. Besides, the inflationary interpretation seems a better fit for the phrase 'looming potentiality', suggesting as the latter does that there is not (merely) a potentiality but one that 'looms'.

How, though, is the posited 'sense of capacity' to be construed, more precisely? One, rather natural, way to go here is to construe the 'sense of. . . ' idiom as patterning with 'thought of. . . ', 'idea of. . . ', etc. That is to take the phrase 'sense of capacity' as purporting to refer to an intentional state of some sort, where the expression following 'of' specifies its intentional content. The sense of capacity would, then, be a mental state intentionally directed at a certain capacity. Yet what would its intentional content be, more precisely?

One might think its content would be, quite simply, that one has the capacity to bring out the relevant as-yet-unarticulated considerations. After all, the intuition we are supposed to capture here, or so one might think, it not just that we have a sense of a capacity to do *something or other* with the inference at hand – translate it into another language, commit it to memory, write it down, or what have you – but that one can spell out, or somehow make clear, that the conclusion holds because certain (as yet unarticulated) considerations. HPA indeed stress the content specificity of chromatic illumination:

[T]he 'getting it' aspect of experience is not some generic feature, such as experiencing oneself laughing or inclined to laugh (perhaps without knowing why). Rather, it is quite content-specific: some particular item(s) of explicitly conscious content (in this case, what the

Conscious Non-Demonstrative Inference 213

guy at the bar is saying, and his obvious consternation) is appreciated as funny by virtue of how those explicitly conscious items are relevantly interconnected with a rich body of pertinent background information. Thus, all those *specific* items of background information are implicitly present in the conscious joke-getting experience, by virtue of the *specific* way that the experience is chromatically illuminated.

(Horgan and Potrč, 2010, pp. 164–165;
original italics)

Suppose, then, that the sense of capacity, in Joke Getting, includes a sense that one could, upon the question of the age of the babysitter being raised, make clear that she is a teenager, where this presumed fact about her age – dub it Teenager – is among one's background assumptions. Teenager, then, turns out to be part of the intentional content of the mental state that is, or constitutes, the sense of capacity.

Yet how is Teenager represented, by virtue of being part of the intentional content of the relevant mental state? If the sense of capacity represents (inter alia) Teenager in a way that is attentive or explicit or otherwise associated with foregrounded assumptions, we would expect the wrong prediction, viz. that Teenager is foregrounded. On the other hand, if it is represented in a way, call it W^B, apt to make for backgrounding, the question arises just what way this is. Recall that a sense of capacity was invoked precisely to account for how assumptions, such as Teenager in Joke Getting, can be implicitly, yet in some sense nevertheless consciously, appreciated in inference, figuring in a backgrounded way. If we invoke a sense of capacity to account for the way, W^B, in which the sense of capacity to offer Teenager if so-and-so queried presents Teenager, we clearly risk vicious circularity or regress. If, on the other hand, we offer some other story of W^B, including, as a limiting case, a view of W^B as a theoretical primitive in the characterization of consciousness, why could we not invoke W^B directly in accounting for how Teenager and kindred assumptions are entertained? To posit a sense of capacity, in which Teenager is represented as part of a representation of what one has a capacity to make clear, would then seem to be a complicating maneuver not clearly called for.

These considerations suggest that, if invoking a sense of capacity is to account for a certain backgroundedness, other than mere inattentiveness, enjoyed by such assumptions as, say, Teenager in a case like Joke Getting, and the sense of capacity is indeed an intentional state, then that state better not be construed as including Teenager as part of its intentional content. How, then, is it to be construed? Could it be simply *de re* with respect to the underlying capacity? That is to say: could it take the form of a sense that one has *this* capacity, where the capacity thereby referred to *is* in fact a capacity to offer (inter alia) Teenager, if so-and-so

214   *Anders Nes*

queried, although it is not *represented* as such? That proposal however seems to offer no account of how a suitable sort of specificity is secured. Although the capacity referred to *is* the specific capacity it is, nothing as yet accounts for how it is that it shows up mentally in some suitable, relevant way, given this *de re* state. Consider the following analogy. A person you are seeing may well *be* your old, red-haired, snub-nosed friend. If that is all we know, however, it is left open whether you are seeing him up-close and recognizably, or in the distance, at dusk, from behind, neither visibly red-haired, sub-nosed, nor even vaguely familiar to you.

Another way of downplaying the specificity of the sense of capacity, not going down the route of *de re*, is as follows. The sense of capacity represents, it might be said, merely a capacity to defend, or anyhow spell out, the inference, leaving open in terms of just what considerations the defense or articulation will proceed. This may seem too unspecific, though. Recall our contrast between Sally and Sally* in Section 4. They both conclude that they have been wasting many months on Sam, for he is a HA member, and. . . . For Sally, thoughts of the criminality of HA would fill out the lacuna; for Sally*, thoughts of their noise and swagger. Part of the motivation for Interesting Views was the notion that this difference in background assumptions might go with a difference in their overall cognitive experience. If their different assumptions show up merely as a sense that they could spell out why Sam has been a waste, we have not captured this difference. If, on the other hand, we take their respective senses of capacity to include the distinct specific considerations in terms of which they would spell out the inference, we are back with the dilemma pointed out two paragraphs earlier.

In view of these difficulties, one might question whether our step of construing the sense of capacity as an intentional state was a misstep. Perhaps the 'of. . . ' in 'sense of capacity' should be taken to pattern with 'sense of joy', 'experience of grief', or 'feeling of despair'. On this construal, the phrase following 'of' serves to classify the mental state in question, but not because it refers to or expresses part of an intentional content attributable to that state.[14]

A parallel worry of specificity arises, however. If the sense of capacity is a non-intentional state – a raw feel, if you wish – we still need to ask how these feels can and do vary. If they are comparatively generic, being, say, common to Sally and Sally*, they do not allow us to draw the distinction we wanted. What about the proposal that these feelings are, instead, highly specific, coming in myriad different flavors corresponding to the different specific background assumptions on which one might be relying? While this proposal avoids the problem for the intentional construal, viz. of embedding the very background assumptions as the intentional content of the feeling, it commits us to a faintly baroque duplication in the mind. Not only can one entertain myriad different contents, such as Teenager: one can also feel in myriad subtly different ways that, while

Conscious Non-Demonstrative Inference   215

they somehow correspond to or are correlated with contents, remain raw feels and are not intentionally directed accordingly. At the very least, it is worth considering whether such a baroque view could be avoided.[15]

7. Husserl on Horizon

HPA's descriptions of how background aspects in conscious thought manifest as 'looming potentialities' recall Husserl's account of what he called the 'horizon' of an act of consciousness. In one of his summary presentations of this aspect of consciousness, Husserl writes:

> Every subjective process has a process 'horizon' . . . – an intentional horizon of reference to potentialities of consciousness that belong to the process itself. For example, there belongs to every external perception its reference from the 'genuinely perceived' sides of the object of perception to the sides 'also meant' though not yet perceived, but only anticipated.
>
> (Husserl, 1933/1960, p. 82)

The horizon of an act of consciousness, as Husserl conceives it, illustrates inattentive backgrounding, as attention is not yet drawn to things that are as yet 'only anticipated'.[16] More to the present point, his view of horizons connects with HPA's views for two reasons. First, although Husserl's paradigm example of horizons in consciousness are from vision – specifically, the implicit sense that there's more to be seen of a chunky object in view before us than what is manifest from our present viewing angle – he takes possession of a horizon to be a feature of any conscious process, which for him includes thinking. Second, and more specifically, there is a striking kinship between HPA's talk of 'looming potentialities', and of our having 'a sense of capacity', and Husserl's phrase 'reference to potentialities of consciousness'. As for HPA on looming potentialities, a distinction can be drawn here between a deflationary and an inflationary construal of Husserl's turn of phrase. One the deflationary reading, the key point is that *there are* certain further potentialities of consciousness associated with an actual conscious process. On the inflationary construal, the key point is not (only) that there are these potentialities, but that something about the actual process or act of consciousness ensures that there is therein 'reference to' (*Verweisung auf*) these potentialities.[17] The questions how such a 'reference' should be understood (as a case of intentional directedness to the things referred, as a raw feel, or something else?), and, in particular, its degree of specificity, thus arises also with regard to Husserl's notion.

Now, out of Husserl's wide-ranging reflections concerning horizon, developed over decades, I shall here rest content with highlighting two putatively central suggestions, that seem helpful in connection with our

216   *Anders Nes*

present concerns. The first has to do, roughly, with what happens when something anticipated comes to pass. Husserl writes that accounts of the horizon of acts of consciousness bring out

> not only the actual but also the potential subjective processes, which, as such, are 'implicit' and 'predelineated' in the sense-producing intentionality of the actual ones and which, when discovered, have the evident character of processes that explicate the implicit sense.
>
> (Husserl, 1933/1960, p. 85)

Husserl's claim about the certain 'evident character' here concerns, in the first instance, the phenomenological inquirer who 'discovers' the relevant features of consciousness. When this inquirer succeeds in linking such-and-such potential conscious acts to so-and-so actual ones, the former will, for her, have that evident character of explicating something implicit in the latter. However, since this inquirer is supposed to discover this through first-personal reflection on (including sympathetic imagination of) the conscious acts or processes in question, one might read Husserl as suggesting that at least some analogous sort of 'evident character' applies to the underlying acts of consciousness reflected upon. If you are seeing what strikes you as uniformly white football, then the experience of seeing more uniform whiteness upon spinning it around, or walking around it, will have a certain 'evident character of making explicit' something implicit in your prior experience. Presumably, this 'evident character' is at least akin to a sense of expectation-fulfilmet upon finding what one anticipated or was on the look-out for.[18]

This idea offers help with the problem, noted at the end of the last section, of suitably distinguishing between Sally's and Sally*'s conscious inference. As we saw, the suggestion that they each have a (fairly unspecific) sense of a capacity to spell out the grounds for their conclusion does not differentiate between them. Yet suppose the relevant capacity is triggered, thanks to a query after the grounds. If thoughts of HA's criminality come to the fore for Sally, they will (the suggestion goes) have a character of making explicit something as yet implicit. If, on the other hand, thoughts of HA's noise and swagger drew her attention, they would lack such a character (though Sally might, of course, still accept them as true). For Sally*, meanwhile, vice versa. Even if the capacity is not triggered, there is a dispositional difference between the two thinkers here that, arguably, helps account for the difference in their conscious thinking.

I am inclined to think there is a dispositional difference of this sort, and that it has a role to play in the story of how Sally and Sally* differ in their conscious inferential thinking.[19] I am less sure, though, whether it is the full story. It is tempting to think that there also is, or at least might well be, a more occurrent, more-than-merely-dispositional difference between them.

Conscious Non-Demonstrative Inference 217

The second aspect of Husserl's account of horizon to which I will draw attention provides clues, I think, for a way in which they can differ, a clue having to do with the degree of specificity in the 'reference to potentialities' of consciousness. Husserl underscores that horizons are characterized by a certain indeterminateness.[20] For example, the perception of a die, from a given angle

> leaves open a great variety of things pertaining to the unseen faces; yet it is already 'construed' in advance as a die, in particular as colored, rough, and the like, though each of these determinations always leaves further particulars open. This leaving open, prior to further determinings (which perhaps never take place), is a moment included in the given conscious- ness itself; it is precisely what makes up the 'horizon'.
>
> (Husserl, 1933/1960, p. 82)

The indeterminateness is comparative: the intentional content of certain anticipations that characterize the horizon is less determinate than the content of some (as yet merely potential) intentional states that correspond to these anticipations. For example, a perception of the backside of the die (as yet a mere potentiality) would give a more detailed and specific presentation of its color, roughness, and so forth, than what is represented regarding these features already at the level of the horizon. Likewise, in conscious non-demonstrative inference, a horizon here would be expected to provide a more indeterminate and generic indication of the considerations in terms of which the inference could be spelled out, and which the thinker may be disposed sooner or later to offer, than the contents of those considerations themselves.

Is there reason to think such comparatively indeterminate representations are in play, in anything like the way suggested by Husserl? The next section finds support thereof in psychological work on gist or schema representations in perception and memory.

8. Gist in Perception and Memory

Our somewhat indeterminate sense of the die's backside, in seeing it from a certain angle, exemplifies what Husserl distinguished as the 'inner horizon' of our perception of that object. That it so say that it has to do with the perceived object itself more than its relations to its surroundings. Our perception also has, Husserl argues, an 'outer horizon': a similarly indeterminate sense of the object's setting (cf., e.g., Husserl, 1948/1973, §8; Smith, 2003, p. 75–79). Thus, in a typical case, the die would be perceived to be resting on an approximately even surface such as table (as opposed to, say, hovering mid-air, as soap bubble might); be located in a furnished room (as opposed to an unfurnished one); be

218   *Anders Nes*

indoors (as opposed to outdoors); be in a built environment (as opposed to a natural scene).

The idea that vision involves such fairly generic representations of setting that objects before us inhabit is, as it turns out, susceptible of experimental confirmation. Work on so-called gist perception indicates that vision provides representations of the overall gist, or generic type, of the scene before our eyes, of varying degrees of specificity, such as its being, say, an office, a room, indoors, a built environment, and so on.[21] Gist representations are extracted very quickly. Interestingly, they seem not asymmetrically to depend or merely supervene on the perceptual segregation and representation of the individual objects making up the scene. This recalls Husserl's view of outer horizons as at least coeval with, and not merely a consequence of, the perception as of determinate individual objects, of various sorts, making up the scene. Moreover, gist representations themselves require little attention, but play a role in directing attention within the scene.

While recent experimental work on gist perception is, in these regards, congenial to some important Husserlian views on outer horizon, there is to be sure the important difference that Husserl purports to be describing conscious experience while recent experimental work on gist perception tends to prescind from claims about consciousness. However, Fish (2013) and Bayne (2016) have recently argued, I believe plausibly, that gist representations can, and often do, figure as aspects of the phenomenal character of perception.

The idea that we form an impression of the gist, or generic type, of scenes before our eyes was much stressed by the psychologist Frederick Bartlett:

> Suppose an individual to be confronted by a complex situation. . . . [I]n this case an individual does not normally take such a situation detail by detail and meticulously build up the whole. In all ordinary instances he has an over-mastering tendency simply to get a general impression of the whole; and, on the basis of this, he constructs the probable detail. Very little of his construction is literally observed and often, as was easily demonstrated experimentally, a lot of it is distorted or wrong so far as the actual facts are concerned. But it is the sort of construction which serves to justify his general impression.
> (Bartlett, 1932, p. 206)

The content of the 'general impression of the whole' here corresponds to the content of a gist representation. Such impressions not only play a role in perception, Bartlett argues, but also, importantly, in memory, where they influence what is recalled. For example, when later trying to recall a story apt to strike one, generically, upon first hearing it, as concerning a battle, one would, other things equal, be more likely to recall – or

Conscious Non-Demonstrative Inference 219

misrecall – certain weapons being used (as one would typically expect to be in a battle) than one would be to remember such putatively irrelevant points of information as the names of the protagonists (Bartlett, 1932).

Several studies on memory, from the 1970s onwards, have supported this point. Taking over a term, 'schema', of Bartlett's, although recasting its theoretical content, these studies posit, under that label, comparatively generic representations of various categories, representations that include, or are linked with, a cluster of tacit expectations of what would typically be go together with the category in question. Thus, a schema for office might include the expectation that it is an indoor space, with desks and chairs, computers, books or papers. Having been presented with a scene apt to trigger this schema, subjects are, other things equal, more likely later to recall it – or misrecall it – as containing schema-related objects of the noted sorts than they are to recall such schema-unrelated objects as, say, a rug on the floor (Brewer and Treyens, 1981; Webb, Turney, and Dennis, 2016). In a similar vein, studies of how classic experiments are reported in the scientific literature, or described by working scientists in the relevant areas, suggest that the findings of these experiments are recalled as skewed in direction of what one expect an experiment stereotypically to deliver (Vicente and Brewer, 1993). These findings fit broadly with the picture Bartlett outlines when he suggests that much, if not all, of the 'probable detail' recalled is served up through an unconscious, constructive process, geared at yielding an overall recollection wherein that detail 'justifies' or, as Bartlett (1932, p. 207) also puts it, 'satisfies' or 'fortifies' the general impression.

As in perception, there is evidence that such schematic, or gist-directed, representations in reasoning and recall require little attention. Subjects are more easily distracted, resulting in poorer performance, in tasks requiring more specific, detailed representations than in those apt to be solved in terms of gist representations (Abadie, Waroquier, and Terrier, 2016).

Again, as in the case of perception, work on schematic or gist-directed representations in memory and reasoning since the 1970s has largely prescinded from claims about consciousness. Bartlett, however, stressed the conscious dimensions of recall. Elaborating on 'the general impression of the whole' posited in the passage quoted earlier, he writes:

> Ask the observer to characterise this general impression psychologically, and the word that is always cropping up is 'attitude' . . . . The construction that is effected is the sort of construction that would justify the observer's 'attitude'. Attitude names a complex psychological state or process which it is very hard to describe in more elementary psychological terms. It is, however, as I have often indicated, very largely a matter of feeling, or affect.
>
> (Bartlett, 1932, p. 206–7)

220 *Anders Nes*

To illustrate, Bartlett says one's 'attitude', in recalling a story, might be characterized by a feeling or sense of the story to be recalled as being 'exciting', 'adventurous', 'like what I read when I was a boy' (1932, p. 207) or meriting some similar, fairly generic label.[22]

In earlier work, I have argued that conceptual content contributes to the conscious character of thinking by providing its thematic unity.[23] For example, suppose you are thinking of a certain school you are contemplating attending. This will not, typically, be not (just) an experience of visualizing such-and-such constellations of shapes and colours (ones typical of school buildings, classrooms, teachers, etc.), having so-and-so phonological strings floating through one's mind (intoning, say, what happens to be the name of the school, or the courses one will be taking), having various ticklish, nervous or excited sensations in one's stomach, etc. In so far as one's thinking implicates such imagery or sensations they are not, typically, experienced as not having anything to do with one another. Rather, in such an episode, the sensory-affective contents would typically be felt to revolve around a common subject matter or theme, viz. one provided by the conceptual content of one's thinking, such as, in this case, a content along the lines of *what would going to this school be like?*

In that earlier work, it was left open how overarching or specific the relevant thematic-unity-providing conceptual contents would be. It is plausible to think, however, that episodes of thinking can have overlapping unities of subject matter, at different levels of grain. Consider the experience of comprehending a story of a Sunday outing. This cognitive episode might be unified overall as concerning a trip to the beach. At more fine-grained levels, it might be unified as having to do with, first, the drive to the beach, then a struggle of parking the car, then finding a place to put up a tent, etc.[24] In such a case, the more fine-grained unities would, typically, be experienced as filling in details of the more coarse-grained, overarching thematic unity. Plausibly, the sense of the detail as 'filling in' an outline here is akin to the feature of recollection alluded to by Bartlett, when he says the detail justifies, satisfies, or fortifies one's general impression.

I will propose, then, that Bartlett's 'attitudes' illustrate, with regard to the content of the 'general impression' they convey of what is there to be recalled, a special case of thematic unity, provided by conceptual content. In particular, it is a case thereof where the unity is of the fairly generic, coarse-grained nature typical of schemas. I will refer to this special case of thematic unity as 'thematic gist'. The next section outlines a role for such thematic gist in conscious inference.

9. Thematic Gist in Conscious Inference

Conscious inferences are, I will assume, conscious in at least the following respects. The conclusion of the inference, C, is consciously entertained,

Conscious Non-Demonstrative Inference   221

as are at least some of the grounds from which C is inferred. Label the grounds so entertained 'G'. Moreover, the subject has some sense, notion, or 'grip', at the level of consciousness, of the relevant grounds G as bearing a suitable support or implicational relation to C.[25] To fix ideas, I will assume the latter relation takes the form of natural meaning, in the sense of Grice, in the cases where the conclusion is categorically endorsed on the basis of the relevant grounds.[26] However, nothing will hang on this choice among candidate support or implicational relations.

The sense of G as meaning (/implying/supporting/. . .) C can, I will propose, go along with, or take the form of, a certain sense of how or why G means C. One's grip on G, C, and their interrelations, can be such that one has a feeling of G as *elucidably* meaning C. To get a rough idea of the kind of 'feeling' or 'sense' at issue here, it may be useful to contrast the non-demonstrative inferences we have been considering with a simple, basic and immediate deductive inferential step. Consider, say, a conjunction elimination inference, from the presumed fact that P and Q to the conclusion that P. Here, if faced with the question how or why the presumed fact that P and Q means that P, one would typically find oneself, straight off the bat, drawing a blank. At least at first blush, one would typically be at a loss for what if anything that even could elucidate how or why this is so.[27] Conscious non-demonstrative inferences are, it seems, typically quite different. In finding the presence of my partner's car outside to mean that she's at home, in Car Means Home, I seem to be alive to the possibility of spelling out or elucidating how or why this is so. I may not already consciously entertain the specific answers I potentially could articulate. I may not already consciously have in mind, even in an inattentive way, such specific assumptions as, say, that she tends to take the car if going out, at least until around mid-to-late afternoon, and at least if it is raining or rain threatens (which it does). However, I might, and perhaps not uncommonly do, already entertain an idea of the gist or drift of these considerations. This gist is one that I could, perhaps, give voice to in some such words as 'The car's being there means she's at home – because, you know, her habits of getting around, and the weather', or perhaps something even more schematic as '. . . because, you know, her habits'.

More generally, then, one could be said to have a sense of G as meaning C, elucidably, viz., along the lines of H. Otherwise put: one could be said to have a feeling of G as meaning, because of H, C. Here, 'H' holds the place for a schema or gist representation, adverting to the drift of a possible elucidation. In Husserlian terms, H predelineates certain further thoughts, spelling out how or why G means C. What fills the place of H are as it were keywords dimly plastered in consciousness.

Having such a sense or feeling would, at least typically, involve or manifests in a disposition, upon the question arising how or why G means C, not only to venture to explain (to oneself or others) that this is so because

222 *Anders Nes*

of such-and-such considerations, H*, having to do with H, but also to find such considerations, when brought consciously to mind, as fitting in with the already assumed gist, H. To speak with Bartlett, the considerations H* occur to one as 'justifying', 'fortifying', or 'satisfying' H. To speak with Husserl, they have 'the evident character' of explicating the anticipated theme.

Such a disposition might be finkish (or, to be precise, 'reverse cycle' finkish, cf. Lewis, 1997): raising the question how G means C might prompt one to reconsider whether G means C at all, or whether, in so far as it does, it has anything to with H.[28] Also, it is a good question to what extent one needs to be able to offer considerations H* that are appreciably more specific or detailed than H itself. Perhaps all one is able to offer, at least in any outwardly articulated way, in a case where Car is taken to mean Home because of travelling habits, would be something like: 'Well, you know, because of the way she tends travel around'. This would effectively amount to a restatement rather than an elaboration of H. However, even in this case, there would, typically, be an awareness of the potential for more to be said about these travelling habits, of relevance to the question at hand, even though one might not succeed in readily articulating these matters or clearly recalling it from memory. This is another reason not simply to reduce the sense or feeling of G as elucidably, viz. along the lines of H, meaning C, to a disposition to offer specifications of H.

What does the view thus outlined imply for fore-v-background structures in conscious non-demonstrative inference? If the generic, gist-like representations, playing the role of H, are a case of thematic gist in the phenomenology of thinking, they partially constitute the phenomenal character of one's thinking. They would, then, not be generically phenomenally backgrounded. However, in as much as such representations demand little attention, they may be expected to be inattentively backgrounded to other aspects of one's inference, such as the conclusion, or certain salient grounds. In proposing that inattention may leave aspect of one's mental life conscious, though peripherally so, the view is, of course, in line with Watzl's picture. However, it offers another account of how these generic representations differ from mere marginal awareness. They differ from the margin not, or not merely, thanks to the causal cum dispositional properties Watzl adverts to in his account of the coloring and sustaining periphery, but because their conceptual content provides a gist – a form of overarching thematic unity – that subsumes, in a putatively illuminating way, the conclusion reached along with any more foregrounded reasons, as well as further information that the subject may be disposed to provide to elaborate the gist in question.

The outlined account agrees with that of HPA in holding that conscious non-demonstrative inference has an aspect well captured by their suggestive phrase 'looming potentialities'. The account seeks a balance between too much and too little specificity in the 'looming'. On the one hand, the

Conscious Non-Demonstrative Inference   223

content of the specific considerations that the thinker, typically, can spell out does not loom to her; on the other, it is not left entirely open what their content might be: their gist, or drift, is what looms. The word 'looming' connotes something approaching, impending, or similarly future-directed, an orientation explicit in Husserl's characterization of horizons as involving a certain anticipation. The role gist-representations have been found, by Bartlett and later researchers, to play in recall fits in with their having a future-directed character, in so far as the representations figure in an 'attitude' felt as playing a role in setting up and controlling the process of retrieving further details from memory. Even if no such further details are immediately forthcoming from the process, it is of a piece with their figuring for in the manner of keywords that there is an awareness as of there being at least the potentiality of such further details turning up.

The more specific considerations, H*, spelling out H are indeed availability backgrounded. However, unlike myriad well-known familiar facts that putatively are not at all on one's mind in the situation at hand – what one's name is, where one lives, whether cars typically weigh more than bicycles, etc. etc. – they are not *merely* so backgrounded. For one thing, they fall under a gist consciously entertained. For another, the thinker is disposed, by virtue of entertaining that gist, to experience them as filling in that gist, upon their consciously coming to mind. We may say, just to put a label on it, that they are condensed-into-gist backgrounded.[29]

How pervasive is thematic gist, and the just-outlined correlative fore-v-background structures, in personal-level non-demonstrative inference? I have not sought to establish it is universal or even widespread. The aim, rather, has more been to articulate a possible structure of consciousness, one that fits with, or at least is in the spirit of, independently plausible phenomenological claims, and that draws on well-attested psychological mechanisms. The phenomenological claims include the idea that attentiveness can make for a fore-v-background structure within phenomenal consciousness; that an important aspect of our consciousness of things, at least often, is an attendant sense that there is more to be gathered or made clear about the things in question; that conceptual content can bestow thematic unity on thinking; and that there can be a feeling of fit or rightness when information occurring to us fits certain expectations. The psychological mechanisms include the role of gist representations or schemas in memory and recall. I take to be plausible that thematic gist actually characterizes at least some conscious non-demonstrative inferences, and perhaps commonly does so. Exploration of its actual incidence must however be left for another occasion.

10. Conclusion

Conscious non-demonstrative inferences often seem to rest on rich body of assumptions that are unequally salient in or available to consciousness.

224 *Anders Nes*

A fore-v-background structure, or several such structures, seems to hold across them. According to Boring Views such structures can be described by specifying, for the various assumptions in question, whether they are phenomenally conscious, or access conscious, or else how easily available they are to such consciousness. Interesting Views hold that this is not the full story of fore-v-background structures. I have gestured at some reasons for thinking Interesting Views at least merit exploration. Building on recent work due to Watzl, and to Horgan, Potrč et al., though modifying, supplementing, or buttressing some their ideas (drawing here on some of Husserl's views on horizons of acts of consciousness, and on psychological work on gist representations in perception and memory), I have outlined a conception of thematic gist in non-demonstrative inference. According to this view, background assumptions in non-demonstrative inferences may be condensed into a consciously, although inattentively, entertained notion of the drift of a possible elucidation of how or why such-and-such salient grounds mean (or imply, or support) that so-and-so conclusion holds. Having such a notion explains why one is disposed, upon seeking to offer such an elucidation, not only to give an account with the relevant gist but also to experience it as filling in an already anticipated outline.[30]

Notes

1. See, e.g., Carroll, 1895; Boghossian, 2014; McHugh and Way, 2016, 2018.
2. See, e.g., Ludwig, 1996; Ludwig and Munroe this volume; Orlandi, 2014; Rescorla, 2015, this volume.
3. The example is adapted from Nes, 2016, which argues for the aptness of using 'means'. Nothing here however hangs on the choice between 'means' and such alternative expressions as 'implies', 'supports', or 'indicates'.
4. This example is due to Horgan and Potrc, 2010, 2011.
5. For overviews, see, e.g., Bayne and Montague, 2011; Hansen, 2019.
6. In particular, the view developed in Sections 8 and 9 builds on aspects of my defence of a liberal view in Nes, 2012.
7. See, e.g., Davis, 2005, pp. 10–13; Boghossian, 2019, p. 102.
8. For such a view, see Carruthers, 2015.
9. See, again, Carruthers, 2015; Cowan, 2000.
10. To be sure, some other aspects of Sally's current thinking, such as Wasting, might be even more highly activated and available for such systems or capacities. So if these notions of access were a matter of more or less, Wasting might be more access conscious than Crime. But Boring Views, we are assuming, are not grading access consciousness in this way.
11. See Horgan and Potrč, 2010, 2011; Henderson et al., 2017; Henderson, Horgan, and Potrč this volume.
12. See, e.g., Lipton, 2018.
13. Cf, e.g., Lakkaraju et al., 2017.
14. It is worth noting that this construal of 'experience of grief' etc., while it allows for a non-intentional understanding of the mental states in question, does not require it. Even so, if an experience of grief is intentional, what

makes it the distinctive intentional state it is is not its being directed at grief itself, but rather certain grievous features of one's life or circumstances.

15. In their most recent work, HPA qualify the assumption of content specificity, writing that 'chromatic illumination sometimes might constitute implicit appreciation of some morphological content or other, without constituting implicit information of any specific, fully determinate, morphological content' (this volume, nt. 11). They do seem to hold, though, that content specificity often or even typically holds for chromatic illumination (and so, presumably, for the looming potentialities in terms of which chromatic illumination is cashed out). If they do *not* hold this, then the account outlined in what follows may turn out to be congenial to HPAs most recent view, at least as far as the issue of content specificity goes. The account outlined in this paper could then be regarded as one that articulates in slightly different terms, and motivates from somewhat different angles, the just cited suggestion of HPA's.

16. See Husserl, 1913/1983, §27, §83. Cf. also Smith and McIntyre, 1982, pp. 236–239, and nt. 20.

17. I do not purport to suggest that 'reference' in these passages of Husserl's means what it means in post-Fregean analytical philosophy of mind and language. The point is just that their inclusion suggests there is more to the horizonal dimension than the mere capacity for or potentiality of such-and-such further conscious acts.

18. In their most recent work, HPA make a closely related point, noting that 'the conscious answers [to probe questions about an inference] are not experienced as arising 'out of the blue,' with no intuitive sense of why or how they are pertinent to the funniness of the joke' (this volume, p. 244).

19. To say the posited difference between Sally and Sally* here is dispositional is not to say that it is merely counterfactual, *pace* Yoshimi's (2016) construal of what a Husserlian horizonal dimension of consciousness comes to. Notoriously, a mere counterfactual difference could be secured by a 'counterfactual intervener' causing Sally and Sally* to have suitably different feelings in the event that so-and-so questions arise even if they are psychologically the same prior to the question arising.

20. Smith and McIntyre, 1982, p. 238 *et passim* stress this aspect of Husserl's views of horizon. They make the further move of distinguishing two sorts of horizon, a 'horizon of indeterminacy' corresponding to the present aspect, and a 'horizon of inattention' corresponding to the aspect of inattentiveness noted earlier (cf. nt 12 and attached text). However, as they acknowledge, Husserl characterizes horizons, under the same heading, is in terms of both inattention and indeterminacy, in such works as *Ideas* (1913/1983). At the very least then, he supposed these forms of horizon to typically go hand in hand.

21. For a review, see Aude, 2015.

22. Though Bartlett says 'affect', it is clear from his examples and discussion that the feeling in question need not have much in the way of affective valence, i.e. a pleasant or displeasant tone, but could be largely cognitive, as in the case of a sense of confidence or hesitation. See also Larsen and Berntsen, 2000.

23. Nes, 2012.

24. Schemas for how activities, of such-and-such types, stereotypically unfold are often referred to as 'scripts', cf., e.g., Schank, 1999.

25. For an argument that these features are required for conscious inference, see Nes, 2016.

226 *Anders Nes*

26. See, again, Nes, 2016.
27. Given some formal schooling in logic, one could come up with something to say here, e.g., invoke a theoretical characterization of logical consequence. The point is that the capacity to offer such a reply seems optional in relation to, and not to be in any direct way reflective of, the structure of one's conscious awareness in competently drawing the inference.
28. Cf. nt. 15 and attached text.
29. The 'condensation' posited here might recall, but should be distinguished from, Siewert's (1998, p. 278) description of thoughts that are 'remarkably complicated, so that to say what one was thinking would require a lengthy syntactically complex utterance – but [that nevertheless] occurs, wordlessly, without imagery, condensed, and evanescent'. For Siewert, 'condensation' does not imply that the complicated content of these thoughts is not, all of it, consciously entertained, but rather relates to how that content is, as it were, lifted out and freed in consciousness from the burdens of the words or imagery needed to articulate it. In contrast, the entire content of thoughts that are condensed-into-gist backgrounded are not consciously entertained, only their gist it. I do not deny some thought are condensed in Siewert's sense, but want to suggest at least some background assumptions that seem somehow to manifest in consciousness are better construed as condensed-into-gist backgrounded.
30. Acknowledgements: Thanks to audiences at Heidelberg University, Central European University, and the University of Oslo for feedback on various versions of the paper. Thanks, in particular, to Tim Bayne, Tim Crane, Frode Kjosavik, Mette Hansen, Terry Horgan, Bence Nanay, Christopher Peacocke, Joelle Proust, Susanna Siegel, Alberto Voltolini, and Sebastian Watzl for comments and discussion.

References

Abadie, Marlène, Waroquier, Laurent, & Terrier, Patrice (2016). The Role of Gist and Verbatim Memory in Complex Decision Making. *Journal of Experimental Psychology Learning Memory and Cognition*, 43.

Bartlett, Frederic C. (1932). *Remembering*. Cambridge: Cambridge University Press.

Bayne, Tim. (2016). Gist! *Proceedings of the Aristotelian Society*, 116(2), 107–126.

Bayne, Tim, & Montague, Michelle (2011). Cognitive Phenomenology: An Introduction. In Tim Bayne & Michelle Montague (Eds.), *Cognitive Phenomenology* (pp. 1–34). Oxford: Oxford University Press.

Boghossian, Paul (2014). What Is Inference? *Philosophical Studies*, 169, 1–18.

Boghossian, Paul (2019). Inference, Agency and Responsibility. In Magdalena Balcerak Jackson & Brendan Balcerak Jackson (Eds.), *Reasoning*. Oxford Oxford University Press.

Brewer, William F., & Treyens, James C. (1981). Role of Schemata in Memory for Places. *Cognitive Psychology*, 13(2), 207–230.

Carroll, Lewis (1895). What the Tortoise Said to Achilles. *Mind*, 4(14), 278–280.

Carruthers, Peter (2015). *The Centered Mind*. Oxford: Oxford University Press.

Cowan, Nelson (2000). The Magical Number 4 in Short-Term Memory. *Behavioral and Brain Sciences*, 24, 87–185.

Crane, Tim. (2013). Unconscious Belief and Conscious Thought. In Uriah Kriegel (Ed.), *Phenomenal Intentionality* (p. 156). New York: Oxford University Press.

Davis, Wayne A. (2005). *Nondescriptive Meaning and Reference*. Oxford: Oxford University Press.

Fish, William (2013). High-Level Properties and Visual Experience. *Philosophical Studies*, 162(1), 43–55.

Fodor, Jerry (1983). *Modularity of Mind*. Cambridge, MA: MIT Press.

Gurwitsch, Aron (1964). *Field of Consciousness*: Pittsburgh: Duquesne University Press.

Hansen, Mette Kristine (2019). Cognitive Phenomenology. In Rocco J. Gennaro (Ed.), *Internet Encyclopedia of Philosophy*. www.iep.utm.edu/cog-phen/

Henderson, David, & Horgan, Terence (2011). *The Epistemological Spectrum*. Oxford: Oxford University Press.

Henderson, David, Horgan, Terence, Potrč, Matjaž, & Tierney, Hannah (2017). Nonconciliation in Peer Disagreement: Its Phenomenology and Its Rationality. *Grazer Philosophische Studien*, 94, 194–225.

Horgan, Terry, & Potrč, Matjaž (2010). The Epistemic Relevance of Morphological Content. *Acta Analytica*, 25(2), 155–173.

Horgan, Terry, & Potrč, Matjaž (2011). Attention, Morphological Content and Epistemic Justification. *Croatian Journal of Philosophy*, 11(1), 73–86.

Husserl, Edmund (1913/1982). *Ideas Pertaining to a Pure Phenomenology and a Phenomenological Philosophy*. Dordrecht: Kluwer.

Husserl, Edmund (1933/1960). *Cartesian Meditations*. The Hague: Nijhoff.

Husserl, Edmund (1948/1973). *Experience and Judgement*. London: Routledge.

James, William (1890). *Principles of Psychology*. London: Palgrave Macmillan.

Lakkaraju, Himabindu, Kamar, Ece, Caruana, Rich, & Leskovec, Jure (2017). *Interpretable and Explorable Approximations of Black Box Models*. KDD (FAT ML), 2017. arXiv:1707.01154.

Larsen, Steen F., & Berntsen, Dorthe (2000). Bartlett's Trilogy of Memory. In Akiko Saiko (Ed.), *Bartlett, Culture, and Cognition*. London: Psychology Press.

Lewis, David (1997). Finkish Dispositions. *Philosophical Quarterly*, 47(187), 143–158.

Lipton, Zachary C. (2018). The Mythos of Model Interpretability. *acmqueue*, 16(3), 1–27.

Ludwig, Kirk A. (1996). Explaining Why Things Look the Way They Do. In Kathleen Akins (Ed.), *Perception*. Oxford: Oxford University Press.

Martin, Michael G. F. (1997). Sense, Reference and Selective Attention II: The Shallows of the Mind. *Proceedings of the Aristotelian Society, Supplementary Volumes*, 71, 75–98.

McHugh, Conor, & Way, Jonathan (2016). Against the Taking Condition. *Philosophical Issues*, 26(1).

McHugh, Conor, & Way, Jonathan (2018). What Is Reasoning? *Mind*, 127(505).

Nes, Anders (2012). Thematic Unity in the Phenomenology of Thinking. *Philosophical Quarterly*, 62(246), 84–105.

Nes, Anders (2016). The Sense of Natural Meaning in Conscious Inference. In Thiemo Breyer & Christopher Gutland (Eds.), *Phenomenology of Thinking*. London: Routledge.

Oddie, Graham (2005). *Value, Reality, and Desire*. Oxford: Oxford University Press.

Oliva, Aude (2015). The Gist of a Scene. In L. Itti, G. Rees, & J. K. Tsotsos (Eds.), *Encyclopedia of the Neurobiology of Attention*. San Diego, CA: Elsevier.

228 *Anders Nes*

Orlandi, Nico (2014). *The Innocent Eye: Why Vision Is Not a Cognitive Process*. Oxford: Oxford University Press.

Rescorla, Michael (2015). Bayesian Perceptual Psychology. In Mohan Matthen (Ed.), *Oxford Handbook of the Philosophy of Perception*. Oxford: Oxford University Press.

Schank, Roger C. (1999). *Dynamic Memory Revisited*. Cambridge: Cambridge University Press.

Searle, John R. (1992). *The Rediscovery of the Mind*. Cambridge, MA: MIT Press.

Siewert, Charles P. (1998). *The Significance of Consciousness*. Princeton: Princeton University Press.

Smith, A. D. (2003). *Husserl and the Cartesian Meditations*. London: Routledge.

Smith, David Woodruff, & McIntyre, Ronald (1982). *Husserl and Intentionality: A Study of Mind, Meaning, and Language*. Dordrecht: Reidel.

Vicente, Kim J., & Brewer, William F. (1993). Reconstructive Remembering of the Scientific Literature. *Cognition*, 46(2), 101–128.

Watzl, Sebastian (2017). *Structuring Mind*. Oxford: Oxford University Press.

Webb, Christina E., Turney, Indira C., & Dennis, Nancy A. (2016). What's the Gist? The Influence of Schemas on the Neural Correlates Underlying True and False Memories. *Neuropsychologia*, 93, 61–75.

Yoshimi, Jeffrey (2016). *Husserlian Phenomenology*. New York: Springer.

9 Morphological Content and Chromatic Illumination in Belief Fixation

David Henderson, Terry Horgan, and Matjaž Potrč

Belief fixation is the formation and maintenance of beliefs. Humans, despite their epistemic foibles, often engage in rational belief-fixation – thereby forming and maintaining doxastically justified beliefs. We will here argue for the following claims. First, rational belief-fixation typically is inferential in a way that draws holistically and abductively upon rich amounts of pertinent evidence possessed by the belief-forming cognizer. Second, much of this pertinent evidence is – and must be – accommodated during belief fixation without getting represented during the process. Nevertheless, third, the doxastic justification of a given belief depends heavily and constitutively upon conscious appreciation of the evidential support that accrues to this belief – even though, typically, much of this evidential support never becomes overtly present in consciousness during belief fixation.

1. Rationality and the Frame Problem

The frame problem in cognitive science, which first arose in the early days of artificial-intelligence research, reveals aspects of human rationality that often have been overlooked in both philosophy and psychology. The frame problem pertains both to 'theoretical' rationality concerning matters like belief fixation and to 'practical' rationality concerning matters like action and planning – while also revealing how deeply intertwined are these two dimensions. These underappreciated aspects of rationality were nicely brought into view by Dennett (1984), in an important and illuminating essay on the frame problem. As prelude and partial motivation for our subsequent discussion, we will begin by quoting Dennett at some length, commenting on quoted passages along the way. He starts the essay with the following parable:

> Once upon a time there was a robot, named R1 by its creators. Its only task was to fend for itself. One day its designers arranged for it to learn that its spare battery, its precious energy supply, was locked in a room with time bomb set to go off soon. R1 located the room,

230 *Henderson, Horgan, and Potrč*

and the key to the door, and formulated a plan to rescue its battery. There was a wagon in the room, and the battery was on the wagon, and R1 hypothesized that a certain action which it called PULLOUT(WAGON, ROOM) would result in the battery being removed from the room. Straightaway it acted, and did succeed in getting the battery out of the room before the bomb went off. Unfortunately, however, the bomb was also on the wagon. R1 *knew* that the bomb was on the wagon in the room, but didn't realize that pulling the wagon would bring the bomb out along with the battery. Poor R1 had missed that obvious implication of its planned act.

Back to the drawing board. 'The solution is obvious,' said the designers. 'Our next robot must be made to recognize not just the intended implications of its acts, but also implications about their side effects, by deducing these implications it uses in formulating its plans.' They called their next model, the robot-deducer, R1D1. They placed R1D1 in much the same predicament that R1 had succumbed to, and as it too hit upon the idea of PULLOUT(WAGON, ROOM) it began, as designed, to consider the implications of such a course of action. It had just finished deducing that pulling the wagon out of the room would not change the color of the room's walls, and was embarking on a proof of the further implication that pulling the wagon out would cause its wheels to turn more revolutions than there were wheels on the wagon – when the bomb exploded.

Back to the drawing board. 'We must teach it the difference between relevant implications and irrelevant implications,' said the designers, 'and teach it to ignore the irrelevant ones.' So they developed a method of tagging implications as either relevant or irrelevant to the project at hand, and installed the method in their next model, the robot-relevant-deducer, or R2D1 for short. When they subjected R2D1 to the test that had unequivocally selected its ancestors for extinction, they were surprised to see it sitting, Hamlet-like, outside the room containing the ticking bomb, the native hue of its resolution sicklied o'er with the pale cast of thought, as Shakespeare (and more recently Fodor) has aptly put it. 'Do something!' they yelled at it. 'I am,' it retorted. 'I'm busily ignoring some thousands of implications I have determined to be irrelevant. Just as soon as I find an irrelevant implication, I put it on the list of those I must ignore, and . . .' the bomb went off.

(1984, pp. 41–42)

This parable illustrates nicely the extent to which ordinary human common-sensical planning and action depend on pertinent background information available to the human agent – information that somehow gets appreciated and accommodated, whether or not it becomes explicitly present in consciousness along the way. It also illustrates the extent to

Belief Fixation 231

which planning and action typically are suffused with pertinent *expectations* about what will happen next if one acts a certain way, and about what *would* happen next if one were to act some other way (e.g., pulling the wagon out of the room without first removing the bomb) – again, whether or not those expectations become explicitly present in consciousness along the way. Such expectations are aptly considered aspects of theoretical rationality, and their presence is intimately bound up with practical rationality – whether or not they qualify as full-fledged *beliefs*. Concerning the robots in his parable, Dennett goes on to say this:

> All these robots suffer from the *frame problem*. If there is ever to be a robot with the fabled perspicacity and real-time adroitness of R2D2, robot-designers must solve the frame problem. . . . [I]t is a new, deep epistemological problem – accessible in principle but unnoticed by generations of philosophers – brought to light by the novel methods of AI, and still far from being solved. . . .
>
> One utterly central – if not defining – feature of an intelligent being is that it can 'look before it leaps.' Better, it can *think* before it leaps. Intelligence is (at least partly) a matter of using well what you know – but for what? For improving the fidelity of your expectations about what is going to happen next, for planning, for considering courses of action, for framing further hypotheses with the aim of increasing the knowledge you will use in the future, so that you can preserve yourself, by letting your hypotheses die in your stead (as Sir Karl Popper once put it) . . . .
>
> But when we think before we leap, *how do we do it?*
>
> (1984, pp. 42–44)

So the frame problem, in short, is the problem of understanding how the human cognitive system manages to bring to bear, in real time, pertinent information it possesses in such a way as to effectively manage these kinds of theoretical-cum-practical tasks. The depth and difficulty of this problem is easy to overlook, precisely because the common-sense rationality that has proved so dauntingly difficult to engineer into robots is so easy and so natural for us humans. But evidently this ease and naturalness belies the complexity of what goes on outside of explicit conscious awareness. Dennett remarks:

> The myth that each of us can observe our mental activities has prolonged the illusion that major progress could be made on the theory of thinking by simply reflecting carefully on our own cases. For some time now we have known better: we have conscious access to only the upper surface, as it were, of the multi-level system of information-processing that occurs in us. Nevertheless, the myth still claims its victims.

232 *Henderson, Horgan, and Potrč*

So the analogy of the stage magician is particularly apt. One is not likely to make much progress in figuring out *how* the tricks are done by simply sitting attentively and watching like a hawk. Too much is going on out of sight. Better to face the fact that one must either rummage around backstage in the wings, hoping to disrupt the performance in telling ways; or, from one's armchair, think aprioristically about how the tricks *must* be done, given whatever is manifest about the constraints. The frame problem is then rather like the unsettling but familiar 'discovery' that so far as armchair thought can determine, a certain trick we have just observed is flat impossible.

(1984, p. 46)

He offers the following mundane example, commenting on it in a way that, like his parable of the three robots, thematizes the richness of background knowledge that needs to be in play in ordinary planning and plan-execution – knowledge of the kind that ordinary common sense typically accommodates without its becoming explicitly present in consciousness. Immediately after the just-quoted passage, and continuing with the analogy of the stage magician, Dennett says:

Here is an example of the trick. Making a midnight snack. How is it that I can get myself a midnight snack? What could be simpler? I suspect that there is some leftover sliced turkey and mayonnaise in the fridge, and bread in the breadbox – a bottle of beer in the fridge as well. I realize that I can put these elements together, so I concoct a childishly simple plan: I'll just go and check out the fridge, get out the requisite materials, and make myself a sandwich, to be washed down with a beer. I'll need a knife, a plate, and a glass for the beer. I forthwith put the plan into action and it works! Big deal.

Now of course I couldn't do this without knowing a good deal – about bread, spreading mayonnaise, opening the fridge, the friction and inertia that will keep the turkey between the bread slices and the bread on the plate as I carry the plate over to the table beside my easy chair. I also need to know how to get the beer out of the bottle and into the glass. . . . [O]ne trivial thing I have to know is that when the beer gets into the glass it is no longer in the bottle, and that if I'm holding the mayonnaise jar in my left hand I cannot also be spreading the mayonnaise with the knife in my left hand. Perhaps these are straightforward implications – instantiations – of some more fundamental things . . . such as, perhaps, the fact that if something is in one location it isn't also in another, different location; or the fact that two things can't be in the same place at the same time; or the fact that situations change as the result of actions. . . .

Such utterly banal facts escape our notice as we act and plan. . . . But if one . . . just thinks . . . about the purely informational demands

Belief Fixation 233

of the task – what *must* be known by any entity that can perform this task – these banal bits of knowledge rise to our attention. We can easily satisfy ourselves that no agent that did not *in some sense* have the benefit of the information (that beer in the bottle is not in the glass, etc.) could perform such a simple task. It is one of the chief methodological beauties of AI that it makes one be a phenomenologist in this improved way. . . . [O]ne reasons about what the agents must 'know' or figure out *unconsciously or consciously* in order to perform in various ways.

(1984, pp. 46–47)

He also stresses, rightly, the important role that doxastic states of *expectation* play in the forming and executing of plans – again, largely without becoming explicitly present in consciousness (not, anyway, as long they do not get thwarted). They are important, *inter alia*, because of how they contribute to the intelligent flexibility with which human agents execute their plans and intentions, adapting aptly to unanticipated contingencies. Continuing with the example of the midnight snack, he writes:

We assure ourselves of the intelligence of an agent by considering counterfactuals: if I had been told that the turkey was poisoned, or the beer explosive, or the plate dirty, or the knife too fragile to spread mayonnaise, would I have acted as I did? If I were a stupid 'automaton' . . . I might infelicitously 'go through the motions' of making a midnight snack oblivious to the recalcitrant features of the environment. But in fact, my midnight-snack-making behavior is multifariously sensitive to current and background information about the situation. . . . [A]n intelligent agent must engage in swift information-sensitive 'planning' which has the effect of producing reliable but not foolproof expectations of the effects of its actions. That these expectations are normally in force in intelligent creatures is testified to by the startled reactions they exhibit when their expectations are thwarted. This suggests a graphic way of characterizing the minimal goal that can spawn the frame problem: we want a midnight-snack-making robot to be 'surprised' by the trick plate, the unspreadable concrete mayonnaise, the fact that we've glued the glass to the shelf. To be surprised you have to have expected something else, and in order to have expected the right something else, you have to have *and use* a lot of information about things in the world.

(1984, pp. 50–52)

In sum, Dennett's observations about the frame problem quoted here, largely focused on his parable of the three robots and his example of the midnight snack, make vivid several crucial points that will be presupposed in our discussion that follows. First, rational agents deploy – and

234 *Henderson, Horgan, and Potrč*

must deploy – extensive amounts of pertinent background information in carrying out even quite mundane everyday activities. Second, such background information typically gets accommodated without becoming present in consciousness – a fact that has often led philosophers (and psychologists too) to seriously under-appreciate the complexity and subtlety of common-sense rationality. Third, 'practical' rationality is much more suffused with elements of 'theoretical' rationality than is often realized – viz., *expectations*, which (like background information) typically are operative in ongoing practical agency without becoming present in consciousness. (Expectations are doxastic, surely, whether or not they always qualify as *beliefs*; and, being doxastic, they fall under the rubric of 'theoretical' rationality.)

2. Morals of the Frame Problem, I: Belief Fixation as Abductively Inferential and Hence as Non-Modular

Belief fixation is the generation of beliefs and the maintenance of existing beliefs. (What will be said in this section about belief fixation applies, *mutatis mutandis*, to expectation fixation too, regardless whether or not one counts all expectations as full-fledged beliefs.) Rational belief-fixation is the generation and maintenance of beliefs under circumstances in which those beliefs (i) are evidentially well supported by one's available evidence, and (ii) arise *because* they are thus evidentially supported. Hence, rational belief-fixation is, in an important sense, *inferential*: it is a process whereby beliefs are generated on the basis of evidence, possessed and deployed by the cognitive system, that supports them. And in general, rational belief-fixation also is *nondeductively* inferential, since normally the pertinent kind of evidential support is abductive rather than demonstrative.[1]

This being so, the frame problem arises in a stark way for belief fixation – a point that long was rightly and emphatically stressed by another influential philosopher who, like Dennett, kept a close eye on pertinent developments in cognitive science – the late Jerry Fodor. Here are some pithy remarks he made at the beginning of an essay of his own on the frame problem, Fodor (1987):

> There are, it seems to me, two interesting ideas about modularity. The first is the idea that some of our cognitive faculties are modular. The second is the idea that some of our cognitive faculties are not.
>
> By a modular cognitive faculty, I mean – for present purposes – one that is 'informationally encapsulated'. By an informationally encapsulated cognitive faculty, I mean one that has access, in the course of its computations, to less than all of the information at the disposal of the organism whose cognitive faculty it is. So, for example, I think that the persistence of the Muller-Lyer illusion in spite of

one's knowledge that it *is* an illusion strongly suggests that some of the cognitive mechanisms that mediate visual size perception must be informationally encapsulated. . . .

It's worth emphasizing a sense in which modular cognitive processing is *ipso facto* irrational. After all, by definition modular processing means arriving at conclusions by attending to less than all of the evidence that is relevant and available. And ignoring relevant and available evidence is, notoriously, a technique of belief fixation that will get you into trouble in the long run. Informational encapsulation is economical; it buys speed and the reduction of computational load by, in effect, drastically delimiting the database that's brought to bear in problem solving. But the price of economy is warrant. The more encapsulated the cognitive mechanisms that mediate the fixation of your beliefs, the worse is your evidence for the beliefs that you have. And . . . the worse your evidence for your beliefs is, the less the likelihood that your beliefs are true. . . .

[R]ational processes have their debilities too. . . . If, for example, you undertake to consider a nonarbitrary sample of the available and relevant evidence before you opt for a belief, *you have the problem of when the evidence you have looked at is enough.* You have, that is to say, Hamlet's problem: when to stop thinking.

The frame problem is just Hamlet's problem viewed from an engineer's perspective. . . . What is a nonarbitrary strategy for delimiting the evidence that should be searched in rational belief fixation? I don't know how to answer this question. If I did, I'd have solved the frame problem and I'd be rich and famous.

(1987, pp. 139–140)

In other writings Fodor elaborated at length on these thoughts, in three respects. First, he argued that typically the degree of evidential support that a potential belief possesses, relative to one's total available evidence, (i) is non-demonstrative and abductive (rather than being a matter of logical entailment by the evidence), and (ii) is highly and multifariously *holistic* (as are evidential abductive-support relations in science). Like confirmation of hypotheses in science, non-demonstrative evidential support for potential beliefs typically exhibits two holistic aspects that Fodor called the 'isotropic' feature and the 'Quineian' feature. In Fodor (1983) he wrote:

By saying that confirmation is isotropic, I mean that the facts relevant to the confirmation of a scientific hypothesis may be drawn from anywhere in the field of previously established empirical (or, of course, demonstrative) truths. Crudely: everything that the scientist knows is, in principle, relevant to determining what else he ought to believe.

(1983, p. 105)

236   *Henderson, Horgan, and Potrč*

By saying that scientific confirmation is Quineian, I mean that the degree of confirmation assigned to any given hypothesis is sensitive to properties of the entire belief system; as it were, the shape of our whole science bears on the epistemic status of each scientific hypothesis.

(1983, p. 107)

Isotropy brings in the whole current belief system: any bit of actual or potential information from any portion of the belief system might, in some circumstances, be evidentially relevant to any other. Being Quineian makes confirmation holistic in a deeper way: confirmation depends upon 'such considerations as simplicity, plausibility, and conservatism' (Fodor, 1983, p. 108), which are determined by the global *structure* of the whole of the current belief system and of potential successor systems.

Second, he urged that human belief fixation is often quite rational, thereby operating in a non-modular manner that successfully brings to bear the holistic, abductive, evidential support for a given potential belief that is actually possessed by the cognitive system. (Likewise for expectation fixation, as it figures in planning and in guidance of action.)

Third, he bemoaned the fact that a tractable computational solution to 'Hamlet's problem,' for creatures who have as much available evidence to draw upon as do real humans, looks unattainable. Hence his ongoing, and increasingly pessimistic, negative attitude about the prospects for what he called the 'computational theory of mind' (CTM). In Fodor (1983) he wrote, concerning processes like belief fixation and planning:

The difficulties we encounter when we try to construct theories of [these kinds of] processes are just the sort we would expect to encounter if such processes are, in essential respects, Quineian/isotropic. . . . The crux in the construction of such theories is that there seems to be no way to delimit the sorts of informational resources which may affect, or be affected by, central processes of problem-solving. We can't, that is to say, plausibly view the fixation of belief as affected by computations over bounded, local information structures. A graphic example of this sort of difficulty arises in AI, where it has come to be known as the 'frame problem' (i.e., the problem of putting a 'frame' around the set of beliefs that may need to be revised in light of specified newly available information).

(1983, pp. 112–3)

In a more recent essay, Fodor (2000), he expressed his ongoing deep pessimism as follows (with our interpolations about what, in context, he clearly had in mind):

Computational nativism [i.e., the CTM] is clearly the best theory of the cognitive mind that anyone has thought of so far (vastly better than, for example, the associationistic empiricism that is the main alternative); and there may indeed be aspects of cognition [viz., informationally encapsulated ones, such as the cognitive mechanisms that mediate visual size perception] about which computational nativism has got the story more or less right. But it's nonetheless quite plausible that computational nativism is, in large part [viz., vis-à-vis informationally unencapsulated cognitive faculties like planning and belief fixation], not true.

(2000, p. 3)

The problem is not nativism (which asserts that human cognitive mechanisms deploy a significant amount of information that is possessed innately), but rather the idea that human cognition is *representation-level computation*, i.e., manipulation of mental representations in accordance with rules that advert to the content-encoding structure of these representations and could constitute a computer program. Tractable representation-level computational processes require modularity – an informationally encapsulated data base – whereas rational belief fixation is highly holistic and non-modular.[2] (The case against the CTM is further articulated in Horgan and Tienson, 1994, 1996.)

3. Morals of the Frame Problem, II: Belief Fixation as Non-Computational and as Essentially Morphological

The human cognitive system somehow accomplishes highly holistic, highly non-modular, belief fixation and expectation fixation. How might it do so? Dennett's analogy of the stage magician is very pertinent here. If one supposes that the trick is accomplished by means of tractable representation-level computation that somehow deploys what Fodor called 'a nonarbitrary strategy for delimiting the evidence that should be searched in rational belief fixation,' then one will find it difficult to avoid concluding (as Dennett put it) 'that so far as armchair thought can determine, a certain trick we have just observed [viz., the holistically rational fixation of beliefs and expectations] is flat impossible.'

The way forward is to follow Dennett's two-pronged advice: 'either rummage around backstage in the wings, hoping to disrupt the performance in telling ways; or, from one's armchair, think aprioristically about how the tricks *must* be done, given whatever is manifest about the constraints.' This was done by Horgan and Tienson (1994, 1996). Aprioristically, they argued that highly holistic, highly non-modular, cognitive processing must operate in such a way that much pertinent background information gets accommodated *automatically without becoming occurrent*, by virtue of the standing structure (the morphology) of the cognitive system. They called information that gets implicitly accommodated this way 'morphological content.' (Here we will refer to information that is being thus automatically accommodated, in generating or maintaining

238 *Henderson, Horgan, and Potrč*

some occurrent mental state or process, *morphologically operative* morphological content – for short, MOMC.)

Rummaging backstage in the wings, at a time when neural-network models had come to prominence in cognitive science, Horgan and Tienson argued that abductively holistic cognitive processing should be understood not as the computational manipulation of explicit mental representations of all the evidentially pertinent information, but rather in terms of the kind of mathematics that goes naturally with neural-network modeling – viz., dynamical systems theory. Morphological content is embodied in the topological contours of the (n+1)-dimensional 'activation landscape' of an n-node neural network – with the activation-level of each node in the network being a dimension in the network's n-dimensional 'state space,' and with 'downhill' on the landscape being the direction of time.[3] Temporal trajectories along the activation landscape from one activation-state to another, as determined largely by the morphological content embodied in the topological contours on the landscape in the vicinity of the initial activation-state, constitute transitions from one occurrent cognitive state to another. (The morphological content embodied in the local topological contours constitutes the *morphologically operative* morphological content – which can figure not only in the initiation of an occurrent mental state, but also in maintaining the persistence of this occurrent state over time.)

Horgan and Tienson argued that two apparent morals emerge from the fact that cognitive processes like belief fixation are richly holistic and highly non-modular. First, such processes are too subtle and too complex to constitute representation-level computation, i.e., manipulation and transformation of mental representations in accordance with programmable rules that advert to the content-encoding structure of those representations.[4] Second, these processes depend essentially and heavily upon MOMC, that is, morphological content that is accommodated automatically by such processes without becoming represented along the way. Although the first of these two apparent morals will not figure prominently in our subsequent discussion in this chapter, then second one will. We will be focusing on two interrelated matters: (i) the question of how the abductively inferential, essentially morphological, nature of rational belief-fixation is related to the conscious, experiential, aspects of belief fixation, and (ii) the question of the potential implications for epistemology of the contention that rational belief-fixation typically is both abductively inferential and essentially morphological.[5]

4. Morphological Content and Consciousness, I: The EOC Assumption

Rational belief-fixation is abductively inferential: rationally generated beliefs are ones that are well-supported – typically non-demonstratively – by

Belief Fixation 239

evidence one possesses. But since processes of rational belief-fixation depend heavily upon essentially morphological aspects, these processes do not constitute *fully explicit* inferences. That is, they do not constitute inferences in which all pertinent evidence, and all of the holistic, Quineian, respects in which the evidence combines to abductively support the given belief, get *represented* during the process of belief fixation.

Prima facie, it seems quite plausible that content that gets implicitly and automatically accommodated during cognitive processing (in the form MOMC), rather than getting represented by an occurrent mental state/process with that very content, cannot be an aspect of conscious experience. This is not to say that all occurrent mental states/processes must be conscious; for, some might be entirely unconscious. Rather, the claim is that being represented by an occurrent mental state/process is a *necessary condition* (albeit not a sufficient condition) for an item of content to be an aspect of consciousness. We will call this claim the *explicit occurrent content assumption* (for short, the EOC assumption).

We next set forth and compare several epistemological positions that presuppose the EOC assumption. Thereafter we will argue that the EOC assumption, despite being initially plausible, is false; and we will consider the apparent import of its falsity for epistemology.

5. Doxastic Justification, I: Three Alternative Positions Each Embracing the EOC Assumption

If one accepts (i) that rational belief-fixation typically is abductively inferential in a highly holistic, isotropic-cum-Quineian way, (ii) that such belief fixation depends heavily upon morphological content, and (iii) that the EOC assumption is correct, then what might all this mean concerning the nature of doxastic justification? We will canvass several alternative potential answers to this question.[6]

First is what we will call *non-experiential reliabilism*. This view holds that the key constitutive feature of a justified belief is the fact that it was produced by a reliable belief-forming process. Although typically the source of this reliability is the sensitivity of the belief-fixation process to holistic evidential support that is possessed by the cognitive system, such evidence-sensitivity is not itself constitutive of doxastic justification; rather, reliability of the operative belief-fixation process is what's constitutive. Moreover, given the EOC assumption and the fact that belief fixation typically is abductively rational in a way that depends heavily upon morphological content, conscious experience is comparatively unimportant in epistemic justification: far too much of the abductive belief-fixing processing takes place outside of consciousness. Hence, this form of reliabilism is aptly called 'non-experiential.'[7]

Second is what we will call *non-experiential evidentialism*. This view holds instead that the key constitutive feature of a justified belief is the

240 *Henderson, Horgan, and Potrč*

fact that it was produced, by a holistically evidence-sensitive belief-fixation process, in response to evidence possessed by the cognitive agent that constitutes strong evidential support for the belief. Although a process of this kind is apt to be reliable, its reliability is a byproduct of the constitutive feature of doxastic justification, rather than being constitutive itself; what's constitutive is evidence-sensitive processing in response to good evidence one actually possesses. But this view nonetheless is similar to non-experiential reliabilism in this respect: conscious experience is comparatively unimportant in epistemic justification because far too much of the abductive belief-fixing processing takes place outside of consciousness. Hence, this form of evidentialism is aptly called 'non-experiential.'

Third is what we will call *evidentially blind gut-feeling experientialism*. This view treats certain conscious epistemic 'gut feelings' – certain conscious experiences as-of a given proposition's *seeming to be true* – as a key constitutive feature of doxastic justification. (In order to be at all plausible, this view presumably would need to impose certain phenomenological constraints on the kinds of epistemic gut feelings that would qualify as justificatory, as distinct from other kinds that would not qualify.) The view also embraces the claim, argued earlier, that much of the abductively inferential belief-fixing processing – processing that generates the epistemic seemings – takes place completely outside of consciousness. Because this view also embraces the EOC assumption, it must treat such a gut feeling (a conscious seeming-to-be-true of a proposition P) as devoid of any significant conscious appreciation of the evidence that accrues to P – even though the gut feeling is *caused* by largely unconscious processes that are responsive to that very evidence. So although the view accords to conscious epistemic seemings a central constitutive role in doxastic justification (a contention to which we will return in Section 7), it treats those seemings as devoid of conscious appreciation of most of the pertinent evidence. Hence, this form of experientialism is aptly called 'evidentially blind.' (One variant of this position would treat the underlying evidence-sensitive processing that generates the gut feeling as being merely causal, rather than as being partly constitutive of justified belief, because it occurs mostly unconsciously. Another variant would treat such processing as partly constitutive of justification, together with the conscious gut feeling that it generates. But either way, the gut feeling itself is construed as evidentially blind, rather than as embodying conscious appreciation of the pertinent evidence.)

Each of these three views denies, in one way or another, that conscious appreciation of a belief's abductively inferential evidential support is constitutive of doxastic justification. The first two positions relegate conscious experience to a peripheral role, constitutively – claiming that very large portions of the crucial constitutive action occur entirely outside of consciousness. The third position, by contrast, treats certain kinds of conscious gut feelings as crucially constitutive of doxastic justification;

but it also construes these epistemic seemings as largely devoid of conscious evidence-appreciation.

None of these views, we contend, is either theoretically satisfying or phenomenologically plausible. Conscious experience plays a crucial and central role, constitutively, in doxastic justification; but it does so in a way that includes conscious appreciation of the pertinent evidence that one possesses. The key to having it both ways is to jettison the EOC assumption.

6. Morphological Content and Consciousness, II: Chromatic Illumination

The EOC assumption, recall, asserts that being represented by an occurrent mental state/process is a necessary condition for an item of content to be an aspect of consciousness. Although this assumption admittedly seems quite plausible initially, nevertheless the following possibility arises concerning the relation between MOMC and consciousness. Perhaps sometimes there occurs a conscious process Φ with these features: (1) an occurrent, conscious, cognitive state S (say, an occurrent belief) is a component of Φ throughout Φ's temporal duration, (2) state S arises within Φ and is sustained within Φ in a way that deploys certain morphologically operative morphological content M that is relevant to S, and (3) the overall phenomenal character of Φ includes a specific phenomenal aspect – an aspect of the total 'something it's like' to undergo Φ – that constitutes *implicitly appreciating* both M itself and M's relevance to S. (The modifier 'implicitly', as used here, means that content M is not represented by any component of the occurrent conscious process Φ.)

In Horgan and Potrč (2010), two of us argued that occurrent conscious experience quite often has such phenomenological aspects, which we labeled *chromatic illumination*. This expression is inspired by a visual metaphor, which is helpful in conveying the nature of such phenomenology. Consider a visual scene that is illuminated in certain ways by light sources that are not themselves visible (from the observer's perspective) within the scene, and that significantly affect the overall look of the scene. Think, for instance, of the famous 1892 painting by Toulouse Lautrec, 'At the Moulin Rouge,' which hangs in the Art Institute of Chicago. Various figures in the painted scene are illuminated in strikingly different ways – e.g., the women more prominently than the men, one woman by lighting to the left but outside the scene, another woman by lighting from the lower right but outside the scene, a peculiar light-induced greenish tint to some of the illuminated faces that blends with the greens in the background of the scene, etc. The presumptive sources of these distinctive features – lighting of various kinds at various positions in the presumptive wider environment, producing light with various different chromatic characteristics – are not present in the visible scene. They are not represented. Nonetheless, they are *implicated* in the scene anyway,

242 *Henderson, Horgan, and Potrč*

in the ways that the figures in the scene are chromatically illuminated by those presumptive light-sources.

The directly visible scene presented in a painting – or in a photograph, or on a stage – can be taken as a metaphorical stand-in for one's occurrent conscious experience. By contrast, the out-of-view sources of the visible scene's various aspects of illumination can be taken as a metaphorical stand-in for what is implicitly appreciated consciously – appreciated not by being actually represented in consciousness, but rather by certain phenomenologically distinctive aspects of *how* what is actually represented is represented. These 'how' aspects of current consciousness, constituting implicit appreciation of pertinent non-represented content and of its relevance to what *is* represented in experience, are what we call chromatic illumination.

Horgan and Potrč (2010) argued, largely by appeal to introspective phenomenological reflection, that conscious experience frequently exhibits chromatic illumination by background information – information that thus is implicitly appreciated experientially. They argued in part, in a way we now reiterate in a somewhat more elaborated manner, by invoking a familiar type of experience: understanding a joke. (An advantage of focusing on a non-sensory cognitive phenomenon is that it is appropriately analogous, so we will maintain, to belief formation.)

For specificity, consider a cartoon by Danny Shanahan that appeared in the *New Yorker* magazine roughly twenty-five years ago.[8] (We will describe it rather than exhibiting it, which underscores the fact that pertinent aspects of joke-getting normally do not depend essentially on specific sense modalities.) Two guys are sitting in a bar, and the one who is speaking looks unhappy and exasperated. He says to the other guy, 'What I don't, like, get is how she, like, figured out I was, like, having an affair with the, like, babysitter.'

Getting this joke, or any joke, is an instantaneous experience. In that instant, normally one needs to appreciate quite a wide range of pertinent background information; also, one needs to appreciate why and how all this information combines, holistically, to constitute an instance of funniness. Each item of that information must be appreciated, together with the ways that all the pertinent items interact with one another to make for funniness – for, otherwise one would not be understanding the joke.

For any reasonably clever joke, typically it is possible to elaborate at some length upon the various items of background information all of which are pertinent. In the example at hand, for instance, probably the most salient such item – the item that one would mention first, in seeking to explain the joke to someone who does not yet get it – is that the practice of persistently inserting the word 'like' into one's spoken English is a distinctive feature of way *teenage girls* talked in the U.S., twenty-five years ago. (Supposedly the practice was initiated by teenage females in the San Fernando Valley, adjacent to Los Angeles – so-called 'valley girls,'

Belief Fixation 243

who are sources of numerous youthful fads in the U.S. Nowadays, regrettably, such 'like'-talk is much more prevalent, so much more so that contemporary American undergraduates frequently don't easily get the joke.)

But that is just the beginning, in terms of pertinent background information that must be grasped in the instant in order to get the joke. Additional such items of information can be made salient by posing suitable questions – questions that might be asked by someone who is persistently deficient at understanding jokes. Whose children did this babysitter care for? Roughly how old is the babysitter? Who is the 'she' who figured out that the guy is having an affair with the babysitter? How did that person react, upon learning this fact? Why is the guy upset that she figured it out and reacted that way? Why doesn't he himself understand how she figured it out? And, of course: What's so funny about all this? One could write a monograph about the pertinent background information and its holistic relevance. Likewise for most any even moderately subtle joke.

In the instant of joke-getting, very little of this kind of information seems to be overtly present in consciousness. Nonetheless, all of it is being *implicitly appreciated* consciously via chromatic illumination that it exerts upon the phenomenological character of one's overall synchronic experience, because otherwise one would not get the joke.

Furthermore – and importantly – the 'getting it' aspect of experience is not some generic feature, such as experiencing oneself laughing or inclined to laugh (perhaps without knowing why). Rather, it is quite content-specific: some particular item(s) of overtly conscious content (in this case, what the guy at the bar is saying, and his obvious consternation) are appreciated as funny by virtue of how that consciously represented content is relevantly interconnected with a rich body of pertinent background information. Thus, all those *specific* items of morphological content are being implicitly appreciated consciously in the joke-getting experience, by virtue of the *specific* character of the phenomenology. This chromatic-illumination phenomenology is supervenient upon the neural activity implementing the experience – neural activity in which the pertinent morphological content is morphologically operative in both the generation and the persistence of the conscious joke-understanding state. The chromatic illumination is thus the supervenient manifestation, in consciousness, of this MOMC.[9]

A chromatically illuminated occurrent mental state is itself rife with dispositional potential, in ways directly connected to the MOMC doing the chromatic illuminating. This dispositional potential includes the capacity to manifest in various ways one's implicit conscious appreciation of this MOMC – with the chromatic illumination constituting the occurrent, conscious, categorical basis of the pertinent dispositions.

One kind of looming potentiality, for example, is the capacity to spontaneously arrive at consciously explicit answers to suitable background-probing questions – in the case of the occurrent state of getting

244 *Henderson, Horgan, and Potrč*

the babysitter joke, for instance, questions like 'Roughly how old is the babysitter?'; 'Who is the 'she' who figured out that the guy is having the affair with babysitter?'; and so on.

Importantly, the emergence in consciousness of answers to such probe questions is itself experienced phenomenologically as arising directly out of the (recalled) joke-getting experience itself, given the probe question. The conscious answers are not experienced as arising 'out of the blue,' with no intuitive sense of why or how they are pertinent to the funniness of the joke. Nor are they experienced as being mere post-hoc *abductive hypotheses* about why the joke is funny and why one laughed at it; that would be different experientially from the phenomenological immediacy with which the answers seem to emanate straight out of the recollected experience.

These introspectively ascertainable features of joke-understanding phenomenology and probe-question-answering phenomenology are just what one would expect if indeed the original joke-getting experience includes rich chromatic illumination constituting implicit appreciation of the information articulable in those answers – chromatic illumination that is the conscious, occurrent, categorical basis of one's capacity to answer the probe questions easily and spontaneously.

On the other hand, this is *not* the phenomenology that one would expect given an alternative hypothesis asserting (i) that the MOMC in virtue of which the babysitter joke is funny contributed to one's laughing *without* the simultaneous supervenient presence in consciousness, at the moment of mirthfulness, of any implicit conscious appreciation of that MOMC, and (ii) that this same MOMC subsequently contributed to the spontaneous emergence in consciousness of accurate answers the probe questions. Rather, what one would expect, under this alternative hypothesis, is both (i) that one's initial mirthfulness-reaction would be experienced phenomenologically as arising 'out of the blue,' and (ii) that one's subsequent, spontaneous and accurate, answers to the probe questions also would be experienced phenomenologically as arising 'out of the blue' (or perhaps as constituting mere hypothetical conjectures about why one laughed). So much the worse for that alternative hypothesis.

The presence of looming potentialities to manifest one's implicit appreciation of MOMC normally is itself a matter of chromatic illumination, rather than something that is represented in consciousness. Moreover, this aspect of chromatic illumination is part of the phenomenological content-specificity of one's experienced mirthfulness, as distinct from the phenomenology of finding oneself laughing with no clue about why. And even when *some* pertinent background information becomes overtly present in consciousness, triggered by the joke-getting experience in combination with some other occurrent mental state (e.g., occurrently considering a probe question), normally much else that one is appreciating remains only implicitly appreciated in consciousness in the form of

Belief Fixation 245

chromatic illumination. In explaining the joke to someone who doesn't yet get it, for example, normally one would bring explicitly to mind, and articulate, only a small part of the pertinent background information – such as the fact that twenty-five years ago, 'like'-talk in English was employed primarily by teenage girls. Explicit information will trigger a joke-getting experience in one's interlocutor only if the interlocutor now undergoes an occurrent conscious mental state that is suitably chromatically illuminated by the various other pertinent items of background information and also is suitably chromatically illuminated by how funniness supervenes, in a holistically Quineian way, on the full body of pertinent information.[10]

Admittedly, it is an empirical hypothesis that joke-getting has the features lately described. But it is a very plausible hypothesis, for at least two reasons. First, it conforms with the deliverances of introspection: when one attends introspectively to one's joke-getting experience (albeit perhaps retrospectively via one's memory of the recent past), it does not seem that all that background information is overtly present – i.e., is actually represented – in consciousness; yet, it also seems, upon reflection, that one would not have *consciously understood* the joke without consciously *appreciating* all that information and its holistic humor-relevance. Second, there are strong theoretical grounds – really the same grounds as in the case of belief fixation – for the claim that the cognitive processes that underwrite joke-getting are essentially morphological: viz., joke-getting exhibits very similar kinds of holistic, Quineian-cum-isotropic, dependence on background information. This means that it is not tractably possible for joke-getting cognition to proceed by deploying, and computationally manipulating, representations of all pertinent items of information and their holistic, Quineian-ishly funny making, interconnections – especially not in the very short time it normally takes to understand a joke.

7. Doxastic Justification, II: Chromatically Illuminated Epistemic Seemings and Chromatic-Experiential Evidentialism

Similar observations apply, *mutatis mutandis*, to the phenomenology of occurrent conscious beliefs. (Indeed, our discussion of joke-getting already illustrates this fact, since the answers one can spontaneously give to pertinent probe-questions constitute epistemically justified *beliefs* about various aspects of the joke's funniness.) Normally, an occurrent belief that P is not experienced as evidentially un-tethered – as arising, for no apparent reason, 'out of the blue.' (That would be the analogue of finding oneself laughing without a clue about why.) On the contrary, normally an occurrent belief that P is accompanied by an occurrent, evidence-sensitive 'epistemic seeming' – a phenomenological aspect as-of

P's *seeming true in virtue of specific evidence one possesses*. Often this aspect will itself figure consciously only implicitly in the form of chromatic illumination, rather than being an occurrent conscious belief alongside the conscious belief that *P*. And although some pertinent items of evidence might be overtly present in consciousness alongside the *P*-belief, much of the isotropic, Quinean, evidential support for *P* that one possesses will be consciously appreciated only implicitly via chromatic illumination. Such chromatic illumination will endow the conscious belief-state with various looming potentialities – often including the capacity to bring explicitly into consciousness, piecemeal, certain specific components of the overall evidential support for *P* that is being appreciated implicitly and chromatically. Normally, however, even when certain evidentially pertinent items of information are overtly present in consciousness and are explicitly being regarded as evidence for *P*, one's consciously so regarding them will take place against a rich background of further evidentially pertinent information that remains only implicitly appreciated via chromatic illumination. Typically, therefore, articulating 'the' justification of one's belief that *P* will be similar to articulating 'the' explanation of a joke: what comes to mind explicitly is only part of the story, and one's appreciation of the (partial) relevance of this part of the story involves a rich further background of holistic, isotropic and Quinean, considerations that are consciously appreciated only implicitly via chromatic illumination.[11]

At the close of Section 5 we urged each of the following claims: first, conscious experience plays a crucial and central role, constitutively, in doxastic justification; but second, conscious experience does so in a way that involves conscious appreciation of the essentially morphological aspects of abductively inferential belief-fixation processes. The key to reconciling these two claims is to embrace the further claim that the conscious phenomenological character of an occurrent belief that *P* can include, in the form of chromatic illumination, implicit appreciation of the holistic, isotropic/Quinean, evidential support that one possesses for *P*. The resulting position, which we will call *chromatic-experiential evidentialism*, asserts that the fundamental constitutive features of a doxastically justified belief that *P* are these: (i) one possesses adequately strong holistic evidential support for *P*, (ii) one experiences an epistemic seeming-that-*P* that is chromatically illuminated by this evidential support, and (iii) one forms the occurrent belief that *P* because of this chromatically illuminated epistemic seeming.

Chromatic-experiential evidentialism, we submit, is much preferable to any of the three accounts of doxastic justification that we canvassed in Section 5. Those accounts, despite their differences from one another, are phenomenologically implausible in essentially the same way: they treat belief fixation as occurring very largely 'out of the blue' in a merely gut-feeling way, as far as consciousness is concerned – rather than arising in a way that involves conscious appreciation of the pertinent evidential support that one possesses. Conscious experience is indeed constitutively centrally important for doxastic justification, but it is important precisely because it includes conscious epistemic seemings that, far from being blind to the essentially morphological aspects of holistic, isotropic/Quinean, evidential support, are richly chromatically illuminated by those very aspects. The neural processes generating and sustaining one's conscious belief include MOMC embodying much of this holistic evidential support, and the chromatic-illumination phenomenology that is supervenient on these neural processes constitutes implicit conscious appreciation of this MOMC and its evidential relevance.

8. Chromatic-Experiential Hierarchical Pluralism

We also maintain that a fully adequate account of doxastic justification should be somewhat pluralistic, acknowledging the pertinence of a hierarchy of goals and subgoals that are constitutively connected to belief (Henderson et al., 2017; Horgan, Potrč, and Strahovnik, 2018). (One reason for this, among others, is that 'evidentialists' and 'reliabilists' in epistemology each seem to be emphasizing something right and important about epistemic justification.) Here we will briefly situate the earlier discussion within the wider context of this pluralistic approach to doxastic justification.

The constitutive goal/subgoal hierarchy can be briefly and approximately characterized as follows – with Level 4 being the principal constitutive *telos* of belief, and each successively lower level constituting an epistemic agent's constitutive best means toward the goal at the level immediately above it:

> Level 4: *Reliable veridicality*. Believing only what is true, by deploying a reliable process of belief fixation.[12]
>
> Level 3: *Objective rationality*. Believing only what is objectively highly likely to be true (relative to one's total available evidence), by appreciating (perhaps implicitly) the objective import of one's evidence and being gripped by belief through that appreciation. (This is one's constitutively best available primary sub-goal as means toward reliable veridicality.)
>
> Level 2: *Sensibility-based subjective rationality*. Believing only what is subjectively highly likely to be true according to one's own deep epistemic sensibility (relative to one's total available evidence), by appreciating (perhaps implicitly) the import of one's evidence (according to one's deep epistemic sensibility) and being gripped by belief through that appreciation. (This is one's constitutively best available secondary sub-goal as means toward objective rationality.)

248 *Henderson, Horgan, and Potrč*

Level 1: *Experiential subjective rationality.* Believing only what accords with one's epistemic seemings that meet certain specific phenomenological criteria, by doing so on the basis of those seemings. (This is one's constitutively best available immediate sub-goal as means toward sensibility-based subjective rationality.)

On this pluralistic approach, normative evaluation of an epistemic agent's belief that P, in terms of the notion of doxastic justification, can be primarily focused on any specific level in this hierarchy, or on several together – depending on one's evaluative purposes in a specific context. (If one is primarily concerned with whether or not someone has formed a certain belief in an epistemically responsible way, for instance, then one's evaluative focus is apt to be primarily upon lower levels; but if instead one is primarily concerned with whether or not one should rely upon someone's testimony, then one's evaluative focus is apt to be primarily upon higher levels.) And in order for an epistemic agent's belief that P to be doxastically justified relative to any given level of the constitutive hierarchy, it also must be doxastically justified relative to each lower level.

Within this pluralistic framework, chromatic-experiential evidentialism would apply most directly to Level-3 normative evaluation, since Level 3 is the optimal kind of epistemic rationality to which an epistemic agent can aspire.[13] However, chromatically illuminated epistemic seemings would figure importantly vis-à-vis Levels 1 and 2 as well – even though one's actual epistemic seemings sometimes might reflect a subjective epistemic sensibility that is imperfectly aligned with objective relations of evidential support (e.g., seemings reflecting a sensibility that is uncritically tethered to the assertions in some putative Holy Book that putatively is divinely inspired), sometimes might fail even to accord with one's own subjective epistemic sensibility (e.g., seemings vis-à-vis the Monty Hall problem that the correct answer is 1/2 rather than 2/3 – cf. Henderson et al., 2017), and sometimes (as with many sincere climate-change deniers) might so ill-accord with the objective rational import of one's available evidence as to be epistemically benighted.

9. Conclusion

The frame problem in cognitive science reveals that rational belief-fixation typically is abductively inferential and non-modular, and hence that belief-fixing cognitive processes typically are essentially morphological: the holistic, abductively inferential, evidential support that accrues to one's beliefs typically contributes to belief fixation in the form of morphologically operative morphological content. Although this MOMC does not itself get represented in belief fixation, nevertheless it does get implicitly appreciated consciously; this appreciation is constituted by the chromatic-illumination phenomenology that is supervenient upon the

Belief Fixation 249

MOMC. A novel kind of experiential evidentialism regarding doxastic justification thereby becomes available, viz., chromatic-experiential evidentialism. This view is considerably more plausible and attractive than are epistemological positions that would sever the connection between doxastic justification and conscious appreciation of the evidence one possesses in support of one's beliefs.[14]

Notes

1. In our view, even perceptual beliefs typically are quite heavily dependent epistemically upon holistic abductive evidential support from one's wider, ongoing, perceptual experience; cf. Henderson and Horgan (forthcoming).
2. In principle, processing that is too subtle and too complex to constitute representation-level computation could be implemented by *sub-representational* computation (e.g., computational processing in and between individual neurons). This can happen if the realization relation from cognitive states to sub-cognitive states is itself sufficiently subtle and complex. (Similarly, representation-level processing that is non-deterministic can be implemented by deterministic sub-representational processing – which can happen if (i) representation-level states are multiply realizable sub-representationally, and (ii) whether one representation-level state Φ evolves to another representation-level state Ψ on a given occasion, or instead evolves to a different representation-level state Ω on that occasion, depends sensitively upon how Φ gets sub-representationally realized on that occasion.) For elaboration of why and how the feature *being computation* can fail to 'transfer upward' from the sub-representational to the representational level, with specific reference to connectionist systems that are sub-representationally computational, see Horgan and Tienson (1996) Section 4.4 (especially p. 66) and Horgan (1997).
3. The *physical* morphology that is characterized by this high-dimensional dynamical system is not the intrinsic physical structure of the neural network or of its successive activation-states. Rather, it is the structure of the network's overall *physical potentiality profile* – the full body of ways it would evolve from any given activation-state to subsequent activation-states. (This profile is subserved, of course, by the intrinsic physical structure of the network.) One can think of such a potentiality profile as the locus of nature's 'engineering design' for intelligent cognizers. For elaboration of how a goddess named Eva – a thought-experimental stand-in for evolution – might implement this design-project, thereby harnessing the enormously rich internal structure possessed by certain dynamical systems and by the physical potentiality profiles they characterize, see Horgan and Tienson (1992), Horgan and Potrč (2008) and Horgan (2012).
4. Horgan and Tienson did not deny, however, that intelligent human cognition needs to deploy occurrent mental representations some of which have language-like structure. On the contrary, they argued in favor of this claim; see Chapter 5 of Horgan and Tienson (1996), entitled 'Why There Still Has to Be a Language of Thought, and What That Means,' and Horgan (2012). Jerry Fodor and Zenon Pylyshyn (1988) had claimed that insofar as cognitive science invokes language-like mental representations that are subjected to structure-sensitive processing, neural-network aspects of cognitive-science models cannot be anything more than an alternative 'implementation architecture' for the classical, computational, conception of cognition. But this reflected a failure to appreciate the possibility that processes like holistically abductive

250 *Henderson, Horgan, and Potrč*

belief-fixation are too subtle and complex to constitute representation-level computation – as indeed is so, argued Horgan and Tienson.

5. See also Potrč (1999, 2000), Henderson and Horgan (2000, 2011), and Horgan and Potrč (2010).

6. Is there any epistemologist, past or present, who might naturally be construed as advocating one of the three positions we will now describe? This is a vexed question, because epistemologists typically have not acknowledged the morals of the frame problem we set out in Section 3.

7. Differing versions of non-experiential reliabilism are possible, depending on how one construes the pertinent notion of reliability. One familiar construal is reliability in the cognitive agent's actual global environment. But Henderson and Horgan (2001, 2006, 2007, 2011) propose an alternative construal, which has the advantage *inter alia* of evading the so-called 'new evil demon problem' for standard reliabilism that was posed by Cohen and Lehrer (1983). Henderson and Horgan's proposal is to construe the pertinent kind of reliability as what they call 'trans-global reliability under suitable modulational control.' More on this matter in note 13 below.

8. This specific cartoon, despite being culturally somewhat dated, illustrates especially well the apparent richness and extensiveness of chromatic illumination in joke-understanding cognition. We authors are constantly on the lookout for a more recent joke or cartoon that could serve this purpose equally well. Suggestions would be gratefully received.

9. The implicitly appreciated content includes both 'long-term' and 'short-term' aspects of morphological content – e.g., the long-term information that 'like'-talk was being deployed (at the time) primarily by teenage girls, and the short-term information that the babysitter is a teenage girl who talks that way.

10. Typically, some aspects of implicitly appreciated morphological content will be more readily accessible to consciousness (albeit normally only in a piecemeal way) than others. Some aspects might be quite resistant to explicit conscious articulability. For instance, in response to someone who persistently fails to understand why one finds the joke funny, even after one has patiently made explicit numerous pertinent items of background information, one might find oneself unable to say anything more.

11. Certain aspects of chromatic illumination sometimes might constitute implicit appreciation of some morphological content or other, without constituting implicit information of any specific, fully determinate, morphological content. Roughly, the less accessible to explicit conscious articulation (even piecemeal) is the actually operative morphological content, the more likely it is that different, non-actual, items of morphological content would have given rise to the very same, phenomenologically indistinguishable, 'seems-true-in-virtue-of-evidence-I-possess' chromatic illumination vis-à-vis P. A plausible 'limit case' of this phenomenon is the (familiar) circumstance in which one has strong seeming-memory that P – strong enough that one believes that P on this basis – with no accompanying seeming-memory about how or when one acquired this seeming memory.

12. In calling reliable veridicality the principal constitutive *telos* of belief, we leave open the possibility that belief has other primary constitutive goals too, such as explanatory understanding or knowledge. (Concerning knowledge, however, we ourselves are inclined to think that it just consists of non-'Getterized' true belief that meets goals 1–4.) Virtue theorists in ethics and in epistemology, invoking one common mode of usage in ancient philosophy, sometimes use the term '*skopos*' for the immediate target of a specific act, while reserving '*telos*'

for a general aim of 'doing well'. (See, for instance, Annas, 2003.) We ourselves maintain that human belief-fixation, although typically non-voluntary, nevertheless is (when rational) an exercise of epistemic virtue: one virtuously deploys one's epistemic competence as a belief-forming agent, in a way that is experienced phenomenologically as occurring in what Sellars (1956) called 'the space of reasons' rather than as occurring in what he called 'the space of causes.' See Henderson et al. (2017), and Horgan, Potrč, and Strahovnik (2018).

13. How does reliability of one's belief-forming processes figure in doxastic justification? First, although there are indeed reliability-involving normative desiderata concerning belief fixation, we maintain that the most fundamental one – the one linked constitutively to objective rationality – is what Henderson and Horgan call 'transglobal reliability under suitable modulational control,' viz., reliability across a wide range of epistemically possible global environments, as modulated by sensitivity to any specific features of one's current experiential situation that are pertinent to the here-and-now trustworthiness of processes that normally are reliable in that way. (The belief-forming processes of your brain-in-a-vat experiential duplicate are no less reliable by this standard than are yours, even though these processes are not reliable within the envatted brain's own actual global environment.) Second, transglobal reliability under suitable modulational control is itself so tightly intertwined conceptually with objective epistemic rationality – i.e., with likely truth, given one's available evidence – that the two cannot come apart. See Henderson and Horgan (2001, 2006, 2007, 2011 Chapters 3–5 and Section 7.1), Henderson, Horgan, and Potrč (2007). Third, global reliability – i.e., reliability within one's actual global environment – is constitutively important too, because it is an aspect of the principal goal in the four-level constitutive means/ends hierarchy: believing only what is true *by deploying a (globally) reliable process of belief fixation.*

14. We thank Vojko Strahovnik and Mark Timmons for helpful comments and discussion.

References

Annas, J. (2003). The Structure of Virtue. In M. DePaul & L. Zagzebski (Eds.), *Intellectual Virtue: Perspectives from Ethics and Epistemology* (pp. 15–33). New York: Oxford University Press.

Cohen, S., & Lehrer, K. (1983). Justification, Truth and Coherence. *Synthese*, 55, 191–207.

Dennett, D. (1984). Cognitive Wheels: The Frame Problem of AI. In C. Hookway (Ed.), *Minds, Machines and Evolution* (pp. 129–150). Cambridge: Cambridge University Press. Reprinted in Z. Pylyshyn (Ed.), *The Robot's Dilemma: The Frame Problem in Artificial Intelligence.* Norwood, NJ: Ablex, 1987 (pp. 41–64). Page citations are to the reprinted version.

Fodor, J. (1983). *The Modularity of Mind.* Cambridge, MA: MIT Press.

Fodor, J. (1987). Modules, Frames, Fridgeons, Sleeping Dogs, and the Music of the Spheres. In Z. Pylyshyn (Ed.), *The Robot's Dilemma: The Frame Problem in Artificial Intelligence* (pp. 139–149). Norwood, NJ: Ablex.

Fodor, J. (2000). *The Mind Doesn't Work That Way.* Cambridge, MA: MIT Press.

Fodor, J., & Pylyshyn, Z. (1988). Connectionism and Cognitive Architecture. *Cognition*, 28(1–2), 3–71.

252 *Henderson, Horgan, and Potrč*

Henderson, D., & Horgan, T. (2000). Iceberg Epistemology. *Philosophy and Phenomenological Research*, 61, 497–535.

Henderson, D., & Horgan, T. (2001). Practicing Safe Epistemology. *Philosophical Studies*, 102, 227–258.

Henderson, D., & Horgan, T. (2006). Transglobal Reliabilism. *Croatian Journal of Philosophy*, 6(2), 171–195.

Henderson, D., & Horgan, T. (2007). The Ins and Outs of Transglobal Reliabilism. In S. Goldberg (Ed.), *Internalism and Externalism in Semantics and Epistemology* (pp. 100–130). Oxford: Oxford University Press.

Henderson, D., & Horgan, T. (2011). *The Epistemological Spectrum: At the Interface of Cognitive Science and Conceptual Analysis*. New York: Oxford University Press.

Henderson, D., & Horgan, T. (forthcoming). Evidentially Embedded Epistemic Entitlement. *Synthese*.

Henderson, D., Horgan, T., & Potrč, M. (2007). Transglobal Evidentialism-Reliabilism. *Acta Analytica* 22(4), 281–300.

Henderson, D., Horgan, T., Potrč, M., & Tierney, H. (2017). Nonconciliation in Peer Disagreement: Its Phenomenology and Its Rationality. *Grazer Philosophische Studien*, 94(1/2), 194–225.

Horgan, T. (1997). Modelling the Noncomputational Mind: Reply to Litch. *Philosophical Psychology*, 10(3), 365–371.

Horgan, T. (2012). Connectionism, Dynamical Cognition, and Non-Classical Compositional Representation. In E. Machery, W. Hinzen, & M. Werning (Eds.), *The Oxford Handbook of Compositionality* (pp. 557–573). Oxford: Oxford University Press.

Horgan, T., & Potrč, M. (2008). *Austere Realism: Contextual Semantics Meets Minimal Ontology*. Cambridge, MA: MIT Press.

Horgan, T., & Potrč, M. (2010). The Epistemic Relevance of Morphological Content. *Acta Analytica*, 25, 155–173.

Horgan, T., Potrč, M., & Strahovnik, V. (2018). Core and Ancillary Epistemic Virtues. *Acta Analytica*, 33(3), 295–309.

Horgan, T., & Tienson, J. (1992). Cognitive Systems as Dynamical Systems. *Topoi*, 11, 27–43.

Horgan, T., & Tienson, J. (1994). A Nonclassical Framework for Cognitive Science. *Synthese*, 101, 305–345.

Horgan, T., & Tienson, J. (1996). *Connectionism and the Philosophy of Psychology*. Cambridge, MA: MIT Press.

Potrč, M. (1999). Morphological Content. *Acta Analytica*, 22, 133–149.

Potrč, M. (2000). Justification Having and Morphological Content. *Acta Analytica*, 24, 151–173.

Sellars, W. (1956). Empiricism and the Philosophy of Mind. In W. Sellars (Ed.), *Science, Perception, and Reality* (pp. 129–194). London: Routledge and Kegan Paul.

Part V

Inference and Perceptual and Introspective Knowledge

10 Experience and Epistemic Structure

Can Cognitive Penetration Result in Epistemic Downgrade?[1]

Elijah Chudnoff

Part of understanding the nature of inference is knowing which mental states can be conclusions of inferences. There are some clear cases. Beliefs can be conclusions of inferences. Headaches cannot be conclusions of inferences. If working through a lengthy bit of reasoning gives you a headache, then your headache is caused by an inference, but it is not the conclusion of an inference. Between beliefs and headaches there are a range of cases that are less clear. Perceptual experiences (from now on just 'experiences') are, or at least have become, one such case.

The orthodox view is that experiences cannot be conclusions of inferences. This is often expressed indirectly in terms of passivity or immunity to rational evaluation. For example, according to John McDowell in having experiences 'a subject is passively saddled with conceptual contents,' and according to Ernie Sosa 'since they are only passively received, they cannot manifest obedience to anything, including rational norms, whether epistemic or otherwise' (McDowell, 1996, p. 31; Sosa, 2007, p. 46). Conclusions of inferences are drawn – not the result of passive saddling – and they do manifest obedience to rational norms. McDowell and Sosa indirectly express the view that experiences cannot be conclusions of inferences.

In her recent book, *The Rationality of Perception* (2017), Susanna Siegel challenges orthodoxy. She defends the view that experiences can be conclusions of inferences. Central to her defense of this view is her interpretation of what she calls 'core cases of hijacked experiences,' among which is the following:

Anger: Before seeing Jack, Jill fears that Jack is angry at her. When she sees him, her fear causes her to have a visual experience in which he looks angry to her. She goes on to believe that he is angry. (Siegel, 2017, p. 67)

Siegel's interpretation of Anger and other core cases of hijacked experience goes like this. There is a baseline of epistemic support for

256   *Elijah Chudnoff*

believing that Jack is angry associated with Jill's visual experience as of Jack being angry. But because Jill's experience is caused by her unfounded fear, the epistemic support it gives to her for believing that Jack is angry falls below this baseline. And the mechanism by which this epistemic support falls below the baseline is not epistemic defeat. That is, Jill's experience doesn't prima facie justify her in believing that Jack is angry, which prima facie justification is then defeated by some other considerations. Rather, the mechanism by which Jill's experience justifies below its baseline is epistemic downgrade. An epistemically downgraded experience is one that has a reduced capacity to even prima facie justify belief. Putting all this together yields the Downgrade Thesis:

Downgrade Thesis: The core cases of hijacked experiences do not prima facie justify their subjects in believing their hijacked contents because their capacity to provide prima facie justification for believing those contents falls below a baseline.[2]

The Downgrade Thesis raises an explanatory question: what is this downgrading mechanism that changes the epistemic properties of experiences? Siegel's elegant answer is that it is just plain old inference: downgraded experiences are conclusions of bad inferences. Believing on the basis of a downgraded experience is like relying on a belief that is the conclusion of a bad inference. The attractions of such an explanation of the Downgrade Thesis constitute Siegel's main positive case in favor of the view that experiences can be conclusions of inference.

Aside from its role in Siegel's case for thinking that experiences can be conclusions of inference, the Downgrade Thesis has come to occupy an independent and central place in recent theorizing about perceptual justification, both by Siegel and others. It is important to distinguish the Downgrade Thesis from some closely related theses. First, there is what I will call the Deficiency Thesis:

Deficiency Thesis: The core cases of hijacked experiences do not prima facie justify their subjects in believing their hijacked contents.

The Deficiency Thesis agrees with the Downgrade Thesis that the core cases of hijacked experiences do not prima facie justify their subjects in believing their hijacked contents, but it doesn't commit to there being any downgrading below an epistemic baseline. Second, both the Downgrade Thesis and the Deficiency Thesis should be distinguished from various proposed explanations of the supposed epistemic downgrade or deficiency. Current proposals differ among each other along a number

Experience and Epistemic Structure   257

of different dimensions, but many are committed to what I'll call the Etiological Thesis:

Etiological Thesis: The core cases of hijacked experiences are epistemically downgraded or deficient because of how they are formed.

Siegel's view that downgraded perceptual experiences are conclusions of bad inferences is just one kind of etiological view. I mention some others from the literature later. The Etiological Thesis itself can seem quite natural: surely what's wrong with hijacked experiences is that they are hijacked and that is a matter of how they are formed. More on why I do not think this is quite right later.

Siegel's core cases of hijacked experiences are imaginary, and it is an open empirical question whether there are any real correlates to them.[3] But the Downgrade Thesis and the Deficiency Thesis command philosophical interest independently of how the empirical question is settled. They do so because their truth about even merely possible cases has implications for theories about the nature of perceptual justification. Consider Phenomenal Conservatism, which, for present purposes, we can simply formulate as follows:

Phenomenal Conservatism: If you have an experience as of it being the case that p, then you thereby have some prima facie justification for believing that p.

As I interpret it Phenomenal Conservatism is supposed to be metaphysically necessary.[4] It holds in virtue of the natures of experiences and justification. So if the Downgrade Thesis or even just the Deficiency Thesis is true, then Phenomenal Conservatism is false because then the core cases of hijacked experiences constitute counterexamples to it. Because Phenomenal Conservatism is supposed to be metaphysically necessary the counterexamples do not need to be or to correlate with actual cases to be effective. Aside from implying that the Downgrade Thesis or the Deficiency Thesis is true, the Etiological Thesis is in additional conflict with Phenomenal Conservatism since Phenomenal Conservatism does not accord any epistemic weight to the causal histories of experiences.

In my view there is much that is right about Phenomenal Conservatism. My aim in this chapter is to set out a picture of perceptual justification that captures what I think is right about Phenomenal Conservatism and explore its implications for the Deficiency Thesis, the Downgrade Thesis, and the Etiological Thesis. What I will argue is that the Deficiency Thesis is true, but the Downgrade Thesis and the Etiological Thesis are false. Of course it is easy to have such a view by having the view that experiences as of it being the case that p never prima justify their subjects in believing

258   *Elijah Chudnoff*

that p. But that is not my view, since that is not a view that captures what is right about Phenomenal Conservatism.

1. What's Right About Phenomenal Conservatism

Phenomenal Conservatism is often combined with a certain view about what it is in virtue of which experiences prima facie justify their subjects in believing their contents. This is what I will call the Phenomenal Grounding view:

Phenomenal Grounding: If an experience as of it being the case that p prima facie justifies you in believing that p, then it does so because of its phenomenology.

In this chapter I am going to assume that Phenomenal Grounding is true.

Phenomenal Conservatism is an unrestricted thesis. It implies that *whenever* you have an experience as of it being the case that p, you thereby have some prima facie justification for believing that p. Some philosophers such as Huemer (2001) and Tucker (2010) accept this. It is possible, however, to develop forms of phenomenal conservatism that restrict when experiences prima facie justify their subjects in believing their contents. The general form of such views is the following:

Restricted Conservatism: If, and only if, you have an experience as of it being the case that p and condition C is met, then you thereby have some prima facie justification for believing that p.

Condition C might include conditions that have to be present for the phenomenology of an experience to make it a prima facie justifier (enablers) or conditions that have to be absent for the phenomenology of an experience to make it a prima facie justifier (absence of disablers). The distinction invoked here can be found in ordinary reasoning about causation (cf. Cheng and Novick, 1991; Cummins, 1995, from which the following example is taken). Pressing on its brake pad causes a car to decelerate. An enabling condition for this is that the brake pad be connected to the brakes. Suppose however you press on the brake pad and the brake pad is connected to the brakes, but there is ice on the road. The presence of ice on the road disables pressing on the brake pad from causing the car to decelerate, but, surface level consideration of the situation might suggest, it does not do so by taking away something that has to be present for pressing on the brake pad to cause the car to decelerate.

The reason I call attention to this distinction is that it helps locate a choice point in developing Restricted Conservatism with respect to the Downgrade Thesis. Suppose you endorsed Phenomenal Grounding and

Experience and Epistemic Structure 259

Restricted Conservatism and took condition C to be the absence of a disabler, say the condition of not being a core case of hijacked experience. Then the Downgrade Thesis follows. Consider a core case of hijacked experience. Given Phenomenal Grounding and its unhijacked counterpart we can find an epistemic baseline. But given the current form of Restricted Conservatism and the fact that it is hijacked we can see that the experience's capacity to prima facie justify its hijacked content falls below that baseline. Siegel's view fits this pattern, as does Lu Teng's (2018). Suppose, however, you didn't take condition C to be the absence of a disabler, but at most the presence of an enabler, which enabler was absent in the core cases of hijacked experience. Then even though those hijacked experiences fail to prima facie justify believing their hijacked contents, this is not because their capacity to do so falls below a baseline. That is, the Deficiency Thesis might be true without the Downgrade Thesis being true.

Suppose we accept Restricted Conservatism and we take condition C to be the presence of an enabler. Let's consider another choice point. Is the enabler a condition on the experience's essential properties or on the experience's accidental properties?[5] One example of an essential property is the experience's phenomenology. Focusing on phenomenology yields:

Phenomenally Restricted Conservatism: If, and only if, you have an experience as of it being the case that p and phenomenal condition C is met, then you thereby have some prima facie justification for believing that p.

Another example of an essential property is the experience's content. Jim Pryor (2000) and Matthew McGrath (2016) develop forms of Restricted Conservatism in which the restriction is on content.[6] The most relevant accidental property for the present discussion is the experience's etiology. Focusing on etiology yields:

Etiologically Restricted Conservatism: If, and only if, you have an experience as of it being the case that p and etiological condition C is met, then you thereby have some prima facie justification for believing that p.

Berit Brogaard (2013), Peter Markie (2013), and, in earlier work, McGrath (2013) again develop forms of Etiologically Restricted Conservatism.[7] If Etiologically Restricted Conservatism is true and the core cases of hijacked experiences have an improper etiology, then the Etiological Thesis is true. Specifically, the core cases of hijacked experiences are epistemically *deficient* because of how they are formed. Note deficient, not downgraded. We have already removed the idea of a baseline by focusing on enablers rather than the absence of disablers. If one endorses Phenomenally Restricted Conservatism rather than Etiologically Restricted Conservatism, however, then the Etiological Thesis is not true.

In a number of places – the earliest being (2011), the most explicit being (2016) – I have defended a form of Phenomenally Restricted Conservatism, which here I'll call Presentational Conservatism:

Presentational Conservatism: If, and only if, you have an experience that has presentational phenomenology with respect to p, then you thereby have some prima facie justification for believing that p.

This counts as a form of Phenomenally Restricted Conservatism because experiences do not have presentational phenomenology with respect to all of their contents. Not everyone uses the term 'presentational phenomenology' so that this comes out true, but that is how I've used it in the past and will continue to use it here. To see what I have in mind consider the kind of experience you would have when presented with a scenario like the one depicted in Figure 10.1.

Figure 10.1 Occluded Dog

Experience and Epistemic Structure 261

You see a dog; you see the rightward part of the dog; you see the leftward part of the dog; but you do not see the middle of the dog, since it is occluded by a bar. These facts about what you see are reflected in the phenomenology of your experience: your experience is also *as of* seeing a dog, seeing its rightward part, seeing its leftward part, but not seeing its middle, since it is occluded by a bar. Though you do not see, and do not have an experience as of seeing, the dog's middle you do represent it. Your experience represents the middle of the dog as having a shape and color appropriate to the dog's seen, and represented, rightward and leftward parts. What constitutes appropriateness and how your perceptual system generates such an experience absent the light array hitting your retina containing information about the shape and color of the dog's middle are good questions. But for now I just want to highlight that your experience would be how I've described.

As I understand the notion of presentational phenomenology we should say the following. Your experience of the partly occluded dog has presentational phenomenology with respect to propositions about the dog's rightward and leftward parts, and even with respect to the whole dog. In having the experience you do not just represent these propositions as being true, but your experience is also felt as making you aware of the bits of reality they are about. This is true of propositions about the whole dog even though you do not see the dog's middle because you can be aware of a whole without being aware of all of its parts. On the other hand we should say that your experience of the partly occluded dog lacks presentational phenomenology with respect to propositions about the dog's middle. In having the experience you do represent these propositions as being true, but your experience is not also felt as making you aware of the bits of reality they are about, that is, the dog's middle, which cannot be seen because it is occluded.

Presentational Conservatism accords epistemic weight to this phenomenal difference that the contents of experience can manifest. According to Presentational Conservatism it is only those contents with respect to which an experience has presentational phenomenology that it prima facie justifies on its own, that is, immediately. If it justifies other contents, then it does so mediately. That the justification is mediate does not mean that it is remote or difficult to attain. Your experience of the partly occluded dog, for example, justifies you in believing various things about the dog's middle both because they are made likely by the propositions about the dog's rightward and leftward parts that it immediately justifies, and even entailed by some of the propositions about the whole dog that it immediately justifies.

Elsewhere I've motivated Presentational Conservatism by its capacity to explain certain patterns in epistemic judgments about cases (Chudnoff, 2016). Michael Veber suggested another such case to me. Suppose you wonder whether the occluded part of the dog is different from how

262　*Elijah Chudnoff*

your perceptual experience represents it due to amodal completion. Suppose, for example, you wonder whether the dog has a bump on the part of its back that is occluded. You couldn't justifiably form the opinion that it does not have such a bump simply because your perceptual experience represents its body as continuing behind the occluder in a regular way rather than in a bumpy way. A good explanation for this runs as follows: your experience does not immediately justify beliefs about the occluded parts; rather it mediately justifies beliefs about the occluded parts; in the context of your inquiry, however, you bracket the background information that would usually allow you to justifiably form beliefs about the occluded parts of the dog, since your inquiry is motivated by a question – does the dog have a bump? – that calls for independently checking the applicability of this background information.

Aside from what it can explain about patterns in epistemic judgments about cases I think that Presentational Conservatism has some intrinsic plausibility. Compare seeing that the dog has a tail, receiving testimony that the dog has a tail, and inferring that the dog has a tail from knowledge of its breed. If you believe on the basis of testimony you have to rely on someone else for your information. If you believe on the basis of inference you have to piece together your conclusion from other things you know. But if you believe on the basis of sight you do not have to do any of these things because you can just point to the state of affairs itself. It is right there before you. It is presented for your inspection. This contrast suggests that your experience on its own suffices to justify you in believing that the dog has a tail. Now compare seeing the dog as having a white middle (albeit an occluded one), receiving testimony that the dog has a white middle, and inferring that the dog has a white middle. Here I think we fail to find a similar contrast. If you believe on the basis of how your visual experience represents the dog you do not have to rely on someone *else* or *explicitly* piece together other information about the dog. But you do have to trust that your own visual system is automatically piecing together information about the dog in a reliable way. Of course you also have to trust your visual system when you seem to see the dog's tail. But there is a difference. When you seem to see the dog's tail you have to trust that your visual system is accurately presenting it for your inspection. When you have an experience as of the dog's occluded middle being white the trust you put in your visual system is not that it is accurately presenting the middle for your inspection. Rather you trust that your visual system is reliably filling in details you can't inspect for yourself. Compare trusting that someone is showing you something without distortion and trusting that someone is telling you the truth about something. So even though you can form the belief that the dog has a white middle just by taking your experience at face value, when you do so you are implicitly relying on more than what the experience on its

Experience and Epistemic Structure 263

own provides for you. A natural way to capture this is to say that your experience on its own does not suffice to justify you in believing that the dog has a white middle. Presentational Conservatism generalizes the foregoing observations.

One might raise worries about Presentational Conservatism from two directions. One might argue that having presentational phenomenology is not a sufficient condition for prima facie justifying believing p. Reflection on the core cases of hijacked experience might suggest this worry. I will argue that this is not so in the next section. Alternatively one might argue that having presentational phenomenology is not a necessary condition for prima facie justifying believing p. Maybe we should treat presented and unpresented contents as epistemically on par. One motivation for this thought derives from the threat of skepticism: do we really have the supplementary background information required for having justified beliefs in the unpresented contents of our experiences? This depends on the scope of presentational phenomenology and the extent of our background information about the world. I've addressed some aspects of the skeptical worry and these related issues elsewhere (Chudnoff, 2016, 2017). Here I set these concerns aside to focus on what we should say about the core cases of hijacked experience.

2. Explaining Epistemic Deficiency

The core cases of hijacked experience are under described. Consider the anger case again:

Anger: Before seeing Jack, Jill fears that Jack is angry at her. When she sees him, her fear causes her to have a visual experience in which he looks angry to her. She goes on to believe that he is angry. (Siegel, 2017, p. 67)

This description can fit two sorts of case. Let us suppose that Jack's face actually looks like the face in Figure 10.2.

Well, really no one's face looks like that. I am simplifying, but nothing will hinge on it. The purpose of the simplification, the reason I didn't use pictures of real faces, is that the simplification will allow easy description of the contents of Jill's experience of Jack. If Jill were experiencing normally he would look to have two horizontal eyes and a horizontal mouth and to not be angry. But Jill's fear hijacks her experience. What happens because of that? Here are two possibilities. First, Jack continues to look to have two horizontal eyes and a horizontal mouth but, in this case, to be angry. In this case Jill's fear hijacks the high level content of her experience but not the low level content of her experience. Second, Jack now looks to have two slanted eyes and a frowning mouth and to be angry. In this case Jill's fear hijacks both the high level content of her experience

Figure 10.2 Jack's Face

and the low level content of her experience. Figures 10.3 and 10.4 show pictures corresponding to the two cases.

The other descriptions of the core cases of hijacked experience also admit these different interpretations. I will not make a case for that here, but I think it is pretty obvious when you go through them.[8] I will continue to take the Anger case as representative.

So which kind of case does Siegel have in mind – Just High or High + Low? Before saying something about that I want to say which sort of case reading her discussions of the Anger case brought to *my* mind. They brought to my mind the Just High case, and when they brought this case to my mind I shared her epistemic judgment about it: Jill's experience doesn't justify her in thinking that Jack is angry. If this is how to read the Anger case, and also how to read the other core cases of hijacked experience, then I believe the Epistemic Deficiency thesis. It is something that needs to be explained. As noted in the previous section, however, that does not commit me to the Epistemic Downgrade thesis or the Etiological Thesis.

I also think Siegel has the Just High cases in mind when she's discussing the core cases of hijacked experience. She says that experiences are hijacked with respect to specific contents. And when she discusses the Anger case she says that Jill's fear hijacks her experience with respect to

Figure 10.3 Just High

Figure 10.4 High + Low

266 *Elijah Chudnoff*

the content that Jack is angry. She doesn't say that Jill's fear also hijacks her experience with respect to low level features such as the orientations of Jack's eyes and the shape of Jack's mouth. In fact she says Jack looks to Jill to have a blank stare (Siegel, 2017, p. 118). So I'm inclined to interpret her as having in mind the Just High Anger case when she discusses the Anger case and the corresponding Just High cases when she discusses other core cases of hijacked experience. And I'm also inclined to think these are the cases that her discussions bring to the minds of most of her readers. And so we all think about the Just High cases and we all share the epistemic judgments motivating at least the Epistemic Deficiency thesis.

But I might be idiosyncratic. Maybe everyone else is really interested in the High + Low Anger case and the corresponding High + Low versions of the other core cases of hijacked experience. Here's one reason I'd find this odd. If it were so, and everyone is also going along with the idea that Jill's experience is at least epistemically deficient with respect to its hijacked contents, then everyone should also be worried about explaining why her experience fails to justify her in believing that Jack's eyes are slanted and Jack's mouth is frowning. But no one seems to worry about that. Nonetheless, I might just be misreading the situation. If that is true, if Siegel along with everyone other than me clearly has the High + Low cases in mind and is making epistemic judgments about *those* cases, then I disagree with their epistemic judgments and I disagree with the Epistemic Deficiency thesis they are supposed to motivate, and so I see no need to explain how it might be true.

Here are two claims summarizing the foregoing. If the core cases of hijacked experience are Just High cases, then the Epistemic Deficiency thesis may be true. If the core cases of hijacked experience are High + Low cases, then the Epistemic Deficiency thesis is not true. I believe both of these claims. But I will not try to argue for them. Our epistemic judgments about cases are typically taken as rock bottom in present discussions of cognitive penetration and perceptual justification. They should be explained, but they needn't be argued for. I will follow this trend here. My aim in the balance of the section is to say how someone committed to Presentational Conservatism might explain Epistemic Deficiency on the assumption that the core cases of hijacked experience are Just High cases.

Consider Jill's experience of Jack's face in the Just High version of the Anger case. It has two representational contents:

(a) Jack's eyes are horizontal, as is his mouth.
(b) Jack is angry.

Jill's experience doesn't justify her in believing (b). Why? Here's the story I think the presentational conservative should tell.

Experience and Epistemic Structure   267

Jill's experience immediately justifies her in believing (a) because it is both represented and presented; Jill's experience doesn't immediately justify her in believing (b) because though represented it isn't presented; Jill's experience would mediately justify her in believing (b) if she had reason to think that if (a) is true then (b) is true; but she doesn't; so it doesn't.

The main premise in this reasoning, after the assumption of Presentational Conservatism, is the claim that Jill's experience represents but does not present that Jack is angry. It does not have presentational phenomenology with respect to the proposition that Jack is angry. I think this premise is plausible. For her experience to have presentational phenomenology with respect to the proposition that Jack is angry her experience would have to have phenomenology reflective of seeing Jack's anger. But were Jack really angry, his anger would be a mental state of his, and mental states are not visible. Some philosophers say things that suggest they think mental states are visible. I find this claim difficult to believe. Mental states do not reflect light. *Expressions* of mental states do reflect light, however, and these are visible. This suggests considering another case.

Suppose because of her fear Jill has an experience that represents the following:

(a) Jack's eyes are horizontal, as is his mouth.
(b) Jack's eyes and mouth express anger.

One might take this case to challenge the presentational conservative explanation of epistemic deficiency. For one might think that this alternative case is another case in which a hijacked experience is epistemically deficient, but in which a key ingredient in the presentational conservative's explanatory strategy is missing. For in this case we may say that Jill's experience has presentational phenomenology with respect to (b). As I've already conceded, expressions of anger are visible and plausibly there is phenomenology reflective of seeing an expression of anger.[9]

Here's my reply. There is indeed something epistemically amiss in this alternative case, but it is not quite epistemic deficiency. I'll name the epistemic trouble in a moment, but first here's the presentational conservative explanation of it. Jill's experience immediately justifies her in believing (a) because it is both represented and presented; Jill's experience immediately justifies her in believing (b) because it is both represented and presented; but Jill's justification for believing (a) defeats Jill's justification for believing (b) because she knows that if (a) is true, then (b) is not true – she knows what expressions of anger look like. So the epistemic trouble is the familiar phenomenon of epistemic defeat. Though Jill's experience prima facie justifies her in believing that Jack's eyes and mouth express anger, all things considered Jill does not have justification for believing that Jack's eyes and mouth express anger because she has justification for

268 *Elijah Chudnoff*

thinking that Jack's eyes are horizontal, as is his mouth and she knows that horizontal eyes and mouth do not express anger.[10]

One might wonder why the defeat doesn't go the other way: why doesn't her justification for believing (b) and her knowledge that if (a), then not (b) constitute a defeater of her justification for believing (a)? We have run into another problem of under description. I have been imagining Jill's experience so that though it immediately justifies both (a) and (b), the justification it provides for believing (a) is stronger than the justification it provides for believing (b). I've been imagining that Jack's eyes and mouth clearly stand out as horizontal. But maybe Jill's experience of Jack's facial features is a bit wobbly. Suppose that if we tried to draw how the low level features of Jack's eyes and mouth show up in Jill's experience then we would have to draw something like the picture in Figure 10.5.

Let us suppose further that the representational contents of Jill's wobbly experience of Jack's face are the following:

(a) (i) Jack's eyes and mouth are horizontal, or

.
.
.

    (ii) Jack's eyes slant and his mouth bends downward.

(b) Jack's eyes and mouth express anger.

Figure 10.5 Wobbly Face

The disjunctive content under (a) captures the wobbly aspect of Jill's experience. The idea is that Jill's experience of Jack's eyes and mouth is compatible with Jack's eyes and mouth having a range of determinate shapes that goes from eyes and mouth being horizontal to eyes slanting and mouth bending downward. If her experience is only so wobbly that it is compatible with Jack's eyes and mouth being horizontal-ish then the case could be treated as shown here. If her experience is only so wobbly that it is compatible with Jack's eyes being slanted-ish and mouth bending downward-ish then there is no epistemic defeat to explain.[11]

Now let us assume for the moment that Jill's wobbly experience has presentational phenomenology with respect to (b) and so prima facie justifies Jill in believing (b). It is implausible that Jill's justification for believing (a.i) defeats her prima facie justification for believing (b). Either her experience does not provide any justification for believing (a.i) or it does and it is weak justification because it derives from justification for believing the disjunction of (a.i) . . . (a.ii). So Jill might retain all things considered justification for believing (b). But, one might now challenge me, doesn't (b) justify believing that Jack is angry and so ultimately the presentational conservative has to say that Jill does gain justification for thinking Jack is angry through fearful seeing?

The problem in this line of reasoning is the starting assumption that Jill's wobbly experience has presentational phenomenology with respect to (b). A facial expression is in part an arrangement of facial features. I do not see how an experience can be felt as making one aware of a facial expression without at least constraining the arrangement of facial features to within one expression appropriate cluster or options. Compare experiencing an octagon. You might have a wobbly experience of an octagon, and indeed a wobbly experience that is felt as making you aware of an octagon. But you couldn't have an experience that is both so wobbly as to leave open the number of sides a figure has and that is felt as making you aware of an octagon. This is not to say that such an experience couldn't represent the seen figure as being an octagon. My point is not about representational content. It is about presentational phenomenology.

3. Non-Core Cases of Hijacked Experience

So far I've focused on core cases of hijacked experience, taking Anger as my representative example. I believe what I have said about Anger generalizes to all the core cases. But there are also non-core cases of hijacked experience, one of which figures prominently in recent discussions of the existence, nature, and significance of cognitive penetration. It is:

Banana: Due to one's true and well-founded belief that bananas are yellow, a gray banana looks yellow. (Siegel, 2017, p. 121. See

270 *Elijah Chudnoff*

also MacPherson, 2012; Deroy, 2013; Teng, 2018; Brogaard and Gatzia, 2017)

I call this a non-core case of hijacked experience for four reasons. First, the terminology of 'core cases' vs. 'non-core cases' comes from Siegel (2017) and Banana is not on the list of core cases of hijacked experience that Siegel gives on page 67 of *The Rationality of Perception*. Second, this is not arbitrary; there is a good explanation for the exclusion. The explanation, I believe, is that all of the other cases are cases in which high level contents – about mental states, natural kinds, and artifactual kinds – are hijacked but Banana is a case in which low level content – about color – is hijacked. Third, and consequent on the second reason, the Banana case does not admit of the two interpretations I distinguished. There is no Just High Banana case and there is no High + Low Banana case. There is only a Just Low Banana case. Fourth, the epistemic claim Siegel makes about Banana is rather different from the epistemic claims she makes about the other cases of hijacked experience. This will take some explanation.

Consider the Anger case again. Siegel's claim is that Jill's experience both represents Jack as angry and fails to justify her in believing that Jack is angry. Now take the Banana case. The corresponding claim would be that one's experience both represents the banana as yellow and fails to justify believing that the banana is yellow. But this is *not* the claim that Siegel makes. What she says is that one's experience both represents the banana as yellow and fails to justify believing that bananas – bananas in general – are yellow (Siegel, 2017, p. 110). So one's experience in the banana case does immediately justify believing its own content – that the seen banana is yellow. Siegel's novel epistemic claim about it is that it does not mediately justify believing another content – that bananas in general are yellow.

Siegel's novel epistemic claim about the Banana case is not inconsistent with Presentational Conservatism, nor even unrestricted Phenomenal Conservatism. But I am inclined to disagree with the novel epistemic claim too.

Siegel's claim that one's experience in Banana does not mediately justify believing that bananas in general are yellow depends on her view that experiences can be conclusions of inference and function like beliefs in reasoning. Everyone thinks that what counts as good reasoning starting from a belief depends in part on the nature of the reasoning that resulted in the belief. Siegel thinks that what counts as good reasoning starting from an experience also depends in part on the nature of the reasoning that resulted in the experience. According to her explanation of the hijacking that goes on in Banana, you reason from the claim that bananas are yellow to the Banana experience that this seen banana is

Experience and Epistemic Structure 271

yellow, and so if you reason from the Banana experience that this seen banana is yellow to the claim that bananas are yellow you would be reasoning in a circle. Reasoning in a circle cannot generate justification. So the Banana experience that this seen banana is yellow does not mediately justify believing that bananas in general are yellow.

This story about the Banana experience wheels in a number of contentious elements of Siegel's overall view. The most important are (1) that experiences result from reasoning, i.e. can be the conclusions of inference, and (2) that experiences do not have special features that make reasoning starting from them independent of the reasoning – granting (1) – that resulted in them. I think that both claims are false. Suppose (1) is true. Still (2) seems false to me because it ignores the presentational phenomenology of experience. Even if experiences result from reasoning their epistemic capacities, in my view, derive from their presentational phenomenology, not from their basis in reasoning.

Further, as has already been noted, Siegel's main argument in favor of (1) is that it fits into an elegant framework within which to explain the Downgrade Thesis. That is, she starts with the core cases of hijacked experience and formulates the Downgrade Thesis, then she develops a framework that includes (1) to explain the Downgrade Thesis, and then in light of that framework she supports the novel epistemic judgment about the non-core Banana case. But I have given reasons to think the Downgrade Thesis is not supported by the core cases of hijacked experience and should be rejected. So there is no need for a framework including (1) to explain it, and so there is no reason to accept the novel epistemic claim about the Banana case. There would be a problem for Presentational Conservatism if the Banana case were an instance of epistemic downgrade or even epistemic deficiency. That is, if one's experience of the banana in the Banana case doesn't prima facie justify one in believing that the seen banana is yellow, then the Banana case is a counterexample to Presentational Conservatism. But I think Siegel's decision to treat the Banana case differently is well-founded. If a gray banana looks yellow to you, then you have prima facie justification for thinking that it is yellow. One cannot draw any contrary epistemic conclusions about the case from the mere fact that the banana looks yellow to you in part because you believe that bananas are yellow. One would need some further specification of just how the belief is influencing the experience and one would need some reason to think that this sort of influence can result in epistemic downgrade or epistemic deficiency. Why not think of the belief as just one among many other epistemically irrelevant causal influences on the experience? Lu Teng (2018) tries to answer this question, but she does so in a way that seems to me to be inconsistent with the Phenomenal Grounding assumption.

272 Elijah Chudnoff

Notes

1. Thanks to Bence Nanay, Berit Brogaard, Anders Nes, Ram Neta, Michael Veber and the participants in the Southeastern Epistemology Conference for helpful feedback on an earlier draft of this paper.
2. Siegel's preferred formulation is: 'The core cases of hijacked experiences are epistemically downgraded in forward-looking power, without defeat' (Siegel, 2017, p. 67). Siegel has reasons for introducing the novel terminology, but I will use the familiar terminology in my formulation. It is sufficient for present purposes and it makes it easier to locate the present discussion relative to the existing literature on perceptual justification. Further, I have also introduced a simplification. I am, in formulating the thesis, ignoring degrees of justification. With reference to the Anger case, for example, I am taking the baseline to be providing some prima facie justification for thinking Jack is angry and the downgraded status to be providing no prima facie justification for thinking Jack is angry. Issues concerning degrees of justification will enter into the discussion later.
3. See (Firestone and Scholl, 2016) and commentary for discussion. They argue for a negative answer. Many but not all of their commentators argue for a positive answer.
4. Thanks to Anders Nes for suggesting I clarify this point.
5. Ram Neta helpfully pointed out to me that the distinction between essential and accidental properties will not cut where I want it to given certain substantive views about the nature of experience. For example one might think that some contents of experience, Russellian contents say, are not essential to them, or one might adopt a form of naive realism on which causal origination in a particular object is essential to an experience. I will not try to develop a more adequate principle of classification here.
6. McGrath restricts to contents about the looks of things. Pryor restricts to what he calls basic contents: these are contents an experience has but not in virtue of other contents.
7. Brogaard distinguishes between seemings and sensations and endorses an etiologically restricted conservatism in which the restriction is to seemings appropriately grounded in sensations. For arguments that one shouldn't make the distinction between seemings and sensations see (Chudnoff and DiDomenico, 2015). Markie restricts to experiences that result from exercise of relevant knowledge-how. McGrath restricts to experiences that do not result from what he calls quasi-inferences.
8. In addition to Anger the cases are Preformationism (attribution of containing an embryo to a seen sperm cell), Gun (attribution of being a gun to a seen pair of pliers), and Vivek (attribution of approval to a crowd of people with neutral faces).
9. One might concede the general point but think that there is something special about Jill's overall experience that prevents it from having presentational phenomenology with respect to (b). I return to this sort of issue later.
10. Berit Brogaard pressed me to consider a variant on the case in which Jill *doesn't* know what expressions of anger look like. There are three variants on the case: (1) Jill has a mistaken view about what expressions of anger look that still implies that if (a), then not (b); (2) Jill has the mistaken view that expressions of anger look the way horizontal eyes and mouth do, so that if (a), then (b); (3) Jill doesn't have a view about what expressions of anger look like. I can tell the same story as I tell in the text about case (1), though I shouldn't call Jill's view about what expressions of anger look like knowledge. In cases (2) and (3) it is not so clear that Jill doesn't gain justification

Experience and Epistemic Structure   273

for thinking Jack's eyes and mouth express anger. These look more like cases of epistemic misfortune: in (2) Jill's experience reinforces her mistaken view; in (3) Jill's experience could be the source of the mistaken view that she has in case (2).

11. Anders Nes alerted me to the worry that the case might then also count as a core case of hijacked experience for which the Epistemic Deficiency thesis is not true. I suspect it shouldn't count as a core case, however. This is not because its low level content is also hijacked but rather because its low level content is already congruent with the high level content that is hijacked.

References

Brogaard, B. (2013). Phenomenal Seemings and Sensible Dogmatism. In C. Tucker (Ed.), *Seemings and Justification*. Oxford: Oxford University Press.

Brogaard, B., & Gatzia, D. E. (2017). Is Color Experience Cognitively Penetrable? *Topics in Cognitive Science*, 9(1), 193–214.

Cheng, P. W., & Novick, L. R. (1991). Causes versus Enabling Conditions. *Cognition*, 40(1–2), 83–120.

Chudnoff, E. (2011). The Nature of Intuitive Justification. *Philosophical Studies*, 153(2), 313–333.

Chudnoff, E. (2016). Epistemic Elitism and Other Minds. *Philosophy and Phenomenological Research*, 92(3).

Chudnoff, Elijah (2017). The Epistemic Significance of Perceptual Learning. *Inquiry*, 61(5–6), 520–542.

Chudnoff, Elijah, & Didomenico, David (2015). The Epistemic Unity of Perception. *Pacific Philosophical Quarterly*, 96(4), 535–549.

Cummins, D. D. (1995). Naive Theories and Causal Deduction. *Memory & Cognition*, 23(5), 646–658.

Deroy, O. (2013). Object-Sensitivity versus Cognitive Penetrability of Perception. *Philosophical Studies*, 162(1), 87–107.

Firestone, C., & Scholl, B. J. (2016). Cognition Does Not Affect Perception: Evaluating the Evidence for 'Top-Down' Effects. *Behavioral and Brain Sciences*, 39.

Huemer, M. (2001). *Skepticism and the Veil of Perception*. Totowa: Rowman & Littlefield.

Macpherson, F. (2012). Cognitive Penetration of Colour Experience: Rethinking the Issue in Light of an Indirect Mechanism. *Philosophy and Phenomenological Research*, 84(1), 24–62.

Markie, P. (2013). Searching for True Dogmatism. In C. Tucker (Ed.), *Seemings and Justification*. Oxford: Oxford University Press.

McDowell, J. (1996). *Mind and World*. Cambridge, MA: Harvard University Press.

McGrath, M. (2013). Phenomenal Conservatism and Cognitive Penetration: The Bad Basis Counterexamples. In C. Tucker (Ed.), *Seemings and Justification*. Oxford: Oxford University Press.

McGrath, M. (2016). Looks and Perceptual Justification. *Philosophy and Phenomenological Research*, 96(1), 110–133.

Pryor, J. (2000). The Skeptic and the Dogmatist. *Noûs*, 34(4), 517–549.

Siegel, S. (2017). *The Rationality of Perception*. Oxford: Oxford University Press.

274   *Elijah Chudnoff*

Sosa, E. (2007). *A Virtue Epistemology: Volume I: Apt Belief and Reflective Knowledge.* Oxford: Oxford University Press.

Teng, L. (2018). Is phenomenal force sufficient for immediate perceptual justification?. *Synthese,* 195(2), 637–656.

Tucker, C. (2010). Why Open-Minded People Should Endorse Dogmatism. *Philosophical Perspectives,* 24(1), 529–545.

11 The Transparency of Inference

Ram Neta

1. The Puzzle of Transparency

How do you know what you believe? Gareth Evans considers this question in the following widely discussed passage:

> in making a self-ascription of belief, one's eyes are, so to speak, or occasionally literally, directed outward – upon the world. If someone asks me 'Do you think there is going to be a third world war?', I must attend, in answering him, to precisely the same outward phenomena as I would attend to if I were answering the question 'Will there be a third world war?' I get myself in a position to answer the question whether I believe that p by putting into operation whatever procedure I have for answering the question whether p.
>
> (Evans, 1982, p. 225)

From now on, let's refer to the phenomenon that Evans observes here as the 'transparency of belief.' And let's also mention a few things about this phenomenon. First, although Evans writes as if this phenomenon occurs *typically* and *commonly* in making a self-ascription of belief, our interest in this essay will be independent of the question of just how typical or common the phenomenon is. We will be interested in explaining the phenomenon, even if it only ever occurs in a small percentage of cases of belief self-ascription. Second, the phenomenon does not concern simply *what we do* when asked whether we believe some proposition; it concerns *what we rationally do* when we consider whether we believe some proposition. In other words, it is not a mere quirk of human psychology that we respond to questions concerning whether we believe some proposition by considering the truth of that proposition. Rather, Evans observes, this kind of response can constitute a rational procedure for answering such questions. Third, the cases in which this kind of response can constitute a rational procedure for answering questions about whether we believe a particular proposition are not confined to those cases in which the proposition queried is a proposition concerning our own psychology.

276 Ram Neta

Indeed, this is precisely what makes the phenomenon itself remarkable: we can rationally attempt to answer a question about our own psychology – in particular, about whether we believe some proposition p (that is *not* about our own psychology) – by considering evidence that bears directly on the question of whether p is true, and only indirectly (if at all) on questions about our own psychology. And finally, the cases in which we can rationally attempt to do this are not confined to those cases in which we have *no access* to evidence that bears more directly on the question of whether we believe some proposition. Perhaps you have plenty of evidence that bears directly on the question of whether you believe that there will be a third world war: for instance, you have not been buying stock in military supply companies, you have not been practicing air-raid drills, you have not been teaching your children basic survival skills, etc. This evidence all indicates – at least to some extent – that you do not believe that there will be a third world war. But even when you are in possession of all this behavioral evidence, you can still rationally consider the question of whether you believe that there will be a third world war, and you can still rationally answer that question in the affirmative, if the geopolitical considerations that you review in response to that question strongly indicate that there will be.

The transparency of belief is as puzzling as it is obvious. While it is no doubt true that we *sometimes* respond – and sometimes *ought* to respond – to questions of the form 'do you think that p?' by considering whether it is true that p, this fact about how we do and ought to respond to such questions is puzzling, and such puzzlement has been articulated as follows:

> What right have I to think that my reflection on the reason in favor of p (which is one subject-matter) has anything to do with the question of what my actual belief about p is (which is quite a different subject-matter)? Without a reply to this challenge, I don't have any right to answer the question that asks what my belief [about, e.g., whether it will rain] is by reflection on the reasons in favor of an answer concerning the state of the weather.
>
> (Moran, 2003, p. 405)

This passage from Moran articulates what I will henceforth call 'the puzzle of transparency'. On the one hand, we have the phenomenon of transparency, which is an obvious fact: the fact that we sometimes rationally attend to our evidence whether p in order to answer the question whether we believe that p. On the other hand, it's unclear how this seemingly obvious fact could possibly be true: how could evidence as to whether p tell us about our states of mind, if p itself is not about our states of mind? This puzzle calls for some philosophy: we need to find a way of understanding the seemingly obvious fact so as to avoid the puzzle of transparency. How to do this?

The Transparency of Inference 277

To see just how puzzling this puzzle is, let's first critically assess some specious solutions.

Some philosophers might think that, in the situations that exhibit the transparency that Evans describes, when I ask you 'Do you think there's going to be a third world war?', what I'm *really* asking – or at least, what you *understand* me to be asking – is rather something like this: Given the evidence currently at your disposal, are you *about* to start believing that there is going to be a third world war? But this proposal cannot be correct. When I ask you if you think that there's going to be a third world war, I am not asking you to make a prediction about what you will believe: a prediction can only be made when the predicted event hasn't yet occurred, but in this case, as soon as you answer my question, you also believe. So there's no time lag between your putative 'prediction' and that which you are, on this proposal, predicting – which implies that it is not a prediction at all.

Perhaps what I'm really asking – or again, what you understand me to be asking – is rather something like this then: Are you *disposed* to believe that there is going to be a third world war? But this proposal also cannot be correct. When I ask you if you have a particular disposition, I am not asking whether that particular disposition is one that you endorse as in any sense correct or trustworthy: but when, in response to my question, you express your belief, you are expressing endorsement of the content of your belief as correct and of your way of forming that belief as reliable. It follows that there's an important difference between reporting your dispositions, on the one hand, and avowing the beliefs that involve those dispositions, on the other. While the avowal of my beliefs may be *an exercise* of the dispositions involved in that belief, it is not *a report* of any such disposition. Notice, by the way, that this particular objection also tells against the 'prediction' hypothesis: making a prediction about what one will believe is not the same as endorsing the predicted belief as correct.

Finally, perhaps what I'm really asking – or what you understand me to be asking – is not a question about my psychology at all, but rather merely, for instance, will there be a third world war? Notice that, if this proposal is correct, then it implicates ordinary speakers in a widespread and systematic misunderstanding. We needn't accept any specific account of the semantics of interrogatives or of the metaphysics of questions to grant the following obvious point: if the truth-conditions for the correct answer to question A differ from the truth-conditions for the correct answer to question B, then A is not the same question as B. Thus, the question whether I believe, for instance, that there will be a third world war, must be different from the question whether there will in fact be a third world war. If what you're really asking – or what I understand you to be asking – is not the question most obviously expressed by the interrogative, that is, 'do you believe there will be a third world war?', but is

278   *Ram Neta*

rather a question about whether there will in fact be a third world war, then your use of the interrogative to communicate that question – or my understanding of it as communicating that question – would either be idiomatic, or a misunderstanding. But it is not idiomatic, since the transparency of belief is not specific to any particular language or language family. Thus, on the present proposal, the transparency of belief involves a widespread and persistent misunderstanding – one for which there is no obvious explanation.

None of these efforts to explain away the puzzle of transparency can succeed. How, then, can we explain the puzzle? Immediately after the passage quoted a few paragraphs ago, Moran suggests a line of explanation:

> What right have I to think that my reflection on the reason in favor of p (which is one subject-matter) has anything to do with the question of what my actual belief about p is (which is quite a different subject-matter)? Without a reply to this challenge, I don't have any right to answer the question that asks what my belief [about, e.g., whether it will rain] is by reflection on the reasons in favor of an answer concerning the state of the weather.
>
> I *would* have a right to answer that my reflection on the reasons in favor of rain provided me with an answer to the question of what my belief about the rain is, if I could assume that what my belief here is was something determined, by the conclusion of my reflection on those reasons.
>
> (Moran, 2003, p. 405)

This passage from Moran can be understood in different ways, depending upon how we understand the auxiliary 'could' in the phrase 'could assume'. On one interpretation, the passage says that my entitlement to regard my reflection on the reasons in favor of some first-order proposition as answering the question of whether I believe that first-order proposition depends upon my being *somehow able* to assume that my belief is determined by the conclusion of my reflection on those reasons. The passage, so understood, is mystifying: how could my being somehow able to make an assumption help secure the entitlement in question?

On a more sympathetic interpretation of the passage, the phrase 'could assume' is equivalent to 'is entitled to assume'. On the resulting interpretation of the passage, Moran is saying that the transparency of belief involves the following features: First, you are asked whether you believe some proposition, and you are not aware of having any behavioral or introspective or testimonial evidence that bears directly on the question of whether you believe it. For instance, you have not heard yourself assert (or deny) the proposition, you have not noticed yourself acting as if the proposition is true (or false), and introspection doesn't immediately disclose to

The Transparency of Inference 279

you any answer to the question of whether you believe it. Second, since you don't have evidence that bears directly on the question of whether you believe that proposition, you check to see if you have evidence that bears on that question *indirectly*. But what evidence could bear on that question indirectly? Third, you assume that, whether or not you believe the proposition in question is going to be determined by your reflection on the evidence for or against the truth of that proposition. Fourth, you reflect on the evidence for or against the truth of that proposition, and take note of how such reflection proceeds, and what conclusion, if any, it delivers. And fifth, in light of your assumption connecting your belief concerning p with your reflection on the evidence for or against p, you report that you believe the conclusion of your reflection on the evidence.

To illustrate the procedure I've just described, we can imagine that you are asked whether you believe that there will be a third world war, and you respond as follows: 'I'm not sure whether I believe that there will be a third world war: I've never said that there will be, nor have I taken any steps to prepare for one, nor can I detect any such belief by introspection. But I assume that my belief as to whether there will be a third world war is a belief that is determined by my reflection on the evidence concerning whether there will be a third world war. Reviewing that evidence now, I recognize that on balance it strongly indicates there will be a third world war. Thus, I conclude that I do believe that there will be a third world war.' Of course, just as ordinary speakers can calculate implicatures very quickly and seamlessly, and without attending to the reasoning that they are doing, so too, we should add, ordinary interlocutors can proceed through the line of reasoning just outlined very quickly and seamlessly, and without attending to the reasoning that they are doing. But, on the present interpretation of Moran's suggestion, what explains the phenomenon of transparency is precisely that it involves our proceeding through a line of reasoning of just this sort.

This interpretation of Moran's suggestion raises an important question, viz., what, if anything, entitles us to make the assumption that Moran mentions, viz., 'that what my belief here is was something determined, by the conclusion of my reflection on those reasons'? Is this assumption somehow a priori guaranteed to be true in every situation in which it is made in the course of addressing a question about what I believe? If so, then why is this? And if not, then what other considerations – either a priori or a posteriori – could entitle us to make the assumption that Moran mentions? Moran's solution to the puzzle of transparency depends on the answers to these questions, and those answers are not obvious.

Before addressing those questions (which I will do in Section 4), I will first put aside Moran's solution to consider an alternative solution that doesn't raise these same questions. The alternative I have in mind has been developed most fully by Alex Byrne.[1]

280 *Ram Neta*

2. Byrne's Proposed Solution to the Puzzle of Transparency

According to Byrne, when our considerations of reasons for or against p lead us to believe that p, we then typically acquire knowledge that we believe that p by making an inference of the form:

P
I believe that P.

Of course, Byrne admits, such an inference is not valid, nor does the truth of the premise in general increase the likelihood of the conclusion being true. Nonetheless, when we make such an inference, we typically acquire knowledge that the conclusion is true, and that is because we know a priori that inferring the conclusion by means of this inference is a perfectly reliable way of coming to believe the conclusion: we cannot infer the conclusion from the premise unless we believe the premise – which is just to say, unless the conclusion is true – and that is all knowable a priori, simply by reflecting on what it is to *infer a conclusion from a premise.* Since we can know a priori that any conclusion reached by making an inference of the form shown earlier is true, we can achieve knowledge of any such conclusion by making that inference. Byrne thus seems to offer a solution to our original puzzle.

One of the benefits that Byrne claims for this solution is that it can explain a wide variety of transparency phenomena. Just as we can know whether we believe that p by attending to whether p is true, so too can we know whether we perceive a particular thing by attending to that particular thing. And so too can we know whether we desire a particular object by attending to that object. And so too can we know whether we intend to pursue a certain goal by attending to that goal. And so on. Each of these cases presents a version of the puzzle of transparency, and one basis on which Byrne recommends his solution to the puzzle of transparency for the case of belief is that it generalizes to solve the puzzles of transparency that arise in each of these other cases. Thus, according to Byrne, our transparent knowledge of what we see is achieved by making an inference of the form:

That thing over there (identified within one's visual field) is F.
I see an F.[2]

And our transparent knowledge of our own intentions is achieved by making an inference of the form:

I will F (where this is something that one knows not on the basis of observation).
I intend to F.

The Transparency of Inference 281

Although such inferences are neither valid nor inductively strong, when the premise of each inference is believed on the grounds mentioned in parentheses, then the conclusion of that inference is guaranteed to be true. And thus, it is a priori certain that anyone who makes such an inference is guaranteed to reach a true conclusion. What more could we want from an epistemic procedure than that it provide an a priori guarantee of the truth of the conclusions it delivers?

Of course, some epistemologists will be tempted to reject Byrne's proposed solutions to transparency puzzles on the grounds that we cannot gain knowledge of the truth of some proposition by inferring that proposition from a false premise. But this is not my objection to Byrne's proposal: I'm happy to grant Byrne that, if I form a belief in a way that I know a priori is certain to lead to a true conclusion if it leads to a conclusion at all, then I'm in a position to know the conclusion arrived at by means of this procedure to be true. So what, then, could be the problem with Byrne's proposed solution?

Recall that, for Byrne's proposed solution to work, it must explain how it is that, *in every case of transparency*, my consideration of reasons for or against believing that p enables me to know whether I believe that p. More generally, the sorts of inferences that Byrne describes must be inferences that I make every time the question of what psychological states I am in is transparent to my reasons for being in those states. Indeed, on Byrne's own view, I must make such inferences just as routinely as my self-knowledge exhibits the transparency phenomenon, since the puzzle about transparency arises for every instance of that phenomenon. Of course, not all of my self-knowledge exhibits the transparency phenomenon in this way: for instance, when I meditate, I do not figure out what thoughts or feelings or sensations are passing through my consciousness by considering any reasons for having those thoughts or feelings or sensations. Indeed, in such cases, I can know what thoughts or feelings or sensations are passing through my consciousness without considering any extra-mental matters of fact. But even if not all of my self-knowledge exhibits the phenomenon of transparency, much of it does – including my knowledge of whether I believe a proposition, whether I intend to do a particular thing, whether I perceive a particular object, and so on. Thus, on Byrne's view, it is by means of perfectly analogous inferences that I routinely come to know my perceptions, intentions, and other attitudes as well. And so, if Byrne's proposed solution works, then I *commonly rationally* make inferences from premises about the extra-mental world to conclusions about what beliefs or other mental states I have.

As ingenious as Byrne's proposed solution is, it will not work. There are at least two serious problems with it, both of which have to do, in one or another way, with inference. In the next section, I will articulate these problems.

3. Why Byrne's Proposed Solution Cannot Do What It Promises

My first objection to Byrne's proposed solution is that it doesn't offer the benefits that Byrne claims for it. In particular, it doesn't generalize to all cases of transparency. This objection is important because much of the appeal of Byrne's solution to our puzzle derives from the solution's purported generality. According to Byrne: inferences of the form that he describes not only account for the fact that we can answer questions about whether we believe that p by considering the evidence concerning p, but it can also account for the fact that we can answer questions about whether we enjoy an experience as of such-and-such objects by considering whether such-and-such objects are before us, and it can also account for the fact that we can answer questions about whether we intend to F by considering the reasons for F'ing, and so on. In short, Byrne recommends his proposed solution to our puzzle on the grounds that it explains how we achieve self-knowledge by means of outwardly directed attention in all the various cases that exhibit the transparency phenomenon. But now I will argue that it cannot explain the whole range of cases of transparency. To see this, let's consider how Evans's observation might apply to the case of *knowing why* you believe something, rather than *knowing whether* you believe it. Imagine that Evans had written the following

In making a self-ascription of one's reasons, one's eyes are, so to speak, or occasionally literally, directed outward – upon the world. If someone asks me '*Why* do you think there is going to be a third world war?', I must attend, in answering him, to precisely the same outward phenomena as I would attend to if I were answering the question 'What indicates that there will be a third world war?' I get myself in a position to answer the question why I believe that p by putting into operation whatever procedure I have for answering the question what indicates that p.

The preceding paragraph, obviously adapted from Evans's paragraph quoted at the beginning of this chapter, makes a point that is just as plausible as Evans's paragraph: just as it is often rational for us to answer the question *whether we believe that p* by considering whether p, it is also often rational for us to answer the question *why we believe that p* by considering what indicates p. But why would it be rational for us to answer the question why we believe p by considering what indicates p? This puzzle is analogous to our original puzzle: both are puzzles of transparency. But how can Byrne's proposed solution to our original puzzle generalize to explain this new puzzle of transparency? Could Byrne propose that we gain knowledge of why we believe that p by making an inference of the form:

E indicates that p.
I believe that p on the grounds that E.

The Transparency of Inference 283

No: the hypothesis that we make such inferences cannot explain why we often rationally answer the question 'Why do you believe that p?' by considering what indicates that p. That's because we can accept that a particular piece of evidence E indicates that p, while consistently granting that E's support for p is defeated – and if we do the latter, then we may grant the premise without drawing the conclusion. And so inferences of the form just sketched do not enjoy the a priori demonstrable reliability of the inferences by appeal to which Byrne proposes to solve our puzzle about how we can know what we believe by considering what is true.

Could Byrne then propose that we gain knowledge of why we believe that p by making an inference of the form:

E indicates that p, and is not defeated.
I believe that p on the grounds that E.

Once again, no: the hypothesis that we make such inferences cannot explain why we can often rationally answer the question 'Why do you believe that p?' by considering what indicates that p. That's because we can accept that a particular piece of evidence E indicates that p, and is not defeated, while consistently granting that E is not strong enough to demand belief in p, and also consistently refusing to take a position as to whether p is true. And again, if we do the latter, then we may grant the premise without drawing the conclusion. And so, once again, inferences of the form just sketched do not enjoy the a priori demonstrable reliability of the inferences by appeal to which Byrne proposes to solve our puzzle about how we can know what we believe by considering what is true.

Could Byrne then propose that we gain knowledge of why we believe that p by making an inference of the form:

E conclusively indicates that p, and is not defeated.
I believe that p on the grounds that E.

Yet again, the answer is no: the hypothesis that we make such inferences cannot explain why we can often rationally answer the question 'Why do you believe that p?' by considering what indicates that p. And that's because we can rationally answer the question 'Why do you believe that p?' by considering what indicates that p, *even when* we do not regard ourselves as having conclusive indication concerning the truth of p. So even if we sometimes do make the inference shown earlier, and even if our making it can explain why it is sometimes rational for us to answer the question why we believe that p by considering what indicates that p, our making such an inference cannot explain why it is rational for us to answer the question in this way even when we don't believe there to be conclusive indication that p. And so, yet again, this proposal fails.

284 Ram Neta

Could Byrne then propose that we gain knowledge of why we believe that p by making an inference of the form:

My total evidence T supports p strongly enough to make it credible that p.
I believe that p on the grounds contained in T.

The answer to this question seems to depend on what 'credible' means. If the credibility of a proposition on one's total evidence amounts to one's total evidence making belief in the proposition mandatory, then this proposal is too strong: we can know why we believe that p even if we don't it to be mandatory for us to believe that p. If the credibility of a proposition on one's total evidence amounts to one's total evidence making belief in the proposition permissible, then the proposal is too weak: we can regard belief in a proposition as permissible even if we don't believe the proposition ourselves. Finally, if the credibility of a proposition on one's total evidence amounts to one's total evidence making belief in the proposition an all-things-considered *good idea*, then this proposal is once again too weak, since we can regard belief in a proposition as an all-things-considered good idea even if we recognize ourselves as unable to believe the proposition ourselves.

We have tried a number of ways to extend Byrne's proposal to explain how it's possible for us to know whether we believe that p by considering whether p is true, so that it could also explain how it's possible for us to know why we believe that p by considering what indicates that p is true. But no such extension of Byrne's proposal has any hope of success. I conclude that one of the main sources of the appeal of Byrne's proposal, viz., its purported generality, is illusory.

Of course this first objection to Byrne's proposed solution is still consistent with its truth, even if not with its generality. But my second objection to Byrne's proposal shows that it cannot even be true. This second objection is *not* the often-voiced objection that inferences of the form Byrne describes cannot be rational:[3] indeed, I think that, *in the right circumstances*, they can be rational. Rather, my objection is that the transitions that he describes can almost never be inferences at all. Not all transitions from one set of beliefs to another constitute an inference – not even if the transition necessarily results in beliefs that are known a priori to be true. To see this, consider a logician who is caused to prove a new (but boring) theorem every time she accepts a premise of the form 'I see something green'. This is a strange causal process, to be sure, but the logician is in a position to know *a priori* that the beliefs formed at the end of this causal process will all be true: they are provable theorems, after all! So the logician knows the theorems that she proves, and her belief in those theorems is caused by a process that she knows a priori will result

The Transparency of Inference   285

in beliefs that are true. But is the causal process by means of which she forms these beliefs an *inference*?

I will now argue that it is not. My argument starts from an observation that Hlobil, 2014 calls the 'Inferential Moorean Phenomenon', or IMP:

> (IMP) It is either impossible or seriously irrational to infer P from Q and to judge, at the same time, that the inference from Q to P is not a good inference.

Why is IMP true? We can answer this question by appeal to a concept that philosophers commonly use in discussion: the concept of someone's being *committed to* a claim by virtue of a move that they make in that discussion. To be committed to a claim doesn't require that one actually accept that claim: one may, for instance, discover oneself to be committed to a claim that one takes to be obviously false. Rather, when one is committed to a claim, one is so committed by virtue of something that one has done or said or thought, and one's failure to accept the claim to which one is thereby committed generates an incoherence. Part of what is involved in an agent's making an inference from premises to conclusion, as opposed to merely undergoing a causal process that takes her premise beliefs as inputs and generates a conclusion belief as output, is that the agent is *committed to* the conclusion belief being justified on the basis of the premise beliefs. This is why an agent who infers q from p while denying that p is a good reason for believing that q is guilty of incoherence.

In claiming that a particular kind of commitment is involved in making an inference, I am not thereby committed to what Boghossian, 2012 calls 'the taking condition' on inference, i.e., the requirement that the causal process must be one that the agent undergoes *in virtue of thinking that the premise justifies the conclusion*.[4] For all I say here, an agent could be *committed to* her conclusion belief being justified by her premise belief, without also *taking it* that the proposition that p justifies the conclusion that q. Indeed, our commitments typically outrun what we take to be true: this is why we can so frequently *discover* what it is that we are committed to when we take certain things to be true.

Still: if an agent is committed to her belief that she believes that P being justified on the basis of her premise P, then she is either severely confused, or else she takes it that P cannot be true without her believing it. Since the phenomenon of transparency involves the agent's *rationally* treating her reasons for being in a mental state as relevant to the question of whether she is in that mental state, cases of transparency cannot involve severe confusion. And since there are very few values of P such that an agent can rationally take the truth of P to require her believing that P, cases of transparency also cannot all involve such values of P. Indeed, if I *ever* manage to form a belief of the form 'I believe that P' by inference

286   *Ram Neta*

from the corresponding premise that P, it will only be because either I suffer from some confusion that prevents me from accurately tracking my own reasoning, or else I take myself to be omniscient with respect to the relevant facts. But neither of these two scenarios obtains very often. So, on the rare occasion when I can make the inference from P to 'I believe that P', that inference will typically be irrational – either the result of my losing track of the inference I'm making, or else the result of my taking myself to be omniscient with respect to P-relevant facts, and the latter is typically irrational.

This is my second objection to Byrne's proposed solution to our puzzle: his solution can explain why Evans's procedure is *often rational* only for those extraordinary agents who often rationally believe that a proposition cannot be true unless they believe it to be true, and it can explain why Evans's procedure is even *sometimes rational for you* only for those extraordinary propositions which are such that they cannot be true without your believing them. And this shows that Byrne's proposed solution is not just insufficiently general, as my first objection showed. It shows that Byrne's proposed solution is also false.

4. The Solution to the Puzzle of Transparency

Recall that, on Moran's proposal, what explains the transparency of belief is our entitlement to assume that what I believe as to whether p is determined by the conclusion of my reflection on the evidence as to whether p. We have yet to see what can give us such entitlement, and so we have yet to see if Moran's proposal can successfully explain the transparency of belief. In this section, I want to offer a suggestion about what can give us the entitlement in question. After doing so, I'll show that the resulting solution to the puzzle can explain the transparency of inference.

What entitles me to assume that what I believe about some issue is determined by the conclusion of my reflection on the evidence concerning that issue? To answer this question, notice that my entitlement can vary in strength for different issues. For instance, I am entitled to be *very* confident that what I believe about the weather in Ulan Bator, Mongolia (a place to which I have no personal attachment) is determined almost entirely by the conclusion of my reflection on any evidence I have concerning the weather in Ulan Bator, Mongolia. In contrast, I am entitled to be much less confident that what I believe about my talents and virtues is determined by the conclusion of my reflection on any evidence I have concerning my talents and virtues. In general, the strength of my entitlement to assume that what I believe about some issue is determined by the conclusion of my reflection on the evidence concerning that issue – the strength of that entitlement is proportional to, and depends upon, the degree to which my evidence indicates that I can think about that issue fairly and impartially. In other words, the strength of my entitlement to

The Transparency of Inference   287

assume that what I believe about some issue is determined by the conclusion of my reflection on the evidence concerning that issue depends on what my body of evidence indicates about my own psychological relationship to that issue. A fortiori, the strength of my entitlement depends upon my total body of evidence.

This suggests – though it does not entail – that what entitles me to assume that what I believe about some issue is determined by the conclusion of my reflection on the evidence concerning that issue is this: my total body of evidence makes that assumption about me credible. That is to say, when it comes to the issue in question, my total body of evidence makes it credible that I form my beliefs on that issue by reflecting on the evidence. It is precisely when my total body of evidence fails to do this – for instance, on issues concerning which I know myself to be partial – that my total body of evidence does *not* make it credible that I form my beliefs by reflecting on the evidence. My suggestion is that what entitles me to assume that my beliefs about some issue are determined by the conclusion of my reflection on the evidence concerning that issue is simply: that my total body of evidence indicates that I do form my beliefs in this way on that issue. We need not grant that there is anything a priori about the entitlement that is central to Moran's solution to the puzzle of transparency. It is just ordinary empirical entitlement – the kind of entitlement we enjoy by virtue of having a lot of evidence about ourselves and our relation to the world around us. Of course, it may be a priori that any agent who can be aware of herself as having evidence at all, or that any agent who can have evidence at all, must have evidence of her own trustworthiness in reasoning from her evidence. In other words, it may be a priori that anyone who can enjoy transparent access to her own beliefs also has empirical justification for taking her beliefs to be determined by her reflection on her reasons for having those beliefs. But, even if this is a priori, what is thereby a priori is simply that agents typically have *a posteriori* justification for taking their own empirical beliefs to be determined by their reflection on the evidence for or against the truth of those beliefs.

I've now supplemented Moran's account of the transparency of belief with an account of the entitlement that his account assumes. Specifically, I've suggested that this entitlement is empirical. I will now show that a perfectly analogous account can explain the transparency of inference. According to the analogous account that I sketch here, the transparency of inference involves the following features: First, you are asked why you believe some proposition, and you are not aware of having any behavioral or introspective or testimonial evidence that bears directly on the question of why you believe it. For instance, you have not heard yourself offer any evidence for or against the proposition, you have not noticed yourself acting as if the proposition can be inferred from some premises, and introspection doesn't immediately disclose to you any answer to the

288   *Ram Neta*

question of why you believe it. Second, since you don't have evidence that bears *directly* on the question of why you believe that proposition, you check to see if you have evidence that bears on that question *indirectly*. But what evidence could bear on that question indirectly? Third, if the proposition in question is one that you believe for a reason, then you assume that the reason for which you believe the proposition in question is going to be determined by your reflection on the evidence for or against the truth of that proposition. (This assumption is made credible for you by your total body of evidence.) Fourth, you reflect on the evidence for or against the truth of that proposition, and take note of how such reflection proceeds, and what conclusion, if any, you reach on the basis of that evidence. And fifth, in light of your assumption connecting your reasons for believing or disbelieving that p with your reflection on the evidence for or against p, you report that you believe (or disbelieve) that p on the basis of the evidence your reflection on which led you to that conclusion.

To illustrate the procedure I've just described, we can imagine that you are asked *why* you believe that there will be a third world war, and you respond as follows: 'I'm not sure why I believe that there will be a third world war: I've never announced my reasons for thinking there will be, nor have I placed any conditional bets that might indicate my reasons, nor can I detect any such reasons by introspection. But I assume that my belief as to whether there will be a third world war is determined by my reflection on the evidence concerning whether there will be a third world war. Reviewing that evidence now, I recognize that on balance it strongly indicates there will be a third world war. Thus, I conclude *from my review of that evidence* that I do believe that there will be a third world war. And specifically, I believe that there will be a third world war on the basis of these specific pieces of evidence. . . .'

Of course, just as ordinary speakers can calculate implicatures very quickly and seamlessly, and without attending to the reasoning that they are doing, so too, we should add, ordinary interlocutors can proceed through the line of reasoning just outlined very quickly and seamlessly, and without attending to the reasoning that they are doing. But, on the present interpretation of Moran's suggestion, what explains the phenomenon of transparency is precisely that it involves our proceeding through a line of reasoning of just this sort, and appealing to our total evidence as we do so.

Readers familiar with Moran's own work on this topic will recognize that I have said nothing at all about several issues that he emphasizes in his discussion of transparency – for instance, his treatment of self-knowledge as involving making up your mind. I ignore these features of Moran's work here not because I find them uncongenial. Rather, it's because I want to show that, at least at the level of abstraction at which I have proceeded here, the solution to the puzzle of transparency doesn't require appeal to those features of his view.[5]

Notes

1. See Byrne, 2011.
2. See Byrne, 2012 for this solution to the puzzle of transparency concerning what we see.
3. See Boyle, 2011; Barnett, 2016.
4. Boghossian states the taking condition as follows: 'A transition from some beliefs to a conclusion counts as inference only if the thinker *takes* his conclusion to be *supported* by the presumed truth of those other beliefs.' (Boghossian, 2012, p. 4). Thomson, 1965 offers what I believe to be the earliest defense of the taking condition on inference. See Neta 2019 for an argument in favor of a specific version of the taking condition that avoids the various objections that have been levelled against the claim that condition is necessary for inference.
5. I am grateful to Christopher Blake-Turner, Eli Chudnoff, Eric Marcus, Anders Nes, Nico Orlandi, John Phillips, William Ramsey, John Schwenkler, and Sarah Wright for comments.

References

Barnett, D. (2016). Inferential Justification and the Transparency of Belief. *Nous*, 50, 184–212.

Boghossian, P. (2012). What Is Inference? *Philosophical Studies*, 169, 1–18.

Boyle, M. (2011). Transparent Self-Knowledge. *Proceedings of the Aristotelian Society Supplementary Volume*, 85, 223–240.

Byrne, A. (2011). Transparency, Belief, Intention. *Proceedings of the Aristotelian Society Supplementary Volume*, 85, 201–221.

Byrne, A. (2012). Knowing What I See. In Declan Smithies & Daniel Stoljar (Eds.), *Introspection and Consciousness*. Oxford: Oxford University Press.

Evans, G. (1982). *The Varieties of Reference*. John McDowell (Ed.). Oxford: Oxford University Press.

Hlobil, U. (2014). Against Boghossian, Wright and Broome on Inference. *Philosophical Studies*, 167, 419–429.

Moran, R. (2003). Responses to O'Brien and Shoemaker. *European Journal of Philosophy*, 11, 402–419.

Neta, R. (2019). The Basing Relation. *The Philosophical Review*, 128, 179–217.

Thomson, J. (1965). Reasons and Reasoning. In Max Black (Ed.), *Philosophy in America*. Ithaca, NY: Cornell University Press.

Contributors

Nicholas Allott Senior Lecturer, University of Oslo

Corine Besson Senior Lecturer, University of Sussex

Federico Bongiorno Doctoral Researcher, University of Birmingham

Lisa Bortolotti Professor, University of Birmingham

Berit Brogaard Professor, University of Miami

Elijah Chudnoff Associate Professor, University of Miami

David Henderson Professor, University of Nebraska, Lincoln

Terry Horgan Professor, University of Arizona

Kirk Ludwig Professor, Indiana University

Eric Mandelbaum Associate Professor, City University of New York (Baruch College and the CUNY Graduate Center)

Wade Munroe Postdoctoral Research Fellow, University of Michigan, Ann Arbor

Anders Nes Associate Professor, Norwegian University of Science and Technology

Ram Neta Professor, University of North Carolina at Chapel Hill

Matjaž Potrč Professor, University of Ljubljana

Jake Quilty-Dunn Research Fellow, University of Oxford and Assistant Professor, Washington University in Saint Louis

Michael Rescorla Professor, University of California, Los Angeles

Index

Note: Page numbers in *italic* indicate a figure and page numbers in **bold** indicate a table on the corresponding page.

abductive inferences, Bayesian account of 3, 75
accessibility 137, 140–141
accessibility-driven system 142
Ames Room Illusion 32
amodal completion 6, 10, 115–116, **118**, 262
anomalous experience 5, 74, 76, 83, 83–85, 84, 86, 89; and delusional belief 90
Aquinas 2
Aristotle 2
association, and thoughts 1
associative symmetry 168n12
associative learning 100
attitude attribution 25
attitude transitions 21
attitudes 20

background assumptions 213–214, 224
Banana case 271, 269
basic logical principle 172–174, 184–186, 189
Bayesian abductive inference 78–80
Bayesian decision theory 40, 45, 60
Bayesian inference 18–19, 83
Bayesian model, objections to 50–55
Bayesian reasoner 18
belief: role of 24; transparency of 275–279, 280
belief fixtation 229, 239
beliefs 5, 35n11, 231; formation and maintenance of 229
Boghossian, Paul 22, 178–180, 180; Carrollian Circularity and 177–180

brain, the 18, 32–33
Brogaard, Berit 259
Byrne, Alex 11, 279; and the puzzle of transparency 280–284

Capgras delusion 78, 80
Capgras model 76
Carroll's Regress 172
Carrollian Circularity 177–180, 180
Carroll-Kripke Adoption Problem (AP) 174–177
causal-functional structure 32
causal-structural information 33
chromatic illumination 210–215, 225n15, 241–247, 248, 250n11
chromatic-experiential evidentialism 10, 245–247, 249; and Level-3 normative evaluation 248
circularities 174–177
Clark, Andy 18
classical inference theory 19
classical or operant conditioning 100
cognition: personal level 15; and subpersonal processes 31
cognitive achievements: and inferences 27–28; and SMI 26–27
cognitive personal state 180
cognitive phenomenology 126, 202
cognitive achievements 15; unconscious inference theories of 16–17
cognitivism 172–174, 180, 182, 190–191
coherence and consistency 1
Coltheart, Max 74, 78

292   Index

Coltheart model 75, 76–78, 83, 86; challenges 82–84
comprehension: pragmatic 3; speech 3
concept, application conditions of 33
concept possession 26, 27–28
conclusion attitudes 20, 21
conditional probability 79
conditionalization 21, 40, 42, 49–50, 60, 79; Bayesian 91
conscious inferences 2
consciousness 2; significance of 2–3
content, application conditions of 33
conversational implicatures 104
cooperative principle 103

Davies, Martin 83, 90–91
deductive inference 2, 7–8, 103, 185, 187, 199–200
deductive reasoning 2, 3, 7–8, 174, 187, 191, 199–200
Deficiency Thesis 257; Epistemic 264, 266, 273
delusional belief 90
delusions 5, 83; empiricist approaches to 84–85; two-factor theory of 74
Dennett, Daniel C. 9, 229, 231–234, 237, 102
description 18
Downgrade Thesis 256–260
dual-processing theory 119

Egan, Andy 31, 83
Egan's terms 31
Ellis, Hayden 76
Emmert's Law 19, 26, 32
endorsement theory 5, 74, 75, 75–76, 92, 93; inference and 86–87
epistemic downgrade 256–258, 264, 271
epistemic justification 239–240, 247
epistemic seemings 240, 245–247, 248
epistemic deficiency 263–269
Etiologically Restricted Conservatism 259
Etiological Thesis 257
Evans, Gareth 275, 277
Evans's route 11
evidence insensitivity 6, 117–119
evidentialism 10, 249; *chromatic-experiential* 245–248; *non-experiential* 239–240
experiences 255
experimental case 113, *114*

explanation, probabilistic account of 79
explanationism 5, 74

facial expression 269
feedback mechanisms 125
First Control Case *114*
fit: mind-to-world direction of 25; mind-to-world direction of 24
Fodor, Jerry 9, 36, 130, 152, 167, 210, 234–235, 236, 249
fore-v-background structure 224
form 3–4, 5–6, 8, 21, 24, 26, 54, 58, 87, 126, 172, 175, 181, 239–240, 259
frame problem 229–234

Gaussian distribution 60
general/particular circularity threat 174, 183–185, 189–190
genuine inferences 24
genuine representations 28
Gestalt properties 108–109, *109*
goals 35n12
Grice, Paul 126, 103–104
Gricean implicature *105*

habituation 111
hard line, the: IO-representation and 28–29; S-representations and 29–30
hearing meanings 99–121
Helmholtz, Hermann von 11, 17, 34, 42, 67, 86–87, 121, 153
heuristics 4, 6, 17, 30, 33, 69, 119, 126–127, 133, 134
high-level properties 88, 108, 109, 120
hijacked experience 257, 269–271
homuncular functionalism 27
homuncular inferences 25–26
homuncular SMI 25
homunculi 27
homunculus, and subpersonal agent 24–25
horizon 201, 215–217, 218, 223, 224, 225
human rationality 229–234
Husserl, Edmund 9–10, 224

icon 7, 151–159, 166, 167
imagery 7, 151–169, 202, 220, 226
inference facsimiles 27–28
inference/inferences: application conditions of 33; awareness of 2; Bayesian 83; conclusions of 255; conscious and unconscious 2–3;

definition 102–103; endorsement theory and 86–87; faculty of 2; putative 3; rule-governed theoretical 23; subpersonal 17, 18–19; and thoughts 1; types of 1; unconscious 2; unconscious subpersonal 17–20
inferential processes, features of 19–20
instrumentalism 55–57, 57–59, 62, 63, 65, 67
instrumental reasoning 99
intelligent 18
interpretation 180–183
INUS condition 109–110
IO-representation 28–29
isomorphism 30

James, Leon Jakobovits 111, 112
James, William 207
justification 1, 3, 10, 34, 60, 117, 171, 185–186, 188, 190, 192, 193, 194, 229, 239, 240, 246–247, 249, 256–257; immediate 101, 261–262, 267–268, 270; mediate 261

Kanizsa Amodal Completion *118*
Kant, Immanuel 2

labor, division of 15–16
language, as a code 126
language comprehension: and amodal completion 115–116; and automaticity 115–117
language center 111
language comprehension, linguistic inference 101–106, 111
Lu Teng 271

Markie, Peter 259
McDowell, John 255
McGrath, Matthew 259
McKay, Ryan 82, 83
meaning comprehension 112
mental states, and inferences 155
metacognition 125, 127, 132
mind-to-world direction 24, 25
modular inferences 35n10
modularity 234, 237
modus ponens 8, 178
monothematic delusions 74
Moran, Richard 276, 278, 288
morphological content 9, 225n15, 237–239, 241, 243, 248, 250

neuroanatomical evidence, and speech comprehension 110–111
non-conceptual content 35n13
non-experiential evidentialism 239
non-human animals 99
non-inferential view 112–115, 115, 101, 110–119; and speech comprehension 106
normative: criterion 80; evaluation 47, 248; model 4, 45–46, 50; properties 102; rule 182

occluded dog *260*, 261–262
ordinary representations 27

Padro, Romina 174
perception 15, 119–120; as intelligent 18; processes and 30–31
perceptual constancies 19
perceptual representation 33
perceptual learning 108
personal level cognition 15
personal level inference (PLI), successful account of 20–23
personal-level cognitive achievements 24
personal-level explanations 102
phenomenal conservatism 258–263
Phenomenal Grounding 259–260
PLS 24–25, 27
Ponzo illusion 19, *20*
pop out effect 112–115
practical inference 21
pragmatic comprehension 3
predictive engine 18
premise attitudes, and conclusion attitudes relationship 21
presentational phenomenology 260–261, 263, 267, 269, 271
prior likelihood 42, 48, 56, 61, 64, 69n18
prior probability 42, 48, 56, 61, 64–65, 79–82, 89
procedural metacognition 125
process 31
propositional attitudes 21, 24
Proust, Joëlle 125, 131
Pryor, Jim 259
putative inferences 3
puzzle of transparency: and Byrne's solutions 280–286; solution to 286–288

ratiomorphic approach/structure 30–32, 33
rational belief systems 78–80

294 *Index*

rational insight 178–180
rational soul 2
rationality 102; human 229–234
reason 2
reasoning, and generality 189–190
Recanati, Francois 140–141
Recanati's bottom-up
   accessibility-driven account 127
recovery, Recanati's bottom-up
   accessibility- driven account of 127
reflection 11, 119, 129, 168n13, 178,
   205, 207, 215–216, 242, 245, 263,
   276, 278–279, 286–288
representation 16–17; application
   conditions of 33; genuine 28;
   ordinary conception of 28
restricted conservatism 258–259
rule-following account 22–23, 188,
   190–191, 194n30; and inferences
   180; intentional view and 180
rule-governed theoretical inference 23

schema 9, 23, 173, 182–184, 193n16,
   201, 217, 219–220, 221, 223, 225n24
Second Control Case *114*
semantic satiation 111–112, 121n9
senses, accessibility of 137
sensory prediction errors 18
Siegel, Susanna 117–118; *The
   Rationality of Perception* 255, 269
Simple Inferential Internalism 178
SMI processes *see* subpersonal
   modular inferential processes (SMI)
soft line, the 28, 30–33
Sosa, Ernie 255
speech comprehension 3; adductive
   inferences to 3; non-inferential view
   of 119, 100; and neuroanatomical
   evidence 110–111; non-inferential
   view of 106, 110–119; pop out
   effect 112–115; and semantic
   satiation 111–112; and the Stroop
   effect 112
Sperber, Dan 137
S-representations 29–30
stimulus satiation 111
Stroop effect 112, *113*
structural representations 29
subpersonal agent 24–25
subpersonal cognitive agents 27
subpersonal inferences 17
subpersonal modular inferential
   processes (SMI) 23–24; argument

against 24; and homuncular
   inferences 25–26
subpersonal processes 30; as
   ratiomorphic 30–31
substitution instances 183
systematic illusions 15

Taking Condition (TC) 22–23, 180
theoretical inferences 20–21, 24, 25
thoughts 1; and the capacity for
   inference 1; transition in 21
transparency: puzzlement of 276–279;
   puzzlement of and solution to
   280–281
transparency of belief 275–279, 280;
   and Byrne's solutions 280–286
truth 1, 56, 57–59, 85, 126, 132, 154,
   181–182, 187, 188, 191, 235, 257,
   262, 275, 77, 279–281, 283–285,
   287, 288, 289n4; truth-preserving
   143, 154, 164, 167n4
Tucker, Chris 258
type-1 cognitive processes 119
type-1 reasoning process 119–120

unconscious inference theories (UIT)
   2, *16*, 27; strategies of 19–20
unconscious inferences 27
unconscious subpersonal inferences
   17–20
universal instantiation (UI) 8, 174,
   175, 177, 183
universal instantiation 8, 174; and
   general logical principles 183;
   versus substitution 183–185
utterance comprehension 121n9,
   125–129, 132, 140–141,
   143–144; and feedback and
   communication 131–132, 133;
   as an ill-structured problem
   129–131; monitoring and control
   in 134–139

validity 173, 179, 181, 183, 185–191
Veber, Michael 261
visual search paradigms 112–115
visual system 26

Wernicke's area 110–111
Wilson, Deidre 11n9, 127, 141
Wilson, John Cook 187, 194n29

Young, Andrew 76